PELICAN BOOKS
GOD AND

An orienta
Beltz is at p
logical sect
German De

Peter Heine
Literature i
He now te
Schenectad
sophy and
spent with
other book

Walter Beltz

GOD AND THE GODS

Myths of the Bible

Translated by Peter Heinegg

PENGUIN BOOKS

Penguin Books Ltd, Harmondsworth, Middlesex, England
Penguin Books, 625 Madison Avenue, New York, New York 10022, U.S.A.
Penguin Books Australia Ltd, Ringwood, Victoria, Australia
Penguin Books Canada Ltd, 2801 John Street, Markham, Ontario, Canada L3R 1B4
Penguin Books (N.Z.) Ltd, 182–190 Wairau Road, Auckland 10, New Zealand

Gott und die Götten first published by Aufbau-Verlag Berlin und Weimar 1975
Copyright © Aufbau-Verlag Berlin und Weimar, 1975
This translation first published 1983
Copyright © Penguin Books, 1983

Quotations from the Revised Standard Version of the Bible,
copyrighted 1946, 1952 © 1971, 1973

Made and printed in Great Britain by
Richard Clay (The Chaucer Press) Ltd, Bungay, Suffolk
Filmset in 'Monophoto' Photina by
Northumberland Press Ltd, Gateshead

Contents

Introduction 9

I. **The Creation of the World**
  1. *The Priestly Account of Creation* 33
  2. *The Prophetic Account* 37
  3. *Liturgical Texts* 38

II. **On God**
  1. *God and Gods* 41
  2. *The Storm God* 44
  3. *The God of War* 47
  4. *The Bull God* 52
  5. *The Fertility God* 53
  6. *The Messengers of Yahweh and Elohim* 57

III. **Myths about Man**
  1. *The Creation of Man* 62
  2. *The Beginnings of Civilization* 68
  3. *The Worship of the Gods* 69
  4. *The Flood: Yahweh's Revenge on Humanity* 72
  5. *The Scattering of the Human Race* 74

IV. **The Emergence of the People of God**
  1. *The Abraham Stories* 79
  2. *The Isaac Stories* 84
  3. *The Jacob Stories* 88
  4. *The Joseph Stories* 96
  5. *The Moses Stories* 102

V. **The Conquest of Canaan**
  1. *The Sea Miracle* 113

2. *Wandering in the Wilderness* 115
3. *The Miraculous Serpent of Kadesh* 119
4. *Stories of the Spies* 120
5. *Balaam's Ass* 122

VI. God Gives the Law
1. *On Sinai* 125
2. *On Horeb* 127
3. *On Ebal* 129
4. *At Shechem* 130
5. *In Jerusalem* 131

VII. The Great Sanctuaries and Heroes of the Early Period
1. *The Ark of the Covenant* 134
2. *The Cities of Refuge* 136
3. *Gilgal, Bethel, Dan and Shechem* 137
4. *Joshua* 140
5. *Deborah* 141
6. *Gideon* 143
7. *Jotham* 146
8. *Jephthah* 147
9. *Samson* 149
10. *Ruth* 151

VIII. Miracles and Other Incidents from the Lives of the Prophets
1. *Samuel* 153
2. *Elijah* 155
3. *Elisha* 157
4. *Isaiah* 159
5. *Jeremiah* 162
6. *Ezekiel* 165
7. *Hosea* 169
8. *Jonah* 170

IX. The Legends of the Kings
1. *Abimelech* 173
2. *Saul* 174
3. *David* 178

4. *Solomon* 184
5. *Jeroboam and Rehoboam* 187
6. *Jehu* 190
7. *Hezekiah* 191

X. **Jerusalem: City and Temple**
1. *The City* 194
2. *The Temple* 198

XI. **The Wonderful Deeds and Adventures of Job, Esther and Daniel**
1. *Job* 202
2. *Esther* 205
3. *Daniel* 208

XII. **The Devil: Satan, Azazel, Beelzebul, and Other Gods**
1. *Satan* 212
2. *Azazel* 214
3. *Beelzebul, the Demons, and the Dragon* 215

XIII. **The Myth of the Redemption**
1. *Jesus of Nazareth* 218
2. *Mary the Mother of Jesus* 226
3. *James the Brother of Jesus* 228
4. *John the Baptist* 228
5. *Peter* 231
6. *Paul* 233

XIV. **The New World**
1. *The New Age* 236
2. *The New Man* 239
3. *The New Earth* 243

XV. **The Evolution of Biblical Mythology** 249

Chronological Table 255
Glossary 261
Index of Personal Names 267
Index of Tribal and Place Names 277

Introduction

This attempt to write a biblical mythology is warranted because one has long been overdue. Pious souls may still shy away from subjecting the myths of the Bible to the same kind of scrutiny as the myths of Graeco-Roman history. But no one who wants to understand the European cultural heritage of almost two thousand years will bypass the Bible, because its myths, like all the myths of antiquity, have been essential sources of world culture until well into the modern period. Even if the Bible recedes still further from our field of vision, its historical significance can only become more distinct.

The need for a biblical mythology is based on the vast amount of time separating the origin of these myths and the modern reader, a gap that bars the way to their ready comprehension. Like Homer's epics, the Bible is unintelligible today without some explanation. Even the believer, for whom the Bible still remains divine revelation, is not spared the detour through commentaries. Nowadays the unprejudiced reader of the Bible can no longer untangle the biblical web of myth, history and the interpretation of both, or distinguish between the original myths and the way the Bible reads them. And so biblical theology undertakes to explain such interpretations, that is, to explain the function that the Bible ascribes to myth. A biblical mythology, on the other hand, will aim at presenting and explaining the myths themselves, at clarifying the historically situated, non-scientific conceptual world of cosmos, man and society.

The Bible, which for almost two millennia has embodied 'Holy Scripture' for Jews and Christians of all denominations, has a long history behind it, whose beginnings can no longer be determined with precision. For the history of the peoples among whom this book acquired its present form has no specific starting point – not least because these small ethnic groups played an active role in the political events of the ancient Near East only for a short time, being otherwise a mere bone of contention fought over by neighbouring countries. The actual greatness of these little groups of people only became evident around the end of the fourth century A.D. Then Christianity, originally a Jewish sect and later elevated by Constantine the Great and Theodosius to the official state religion, included the religious literature of Judaism among its sacred writings, naming it the Old Testament in contrast to its own much smaller body of literature, the New Testament. The great historical achievement of Israel lies in having passed down this literature, which the Christian Church brought out of narrow national confines into the universality of a world religion.

The nations in which the Bible originated, Judah and Israel, and their location on the land bridge between Eurasia and Africa, in the midst of the ancient empires on the Euphrates, Tigris and Nile, show clearly the importance this region has always had for the inhabitants of the Mediterranean coast and the other neighbouring peoples.

At the time that Israel and Judah were emerging, the 19th Dynasty ruled in Egypt. Its most eminent pharaohs, Seti I (1308–1290 B.C.) and Ramses II (1290–1223 B.C.), restored Egyptian hegemony over Syria and Palestine, which their predecessors had partially lost. The kingdom of Egypt controlled a highly developed culture, a well-organized system of finance and taxes and a good army. The pharaoh, as the son and deputy of the gods, and king of Upper and Lower Egypt, ruled through the priests. Both the land and its people were the property of the gods, that is, of the temples and the temple priesthood. At one time the kingdom extended from Lebanon to the Sudan. By the 3rd Dynasty (*c.* 2700 B.C.), the patriarchal order was already in place, with its institutions of religion, technology and writing. The individual districts or provinces of the kingdom enjoyed a considerable degree of autonomy, and in fact the post of governor was hereditary during certain periods. The Egyptian pantheon was the assembly of the old sacred kings – matriarchy had already vanished with the pre-dynastic history of Egypt.

To the north of Israel and Judah, the great empires were those of Assyria and Babylon, which were forever trying to spread their influence southward. Assyria and Babylon were the heirs of the kingdom of Akkad (*c.* 2340–2150 B.C.), which was preceded by the kingdom of Sumer. The culture of the early historical epoch in Sumer was that of the Neolithic and Bronze Age. Sumerian cities still had no walls, their inhabitants lived by farming in extended family groups. Matriarchy still prevailed. The sacred queen, in her role as the goddess Innana, represented the populace, the city and the land itself. Only with the end of the kingdom of Sumer did patriarchy finally triumph. The 'old gods' of late Sumerian tradition were without exception goddesses. Antum, Ninlil, Damkina, Ishtar and Baba, the sacred queens of the five ancient cities, Uruk, Ur, Eridu, Larsa and Lagash, were older than their husbands, Anu, Enlil, Enki, Utu and Nergal. Their spouses were all of lower rank. Sacred queens used to have two husbands, a fact that emerges from an inscription by Urukagina of Lagash, who, however, rejected the custom for his own day. We know that after the passage of a year the sacred king was sacrificed and a new one chosen in his stead, to preserve the matrilinear succession. This necessary cycle of replacements was first inter-rupted by sacrificing a substitute for the king, and then permanently done away with.

The first sacred kings came from the nomadic peoples who entered Sumer in dribs and drabs from the interior of the Arabian peninsula. Their Semitic language won out over non-Semitic Sumerian. The arrival of the patriar-chate meant private property, class distinctions, exploitation and emergent state authority. Innana of Uruk, who as daughter of the moon god was herself a moon goddess and a sovereign goddess of fertility, was banished from Ur by her masculine replacement Eanna. She became a Venus, her powers limited to love and procreation.

The Akkadian empire, created by Sargon (2340–2284 B.C.), recognized these same divine couples, the old sacred kings and queens, in its individual kingdoms of Isin, Larsa, Babylon, Assyria and Elam (c. 1900 B.C.). The Akkadians clung to these gods – but now the goddesses retreated to second place, while Enlil, Anu, Sin and Shamash took precedence over them. The empire of Akkad undoubtedly came about as the result of a massive immigra-tion of Semitic-speaking nomads into Mesopotamia from the interior of the Arabian peninsula. Mesopotamian kingdoms, both small and large, had constant dealings with such nomadic peoples. It is certain that several tribes from the future people of Israel also came from Arabia, for the fertile alluvial soil of Mesopotamia held a magnetic attraction, both for the nomadic Cassites from the mountains on its northern border and for the wandering peoples from the southern wilderness of the Arabian peninsula.

Around 1550 B.C., the Cassites put an end to the Mesopotamian kingdoms, and a thousand years later the Elamites and Persians overturned the Baby-lonian empire. In contrast to these northern peoples, the nomads who kept trickling into the zones of arable land on the edge of the wilderness were less aggressive. They infiltrated these regions by occupying unclaimed areas in between the various city-states, often making defence treaties with the latter. As time went on, the less culturally developed newcomers adopted the customs and habits of civilization, until, in the end, they became the deter-mining influence on the native language, culture and economy. They made a crucial contribution to the rise of patriarchy. These nomads are what the Bible has in mind when it speaks of Israel as a name for the confederation of twelve tribes, without giving a concrete explanation of the name. Such nomadic tribes as these from the Arabian peninsula did at one time im-migrate into the country, and later narrators considered them children of a single father, Jacob, also called Israel. But nowadays the meaning of the name is just as obscure as the whole early history of which it is part. Biblical prehistory – everything prior to the enthronement of Saul, the first king, *c.*

1000 B.C. – is made up of myth, aetiological tales and legends. The brief notices we find concerning the land of the Bible in Egyptian and Mesopotamian documents still remain unclear. We don't know, for example, what the phrase, 'the foreign nation of Israel', on the stele of Merneptah in Thebes from *c.* 1200 B.C. refers to, whether it means a single tribe of nomads or an alliance of several tribes.

It is safe to assume that these nomadic tribes were patriarchally organized. Just as the Hellenes attacked the matriarchal inhabitants of Attica, and from this clash of two conflicting kinds of society Greek mythology received its most powerful impetus, so the mythology of the ancient Near East was profoundly stimulated by the encounter of different social structures. This is reflected in the Bible itself, which is full of myths about the encounter between the nomadic tribes of Israel and the agriculturalists inhabiting Canaan. The immigration of the Israelite nomads into Canaan (modern Palestine), began in about 1300 B.C., when both the New Kingdom in Egypt and its two rivals, Assyria and Babylon, were undergoing internal crises.

There is no way, of course, that we can plot out exactly the time frame for the tribes' nomadic existence, either when it began or when it ended. We can only ascertain the rough period of between 1300 and 1000 B.C., during which the tribes penetrated into the territory of Canaan, in loose succession, at longish intervals, arriving at different places from various directions. These individual tribes kept a clan-based sense of identity, which is a characteristic feature of such nomads. Even later, after the destruction of the first temple of Jerusalem in 586 B.C. by Nebuchadnezzar of Babylon, the priestly trained narrator of the Books of Chronicles still believed in this tribal self-consciousness: he reckons the number of returnees from the fifty-year Babylonian captivity and of volunteers in the rebuilding process by the old tribal connections, which by then were long since gone – if they had ever really existed. But for half a millennium this sense of tribal identity left its mark on the historiography of the Bible, and in this the years of hard labour in Egypt played a critical part. For, according to tradition, Moses freed the Israelites from the Egyptian bondage into which they had innocently fallen. The miraculous liberation from Egypt, and the Joseph stories preceding it, were presumably modelled on the history of a tribe that, like many other nomadic peoples from the desert, had been given shelter and grazing rights in Egypt in exchange for certain services. And so Moses, one conjectures, emancipated such Israelites from exploitation by the Egyptians.

In the history of civilization, the tribal invasion of Canaan coincides with the beginning of the Iron Age. The archaeological remains of the cities which the tribes found in their path reveal the typical characteristics of the Late Bronze Age. Pots and shards from different sources testify to extensive trade on the land bridge between Asia and Africa, and to the presence of various peoples, now long forgotten, speaking a variety of languages. The population of Canaan was Semitic, but when the Israelites entered the country, its ruling class was still made up in part by the descendants of the Hyksos. These were a people from the Hurri-Mitanni mountains who ruled Syria-Palestine, Assyria and Egypt in the middle of the second millennium B.C. The descendants of the Hyksos, once they were seated on the thrones of Palestine, were loyal vassals of Egypt, which had in the twelfth century grown too weak to protect them. The nomadic tribes at first only occupied the parts of Canaan that were, in the Bronze Age, unpopulated or only thinly settled, as we see from biblical remarks concerning the boundaries of the individual tribes. The power of such tribes did not permit more ambitious conquests: the nomads seldom had more than 300 fighting men. Thus, according to Chapter 15 of the Book of Joshua, the tribe of Judah settled to the south of Jerusalem, but Hebron already belonged to the Calebites, as Chapter 14 shows. Other peoples settled in this region included the Othnielites, the Kenites and the Jerahmeelites, likewise mentioned in Joshua 15 and I Samuel 27: 10.

According to the fragmentary information provided by the first chapter of the Book of Judges, the tribe of Simeon occupied the far south (though we know nothing further about them). If Judges 15 may be trusted, the tribe of Dan dwelt in the extreme north. The most important tribes were those of the so-called 'House of Joseph', namely Ephraim and Machir-Manasseh (see Joshua 16–17). Ephraim had the largest territory, Benjamin the smallest, according to Joshua 13. In the country east of the Jordan lived the tribe of Gad, and also, presumably, of Reuben, although here, too, we have no more specific information about that tribe (Joshua 13). In the north lived members of the tribes of Asher, Zebulun, Issachar and Naphtali (Joshua 19). These regions had only a very few far-flung Canaanite settlements, which in the course of time were slowly absorbed by the tribes. A regular conquest of the land – something comparable to, say, the wars waged by Tukulti-Ninurta I of Assyria (1243–1207 B.C.) or Ramses II of Egypt (1290–1223 B.C.) – never took place. Both those kings had proper armies. In his campaigns, for instance, Ramses copied the technique of fighting from war chariots as practised by his enemies, the Hittite kings. He improved on it and conquered the Palestinian region of the Hittite empire. The rock cliff temples of Abu Simbel today proclaim his glory. Tukulti-Ninurta of Assyria had at his disposal a mercenary army with the finest armour, measured against which the individual nomadic tribes were small and weak. One of the tribes, Levi, evidently suffered the fate of being 'scattered among all the tribes' by the Israelites entering Canaan along with it.

Perhaps the only bond uniting these tribes was worship at a common sanctuary. The sayings in Genesis 49 and Deuteronomy 33, where all the tribes are mentioned in a liturgical hymn, could be read as a religious service or ritual text. For the account in Joshua 24, despite its bias, seems to attest to a collective celebration at a shrine. But the tribes – and in this they resembled the Greek amphictyonies – were only very loosely grouped around the sanctuary, in this case the ark of the covenant. The Greek amphictyonies were leagues of different states designed to protect a given shrine. The league of Delphi also had twelve member states, but the numbers three, six and twelve grew out of calendrical calculations. Queen and king, moon goddess and sun god, once ruled by taking turns, three or six months at a time. If the sanctuary was abandoned or destroyed, the bond between the tribes generally fell apart and new groupings arose around a new central shrine, in which case all the tribes naturally kept their own local and family cults. Each tribe also worshipped its own progenitor, royal ancestor and god. The details concerning these cults and festivals at the old tribal sanctuaries have been expunged from the Bible by the priestly editors of the Jerusalem school. They did this in the third century B.C. when they were gathering and arranging the biblical myths in order to justify the dogma to which they owed their livelihood, namely that the sacrificial rite at the temple of Jerusalem was the only correct and divinely ordained form of worship. This is why tradition is silent about the old tribal arrangements and institutions. For a like reason we have little traditional material about the Judges in Israel.

The Judges are the conspicuous tribal authorities, the safeguards of independence from the monarchy and the temple priesthood, and hence their opponents. Although a biblical book was named after them, it is no longer possible to determine their function with any accuracy. They were either charismatic military commanders or guardians and interpreters of divine law, i.e. arbitrators for cases affecting the entire confederation. At times the tribal elders pronounced judgement, as is shown by the patriarchal structures and subdivisions mentioned in Joshua 7: 16–18.

The straggling nature of the immigration also led to the tribes' reaching a peaceful modus vivendi with the Canaanites. They took part in the local economy, adopted the traditional agricultural festivals and appropriated the ancient Canaanite cult sites. They did have problems, however, in defending themselves, especially against the attacks of camel-mounted nomads from the deserts of the Arabian peninsula, such as the Midianites, as well as against the Philistines, the Sea Peoples. In such periods of crisis the sturdy tribal confederation was always active.

The Israelites, it is certain, raised small livestock. The camel nomads were, by contrast, well-organized fighters who supported themselves mostly by trading and providing military services to various kings. The Philistines invaded the country at about the same time as the Israelites. They came by sea from Crete, Cyprus and Asia Minor, retreating in the face of the Dorian invasion. Like the Israelites, they fought for the land, but they were already solidly organized into kingdoms, whereas the Israelites remained independent nomadic tribes until they too chose a king.

The reports in I Samuel 9–11 suggest that the monarchy was established in Israel in the wake of a military victory of certain tribes led by Saul, a Benjaminite, over East Jordanian desert tribes, the Ammonites. The legend has it that Saul was appointed king thanks to the efforts of Samuel, the man of God. The proclamation occurred in about 1000 B.C. in Gilgal, an old Canaanite sanctuary. Saul's was a military kingship, that is, his role was limited to leading the tribal army in campaigns against their enemies. Saul was a successful commander, and, according to the legend, his son Jonathan didn't lag behind him in heroic deeds. The Israelites under Saul apparently managed to secure the frontiers in the north, east and south of the country. The biblical accounts seem to agree on that point. But only the next king in Israel, David, succeeded in making the western border safe against the aggressive Philistines. Saul's brief two-year reign did not last long enough for a loose tribal confederation to develop into a strong military despotism. The biblical accounts sound credible when they say that the establishment of the monarchy met bitter resistance from the old tribal priests, who were keen on the security of their cult shrines but not on the erection of a new power structure like that of the Canaanite kingdoms. There, as they could see, the king was also the supreme high priest and deputy of the city's god, was indeed the son of the gods and hence a god himself. Old Samuel therefore plotted against Saul's kingship which ended in catastrophe: Israel was defeated by the Philistines, and Saul and his sons fell by the hand of an assassin.

David probably came to power, starting in Judah and Hebron, with the help of the same country priests who overthrew Saul. His kingship was a military one, his rise that of an oriental despot. Through bribery, cunning, perfidy and, on occasion, murder, he got rid of all his rivals. By marrying one of Saul's daughters, he laid a seemingly legitimate claim to Saul's throne, which he ultimately ascended. After being chosen king of Israel, David transferred the seat of power from the northern part of the country to the south, to the fortress of Jerusalem which he had just conquered. He then claimed the rights of king and high priest, in the manner of his Middle Eastern colleagues, without, however, interfering in the functions of the local priestly cults.

David was successful in foreign affairs. Within the country he fought the resistance of the old conservative tribal princes. He did not succeed in fusing the two kingdoms of Israel and Judah, which were bound together by their loyalty to him, into a national unit, as is shown by the conclusion of Absalom's rebellion in II Samuel 20. It was true that the ark of the covenant was brought to his royal city of Jerusalem, an old Canaanite cult site. But the priests who served the ark were not yet in complete control because the old regional holy places and their sacrifices were still in business, both in the former tribal regions of Israel and Judah and in the parts of the country conquered by David and integrated into his kingdom. II Samuel 24 gives the boundaries of the kingdom subject to David's military conscription. The census figures reveal a sizeable population, but they cannot disguise the real political weakness: a state made up of various peoples whose distinctive features were very much intact. It was held together only with difficulty, through the power and authority of the king and his troops.

Aside from the crowns of Judah and Israel, David also bore those of Damascus, of the Ammonite kingdom east of the Jordan, of the kingdoms of Edom, Moab and Zoar south-east of the Dead Sea. This empire managed to see the light because around the beginning of the first millennium B.C. there were no large kingdoms bent on expansion in either the land of the Nile or Mesopotamia. Between 1085 and 950 B.C., for example, Egypt was divided, and the pharaoh of Thebes reigned in opposition to the pharaoh of Tanis. In Mesopotamia, the heirs of Tiglath-Pileser I of Assyria (1112–1074 B.C.) could not keep the empire together, and Assyria would not regain its strength till the ninth century. David exploited this pause in the quest for power by the two great river valley civilizations. Even the struggles over succession to his throne (II Samuel 7, 9), which might otherwise have led Israel's nearest neighbours to intervene, ran their course without damaging the kingdom. These dynastic struggles cost the lives of two of David's sons. By means of a clever cabal, the priestly-prophetic party finally managed to win David's approval of their pretender Solomon, who then ascended the throne around 972 B.C.

Solomon's first act as king which the Bible informs us of was to have his brother Adonijah and his partisans at court put to death. Power was also seized by Benaiah the son of Jehoiada, who was both chief of the royal bodyguards and commander of the army. In David's time, these two functions were still separate. David's troop of professional soldiers, the Cherethites and Pelethites (Cretans and Philistines), and the volunteer fighters from the adult men of Israel, groups which had been rivals till then, were forcibly united. Thus an all-important privilege and weapon of the individual tribes was taken from them. This was a political error on Solomon's part, a tribute he had to pay to his paladins, and it soon cost him dearly. Edom and Damascus defected and were not won back. The northern tribes attempted an uprising. Solomon was able to put down the rebellion, but it did grievous harm to the body politic. The voluntary supply of conscripts to the army by the tribes was an expression of the old nomadic way of life, which throve more vigorously in the north than in the south, in Judah, David's ancestral home, where economic development was more advanced than in the north. Demeaning conscripts to the level of the royal mercenary army, and Solomon's attempt to imitate the luxury and splendid display of oriental potentates, for which he necessarily had to introduce taxation, weakened the only instrument available to hold the state together, namely the tribes' former readiness for battle.

Under Solomon's rule, reforms were carried out with the primary purpose of covering the costs of the monarchy by collecting higher taxes and duties. Above and beyond the military draft, Solomon's subjects were now mobilized for the corvée. By building the temple in Jerusalem, in whose inner sanctum the old ark of the covenant was set up, Solomon trespassed upon the internal relations of the individual tribes, which had up till that point tended their own local shrines. The great Old Testament prophets arose from the circles of these local cult priests. The proverbial 'wrath of the prophets' expressed the political opposition of the old clan associations to the central government of king and temple priesthood in Jerusalem. The prophets preached and fought in the name of a god called Yahweh Sabaoth, that is, Yahweh of the hosts (stars, tides, natural forces). This god acted and ruled as a sovereign, independently of priests, temples, sacrifices and feasts, which were hateful to him. He spoke and acted amid thunder and lightning for old-fashioned justice (i.e. tribal interests), because the ancient clan arrangements that took care of all members of society had broken down over the course of time. Solomon tried to combat the dissatisfaction arising from his policies with a strong military build-up, as is seen in the construction and fortification of garrison cities in the countryside. But this provoked the old conservative forces to lively resistance. The extensive trade and merchandise traffic, as well as the new urbanized lifestyle, which ran contrary to the older tribal customs and interests; a class of officials no longer exclusively Israelite who exercised enormous power throughout the country, and who also represented the interests of the kings of Tyre, Sidon and Egypt – all this stirred up a swelling wave of hostility towards the absolute monarchy during Solomon's reign.

The split between Israel and Judah broke wide open after the death of Solomon in 932 B.C., when his successor Rehoboam, who had already been anointed king in Judah, went to Shechem to receive the homage of Israel along with its royal crown. But the tribes of Israel rejected him as king, when Rehoboam, totally misunderstanding the actual balance of power, turned down the proposed reforms, which dealt mainly with ending conscription and the high taxes. The northern tribes chose another king, and the alliance between the two states disintegrated. In the southern kingdom of Judah, the Davidic dynasty continued to rule until its downfall in 586 B.C. In the northern kingdom, the old elective monarchy, with Jeroboam as its first ruler, was revived, but, in terms of historical development, this unquestionably represented a step backwards.

Jeroboam also detached the northern kingdom from Jerusalem in cultic matters. He restored the old bull-god shrines at Bethel and Dan, and tried to conduct ceremonies in these sites as in Jerusalem. Both this and his effort to strengthen the king's central authority – in the north – lost him and his successors the initial sympathy and support of the clans. This becomes especially clear in the prophets, for example, in Amos, who now spelled out in detail all the mistakes and weak points of the king of Israel and proclaimed them aloud on the street, just as had been done to the kings in Judah.

The history of the northern kingdom of Israel all the way till its downfall in the year 722 B.C. was merely a series of struggles between rival factions contending for the throne. Beneath this lay the interests not only of the northern tribes themselves, but also of the surrounding nations. Only two attempts were made to found a royal dynasty in the north, and they failed to arrest the break-up of the kingdom. In the southern kingdom of Judah, which survived for another century, political developments followed a more regular pattern. The northern kingdom remained dependent on the policy of the kings of Assyria until finally, in 722 B.C., it was broken up by Sargon II. Meanwhile Judah had taken the timely step of becoming a vassal state of Assyria, as Assyrian royal inscriptions attest. Occasionally, it is true, the Jerusalem kings tried to exploit the disagreements between Egypt and Assyria to win an interval of relative independence. For instance, in about 700 B.C. King Hezekiah dared to remove from Jerusalem the ensigns that symbolized both the foreign nation and the supremacy of its foreign god. In about 630 B.C. King Josiah even incorporated some Assyrian provinces into his confederation of states. During his reign the historical identity of Judah was revived by the sudden rediscovery of the 'Law'. But Josiah and his political plans fell prey to Egypt's expansionist drive northwards. And then, in 587 B.C., Nebuchadnezzar of Babylon, in the course of a quarrel with Egypt, absorbed Judah into his empire as a provincial state. After that the Davidic dynasty was deported to Babylon, together with the upper classes, that is, the artisans, traders and government employees. The only ones who remained in the country were the farmers and a small percentage of the urban population.

The deportation was reversed after the Persians conquered the Neo-Babylonian empire in 537 B.C. For the Persians took a different approach with their subject nations from that of the Babylonians and Assyrians: they tolerated their vassals' religious and economic customs, and, apart from taxes (which were slight, compared to what the Babylonians imposed) they demanded only the abandonment of anti-Persian political activity. By royal Persian edict, the temple in Jerusalem was rebuilt and most of the stolen cult objects were replaced.

The reconstruction of the city proceeded at a sluggish pace. The Jews themselves were not greatly interested in it, if we may believe the prophet Haggai (Haggai 1). They had become mistrustful, and pinned their hopes for the future on other things. Only when Darius I assured them that the temple would be considered a royal shrine did interest grow. The nation now rallied around the temple as a cultic community, whose members were scattered all over the ancient world, from Babylon to Thebes. The tribal priests developed into a new caste presided over by a high priest. This caste, upon which devolved the duty of preserving the old traditions, may have aroused the ire of the conservatives, as we see in the Book of Malachi (composed perhaps *c.* 480 B.C.). But, to its credit, the group stimulated historical writing in Israel and drew up the binding version of the great traditions. By the end of the fifth century B.C., the province of Judah with its rebuilt capital and its Jewish governor had become so strong and stable that the neighbouring governor of Syria felt obliged to send an anxious report of this to the Persian court.

Under their governor Nehemiah, the Jerusalemites now introduced the rule of rest on the Sabbath, which had never been applied with such strictness before. While Artaxerxes I was still alive, Ezra, 'the scribe of the law of the God of heaven' (Ezra 7:12), arrived in Jerusalem from Babylon and introduced a new cultic law. The basic elements of this law originated, presumably, during the Jewish diaspora in Babylon, but we can only speculate as to its contents. From this point on only the priest and levites performed sacrifices in the temple. Lay people were forbidden to participate in any way.

Israel's internal development was unaffected by the events surrounding the foundation of the empire of Alexander the Great and the conflicts among his successors. Israel and Judah – the provinces of Samaria and Jerusalem – fell to the kingdom of the Ptolemies, and many Jews voluntarily moved to the new capital city of Alexandria. There they formed a numerous community, inhabited a quarter of the city all their own, and made themselves a Greek translation of their 'Law' (the five books of Moses), because most of them no longer had a command of Hebrew. We may assume that the final redaction of the Pentateuch coincided with the end of the Persian period, because the cultic severance of the province of Samaria from Jerusalem and the revival of the 'high places' on Mount Gerizim at the beginning of the Alexandrian era occurred with both sides in possession of the completed Pentateuch. From

that day till the present there have been two groups claiming that each is the true Israel: the Samaritans in and around modern Nablus, who have shrunk into numerical insignificance, and Judaism, one of the world religions. This separation keeps alive the old split between Israel and Judah, between north and south, conservatives and progressives.

The Samaritans seldom or never came into conflict with the foreign powers occupying their country, but such clashes took place more frequently among the Jews. After a long period of quiet and deliberate promotion of the Jerusalem cult by the Seleucid Antiochus III, who in 198 B.C. wrested Palestine and Phoenicia from the Ptolemies, the first great uprising occurred under his successor Antiochus IV Epiphanes, who forbade the cult, having already auctioned off the post of high priest to the highest bidder. The Maccabean revolt, named after the man who led it, was crushed, but it fought successfully for freedom of worship, and this right remained intact. Although not by birth a priestly family, the Maccabees obtained the office of high priest, and they had the skill to safeguard the existence of the cultic community in Jerusalem through all the dynastic struggles of the Seleucids. Simon Maccabeus even managed to win a relative independence for his province and widened its territory considerably. His son John Hyrcanus I, amid the confusion accompanying the downfall of the Seleucids in 128 B.C., virtually made the province into an autonomous kingdom. There literature too experienced a vigorous renaissance. But ever since the days of Ptolemaic supremacy, Jews had felt a great attraction towards the Diaspora.

After 65 B.C., Judah's independence was a mere farce. In reality the Romans already controlled the country as part of the province of Syria. The emperors made broad concessions to the Jews, but in 37 B.C. Herod was the first ruler to acquire an almost independent kingdom from the Romans. He was an 'allied king' of Rome, and in his own territory he was quite free to do as he liked. Even today many imposing ruins remind us of his busy career as a builder. A typical Hellenistic monarch, he naturally drew angry fire from the pious folk. Even his splendid renovation of the temple did nothing to mollify them because he treated the high priests like slaves. He installed them, dismissed them and had them murdered if he saw fit. After his death, the Emperor Augustus ordered Herod's kingdom to be divided up. In A.D. 6 Jerusalem and Judah formed a procuratorial province: a procurator governed it from Caesarea, with both the provincial troops and ruling authorities subject to his command. Only the procurator could pass death sentences, for example. The cultic institutions of Jerusalem were not assaulted, were in fact treated indulgently, but this was after the introduction of Roman taxes had already stirred up a good deal of unrest among the population.

It was during this period that Jesus of Nazareth lived, following the tradition of the old prophets. His work was limited at first to the area between the sub-provinces of Galilee and Judah, a typical frontier region with quarrelsome neighbours on either side of the border, tax stations and a Roman army of occupation. The last visit Jesus paid to Jerusalem ended with his death on the cross. The cultic community of Jerusalem, as represented by its spiritual tribunal, the Sanhedrin, condemned him to death and had the sentence confirmed and carried out by the procurator Pontius Pilate. They probably took this step for fear that Jesus might damage the religious community with his teachings, and might disturb the carefully tempered political climate, the delicate relationship between Rome and Judah. In the years that followed, the Sanhedrin was able to get a few of Jesus' supporters executed – they were evidently seen as a threat to both the internal and external security of the country. Finally, as a result of the uprising of the province in A.D. 66, the Romans under Vespasian and Titus not only visited total destruction upon Jerusalem but ended the city's function as the religious centre of Judaism. At Jamnia, north of Jaffa, a new centre was created, where the synagogal canon of the Old Testament was put together and translated into Greek (the translation of Aquila). At the time Christianity had no such focal point, consisting, as it did, of a great many loosely knit cultic communities in various parts of the Roman Empire. These groups circulated and made use of both the Old Testament and other sacred writings. In A.D. 135 the Jews, under Simon bar Kochba, once again tried to rise up against Rome. This revolt was also crushed, and from then on the Jews were forbidden to set foot in their former holy city, which now bore the name Aelia Capitolina. The provincial title of Judea was abolished, and the country now called Palestine. The Romans would not even leave names as clues to the past. Reality disappeared once and for all into the realm of legend, fable and myth – but myth outlasts the ages.

This period of a thousand years saw the composition of the entire biblical corpus. The earliest Old Testament manuscripts date from around the beginning of the Christian era, the oldest New Testament papyri from the beginning of the second century A.D. In each case the texts themselves are older than their transcriptions.

It is beyond dispute that some of these Old Testament texts preserve living traditions which may be traced back to the historical situation of the tenth century B.C. They can be lumped together under the term 'Lay Source'. They mirror the life of a cohesive nomadic society, patriarchally structured, which confronts the legal patterns of the matriarchy in Canaan. The matriarchy is characterized by 'maternal law': the mother of the tribe, the ruling queen, is the holy divinity. The man plays only a subordinate role, while the woman has the right and the option of having several husbands. Fathers have no influence on the fate of their children.

In the patriarchy, man takes over from woman. The sacred king becomes a god and appropriates the functions of the mother goddess. He wears women's clothes. He introduces private property, along with bloody battles over royal succession. Patriarchy is the primeval form of alienation, and so there appear along with it class distinctions, private property, exploitation and the state. The confrontation between these two cultural modes was the most powerful influence on the traditions of what is called the 'Lay Source', which includes the oldest myths in the Bible. These traditions remained faithful to their origins because they were handed down in the most southerly inhabited areas of Palestine, where the nomadic way of life lasted into the fifth century B.C. When the five books of Moses were codified, the Lay Source was melded with the other sources.

The second oldest traditional source of the Pentateuch is termed the 'Elohist Source'. In these texts the name of God is always given as Elohim. The god Elohim was very lofty, very kind, and dealt directly with men. The texts of this branch of scripture show by their style that they derive from the tradition of the old Canaanite local cults, which continued to survive and to undergo less interference in the tribal regions of the north than in the south (the neighbourhood of Jerusalem). Elohim would have nothing to do with war. He loved the order and harmony of agricultural society, still closely connected to matriarchy.

In direct contrast to Elohim stood the Yahweh cult of Jerusalem, which institutionalized the priesthood. The Elohist tradition held that all of Israel was to be a nation of priests. It rejected the centralized monarchy in Jerusalem and the special priestly caste associated with the temple there. The group represented by the Elohist texts – a remnant of the old Canaanite population, in particular its priestly caste – did not at first lose its social position when the nomadic tribes of Israelites took possession of the land. This is evidenced by the important role that women still play in the Elohist source: the wife names the children and exercises her marital rights. Such traditions were rooted, above all, in the northern and western parts of the country, where they were attentively cultivated.

They survived there thanks to the influence of Phoenician coastal cities such as Tyre and Sidon. The Elohist group had a part in the northern kingdom's breaking away from the south in 932, just as it did when the Samaritans separated from the Judeans after the Exile. It is difficult, however, to specify the age of individual texts and the traditions behind them. The conventional date of the mid ninth century B.C. makes sense because it provides an approximate time-frame for the close preliminary contacts between the immigrant Israelites and the population of Canaan. In any case, the Elohist texts are surely as old as the myths of Ugarit. Ugarit was a city-state in Asia Minor with an important harbour; it lay on the mainland across from the north-eastern tip of Cyprus. About fifty years ago scholars began to explore the language and literature of Ugarit, which provide us with a self-contained Canaanite mythology from *c.* 1000 B.C. The modern name of Ugarit is Ras Shamra.

An equally ancient tradition is found in the 'Yahwist Source', in whose texts God is always called Yahweh. Yahweh is the god of nomads and of war. He looks after the aims of the patriarchy, where males have seized and hold power. The matriarchal 'Golden Age' was over, the *pax cretensis* (as this phase of social organization has been called, after the place of matriarchy in Cretan culture) broken forever. Now wars were waged, lands conquered, foreigners exploited, centralized political authority established. All this required laws and regulations, and Yahweh enacted them. In order to maintain such laws and guarantee their observance, judges and soldiers were brought in. Private property, family law, exploitation and statist ideology all underwent a broad development. The Yahwist texts reflect the transitional period when nomadic Israelite society turned to the ways of Canaanite farmers. The Yahwist viewed work in the fields as a punishment but praised and glorified the land and its cultivation, because Yahweh himself had bidden the Israelites seize it. It was an act of virtue to wage war. The monarchy was a God-given institution, and obedience to the royal priests was commanded by law. Woman were looked upon as less valuable, important only as the mothers of children.

We can be certain that this ideology arose and was perpetuated in the new warrior caste and the royal officialdom, which were concentrated in Jerusalem and Judea, the monarchy's home base. The doctrine of the one jealous god, Yahweh, who wanted a unified people, dwelling in and farming a single land, surely had its historical point of departure in the ninth century. Yahweh would suffer no woman at his side. This zealously promoted monotheism was characteristic of the early patriarchate. Yahweh himself assumed the traits of the ancient sacred queen (cf. Isaiah 66: 13). On the one hand, the Yahwist tradition flourished in the Jerusalem temple priesthood, whence it exerted the strongest influence on the formation of Old Testament mythology. On the other, it also persisted in the old local tribal centres, and from there the Yahwist ideology of the prophets set forth to do battle with the Yahwist ideology of the priests. As power was increasingly concentrated in Jerusalem, so opposition to it swelled in the tribal centres, which saw their influence and importance dwindling away. In the name of a Yahweh fundamentally different from the god of the Jerusalem priests, prophets like Amos, Isaiah and Jeremiah defended the rights of the poor and the oppressed country folk against the priestly caste, which countenanced and shielded the exploitation.

The last great complex of traditional material arose after the Babylonian Exile in the sixth or fifth century B.C. It sprung from the priestly tradition of Jerusalem, embraced the whole history of Israel, and contained primarily legal texts. The narrative elements worked up in it chiefly served the purpose of stressing the significance of the laws. In contrast to other great biblical traditions, the 'Priestly Source' reveals a clear schema. First, it recounts the origin of all the creatures of earth, then of human beings. The only humans that interest it, however, are those belonging to the family tree of Jacob/ Israel, for the priests wished to prove that only Israel, the sons of Jacob, represented the true people of God. Owing to the sort of closure we find here, the Priestly Source has been seen as the core of the Pentateuch. It has the declared purpose of showing that the sacred worship practised by the priests in Jerusalem was the only kind in accordance with the laws of God. But this cultic practice was only a smokescreen for political ambitions, the quest for power that hid behind the royal foundation of the temple as the central shrine of Israel. Only the sacrifices offered in Jerusalem were valid, hence the entire populace had to come to Jerusalem at least once a year to be purified of their transgressions against the laws of the sacred king Yahweh.

In this source the god, generally called Elohim, is a learned man. He creates the world through his word, he writes down his law. But only the priests were capable of interpreting those words and texts. The mythology of the priestly tradition, which adapted many other contemporary myths, is distinguished above all by its editorial method: the priestly authors interspersed theological reflections among the old myths and thus made them serve their own goals.

This priestly core of the Pentateuch is not as ancient as the traditional material of the so-called 'Deuteronomist'. That source comprises mainly the entire Book of Deuteronomy (=repetition of the Law). Apart from its cultic-religious bias against every sanctuary but the one in Jerusalem, this tradition was characterized mainly by its social nature. This has led some interpreters to claim that it emerged from the intermittently active groups of rural Yahwist priests, who had once served as tribal delegates at the temple in Jerusalem, but were displaced by the resident priests and nursed their discontent in the countryside. The Deuteronomist Source dates from the middle of the sixth century B.C., and the views it represents show strong similarities with those of such men as Jeremiah and Nahum. These prophets, it is practically certain, were the instigators of the reforms carried out by King Josiah (638–608) of Judah. To achieve their purpose, we may surmise, they wrote up a memorial and termed it the original Law of Yahweh. Their intrigue had the desired results: Josiah destroyed the whole elaborate structure of the Jerusalem temple hierarchy, including its rural branches. But in so doing he also destroyed his own power base and fell shortly thereafter. The Deuteronomists aimed at making the central sanctuary in Jerusalem the bulwark of social justice, and at ending exploitation by the royal priests. But their resistance movement had no success, because it was geared to outdated models of the ideal society.

These major bodies of tradition are clearly discernible in the Pentateuch and the Book of Joshua. They also influenced the Book of Judges, the two Books of Samuel and both Books of Kings, but their effect on the remaining books of the Old Testament was not nearly so pronounced. During a long process of development, the five sources telescoped and fused together, following a pattern analogous to the formation of the various territorial groups. Thus the Lay Source and the Yahwist tradition fused together before the Elohist Source was worked into them. Finally, the learned, zealous priests of Jerusalem concluded the task of editing the biblical texts. They let contradictions stand unresolved and admitted parallel versions of a single episode. They collected the legacy of the many scattered tribes and dissolving interest groups, unified it and preserved it. It was their last attempt to lay the foundations for a new kind of unity for Israel now that the old one was shattered.

The foregoing account of the Bible's origins is hypothetical, to be sure, for we have no precise information about how the Pentateuch was composed, but it is the best possible explanation.

Over the past two centuries, textual criticism of the Bible has developed criteria that enable us to distinguish clearly between different sources. In the New Testament, for example, there are certain items common to all four gospels and others found only in one. Thus, in reading the first three gospels, the Synoptics, a number of common topics and events are treated in texts so broadly similar that one is forced to assume they all share the same source.

With the Old Testament, of course, this discriminating between sources is more difficult. In the Pentateuch the previously mentioned sources are easily detectable. The criteria for identifying them derive from the observation that the name of God plainly varies from passage to passage, as in Genesis, for example. Secondly, the Bible sometimes assigns the same event to two different places. Thirdly, in specific verses of the biblical text two different syntactic units will be found side by side but uncoordinated. In such cases, the verb tenses and the verbal prefixes that govern the relation between subject and predicate make it obvious that two different sources have been stitched together.

The method used in editing the Bible was cumulative: both new material and fresh interpretations of old material were added on to the traditional corpus, regardless of any ensuing contradictions. Newer texts explained,

altered or even repudiated the older ones. Accordingly, in the fourth century
A.D., Christian tradition could put the various gospels concerning the career
of a Son of God, together with letters and other theological writings, alongside the great Old Testament sermons on the uniqueness and oneness of God,
without Christian dogma running the risk of collapsing in self-contradiction.
The disparate elements of the Bible were held together only by the continually repeated assertion that the many different gods were, in the final
analysis, one and the same God. In its climactic assertion, fourth-century
Christian theology will claim that this God can even have two natures, one
human, one divine, and can appear in three persons, God the Father, God the
Son and God the Holy Spirit, but that – to save the concept as a whole – God
was still only a single essence. This pious construct, which belongs to post-
biblical Christian mythology and will therefore not be discussed any further
here, reflects once again the great theological topic of the Bible: shaping the
many perceptions of the gods into a singular image of God.

This theme emerges in all the Bible's literary genres. The genres themselves all go back to a pre-literary form whose exact time of origin and whose
contents lie beyond our grasp: the many migrations and population shifts
have erased any firm contours. The biblical forms were influenced not only
by the homeland they shared with other Semitic peoples but also by the
cultures of Babylon, Egypt and Anatolia, which the Israelite tribes were
forever confronting. The original literary units were undoubtedly very short,
but thanks to these encounters they underwent a manifold expansion and
alteration.

If we accept a crude division into poetry and prose, the latter category
would include the speeches, long or short, of the great heroes, such as
Joshua's farewell address in Joshua 24, Samuel's farewell in I Samuel 12,
Jesus' Sermon on the Mount in Matthew 5–7, the apocalypse in Matthew 25,
Peter's sermon in Acts 11. In the same class belong large sections of the Old
Testament prophetic books which, although in context they appear to be
speeches, were more probably conceived as letters, that is, as written
discourse.

The theological speeches described as sermons were late-comers to biblical
literature. Beginning in the middle of the seventh century B.C. they pressed
their way into the prophetic and legal texts, and from then on became their
dominant feature. In the process, the sermon topics took a noticeable turn
towards the metaphysical. With the power of the holy God and of his deputy,
the king, fading away, the power of the temple diminished as well. External
decline and fall was matched by internal. Now that the sacred king was no
longer visibly present, he had to be conjured up by the magic of the word,
by myth. This is when 'sacred history' first saw the light of day. Myths were

detached from their usual setting in religious ritual, because these rites could no longer be performed. Since Israel had lost its historical, national and political significance, priests and prophets concluded that the importance of their people lay in their being 'chosen by God', which would become gloriously manifest to all nations at the end of time. A once secular nation was to be a holy, consecrated people, for whom a 'Holiness Code' (Leviticus 17–26) was drawn up. Hence Ezekiel prophesied to the exiles and deportees that their only chance of survival was to pursue radical, cultically regulated holiness. Isaiah prophesied that Yahweh would soon create a mighty, infinite kingdom of peace and justice; he would put his servant, the Messiah, in charge of it. New Testament sermons, as we find them reported in, say, the Acts of the Apostles, proceed to install Jesus in the place where Yahweh, the Holy One of Israel, used to be enthroned.

Besides the above texts, the prose category unquestionably includes prayers not composed in metre, such as the prayers of Solomon in I Kings 3, 8. The Bible has few specimens of various other kinds of documents frequently encountered elsewhere in ancient Near Eastern cultures. It often mentions contractual agreements, but it does not transmit the text of such contracts. The epistolary material is equally rare. One example of an almost complete letter can be found in Jeremiah 29: 1–23. The letters in Ezra 4–6 seem to be genuine, as do the New Testament epistles, such as those to Titus and Timothy.

One genre the Bible has in much greater abundance is lists. Above all, there are the genealogical tables, such as those in Genesis 10 and I Chronicles 1–9, as well as the catalogue of officials, places and sacrificial offerings in the Books of Samuel and Kings. Many seem credible, while others are readily shown to be artificial constructions.

The most voluminous body of prose is made up of laws and cultic prescriptions. These were important at every stage of the history of Israel, and were formulated in accordance with the needs of each period. The most important collections are the so-called Book of the Covenant (Exodus 20, 22–3, 33) from the ninth century B.C., the Book of Deuteronomy from the sixth century, the Holiness Code in Leviticus 17–26, also from the sixth century, and the legal material from the priestly tradition, dating from the sixth or fifth century.

Biblical poetry is generally seen as comprising the group of stories about the gods, folk tales, fables and legends, the sayings of the prophets, songs, hymns, psalms and poems, fables, parables and allegories. These forms appear recurrently in all the books of the Bible. Even the books that profess to deal with the history of the tribes must all be assigned to the poetic genre, save those texts whose documentary character makes them properly historical. References in the two Books of Chronicles to the annals of the kings of Israel and Judah suggest that fully fledged historical works existed in the Israelite period.

The historical books of the Bible (the Pentateuch, Joshua, Judges, Samuel, Kings and Chronicles, as well as the New Testament gospels) have to be reckoned as poetry, because their contents are in large part poetic fictions. In so far as in these stories the gods – e.g. Yahweh, Elohim, El Shaddai, the God of the Fathers, and even Jesus Christ – play an active role, such tales are myths. That is, they transform a cosmic chaos into an ordered world, they appoint a given people to bring civilization and salvation to the rest of mankind, they shape and control the forces both of nature and society, they promise the coming of a new world. But unlike Greek or Roman mythology, the Bible hardly ever takes us to the heavenly realms or shows us the private lives of the gods.

The Bible prefers to speak about God, gods, angels, and heroes indirectly, in the context of stories concerning human beings involved in the vicissitudes of life, political, economic and social. For this reason, biblical mythology is preponderantly a kind of political-religious history. It is not theology, which would have to abstract and expound its teaching about God from many Old and New Testament texts, but rather a presentation of the various individual stages and environments, in and from which myths emerged. It is also not anthropology, which would have to analyse the numerous contradictory observations by biblical authors on the essence, function, value and meaning of humanity. Neither does biblical mythology describe the philosophies or world views present in the Bible (there are more than one), nor attempt to take the place of a history of biblical literature, which would deal with texts not discussed in this book. Finally, biblical mythology does not portray the history of the pious 'people of God'.

Biblical mythology, then, will be exclusively concerned with self-contained myths that describe the dealings of a god with the world and with men. It will address itself to the symbolic accounts of the creation of the world, of miracles great and small, of gods, angels, men and women, of this world and the next, of 'eternity'. Biblical mythology will have to cover a broad span, overarching many nations, periods and places. It will show that the one God is only a sort of fascinating curtain behind which many gods, once a part of the lives of various tribes and peoples, play out their drama. And so biblical myth, in which the experience, both corporate and personal, of the human environment in all its dimensions has taken on concrete form, provides us today, as does all ancient myth, with a feasible model for the original vision that integrates concept (or idea) and image, of the kind Lessing tried to conjure up in *Laocoon*. The biblical myths themselves, presented in this way, disengaged from their strictly religious function (on which level the modern mind can only view them as false), become then not just the key to understanding a good deal of European cultural and intellectual history, but a colourful plot in their own right in the garden of the ancient Near Eastern world.

The 'and' in the title of this book precisely defines the standpoint of its author, who has to pilot the bark of biblical mythology through the straits between monotheism and polytheism. The passage between Charybdis, spewing out its all-destructive waters, and the six-headed, man-eating Scylla is a narrow one. When Odysseus sailed through it, he preferred to sacrifice six of his companions rather than go down with all hands. And, in the Bible, King David likewise sacrificed thousands of his people to the plague in order to save his own life. If my biblical mythology now skirts the shore close by to Scylla, the many headed divinity, the reader should remember that Scylla at least spared Odysseus' life, that only polytheism keeps biblical mythology alive.

Myth is at home in cultures where the world is not explained by logic. Biblical mythology derives in all its abundance from the pre-literary period in the history of Israel and Judah, that is, from before the formation of the monarchy and its centralized government. But it drew its vital force from the persistent human trait of using poetry, however illogically and unscientifically, as a way of knowing nature, history and society. The fundamental social structure of biblical mythology – man's dependence upon his holy fathers, the sacred kings, the gods – never changed, whereas the specific image of the divine was always changing from age to age. In turn, these changes, or more properly differences, were contingent upon the social development of the various groups represented in the texts. Hence the modern reader of the Bible finds a pastoral god enjoying equal rights with a warrior god, a fertility god side by side with a lawgiver god, a national juxtaposed to an international god. The family of the gods – divine fathers, sons and mothers – stage among themselves the battles that take place on earth. The father god, Yahweh, dethrones the divine mother, queen of heaven, and the kindly Elohim watches in vexation as the struggle between the nomads and Sea Peoples lays waste his fair land. The period of Yahweh's hegemony after the Flood, when Israel, having migrated across the sea, conquered Canaan, began peaceably, but this did not last long, for Yahweh took revenge on his rebellious children. Just as Zeus sent his disloyal sons Poseidon and Apollo into slavery at Troy, so Yahweh sent his people to Babylon.

But, during the Babylonian captivity, the Israelite priests proclaimed that their god was the creator of the world, who made humanity for the purpose of mastering that world. In the days when they were living in their own country and suffering beneath the yoke of their own kings, these same priests had preached that man, the farmer, was a serf and God was a king. But now, having lost both temple and independence, they taught that their god was holy, absolutely invisible, dwelling in transcendence, that his chosen ones should sanctify themselves, to live in a state of moral isolation from the world. In the second century B.C., the priests were deprived of their social position and economic power, whereupon they consoled themselves with the thought that their god would some day make a new world inhabited by new men. For that purpose he would send his servant, the Messiah, to fashion a new realm, the Kingdom of God. Until then, however, pious Jews were to gather faithfully around the priests and obey them, for priests administered the law, the observance of which would positively guarantee admission into this kingdom.

That was the moment of Utopia, for 'sacred history' was now left behind. Even the memory of the sacred king was superseded – the 'Age of Brass' was at its zenith – by the vision of a new world that had never existed.

The last group of biblical writers, namely, the authors of the New Testament, cannot be understood apart from the background of the Roman Empire and its slave-holding society. The increasingly grim historical situation, which greatly enriched biblical eschatology (doctrine of the last times), gave rise to the notion of the transcendent Saviour. God himself would put an end to the intolerable conditions on earth by sending the divine hero, the Messiah. Jewish concepts of the Messiah are a sort of clamp binding the Old and New Testaments together. At the same time they reveal the great distance separating later writers from their predecessors among the prophets. The god-like man who was to rule the world became the weak sinner who could change neither himself nor the world without divine assistance. The master-slave relationship dominant in society now determined the image of God. And when a human being, Jesus of Nazareth, took it upon himself to break out of such fatalism, he was made a son of God, and even God himself. There was no other way to endow him with authority. Like Heracles he was elevated after death to the status of son of God, though during his lifetime he had merely been a great hero, a man who accomplished divine miracles and performed the lowly tasks of a slave.

Before the laws, tales, sayings, sermons, songs and hymns were permanently written down, they had been passed along by word of mouth, as was usual in antiquity. Oriental peoples love to tell stories, and the campfire is the home of tradition. On Moses' authority, God was quoted (Deuteronomy 4: 9) as saying, 'Only take heed, and keep your soul diligently, lest you forget the things which your eyes have seen, and lest they depart from your heart all the days of your life; make them known to your children and your children's children.' Tradition, therefore, was a repository of lived experience from the major civilizations – on the Euphrates, Tigris, Nile and Mediterranean – surrounding Israel. In this process, however, the legends, fables and myths acquired their binding force only by changing certain names and terms. But this priestly (and later churchly) editing often dimmed their pristine power and freshness. A wide range of theological reflections, inserted into songs and hymns, displaced the standard mythologems. Mythical motifs are missing altogether in the contractual documents, in the geographical, historical and economic lists, as well as in the collections of laws, and hence such texts will not be further discussed. At one time myths, fables and parables could be freely retold and altered, but when used as accounts of divine omnipotence and human helplessness, they fell under a taboo. They were turned into 'Holy Writ', whose letters were numbered and could never be changed.

The canonization of texts by church and synagogue had the effect of severing the ties between biblical tradition and the various popular mythological sources. The mythical evolution of this tradition went on in the pious writings of Christians and Jews, in dogmas and official teaching, which grew out of the encounter, in one country or another, with new and different situations and cultures. But the canonical form of Scripture has remained unchanged till this day. The manuscripts found at Qumran (1946), which date from some time around the beginning of the Christian era, agree almost verbatim with certain passages in the hitherto oldest Hebrew manuscripts (from the eighth and ninth century A.D.) of the Old Testament. On the other hand, there are also a number of discrepancies, which leads us to conclude that there must have been several written versions of individual books of the Bible, the same being true for the New Testament.

Since 1937, Codex B19A in the Public Library of Leningrad, a manuscript dating from A.D. 1008, has been considered the definitive scholarly edition of the Hebrew text. This MS. is some three or four centuries older than the relatively corrupt texts used by Luther and the Reformers. The countless translations of the Old Testament into Greek, the first of which was presumably made in the third century B.C., and other languages as well, are further proof that there must have been different versions circulating of the individual books of the Bible. Hence we can understand why Jews and Christians wished to establish a binding canonical text. For the Roman Church, this was Jerome's Latin Vulgate, a translation he made in about A.D. 400 from the Hebrew and Greek. But when Luther translated the New Testament in 1522, he used the Greek edition of Erasmus, who had compiled it from the manuscripts at his disposal in Basle. With a few exceptions, this edition is still the standard scholarly text. The division of the biblical books into chapter and verse was adopted from the Vulgate and has been kept to this day for purely practical reasons. It was not originally present in the Bible nor in any other ancient works of literature.

The main body of this book, which deals with the sources of biblical mythology and their interpretation, is structured as follows. Each of the chapters presents related individual myths. The lower-case letters marking each section of text, like the small roman numbers marking each section of commentary, are simply designed to facilitate cross-references. So, for example, the notation II,1,**b**,ii means that further material on the theme in question may be found in Chapter II, section 1, paragraph ii of the commentary on text **b**.

I have rendered the biblical texts freely and as briefly as possible, offering a literal translation only when necessary to convey the mythological meaning. This handbook is not meant as a short Bible with explanatory notes, but as an aid in understanding the mythological parts of the Bible. For this reason, it aims to analyse only the actual biblical texts. It makes no attempt to invent a lovely mythological world of the Bible – of the sort that Herder did not hesitate to make up, or like the one Kerényi invented for Greek myths – because such a mythology never existed.

The commentary tries to determine the original form and meaning of the myths and to elucidate them, as far as possible, by means of literary analysis and the history of religion. Naturally the connections between the Bible and ancient Near Eastern mythology will play a key role here. The Bible's own interpretation of the various myths will be noted only to show how their meaning evolved. Obviously a commentary such as this cannot go into specialized textual and exegetical problems. Hence only the generally accepted findings of biblical scholarship will be mentioned in the notes. The glossary briefly explains some unavoidable technical expressions as well as the most important mythological and cultic terms.

Like the Bible itself, biblical mythology bears witness to a religion already far removed from that 'primeval time' (Engels) in which all religions originated. In its gods – whether Yahweh, Elohim or Jesus Christ – it embodies a complex of human capacities, for love and hate, work and rest, building and destroying, enslavement and liberation. Like Graeco-Roman mythology, the myths of the Bible incarnate in their gods a perfect man, they speak explicitly of 'God becoming man' (Philippians 2:7) and confess that Paul and Barnabas could be mistaken for Hermes and Zeus (Acts 14:8–15). The enduring meaning of biblical mythology may be found not least in its god/man dialectic. It is like other mythologies in that it uses this dialectic to fashion the image of the perfect human being.

I. The Creation of the World

I.1. *The Priestly Account of Creation*

First Elohim created the heavens and the earth. But the earth was desolate and void, and darkness lay over the primeval sea. Yet the spirit of Elohim blew over the waters. And Elohim said: Let there be light. And there was light. And Elohim saw that the light served its purpose. Then Elohim separated light from darkness, and Elohim called the light Day, and the darkness he called Night. So there was evening, and there was morning, the first day. And Elohim said: Let there be a vault amid the waters to separate them. Elohim made the vault and separated the water under the vault from the water above the vault. And so it was done. Then Elohim called the vault Sky. So there was evening, there was morning, the second day. And Elohim said: Let the water beneath the sky be gathered in one place, that the dry land may be seen. And so it was done. Elohim called the dry land Earth, and the gathered waters he called Seas. And Elohim saw that it served its purpose. Then Elohim said: Let the earth put forth greenery, plants that bear seed, trees that bear fruit according to their kind, with their seeds in the fruit. And so it was done. The earth brought forth grass and plants, bearing seeds, each according to its own kind, and trees bearing fruit with their seeds in it. And Elohim saw that it served its purpose. So there was evening, there was morning, the third day. And Elohim said: Let there be lights in the vault of the heavens, to separate day from night. Let them be signs to mark the festive seasons, the days and years, and lamps in the vault of the sky to illumine the earth. And so it was done. Elohim made two great lamps, a large one to rule the day, and a small one to rule the night, and the stars as well. Elohim set them in the vault of heaven to shed light on the earth, to rule over day and night, and separate light from darkness. And Elohim saw that it served its purpose. So there was evening, so there was morning, the fourth day. Then Elohim said: Let the waters teem with a swarm of living creatures, and in the vault of the sky let the birds fly over the earth. And Elohim also created the great beasts that dwell in the sea, that gambol about and swarm in the waters, all according to their kind, and the feathered birds. And Elohim saw that it served its purpose. Then Elohim blessed them and said: Be fruitful, and multiply, fill the waters of the sea with life. Let the birds multiply on the earth. So there was evening, there was morning, the fifth day. And Elohim said: Let the earth bring forth living creatures according to their kind, cattle, creeping things and wild animals, each according to its kind. And so it was done. Elohim made the wild animals according to their kind, the cattle according to their kind, and the creeping things of the earth according to their kind. And Elohim saw that it served its purpose. Then Elohim said: Let us make man, in our image, like unto us. Let him rule over the fish in the sea, over the birds in the air, over the cattle and the beasts of earth, over all creeping things on the earth. And Elohim made man in his image, he created him in the image of Elohim. He created a man and a woman. And then Elohim blessed them. Elohim said to them: Be fruitful and multiply and people the earth, conquer it and rule over the fish of the sea, the birds of the air, and all living creatures that frolic on the earth. Elohim said also: I give you every plant that sows seed on the earth for your food, and every tree with seed in its fruit. But to all the beasts of the earth, all the birds of the air, and all creeping creatures that live on the earth, I give all the grass and green plants for their food. And so it was done. Then Elohim looked at everything he had made, and it served its purpose very well. So there was evening, there was morning, the sixth day. Thus the heavens and the earth and all their hosts were finished. On the seventh day Elohim finished the work that he had done, and on the seventh day he rested from all his work of creation. And Elohim blessed the seventh day and hallowed it, because on it he rested from the work that he had done.

[Genesis 1: 1–2: 3]

(i) The text of this myth comes from the Jerusalem priestly tradition. Although it acquired its present form in the fifth century B.C., its component parts are older and belong to the common fund of Middle Eastern mythology, as we know it, for instance, from the Babylonian creation myth 'Enuma Elish'. But the biblical author deliberately frames his story in contrast to the Babylonian myth. The Babylonian writer begins: 'At the time when the sky above and the earth below had not yet come to be, there was only Apsu, the very first of all beings, and Tiamat, the primeval water, and the waters of these two mingled.' The biblical author wished to draw a clear distinction here, and so he chose as the 'headline' of his narrative, 'In the beginning Elohim made heaven and earth.' But as he goes on to tell the story, he cannot help following a path parallel to the Babylonian epic. The world was desolate and void (*tohu wa bohu*), and darkness lay over the primeval sea, i.e. like Apsu on top of Tiamat, fertilizing her. The actual account of Elohim's creative activity does not begin until the creation of light. Hence, because the world was already there – formless to be sure, but in existence – his creating was not originally a *creatio ex nihilo*, from nothingness. The meaning here must be, 'The world was desolate and void', even though the Hebrew writer uses the same word for both world and earth as opposed to sky. In so doing he echoes his Babylonian counterpart, but he differs from the latter in that his description is more pallid. The Babylonian author makes the union of Apsu and Tiamat lead to the birth of the gods, among whom a quarrel soon breaks out. Then, in a battle, Marduk overcomes the primeval mother Tiamat, who seeks to avenge the death of her husband Apsu upon his murderer Marduk. 'With raging winds he filled her belly so that her body swelled up. Then Marduk sent his arrow whirring down, smashed her belly, split her body into two, clove through her innards, and set up one half of her as the sky, the other as the earth', separating the two parts with a barrier, with guards to watch lest the water force its way up on the land. Marduk then creates the moon god, the sun god and the rest of the world. Out of Tiamat's partner, Kingu, Marduk proceeds to make men, so that they can serve the gods. The Babylonian writer is justifying a theocratic social order: land and people are the property of the gods, as represented by the divine king and the priests of Ea, Marduk and Ishtar. Some vestiges of this creation story, which is common to Semitic peoples, may still be seen in the biblical myth. The Babylonian version has Marduk impregnating Tiamat by means of the winds; in the biblical myth, the *ruach* of Elohim impregnates the waters. The Hebrew word *ruach* means both spirit and wind, and the verb, sometimes translated as 'hover', means 'to move (something) back and forth' or 'to touch'. In Syriac, the same word also means 'to brood'. But the archaic context makes it certain that the reference is to an action taking place during sexual intercourse. Marduk creates men out of the divine Kingu; Elohim, one gathers, creates them out of himself. Both myths testify to man's divine nature, but they differ in their view of man's destiny: the Babylonian author sees man as the servant of the gods, the biblical writer considers him the equal of the gods and lord of the world.

(ii) Another distinctive feature of the priestly account is its placing of creation in the framework of a week, thereby making it an aetiological explanation of the sabbath. The Israelites are to abstain from work on the seventh day of the week and hallow it, because Elohim rested on that day.

The stylistic keynote of the biblical account is the formulaic use of Elohim's creative word which precedes each act of creation. This harkens back to Egyptian sources, according to which the god creates through the word that he speaks: 'After he came to be, he says: I have come to be, so that what exists can come forth. Everything in existence arose after I came to be. Many are the works that came forth from my mouth.' (Creation myth from Thebes.)

(iii) Elohim (plural of the Semitic *el*, meaning 'god') is surely a personal name here rather than a generic term. In the context of the ideological conflicts of the sixth century B.C., the word in its plural form incorporates, as it were, all conceivable Semitic *els*, together with their theogonies and cosmogonies. The hand of the biblical writer then gradually shapes the abstract plural into an absolute singular, which is both a name and a programme. But in Elohim's statement, 'Let *us* make man', the plural refers to the community of the gods that Elohim belongs to. The earliest narrators took it for granted that this community existed before creation. Elohim was at first merely the god who made the world habitable. The formulaic expression that Elohim looks and determines that each newly created thing serves its purpose contains in addition a deliberate challenge to Babylonian ideas. For Israel's neighbours, sun, moon and stars were the outward manifestations of the gods, but this text presents them as objects designed to make the world fit for human habitation, since man is to rule this world. That explains why man is said to be made in the 'image and likeness' of God. As the priestly account sees it, man's life and work are not blighted by a curse, but have a divine commission to take care of the earth and its living creatures.

Elohim lays down binding rules for life on earth. He not only regulates the time for work, but commands that men and animals should feed on trees and plants. Cattle have to be spared, because large herds are the basis of rural prosperity. We can understand the priestly doctrine of God's commands in the light of the wars that Israel lost, its two major resettlements, and its continued state of political dependence. Like all of priestly literature, this story, which culminates in the establishment of the sabbath rest (the hallmark of a cultic community), aims to prove that the remnant of Judah is the true people of God. Later generations forgot the precise circumstances that gave rise to this myth and understood it as an account of the wondrous creation of the world.

The real creation story from the Priestly Source may be found in Genesis 5: 1–32. There, in its characteristically sober style, the source tells us: 'This is the book of the generations of Adam. When God created man, he made him in the likeness of God. Male and female he created them, and he blessed them and named them Man when they were created.' After that lapidary statement there follows the list of Adam's descendants up until Noah. Even more prosaic is the roster in I Chronicles 1, which was taken over and used a second time in the gospel according to Luke, in order to identify Jesus as the descendant of Seth, Adam's god-like son. The Book of Chronicles mentions neither creation nor the Fall, neither the building of the Tower of Babel nor the catastrophe of the Flood. This was possibly because Israel and Judah had no obligatory doctrine about the beginning of the world. The only justification for grouping the priestly account of the founding of the sabbath (viewed as the original distinctive mark of God's chosen people) with creation stories is the undeniable connection with ancient Middle Eastern myths about the beginning of the world. But the priestly account took these myths and deliberately transformed them.

(iv) But the biblical author's real purpose in dividing creation into a week-long process was to present the sabbath as its goal. The strong central government of the monarchy, which guaranteed the power of the priests, had been broken, never to be restored. The priests could only salvage their influence by rallying the people to their side, whence the importance of inserting the sabbath commandment into the creation myth: man is supposed to rest from servile labour and busy himself with the word of God – which, after all, was responsible for the creation. But the word of God is in the custody of the priests. The priests and the scholars of the priestly schools are the only ones who can teach it. The myth of the origin of the world, put in its present form by the priestly source, requires that a man dedicate one day in the week to the priests: an obvious bid for power by the Jerusalem temple priesthood. At the same time the priests used this myth to oppose political dependence on Babylonia and Persia.

(v) Genesis 2–3 has been traditionally called a creation narrative, although it is actually a myth about the origin of man, and hence will be treated elsewhere (see III.1 (p. 62)). This text derives from a quite different source, the Yahwist, which certainly had no creation story dealing with the origin of the world. In it Yahweh is seen as a god of the people, whose primary concern is for human beings, not for the world or the universe.

I.2 *The Prophetic Account*

Yahweh is the lord who made the earth by his power. He established the world by his wisdom. By his understanding he stretched out the heavens like a tent. The waters of the heavens are in tumult, when his thunder roars. He is the lord and there is none but him. There is no God beside him. He made light and darkness, he is the cause of all things. If the heavens drop rain from above and the clouds stream, if the earth opens up, it is because Yahweh alone has done this. He made the earth and created man upon it. His hands stretched out the heavens, and he commanded all their host.
[Jeremiah 10: 12–13; Isaiah 45:5, 8–12]

(i) This text is a montage of sayings used by the prophets to open their sermons. Such sayings are designed to clothe the prophets (who levelled their attacks chiefly against priestly practices in Judah and Israel) with the authority of Yahweh. In the prophets' eyes, Yahweh is a god more accessible to the farmers and small herdsmen of the countryside, a god more 'homely' than the Yahweh of the Jerusalem priests, whose realm is in the ordinances of ritual law.

(ii) Yahweh speaks directly to the people through natural phenomena, which are familiar to the country dweller. The farmer feels more at ease with old images from the local Canaanite mythology than with the artful abstractions of the Jerusalem priestly theology. Yahweh rules by means of the heavenly hosts, and as their lord he needs no earthly priests and no temple economy. Yahweh's title of 'Lord of Hosts' is hence an expression of the prophets' resistance to the temple of Jerusalem and its power hunger (see also II.1.d (p. 43)).

(iii) The prophets came from the groups of local tribal priests who had lost their power to Jerusalem. They stood in open opposition to the central government, and manifested this by radically reinterpreting official Jerusalem doctrine.

(iv) This explains the well-known fact that, in the final redaction of the Old Testament, the priests assigned the prophetic corpus to the less important category of 'Writings'. By then the social position of the prophets had collapsed, while that of the priests was still solid. The priests could not overlook the ideological opposition from the prophets, which was dangerous even though it had passed its prime.

I.3 *Liturgical Texts*

Thou, Lord, coverest thyself with light as with a garment. Thou hast stretched out the heavens like a tent. Thou didst set the earth on its foundations, so that it should never be shaken. The deep covered it as with a garment, and the waters stood above the mountains. The mountains rose, the valleys sank down. Thou didst set a bound to the waters which they should not pass, so that they might not again cover the earth. Thou makest springs gush forth in the valleys; they flow between the hills. They give drink to every beast of the field, and on their shores the birds nest in the shadowy trees. Thou, Yahweh, dost cause the grass to grow for the cattle, and plants for men, bread and wine, to strengthen man and gladden his heart. Thou hast made the moon to mark the seasons, and the sun to measure the day, and the night, to give living space to the forest animals and the beasts of prey. The day is made for man to work, the night for rest. Thou makest life to begin and to end and the living creatures to return to the dust.

[Psalm 104]

(i) This text surely comes from the priestly tradition. Yahweh's creative attributes were firmly fixed in the Jerusalem ritual, just as they were a component of the old Canaanite ritual poetry encountered by the invading tribes of nomads. Here we find that the world Yahweh has created is free from war and any divine curse. Man's work is part and parcel of nature's harmonious course. Man fits into the cosmos like the birds and animals. The text gives no indication of any falling away of creation from God. Death and the natural renewal of the world are taken for granted.

Other biblical songs contemporary to this one which praise Yahweh as creator, sometimes using the same expressions, are Psalms 19:1–7; 24:1–2; 136:5–9; and Job 38–9.

(ii) This hymn displays surprising similarities to extra-biblical writings, for example, the hymn to the sun of Pharaoh Amenophis IV, which was found in the Amarna texts. Amenophis IV (1377–1358 B.C.) also called himself Ikhnaton, after his attempt to replace the old god Amon with the spiritualized sun god Aton. He founded a new capital, Amarna, between Memphis and Thebes, but came to grief as a result of opposition from the traditionally minded priestly groups. After his death Amarna very rapidly fell into ruin. Amid the debris of the royal palace, alongside the bust of his wife Nefertiti and a large number of letters and literary texts, excavators found the hymn to the sun, containing such things as:

> Thou appearest in beauty on the horizon of heaven, living sun-disc [Aton], the first of all living things ... Thou art beautiful, thou art great ... thou art exalted high above earth. The earth brightens when Thou goest up on the horizon and shinest as the sun-disc of the day ... All cattle rejoice in their fodder. The trees and plants grow green, the birds fly out of their nests, their wings praise thee ... Thou madest the world in accordance with thy wish, while Thou wert alone, with men, herd animals, and small livestock ...

This hymn is closely related to the priestly account of creation (see I.1 (p. 33)), which says that Elohim too, while all by himself, wishes for something and it comes to be, as in the Amarna texts concerning Aton. All this is lofty abstract thinking, in the priestly manner. Egyptian hymn literature was surely transmitted to the Jerusalem priests by way of Canaanite religious literature, which the Israelites discovered upon entering the country. The Yahweh cult was *not* directly dependent upon Egypt, despite the oft-repeated hypothesis that the flight of the Israelites from Egypt was tied in with the persecution of Ikhnaton's supporters. Rather, the similarities between the priestly texts of the Bible and those from contemporary Canaanite sources urge the conclusion that the Israelites adopted the literature, even as they adopted the culture, of the Canaanites. This is all the more likely since the text also resembles other contemporary sources, such as the Babylonian hymns to Shamash, thus excluding any straightforward links with Egypt.

In all probability, these hymns represent the final stage of a long development in various theologies of creation, all of which were fused and related to a single god.

(iii) Cultic practice turned this hymn into a specialized sort of liturgical text. Only trained priests could sing such virtuoso hymns, which were never in common use. In Judah and Israel the genre was certainly not 'naturalized' until after the construction of the temple under Solomon, that is, *c.* 800 B.C. The hymn is completely lacking in the social references characteristic of the psalms and prayers deriving from the non-priestly population both of the city and the countryside.

II. On God

II.1. *God and Gods*

a. When men began to multiply on the face of the ground, and daughters were born to them, the sons of the gods saw that the daughters of men were very beautiful; and they took to wife such of them as they chose. In those days and also afterwards the giants were on the earth. The sons of the gods came in to the daughters of men, and they bore children to them. These were the famous heroes of old.

[Genesis 6:2, 4]

(i) This text belongs to the Lay Source and dates from about the tenth century B.C. In its plain-spoken way, the myth tells about the times when peace and concord still prevailed between gods and men. It has no notion of the doctrines of the Fall and the curse laid on man, describing instead the untroubled harmony of a life governed by the patrilineal clan. The text makes no bones about sexuality, human or divine, but accepts it as a matter of course. This myth surely derives from Canaanite tradition.

(ii) The myth takes us back to the primeval 'days of old', also a familiar topic from Greek mythology. The priestly editor wants us to see the story as the reason for the coming of the Flood, and so in an interpolated verse (Genesis 6:3) he expresses Yahweh's displeasure with these doings. But this interpretation does not really fit the myth, which must be altered and broadened to accommodate it. The original myth undoubtedly described the historical transition from matriarchy to patriarchy. The sons of the gods – the sacred kings – invade the arable land of Canaan and conquer it. These invaders are definitely not the nomadic Israelite tribes, they seem rather to have some connection with the invasions by the Cassites, Hittites and Egyptian Hyksos (all *c.* 1500 B.C.), who conquered Syria, Palestine and Egypt. The rape of the daughters of men by the sons of the gods refers to marriages between tribal princes and the indigenous sacred queens. The mountain peoples from central Asia Minor and the Caucasus presumably had extremely close contacts with the agricultural inhabitants of Canaan. In this the myth resembles others from early Greek history, concerning, say, the encounters between Aeolic and pre-Hellenic peoples.

b. Once when Abraham happened to come with his herds to the territory of King Abimelech of Gerar, the king took away Abraham's wife from him (Abraham had given out that she was his sister). But in the night Elohim appeared to Abimelech and told him that the woman he had taken was Abraham's wife. Thereupon Abimelech called Abraham to account, and he justified himself by saying: When the Elohim (pl.) bade me go from my father's house I counselled her to say she was my sister, for I feared that I could be killed on account of my wife. Abimelech believed the warning given him in the dream and gave Sarah back to Abraham with a rich indemnity.
[Genesis 20]

(i) The story about Abraham belongs to the Elohist Source and dates from the ninth century B.C. The original narrator has learned from the Canaanite elders in his country that there once were many gods involved in the life of man. With characteristic straightforwardness the narrator has Abraham (invoked by others as a star witness for the true and strictly monotheistic faith) acting at the behest of the gods. It was clear to the narrator that there were as many gods as there were cities (Jeremiah 11:13). Elohim is a kindly god, greatly concerned lest evil befall Abraham and his wife. Abimelech must compensate Abraham handsomely for the wrong done him, but in exchange he receives from Elohim a bountiful blessing of children, for Elohim esteems human fecundity.

(ii) The story shows that the idea of monotheism was foreign to the unsophisticated popular piety of the ninth century B.C. Abraham lives with many gods. To be sure, in this passage as in many others the translators have erased the presence of polytheism. Thus the pious reader is obliged to view the 'living Elohim' (plural, i.e. the living gods, as in, say, Deuteronomy 5:26; I Samuel 17:26; Jeremiah 10:10; 23:36), and to take the 'holy Elohim' (the holy gods, as, for example, in Joshua 24:19; I Samuel 2:25; II Samuel 7:23; Genesis 35:7; I Samuel 4:8) for none other than 'the one holy God of Israel', as the dogmatic teaching of the Jerusalem Yahweh priests prescribes. But stories like this one demonstrate that old Canaanite religious beliefs survived in places remote from Jerusalem. The Jerusalem priests, in fact, never completely succeeded in uprooting this ancient Canaanite religious feeling, which was sustained above all by the political resistance movements among the long-term inhabitants of the country.

c. One day the sons of the Elohim came to present themselves before Yahweh, and Satan too was among them. Yahweh asked him: Whence have you come? Satan answered him: From going to and fro on the earth, to observe men, which is the task of the gods. And Yahweh asked Satan about Job, the most pious man on earth. Satan answered: Why, think you, does Job lead such a virtuous life? You have poured all sorts of blessings over him. His piety will look very different, if you take your hand from him. – Thereupon Yahweh gave him freedom to do as he pleased, and said: You may take everything he has away from him, but you may not touch his life. Then Satan went off, did harm to Job and tortured him dreadfully.

[Job 1:6–12]

(i) The Book of Job was presumably composed in the fourth century B.C. Its frame story contains an older legend about the unshakeable faith of a man named Job. The author of this poetic work was not scandalized, any more than his listeners and readers, by the idea that Yahweh had active dealings with the gods, the Elohim. 'Sons of the gods' means, in general, 'belonging to the race of the gods', and this includes Satan too. Like the other gods, Satan performs a positive function, i.e. he keeps an eye on the earth and reports to Yahweh (that being the mythological background to this tale). Yahweh is the lord of heaven and president of the council of the gods. Satan plays his negative role, as the spirit who plagues Job, on orders from Yahweh. Jewish dogma in the fourth century B.C. could not admit that Yahweh had a divine opponent or counter-god (see also XII.1 (p. 212)).

(ii) Only in playing his cruel tricks on Job does Satan fall into the negative associations that have since become his permanent character. After the introduction comes the story of Job's trials. The images here surely derive from the period of the Diadochi, so filled with brigandage. Job loses all his possessions, his reputation and his health. His only hope of deliverance lies in Yahweh's reversing the sentence passed on him. The fate of the individual symbolizes that of the believing community. The myth goes beyond its own generic boundaries and becomes an undisguised sermon on Yahweh's will to redeem. In addition, the book attacks the priestly theory of sin and guilt and advocates the old prophetic principle of Yahweh's utter transcendence.

d. When the Persian king Cyrus fell upon Israel, Yahweh revealed himself to him, the man whom he had chosen to be his Messiah, his Anointed One, and promised to help him. For this reason the pious men of the house of Israel chided Yahweh. But Yahweh answered these reproaches: If you wish to take me to task on account of my sons and of the work of my hands, know then that I am Yahweh, the Lord of Hosts, who made the earth, who created men, whose hands stretched out the heavens like a tent, who commanded all their host.

[Isaiah 45:1–13]

(i) This prophetic utterance by Isaiah, from the sixth century B.C., uses the term Yahweh in connection with that of Sabaoth, which must be translated as Lord of Hosts. The idea is that Yahweh has sons, and their actions, like the work of his hands, can be perceived and judged by men. The son of Yahweh is in this case Cyrus. The Anointed One = the son of god or the king = the Messiah.

(ii) Some notion of the erstwhile multiplicity of the gods has survived in Jewish tradition and may be seen in the person of Yahweh. For the Jews never pronounced the name of God. Every time the word appears, they read 'Adonai', which literally means 'my lords'. So, like the tip of an iceberg breaking the surface of the ocean, the full variety of ancient religious beliefs about the gods breaks through the monolatry of a later period. We have here living proof that the efforts to impose monotheism failed.

(iii) This prophetic text also shows very well the political opposition that the prophets brought to bear against the priests of Jerusalem. The prophets, representatives of the old-time priests who used to serve at the tribal sanctuaries before being deprived of their rights by Jerusalem, openly side with the party of Cyrus against the central government in Jerusalem. They not only invoke Yahweh as the Lord of Hosts (see I.2 (p. 37)), that is, the planets, constellations and heavenly powers such as lightning, thunder and rain, but they also teach that Cyrus, a pagan, is a son of Yahweh. It is obvious that the prophets collaborated with him and thereby materially contributed to the fall of the Babylonians and their priestly vassals from, among other places, Judah and Jerusalem.

II.2. *The Storm God*

a. When Moses and the people who had wandered with him had gathered around the mountain in the Sinai wilderness, on which Yahweh wished to proclaim his law, Yahweh said to Moses: I shall come to you in a thick cloud, so that the people may hear when I speak with you. – On the third day thunder and lightning burst out, and a thick cloud lay upon the mountain, which was entirely veiled in smoke, for Yahweh had come down upon it in fire. But when the people heard the claps of thunder and saw the lightning and the smoking mountain, they were frightened and remained behind, for they were afraid of dying. Only Moses came right up to the dark cloud in which Yahweh was concealed.

[Exodus 19]

(i) Yahweh, it seems certain, was a storm god, like the Near Eastern gods Teshub and Hadad, or Zeus and Jupiter. Weather gods have always been closer to man than astral or cosmic gods. They are most often seen as inhabiting mountain peaks, which tower into space and are swathed in clouds. Olympian Zeus, the Phoenician Baal-Zaphon and Yahweh of Horeb or Sinai all share this trait. Apart from their role as storm gods, they have other mythological functions: they are judges or law-givers, as in this case, where Yahweh comes to Sinai to promulgate the ten commandments.

(ii) The Yahwist myth of Yahweh's revelation on the mountain in the Sinai wilderness was surely a local tradition. The eighth-century narrator places the myth there, in a deliberate effort to distance it from Jerusalem, even though the narrative is no longer concerned with the regulation of meteorological conditions that ensure the life of the herds, but with an act of law that aims to ensure the human order. Yahweh has already become, like Zeus, the guardian of justice who 'sees all men's undertakings and punishes all sins', as the *Odyssey* puts it. But he is still the storm god of Sinai, not the god of the Jerusalem priests.

b. As they fled before the Egyptians and on the way through the land east of the Jordan, Yahweh went in the van of the Israelites. In the day he wrapped himself in a pillar of cloud, and in the night he appeared to them as a pillar of fire, which pointed the way for them, so that they could travel both day and night. In these two forms he remained at the head of the march. With clouds and winds he cleft the sea asunder, so that the people could walk through the Sea of Reeds, but the troops of Pharaoh following after them drowned in the waves that flooded back.

[Exodus 13–14]

(i) Yahweh in his role as storm god was a vitally important partner for a group of livestock owners. Increasing conflicts and disputes over pasture land led to his acquiring the function of god of war. The king of the tribe becomes king of the army. Thus Yahweh rides on the clouds, when he comes to help Israel in its hour of need (Deuteronomy 33:26; Isaiah 19:1; Psalms 68:5, 68:34), just like his rival from the Ugaritic pantheon, Aleyan Baal, who also 'comes riding on the clouds'. Just as Perseus liberates Andromeda, so Aleyan Baal frees Astart from the captivity of Yam, who rules over the waters of the deep. Baal smashes and shatters Yam, finally destroying the ruler of the floods. From heaven on high Astart cries aloud, 'Smite away, O Aleyan Baal, smite away, you who ride along on the clouds.' The biblical myth of the rescue from the Sea of Reeds unites both functions – storm god and war god – in Yahweh.

(ii) This text belongs for the most part to the Yahwist tradition. According to Isaiah 51:9–10, Yahweh splits the sea in half with one blow. Just as

Perseus or Marduk employs the marvellous steed of the sun, so the sun-god king uses pillars of cloud and fire to accomplish his work. Hence it is no accident that, as we read, Perseus was miraculously rescued in an ark, like Moses. The archetypal mythological pattern here is the Egyptian story of Isis, Osiris and the child Horus. In the revolt of the 'children against their father', the myth plainly echoes the rebellion of the Hebrews against the Egyptians, with whom they once had lived in peace. The Hellenic invaders fought the pre-Hellenic Thessalians and eventually conquered them (mythically represented by the defeat of Cronus).

c. Once when Moses was tending his father-in-law's sheep on Mount Horeb, he saw a thorn bush on fire, but not burning up. Out of curiosity he came up to the spot to find out why the bush was not consumed. But as he drew near he heard a voice that seemed to resound from within the burning thorn bush: Come no closer, but take off your shoes, for you are standing on holy ground. Moses obeyed and veiled his face with his cloak, for he feared to look upon Yahweh. But Yahweh summoned him to free his people, the Israelites, from slavery.

[Exodus 3]

(i) The Yahwist narrative of the divine election of Moses on Horeb has the same meaning as the command that Marduk's parents give their son to kill Tiamat, or the help that the goddess Athena gives Perseus: at stake is the politico-religious motivation of a rebellion against an oppressor. The god of war makes his appearance as the storm god.

(ii) Yahweh's theophany on Horeb is an attempt to anchor the god's first 'revelation' on that mountain. The narrator sides with the old local cults in the quarrel over the holy places. This conflict, something often seen in other religions, was an inevitable side-effect of the priestly cultic organization and of the priests' desire for power. The myths of Yahweh the storm god are a feature peculiar to the Bible. The Yahwist author employs the generally accepted mythologems of ancient Canaan, which were still familiar to the indigenous country folk. This is the key to some powerful passages in the prophets, such as Micah 1:3–4: when Yahweh comes forth from his dwelling place to tread upon the earth, mountains melt beneath his steps and the valleys split open. Or Nahum 1:3–4: he makes his way in whirlwind and storm, the clouds are like dust beneath his feet. He dries up the seas and causes floods to cease. Or Ezekiel 1:4: when Yahweh revealed himself to the prophet, stormy winds from out of the north drove a great cloud before them, which was surrounded by a gleaming radiance and a continual blaze of fire, with lightning bolts shooting out from its midst.

d. As Job pondered, along with his friends, over his fate, his friend Elihu tried to get him to recognize God's almighty power, by reciting to Job the words of a hymn. Yahweh, said the hymn, makes the sun shine and the rain fall. He covers his hands with lightning, and behind him the thunder roars. And he thunders with his mighty voice, and does not restrain the lightning. Yahweh makes it snow, and makes frost come over the earth, so that the waters freeze. – And Yahweh himself appeared to Job and answered him from out of the whirlwind.

[Job 36–8; 40:1]

e. After the great flood Elohim spoke to Noah and his sons: I will establish a covenant with you and your descendants, and it will hold for all beasts and birds as well. For in time to come no flood shall ever again come over the earth, to destroy life. I shall set my rainbow in the clouds, to attest to the covenant between me and the earth, that never again will a flood come over the earth. When the rainbow appears in the clouds, I will remember my promise.

[Genesis 9]

(i) By the fourth century B.C., when the Book of Job was composed, the myth of the storm god was no more than a great pictorial device for glorifying the righteousness of Yahweh. For Yahweh gets Job the justice he deserves. The accent has already shifted here, as it has in the post-exilic account of Yahweh's covenant with Noah and his family after the flood (see III.3.**b** (p. 70)), where the miracle of the rainbow is only a pale symbol of the great covenant between God and the earth, guaranteeing the safety and survival of living creatures. But the narrator of the Book of Job still has a polemic bias: in accord with the old prophetic tradition (see II.5 (p. 53)) he launches a vehement assault against the atonement theology of the Elohist narrator in Genesis 9.

II.3. *The God of War*

a. Yahweh is a warrior, Yahweh is his name. He cast the chariots of Pharaoh into the sea, and his whole army with it. Pharaoh's chosen champions drowned in the Sea of Reeds, the waves covered them, while Yahweh safely led his people through the waters.

[Exodus 14–15]

(i) The Yahwist narrator stresses that Yahweh has acted as a god of war. The narrator represents the old tribal traditions, and hence he opposes the aristocratic military caste of Jerusalem and their powerful position, acquired during Solomon's rule. The praise of Yahweh's strength in Exodus 15:1–8 is a song of victory, but this text, of course, dates from the late monarchical period, since it has Israel already inhabiting Canaan and the temple already built. The song is only invested with Moses' personal authority to assure it a fitting place in the sacred text (after the great drowning of the Egyptians). As far as content is concerned, the song does two important things. It establishes the fact that Yahweh, and not Moses, Joshua or even David or Solomon is the conqueror; and it states that the goal of immigration into the fertile land on the Mediterranean is not to be the erection of a hereditary monarchy, but rather a theocracy, a system dominated by the temple. The song is part of the tradition of the pre-exilic Jerusalem priests. The latter, in the face of the threat from Babylonia, tried to make a pact with the tribal princes. This was an ideological compromise; it also aimed at offering the Babylonian invaders evidence that Israel was not a political power but a cultic community. Similar ideas recur in the Psalms, e.g. Psalms 24:8 and 44.

b. Yahweh Sabaoth (that is, the Yahweh of hosts) is mustering an army for battle. His warriors come from a distant land, from the end of the heavens. Yahweh arms himself with the weapons of his indignation to destroy Babylon utterly.

[Isaiah 13:2–5]

(i) This song dates from the middle of the sixth century B.C. The downfall of Babylon, which the author has personally experienced, is here passed off as a prophetic prediction. The text is supposed to validate Yahweh's claim to be the cause of Babylon's fall and the ally of the king of Persia. Taking the myth of Yahweh the unconquered (who had already lost his people and their land to Babylon), the poet reworks it. This interpretation of history aims to get Israel into the Persians' good books. The song was one of the religious hymns used by the Jews who were not carried off into exile.

c. Yahweh always kept faith with his people in their battles, when his people obeyed him. When the Israelites stood before the fortress of Jericho, which seemed impregnable to them after the spies they sent out had returned with their report, Yahweh advised them to march around the city in silence once a day for six days, then, on the seventh day, to sound the trumpets and blow the ram's horn. The walls would collapse and the city would be taken. And so when on the seventh day they raised the battle cry, and rams' horns and trumpets sounded, the walls fell down, and the city was destroyed, its inhabi-

tants wiped out except for the harlot Rahab and her family, who had harboured the spies. The city's wealth was placed in the priestly treasury.
[Joshua 6]

(i) The story of the conquest of Jericho is a conflation of at least two different groups of texts. One tradition is designed as a showcase for the brilliant military achievements of Joshua and his men, while the other aims to extol the pivotal role of the priests and the ark of the covenant. The second strain belongs to the anti-royal Elohist tradition, while the first belongs to the Yahwist tradition, which represents the new upper class from the monarchical period, favouring both the kingship and agriculture. Archaeological excavations have shown that, at the time in question, Jericho was already in ruins. The story is therefore actually an aetiological legend, in so far as it was supposed to explain to people in the ninth century B.C. why the ruined city could not be rebuilt, under pain of death. Out of this aetiological tale the narrator has drawn proof for his myth of Yahweh the only lord and god of war, although it was originally a heroic legend concerning Joshua.

d. In the battle at Gibeon, Yahweh made such a tremendous hailstorm fall on Israel's enemies that six times as many men were slain by the hail as by the force of arms. But the battle was bloody enough by itself, for the sun stood still in the midst of heaven and did not go down. It delayed its setting for almost one whole day. For Joshua had conjured the sun to stay its course, and had threatened the moon, bidding it stay away until he had finished the slaughter. And Yahweh, the lord of the sun and moon, listened to Joshua, for he himself fought for Israel, as it is written in the old Book of Heroes: Sun, stand thou still at Gibeon, and thou Moon in the valley of Aijalon. And the sun stood still, and the moon stayed, until the nation took vengeance on their enemies.
[Joshua 10]

(i) The myth of Joshua's battle at Gibeon is a characteristic piece of evidence showing how the central government in Jerusalem, the priestly-monarchical alliance, manipulated the writing of history. The Book of Heroes, which has disappeared, presumably retold the great legends of the primeval mythic heroes from the northern tribes without any theological embellishment. This book is mentioned again in II Samuel 1:18–27, but otherwise it has been suppressed. For the ancient Near East, the idea of the sun and moon standing still was altogether believable. Nevertheless the narrator, who has the interests of the Jerusalem priestly caste at heart, immediately reins in his listeners' fantasy: never again, he says, will Yahweh hearken to the voice of man in this way. If the old story could not simply be passed over in silence, the priests could only blunt its edge with theological censorship. The myth is still working on the assumption that the sacred king/sun god and sacred queen/moon goddess obey the bidding of their son, King Yahweh, in order to help him.

e. Yahweh claimed all the booty of war for himself. No one could lay his hands on it with impunity. Once when Achan the son of Carmi, of the family of the Zerahites, a member of the tribe of Judah, took a Babylonian mantle and some silver and gold from the spoils of war, Israel lost the first battle of Ai. Achan's guilt was confirmed by lot. The whole people stoned him and his property, including his cattle and children. With that the wrath of Yahweh was appeased, and he gave them the city of Ai the next day. And when King Ahab of Israel spared the life of Ben-hadad, whom he had conquered, he had to give Yahweh another life in exchange for the king. His own son was sacrificed in expiation of the sin.

[Joshua 7; I Kings 20]

(i) The stories of Achan and Ahab are taken from the northern Hebrew corpus of legends. They illustrate the myth of the one and only God who is Yahweh. They reveal the north's resistance to the central authority of king and Temple in the south, as opposed to the power of the individual tribes and the prophetic office. The north was only too happy to tell stories about impious kings and ungodly characters from Judah. The importance of the prophets flows out of their objective historical situation. The erection of the central shrine in Jerusalem took away the power of many members of the middle and lower priestly classes, especially in the north, in Israel. Out of this group came the prophets, who, like Amos and Jeremiah, were passionate defenders of the people. The prophets represented the old social order based on the clan in its struggle against theocratic exploitation.

f. Yahweh was a merciless warlord. He himself directed the battles but he had generals appointed to lead the army. Thus David was a general in the wars of the Lord, as were Joshua and Moses. Yahweh's wars were waged against entire peoples and to the point of extinction. When the Amalekites tried to attack Israel on its way into the promised land, Yahweh swore to them that he would wage war against them throughout all generations. Moses, Joshua and their descendants were bidden never to forget this oath.

[Exodus 17:8–16]

g. Yahweh always went out to do battle together with his people, so that he could fight for them and win the victory. For this reason he also laid down a holy law for the conduct of war. Whoever went with him to do battle was holy.

In his wars Yahweh could use only those men who had been hallowed. Once when he was fleeing from Saul, David and his companions were hungry. He came to Nob and asked the priest Ahimelech for bread. But the priest had nothing but the holy bread of the Presence, which could be eaten only by consecrated or hallowed men. Hence his first and only question to David was whether the men had refrained from sexual intercourse. David was able to assure him that they had and took the bread.

Even the Hittite Uriah, who as a non-Israelite was not absolutely bound to observe the law of holiness, respected it. For when David committed adultery and impregnated Bathsheba, Uriah's wife, he wished to lure Uriah home and into his wife's bed, to conceal his lapse. But Uriah pleaded the fact that the ark of the covenant and all of Israel were in the field, and so did not go to his own house, but slept at the door of the king's house. He paid for this fidelity to the law with his life, for the king had him murdered, when his attempt to foist the child on Uriah failed.

[Deuteronomy 20, 23:9–14; Jeremiah 6:4; Micah 3:4; I Samuel 21; II Samuel 11]

(i) The story reported in Exodus 17 belongs to the Elohist tradition. The episodes concerning David in the Books of Samuel stem, like the Elohist source as a whole, from the traditions of the northern tribes, which were always very cool to the central government in Jerusalem. These episodes openly propose to use the laurels of victory, not to adorn the crown of the king of Judah, but to wreathe about the altar of Yahweh. They date from the middle of the eighth century B.C. or thereabouts.

(ii) The law of the holy war is no older than the monarchy with its standing army. War now becomes a sacred activity. Shortly before the end of the southern kingdom of Judah, when no one could wage the holy war any longer, priests and prophets, recalling Israel's bygone glories, reached a compromise that was also known as the second law or Deuteronomy. It comes from the mid sixth century B.C.

(iii) The law sanctifying the warrior had an unambiguous political purpose. The independent nomadic tribe could still protect and defend itself without laws, but the farmers drafted for military service feared for the property they had left defenceless behind, for their wives. The priestly law painted a nimbus of sanctity around its basic interests. The priests used this law to do battle against the old Canaanite piety. In Canaan, as in the rest of the ancient Middle East, the function of the deities of fertility and death were united in a single person. In the creation story found in Genesis 2–3, this double role is still visible in the paradisiacal fruit, which brings both sexual pleasure and death into the world.

The priestly law was designed to displace ancient Middle Eastern religious ideas, which were thoroughly familiar to the agricultural population of the country. The old Canaanite gods, for example, engage in sexual intercourse before setting off for battle, as can be seen in the myths of Ugarit. Thus the goddess Anat says to her warrior Itpn, before she sends him into battle: 'Be docile, Itpn, and listen: I am placing you in my bosom in the form of an eagle, as a bird of prey in my vagina.'

II.4. *The Bull God*

a. When Moses went up to Yahweh on Sinai to receive the ten commandments from him, the people, who had camped about the mountain, grew restless. Thinking that Moses would not come back, they implored Moses' brother, the priest Aaron, to make them a god to march before them. Aaron agreed, and so they gathered gold ornaments in the camp and moulded the image of a calf, which they worshipped with song and dance. 'These are your gods, O Israel, who brought you up out of the land of Egypt!' But Moses, full of indignation, shattered this image of the gods when he came down from the mountain.

[Exodus 32]

b. After the death of King Solomon, the northern kingdom of Israel split away from the southern kingdom of Judah. Jeroboam, the new king of the north, wanted his state to have its own cult places and he had golden bulls set up in Dan and Bethel, two old cult sites in his kingdom, and he proclaimed to the people, 'Behold your gods, O Israel, who brought you up out of the land of Egypt.' These images were worshipped until after the nation's defeat in 722 B.C. when the victors took them back with them to Assyria as a present for the emperor. This caused great wailing and mourning in the land on the part of the priests and the people.

[I Kings 12; Hosea 10:5–6]

(i) Both stories attest to the fact that the central government in Jerusalem subjugated the old Canaanite tribes. The Elohist text assumes that Yahweh's symbol is the bull, as it was for the god El of Ugarit. But the Yahwist source is the dominant influence in all accounts; and inculcates the idea that Yahweh is not a bull, but is entirely without form.

Both stories take for granted the fact that – as we see in the polemic by the prophet Hosea – even as late as the seventh century B.C. there were people who considered a bull the embodiment of Yahweh. On this point they were in full agreement with their closest neighbours. In Egypt, the moon was invoked as a 'rutting bull'. In the myths of Ugarit, El, the patriarch of the gods, is called the 'god-bull': 'Let him bellow, the bull, El, his father, the king who begot him!' El's son, Aleyan Baal, likewise appears as the bull of the goddess Anat and copulates with her. She then tells him, full of joy, 'Ah, a bull has been born to Baal, a bullock who comes riding in on the clouds! Aleyan Baal rejoiced over it.' The abundance of bull images discovered in Mesopotamia, like these extra-biblical mythological texts, leaves us with only one conclusion: the Bible's assault on bull worship was based on the presence of that worship in Israel itself.

The battle against Yahweh the bull god and in favour of Yahweh the god without shape or form was led by the king and priests of Jerusalem along with their followers. Its chief target was the quest for autonomy by the tribes and certain regions of the nation, an autonomy which is manifest in the bull cult and which ran directly counter to Jerusalem's plans. Those who adored Yahweh as a bull were to be denied Yahweh's friendship. Yahweh wished to reveal himself only through his law, as handed down from Moses to the priests and as administered by them. Yahweh was no longer to be worshipped with licentious freedom in orgiastic round dances, but in a carefully regulated sacrificial cult, whose rituals had to be celebrated by the priests in Jerusalem. All these texts graphically illustrate the conflict between the older inhabitants, the Canaanites, and the Yahweh-worshipping invaders.

II.5. *The Fertility God*

a. Elohim created the earth as a wonderful, well-ordered garden. But when he saw that men did not comply with his commands, but dealt with one another and with the earth in a wilful, self-reliant manner, he determined to wipe them off the face of the earth. Only Noah and his family were to be spared, for which reason he ordered him to build an ark, water-tight and with many chambers, in order to take with him some of all living creatures, all seeds and all kinds of food, so that after the great catastrophe of the flood the world would once again be habitable [cf. III.3.b (p. 70)]. After the earth had dried up, Elohim bade Noah go forth from the ark with everything else, and he blessed them with the wish: Be fruitful and multiply and people the earth. Man now received permission from Elohim to eat meat, provided he poured out the blood of the animal when he slaughtered it. For the blood contained the soul, the life which Elohim reserved for himself.

[Genesis 8–9]

(i) This Elohist text from the ninth century B.C. clearly shows signs of interpolation by the third-century B.C. priestly editor. For, by introducing the catastrophic flood, the priest has destroyed the myth. In accordance with the old tradition of the Canaanite farmers, El is described as a good gardener. Elohim resembles the El of Ugarit, 'the kindly One, El the tender-hearted'. He is more disturbed by the disorder in his garden (the land of Canaan) than by the people who caused this disorder, evidently the bedouin, the Israelites from the Arabian peninsula and the Sea Peoples, the Phoenicians and Greeks of the twelfth century B.C. Elohim therefore speaks like a farmer to other farmers: 'Be fruitful and multiply and populate the earth'; that is, work it. The farmer is also allowed to eat meat, provided he pours out the blood on the earth in the slaughtering process, thereby showing his respect for Elohim's command by giving him the blood, i.e. the life. Sacrifice offered by men is wholly valid, no temple is needed for it, nor altar, nor priests, nor ritual. Thus the claims of the Jerusalem priests are rejected.

The priestly editors, one assumes, let the Elohist account pass because, as a fertility god, Elohim, with his categorical command that humans multiply (Elohim decides whether women bear children or not – see I Samuel 1:5–6) took on extraordinary importance at a time when the cultic community was at a very low point.

b. After Sarah, advanced in age as she was, had borne a son to Abraham, Elohim wished to test Abraham and demanded that he sacrifice his son Isaac. Abraham obeyed and prepared for the journey and the sacrifice, as Elohim had required of him. For three days he journeyed through the country till he came to the place to which Elohim had directed him. And Abraham got everything ready for the sacrifice. But when Abraham lifted up the knife to obey Elohim's command, Yahweh suddenly intervened. Through his angel he prevented Abraham from completing the sacrifice. He sided with Abraham and vouched for him and bade him offer a sheep in place of Isaac. Abraham went back with his child and his servants and from then on dwelt in Beersheba. [See also IV.1.b (p. 81).]

[Genesis 22:1–19]

(i) In the Yahwist story of the sacrifice of Isaac, we find the reflection of extremely ancient myth. The sacrifice of the first-born male was customary not only among the nations of the Bible (Exodus 13:12–13; 22:29–30), but also among the Phoenicians and the Moabites. The practice was a survival of the old matriarchal traditions with which Abraham is obviously familiar and ready to follow. But the god Yahweh, who stands for a new patriarchal order, decrees that human first-born males are to be ransomed. The story of this miraculous encroachment by Yahweh upon the rights and dominion of Elohim was evidently not widespread, because the narrator of Exodus 13 is unfamiliar with it. His explanation why the first-born male child was ransomed rather than sacrificed is that this serves to bear witness to the fact that Yahweh led the Israelites out of Egypt with a mighty hand. One thing certain in all this is that, at an earlier time, the old Yahweh too had demanded first-born human males for himself. He also probably got these offerings, as the name of the sacrificial site where Isaac was taken (Moriah = God chooses) seems to indicate.

(ii) Pious interpretations of the story have always underlined the testing of Abraham's faith and Yahweh's gracious intervention, and asserted that this is the point of the myth. But the original myth describes the battle between two gods, won by Yahweh, who represents the more progressive patriarchy. This is pure Middle Eastern mythology. In Ugarit, Aleyan Baal overcomes old El and succeeds him; in Babylon, Marduk overcomes Ea and Anu; in Greece, Zeus overcomes Cronus.

(iii) The myth of the sacrifice of Isaac and the atoning power of bloodshed takes on great importance once more in Christian mythology. The first Christians tried to find meaning in the death of Christ by comparing the sacrifice of Isaac to Jesus' death on the cross (Matthew 26:28; 20:28; Hebrews 9:20–28; see also XIII.1 (p. 218)).

c. After Moses married Zipporah, she bore him a son. As they went their way with the herds, at a lodging place Yahweh met him and sought to kill him. Then Zipporah took a flint and cut off her son's foreskin, and touched his genitals with it, and said: You are my bridegroom of blood. And he left him alone.

[Exodus 4:24–26a]

(i) Translators have always attempted to make sense of this brief episode concerning Moses' wife Zipporah by various additions and explanations. Since, in these two verses, Yahweh appears only once as a noun subject, of masculine gender naturally, the masculine personal pronouns must refer either to him or to the son. They cannot refer to Moses, because there is no mention of him in the passage immediately preceding this one. There the topic being discussed is Pharaoh's first-born son, which obviously gave the narrator a cue to bring up his story. Hence the meaning must be that Yahweh wished to take Moses' first-born son because the first-born male belonged to him by rights. He was entitled to the boy. Zipporah, his mother, circumcises her son – an old relic of the matriarchy – and touches the foreskin to Yahweh's genitals. This is the only way to make sense of her pronouncing the formula, 'You are my bridegroom of blood', as she performs the act. For she is initiating Moses' child into a marriage with Yahweh, and he becomes Yahweh's child. Instead of the life of the boy, only a part of the penis is sacrificed. The biblical editor was still aware of this meaning, as we see from his comment, 'Then it was that she said, "You are a bridegroom of blood", because of the circumcision'. But devout readers were always scandalized by anthropomorphic treatment of Yahweh, and tried to smooth over the offensive reference to his genitals by inserting the name of Moses. Elsewhere, however, old portions of biblical mythology do not shrink from anthropomorphizing Yahweh, for example, in Genesis 32 (Jacob's wrestling with Yahweh; see IV.3.**d** (p. 93)).

(ii) The original myth present in this passage unmistakably points to the fact that Yahweh, as an ancient fertility god, had a claim on first-born males. In Crete and Phoenicia, boys were at one time sacrificed to the supreme goddess, after the priestesses had engaged in cultic intercourse with them (the 'sacred marriage'). This story of Zipporah's touching the god's genitals with her child's foreskin and saying, 'You are my bridegroom of blood', fits in with such ancient notions.

d. After Eve had borne Cain to Adam, she said: I have gotten a man, that is, Yahweh. After this she gave birth to her second boy, Abel. Abel was a shepherd, but Cain a farmer. And when they both grew up, they sacrificed to Yahweh. Cain offered the fruits of the field, Abel the first-born of his herds. Yahweh had regard for Abel's offering, but he disdained the offering of Cain. Cain was very angry at this and slew Abel out in the field. But then Yahweh came thither and asked Cain: Where is your brother Abel? Cain answered: I do not know. Am I my brother's keeper? Yahweh's answer was a curse: The voice of your brother's blood is crying to me from the ground. And now you are cursed. When you till the ground, it shall no longer yield to you its strength. You shall be a wanderer and fugitive on this earth. But no one may strike you dead, for I shall take sevenfold vengeance on anyone who dares to do so. – And Cain went away from the presence of the Lord, into the land of refuge east of Eden.

[Genesis 4–16]

(i) The myth of Cain and Abel is not primarily a myth of fratricide. Originally the myth dealt with the murder of a son of the gods. In this story from the Lay Source, Eve appears as the ancient sacred queen or divine primeval mother. For, with the conception of her second son, Eve has 'gotten' a man, who is none other than Yahweh. And from their union the boy Abel is born, whom the myth, logically enough, shows Yahweh favouring. Yahweh condemns his son's murderer to the most horrible punishment imaginable: Cain is doomed to be a lifelong fugitive, and no one can give him the *coup de grâce* without paying retribution seven times over for it.

Only pious souls would have found Yahweh's sexual nature repulsive. After all, they knew that the sons of the gods had sexual relations with the daughters of men (Genesis 6:1–4; cf. II.1.a (p. 41)). But early translators of the Bible took offence at the plain tenor of the text and tried to get around it by claiming difficulties with the original, such as the ambiguous meaning of the verb 'get' in the context of this passage. Later commentators have echoed this argument, and so the impression has been created that the myth of Cain and Abel is a story about the crime of brother killing brother. But the myth only took on the characteristics of a moral fable by means of a doctrine of sin that was originally alien to it.

(ii) The myth of the conflict between Cain and Abel may be compared with the struggles between Pelias and Neleus, Eteocles and Polyneices, Heracles and Iphicles, Romulus and Remus, and other sets of mythological twins in that its picture of discord among the gods symbolizes the breakdown of the system by which kings and their deputies ruled by turns. After the struggle, the stronger man ruled all by himself. Once again we have the patriarchy taking over from the matriarchy. For it is Yahweh who destroys the primeval peace of matriarchal society. He prefers his son, thereby laying the groundwork for patrilineal succession, recognizing private property, and at the same time establishing the state; when he banishes Cain.

(iii) The myth is expanded through the addition of the sign of Cain, 'lest anyone who came upon him should kill him'. This supports the so-called Kenite hypothesis, namely that the myth was a tribal legend of the Kenites, neighbours of Israel who lived on the edge of the cultivated land. For his part, the ancient narrator is trying to explain the division of society into farmers and nomads, with the nomads enjoying the special protection of Yahweh.

II.6 *The Messengers of Yahweh and Elohim*

a. One day while Abraham was living in Mamre, his family's tent village, Yahweh appeared to him, accompanied by two men. Abraham immediately recognized Yahweh, and invited him and his companions to a banquet, where in keeping with the old custom the guests' feet were washed before the meal. After the meal Abraham went with the three men part of the way to Sodom, but he returned before evening.

[Genesis 18]

b. Joshua and the army of the Israelites were camped before the city of Jericho on the Jordan, preparing to take the city by storm [cf. II.3.c (p. 48)]. One day a man with a drawn sword suddenly stood before Joshua. Joshua did not know him, and so asked his name and descent. The man explained to him that he was a messenger of Yahweh and commander of Yahweh's army. Then Joshua fell on his face to the earth and worshipped him, for the place where he stood was holy.

[Joshua 5:13–15]

(i) Both texts come from the Yahwist tradition. It is customary to identify Yahweh's companions on the road to Sodom as angels, but this is incorrect. The text speaks unequivocally of men, for the Yahwist narrator is not surprised that Yahweh should deal with men and through men. The commander of Yahweh's armies who appears to Joshua before Jericho is no angel, but a man. Joshua treats him as an army officer might treat his commandant. He performs the *proskunesis* (obeisance) before him, takes his shoes off, and listens to what the deputy of his great king has to say, the latter having already hallowed the place through his presence.

c. In Zorah, in the region allotted to the tribe of Dan, lived a man with his wife. An angel of Yahweh appeared directly to her and promised the childless woman that she would soon give birth to a son. This son, he said, was to be dedicated to God from birth. The woman told the wondrous event to her husband, Manoah, and he asked Yahweh to let the angel bring this message to him too. Thereupon the angel of Yahweh appeared and assured him that his son Samson would be a great hero in Israel. Manoah believed the angel, who disappeared in a cloud of smoke.

[Judges 13]

(i) The stories of the messengers (angels) sent by Yahweh and Elohim clearly illustrate the distance separating the individual narrative traditions. With the end of Solomon's empire, the image of God began to undergo a process of increasing spiritualization. No longer do the gods intervene directly in human history, they have their messengers. These can be men, gods or even fabulous creatures such as the Seraphim and Cherubim (see also VII.9 (p. 149)).

d. When Jacob went to the land of his fathers in search of a bride, he had to spend the night out on the steppes. There he dreamed that a ladder stood on the earth reaching up to heaven. And on this ladder the messengers of Elohim were going up and down. Jacob grew very frightened and thought that this place must be the gate of heaven, Elohim's dwelling place. Upon awakening the next morning he therefore took the stone, in whose shadow he had rested, and set it up as an altar, and named the place Bethel, the house of God. He made a vow to build a temple, a house of God, on the site, if Elohim let him return safe and sound to his father's tent.

[Genesis 28]

(i) This ancient Elohist text presents the cultic legend of the northern sanctuary of Bethel. The priestly editor has given the story a new, non-Canaanite twist by inserting the theme of the promised land.

(ii) God's messengers (our word 'angel' is borrowed from the Greek via the Latin *angelus*) had no wings in the ancient representation: to make their way from heaven to earth and back they had to use a ladder. They became the winged creatures of legend in biblical mythology only after the Babylonian exile. When 1 Chronicles 21:16 says that the angel of Yahweh, the destroying angel, appeared to David 'standing between earth and heaven', and when the Seraphim and Cherubim cover themselves with their wings, we know for certain that these mythical images come from Mesopotamia. Extra-biblical Jewish religious literature found in angelology one of its favourite topics and dealt with it at great length. Christianity inherited this interest. According to the *Testament of Adam*, the lowest order of angels (called simply Angels) is assigned to take care of individuals. The second order is that of the Archangels (the Church included Gabriel, Michael and Raphael in this group). The third is the Principalities, who rule over clouds and storms. The fourth is the Powers, who attend to the stars and the seasons. The fifth is the Virtues, a category for the demons and other non-Jewish gods. The sixth is the Dominations, whose responsibilities are the kings and the political life of nations. The remaining orders, Thrones, Cherubim and Seraphim, serve the heavenly throne. The doctrines of angelology reflect the social structures of the Hellenistic kingdoms.

(iii) In Christian mythology, the angels are gathered around God's heavenly throne. There each person has his own individual angel to care for him (Matthew 18:10) or even to take his place on earth (Acts 12:15). The angels of the nations also dwell in heaven (Daniel 10). It is part of the myth of Jesus' divinity that, after his birth, the heavens open, angels descend to earth, and salute him with the greeting of peace (Luke 2:13–15).

e. And the prophet Micaiah saw Yahweh sitting upon his throne. All the host of heaven was standing beside him as he held court. Someone was needed to entice King Ahab to his destruction. Then the *ruach*, the spirit (see I.1 (p. 33) and I.1.i (p. 34)) came forward from the ranks of heaven's royal household and accepted the assignment. He took on the form of a lying spirit and confused Ahab's counsellors. And the king fell.

[I Kings 22:19–40]

f. After David had made the borders of his kingdom secure, he had a census taken of his people, to get the information needed to assess taxes and duties. But then plague broke out in the land. This was one of the punishments with which Yahweh had threatened David, the one David had chosen as the wisest course. But when the angel of Yahweh, after smiting the land with the plague, stretched out his hand to destroy Jerusalem as well, Yahweh suddenly repented of the evil, and he caused the pestilence to abate.

[II Samuel 24; I Chronicles 21]

(i) This text belongs among the Yahwist traditions of the northern kingdom, which was also the home of the great prophets. The fact that army officers conducted the census makes its purpose evident. It was to serve military conscription and the tax system of the king's central government. Priests and tribal elders lodged protests against the census, which they saw as an attack on their rights and privileges. Naturally they had Yahweh on their side. Hence we see King David here in a remarkably ambiguous light. At first he chooses to sacrifice as many people to the plague as it can strike down in three days, but then he proposes to Yahweh to take his life instead. But his prophet Gad gets David to build a new shrine with a sacrificial altar, in order to placate Yahweh.

g. In the year that King Uzziah died Isaiah had a vision. He saw Yahweh on a throne, high and exalted; and his train filled the temple. Seraphim hovered over him, each with six wings: two covered the seraph's face, two his feet, and with two he flew. And one called to another: Holy, holy, holy is Yahweh of the hosts! The whole earth is filled with his glory. – One of the Seraphim flew to Isaiah with a burning coal, which he had taken with tongs from the altar. He touched it to Isaiah's mouth and thus helped him to hear Yahweh's voice, to obey it, and to repeat Yahweh's message to the people of Israel.

[Isaiah 6:1–8]

(i) Isaiah's vision dates from about the year 740 B.C. The prophet raises the royal splendour of Jerusalem to the level of Yahweh's indescribable glory. The Seraphim who surround the throne are serpentine creatures. Yahweh occasionally sends them to punish his people with death (Numbers 21:6). In the history of religions, snake goddesses belong to the matriarchy. The presence of snake-like beings in the entourage of masculine gods shows that they have come over to the patriarchy only in the role of servants. The angelic chorus, 'Holy, holy, holy', drowns the voice of Yahweh until man is ritually prepared to hear him. (See also VIII.4 (p. 159).)

h. Yahweh not only hovered on the wings of the wind, the *ruach*, but he also rode on the Cherubim. Thus Ezekiel saw in a vision how four Cherubim, each with four wings, carried above their heads something resembling a plate, shimmering like crystal, on which stood Yahweh's sapphire throne. Beneath their wings, whose beating sounded like the voice of Yahweh, the Cherubim had human hands. All four Cherubim seemed to have the same shape. Beside them, wheels could be seen, which enabled the throne to speed about in all directions. And the Cherubim were covered all over with eyes, on their backs, their wings, their hands – Ezekiel could see them even on the wheels next to them. Each Cherub had the eyes on his four faces, of which one was that of a bull, one of a man, one of a lion and one of an eagle.

[Ezekiel 1; 10]

(i) Ezekiel's vision is impenetrably obscure. All attempts to trace this detailed description back to a Babylonian source (a job not made easier by the damaged state of the text) have failed. It is conceivable that the prophet was inspired by the legendary creatures of Babylonian mythology when he lived in Babylon, around the beginning of the sixth century B.C. Ishtar rides on a lion, the bull is the sacred animal of Adad, and the city-god of Babylon rides on a scaly-bodied monster, like a dragon with a snake's head. We are also familiar with the winged bulls with human heads from Assyria. These creatures were once gods in their own right, representatives of independent monarchies. In the Babylonian pantheon, they had already been turned into vassals of the greater kings Marduk, Adad, Ishtar and Ashur. But now Yahweh reigns over them, and they are his subjects. But Ezekiel presents all this in a fantastic manner. The dominant feature of the vision, the fire in the midst of the living creatures, is Yahweh himself. We see here a fore-shadowing of Persian religion: the prophet uses code language to speak of the future rulers of the land. This Yahweh is so inaccessible that his followers dare to enter his presence only after extensive ritual purifications. Ezekiel is the prophet-founder of the exclusive cultic community of Jerusalem. (See also VIII.6 (p. 165).)

III. Myths about Man

III.1. *The Creation of Man*

On the day that Yahweh made the earth and the heavens, when no plant of the field was yet in the earth and no herb of the field had yet sprung up – for Yahweh Elohim had not caused it to rain upon the earth, and there was no man to till the ground; but a mist went up from the earth and watered the face of the ground – then Yahweh Elohim formed man (Adam) of dust from the ground, and breathed into his nostrils the breath of life; and Adam became a living being.

Then Yahweh Elohim planted a garden in Eden, in the east; and there he put Adam whom he had formed. And out of the ground Yahweh Elohim made to grow every tree that is pleasant to the sight and good for food. And Yahweh Elohim took Adam and put him in the garden of Eden to till it and keep it. And Yahweh Elohim commanded Adam: You may freely eat of every tree of the garden; but of the tree in the midst of the garden you shall not eat. In the day that you eat of it you shall die.

And Yahweh Elohim thought: It is not good that Adam should be alone; I will make him a helper fit for him. So out of the ground Yahweh Elohim formed every beast of the field and every bird of the air, and brought them to Adam to see what he would call them. Adam gave names to all cattle, and to the birds of the air, and to every beast of the field; but for Adam there was not found a helper fit for him.

So Yahweh Elohim caused a deep sleep to fall upon Adam, and while he slept took one of his ribs and closed up its place with flesh; and the rib which Yahweh Elohim had taken from Adam he made into a woman and brought her to Adam. Then Adam said: This at last is bone of my bones and flesh of my flesh; she shall be called Woman (*ishshah*), because she was taken out of Man (*ish*). And Adam and his wife were both naked, and were not ashamed.

Now the serpent was more subtle than any other wild creature that Yahweh Elohim had made. He said to the woman: Did Elohim say, You shall not eat of any tree of the garden? And the woman said to the serpent: We may eat of the fruit of the trees of the garden, but Elohim said, You shall not eat of the fruit of the tree which is in the midst of the garden, neither shall you touch it, lest you die. But the serpent said to the woman: You will not die. For Elohim knows that when you eat of it your eyes will be opened, and you will be like Elohim, knowing what is sensible and what is senseless. So when the woman saw that it was sensible to eat of the tree, for it seemed to her that the tree was to be desired to make one wise, she took of its fruit and ate; and she also gave some to her husband, and he ate. Then the eyes of both were opened, and they knew that they were naked; and they sewed fig leaves together and made themselves aprons.

And they heard the sound of Yahweh Elohim walking in the garden in the cool of the day, and Adam and the woman hid themselves from the presence of Yahweh Elohim among the trees of the garden. But Yahweh Elohim called to Adam and said: Where are you? And he said: I heard the sound of you in the garden, and I was afraid, because I was naked; and I hid myself. He said: Who told you that you were naked? Have you eaten of the tree of which I commanded you not to eat? Adam said: The woman whom you gave to be with me, she gave me the fruit of the tree, and I ate. Then Yahweh Elohim said to the woman: What is this that you have done? The woman said: The serpent beguiled me, and I ate. Then Yahweh Elohim said to the serpent: Because you have done this, cursed are you above all cattle, and above all wild animals. Upon your belly you shall go, and dust you shall eat all the days of your life. I will put enmity between you and the woman, and between your seed and her seed. He shall bruise your head, and you shall bruise his heel. To the woman he said: I will greatly multiply your pain in childbearing; in pain you shall bring forth children, yet your desire shall be for your husband, and he shall rule over you.

And to Adam he said: Because you have listened to the voice of your wife, and have eaten of the tree of which I commanded you, you shall not eat of it, cursed is the ground because of you. In toil you shall eat of it all the days of your life. Thorns and thistles it shall bring forth to you; and you shall eat the plants of the field. In the sweat of your face you shall eat bread till you return to the ground, for out of it you were taken. You are dust, and to dust you shall return.

And Yahweh Elohim made for Adam and his wife garments of skins, and clothed them. Then Yahweh Elohim said: Behold, Adam has become like one of us, knowing what is sensible and what is senseless. And now, lest he put forth his hand and take also of the tree of life, and eat, and live for ever – therefore Yahweh Elohim sent him forth from the garden of Eden, to till the ground from which he was taken. He drove out Adam; and at the east of the garden of Eden he placed the Cherubim, and a flaming sword which turned every way, to guard the way to the tree of

life. Then Adam called his wife's name Hava [Eve], because she was the
mother of all living.

[Genesis 2:4–3:24]

(i) We have here an unprecedented juxtaposition of two names for God.
God's original name was surely Elohim, as is clear from the conversation
between the serpent and the woman. Pious editors of a later generation had
the idea of changing the name into a generic term and adding on the divine
name of Yahweh. Scholars generally agree that the text comes from the
Yahwist source, but so far they have had to resort to strained interpretations
to explain why the name of Yahweh is missing in the previously mentioned
passages. We have left the names of both gods side by side in order to show
the phases of development a myth (which was certainly Elohist to begin with)
can pass through.

(ii) After the clause, 'And out of the ground Yahweh Elohim made to grow
every tree ...', the Bible adds, 'the tree of life also in the midst of the garden,
and the tree of the knowledge of what is sensible and what is senseless'. We
have omitted this conclusion to the sentence because it is an editorial gloss,
which awkwardly anticipates the point of the myth. Likewise, the geographical description of Paradise, locating it at the source of four rivers,
Pishon, Gihon, Hiddekel and Phrat (Genesis 2:10–14; the rivers are thought
to be the Indus, Nile, Tigris and Euphrates) is an amplification by the editor,
and so has been dropped. This mythical geography (and more such names
can be found in the mythical list of nations in Genesis 10) is closely related
to the thought of the Babylonians, who believed that the world was an
oblong surface surrounded by four streams, which encompassed all the
riches imaginable and everything desirable in nature. Interpolated into the
myth, the reference to the rivers only slows the pace of the story.

(iii) 'The tree in the midst of the garden' is more correct than the traditional
'tree of the knowledge of good and evil'. In this passage, the theologically
minded editor has sought to disclose the mystery of the tree lest the serpent
be the first to reveal to man the true qualities of the trees. Furthermore, 'good
and evil' are only weak attempts to explain Yahweh Elohim's knowledge of
the entire world, and hence the translation 'sensible and senseless' is prefer-
able. Christian mythology has tried to ground an ethical system on this pair
of terms in connection with the doctrine of original sin. But the myth deals
primarily with the nature of God, who as creator of the world judges his work
not ethically (good and evil) but pragmatically. We may only assume that all
the other trees of the garden – unless there is another special tree in addition
to the one in the midst of the garden – bear fruit that gives eternal life to the
man who eats them. For from now on man is to eat only the plants of the

field. We can be sure, then, that the narrator had the mythologically univocal tree of life in mind.

(iv) The sentence which follows 'because she was taken out of Man' – 'Therefore a man leaves his father and his mother and cleaves to his wife, and they become one flesh' – has also been omitted here. Even its language shows that it does not belong to the myth. It may date from a period that saw in the myth an argument for marriage on matriarchal lines.

(v) The Hebrew word used here for 'wise' (or 'subtle') can also mean 'naked'. Adam and his wife were naked, as the course of the story makes plain. The serpent was also considered a naked animal, because it has neither hair nor feathers. The fact that Adam and Eve have just been described as naked might suggest that the serpent's nakedness was likewise being stressed, except that the usual translation, 'subtle', conveys better the original positive meaning of the myth. The sentence, 'Then Adam called his wife's name Hava [Eve], because she was the mother of all living', has been placed at the end of the myth, because its sententious character interrupts the story, which like all genuine Middle Eastern myths originally had no moral. (Linguistically, the biblical etymology, Hava = mother of all living things, is untenable.)

(vi) Contrary to traditional usage, the text here speaks of 'Adam' rather than of 'the man', despite the definite article before 'Adam'. This is to under-line the character of the myth. Since *'adamah* means earth, the Hebrew narrator naturally evoked in his audience a connection between the 'man', Adam, and 'earth'. Hence, to translate the name Adam and the term 'man', the phrase 'the earthly one', would have to be used.

(vii) The myth of man's origins was originally an Elohist text. It is not a myth about the creation of the world, because the world does not really interest the god Elohim very much. He is the gardener of agricultural land, and intent on keeping order in it. For this reason he takes special care of man, and the creation of man is described in detail, in marked contrast to the priestly account (see I.1 (p. 33)) of the creation of the world.

But, in its present form, the myth has already been reshaped by Jerusalem theologians loyal to the monarchy. To check the influence of their opponents – the old Canaanite priests, who were still operating, particularly in the north among the Israelite tribes – it is now claimed that Yahweh created men. Yahweh is the sacred king who strolls in his garden, while men must live in drudgery. The golden age of Elohim is past, when men, as the myth imagines it, lived and worked with neither care nor fear. For them death held no more terror than sleep. But that is gone for good. Yahweh demands obedience and work.

(viii) The Yahwist myth as we now have it deals only with the creation of the first couple. Its summary introduction stresses that man was there before anything else in the world had yet existed.

The first man is called Adam, because he was formed from the arable soil, the alluvial land in the river valleys of the Middle East. Woman too is man (human), because she comes from Adam, which henceforth will be the term for man (male).

Yahweh creates them both. The myth once had a positive accent: Adam and Eve are to be in charge of the garden as the deputies of God. Adam receives the divine right to name the animals. He is a lord, and his wife Hava is a lady. She bears the name of the Phoenician snake goddess, who is also known elsewhere in mythology as the mother of humanity. In Aramaic and Syriac, for example, the serpent is called *hevya*. This coincidence is important for understanding the myth, because in its original form it took a positive view of the woman's longing to be wise. And Elohim is not distressed to see that man has become like a god. Elohim takes away from him the management of the garden and assigns the earth to him instead. But man loses immortality, which he had possessed by eating the fruit of the trees in Paradise, for all the trees there confer immortality. This notion is still alive today in Islam.

(ix) Adam and his wife were made for work. The myth views work negatively, but its fatalistic tone comes from the theological maxims which are presented as Yahweh's sentence of the man and the woman. Only the serpent is cursed, 'because you have done this'. The judgement of the serpent is introduced by the formulaic curse (Heb. *arur*). The Yahwist formulas for the destiny of men and women turn the ancient myth of the creation of the first godlike human couple into an aetiological legend, to explain why the farmer's daily work and woman's pregnancy are so exhausting. The sentences express the religious views of the Yahwist tradition, which during the regime of Solomon wished to account for the fate of the peasants, condemned to grinding toil, and so shaped the biblical myth in this direction.

The curse on the serpent has, in addition, another concrete application. Any unprejudiced reader can see that the myth as it has been handed down shows the serpent playing a positive role in the humanization of man. This myth was still alive in the ninth century B.C., as were the old Middle Eastern snake cults. The tale of the 'bronze serpent' in Numbers 21 reflects the Canaanite custom of venerating snakes. Athena, too, was originally a Cretan-Mycenaean serpent goddess; in Crete she was considered the mother of life. This political reference gives the myth a double function, a meaning both political and religious. The serpent, symbol of the culture-bearing coastal peoples, is granted a part in enabling man to turn from a nomadic existence to agriculture. But, at the same time, the creature is cursed.

Yahweh must triumph over it, the tribes of Israel must conquer Canaan, must trample it down, even if this arouses an inextinguishable hostility that will cause the serpent to 'bruise his heel'. This is how the statement concerning the 'enmity' must be understood. (See also V.3 (p. 119).)

(x) Christian dogmatists, operating under the assumption that the Old Testament proclaims in advance the Christ of the New Testament, have naturally found a proto-evangel in this text. The seed of the woman is supposed to be Christ, and the serpent is the devil. The way is already paved for this interpretation in Revelation 12, but strictly speaking it is just an element of Christian mythology, irrelevant in this context.

(xi) The foregoing exegesis brings out a further meaning of this ancient myth. It served as yet another justification of the older matriarchal social structure, where woman plays the clever, decisive, enterprising role. For her sake, the man leaves father and mother and enters his wife's family. But the expanded form of the myth alters this, as the Yahwist reverses the statement: despite the hardships of pregnancy the woman will desire her husband, and he will be her lord and owner, and she his property.

(xii) The myth's original assessment of sex (like the myth as a whole) was positive. After the couple eat from the tree of knowledge, they recognize the purpose of their own bodies, their sexuality. With complete naturalness the narrator reports how, in his opinion, lovers behave. The lover tries to hide himself and his beloved from the eyes of potential rivals – and for Adam, who knows now what is sensible and what is not, Yahweh is a rival. To the Yahwist narrator, Yahweh is a man, even if he is also a lord, a mightier king than David. After all, David did not scruple to take the wife of another man (see II.3.g (p. 150)), and the sons of the gods, as the narrator sees it, once paired wantonly with the daughters of men (cf. II.1.a (p. 141).

One can call this myth of the creation and humanization of man 'the story of the Fall' only by a drastic reinterpretation. In the ninth century B.C., people living in Judah used it to explain the contemporary situation. Yahweh, the almighty lord and king, sits majestically in his marvellously beautiful garden, surrounded by all the world's riches, while the farmer and his wife have to work hard. The lovely garden (our 'Paradise' is the Septuagint's version of 'garden') remains inaccessible to them. The farmer naturally yearns for the garden, for its shade and water, in the dry heat of his everyday toil. But he doesn't lose heart, for he has his fitting helpmate, Eve, the mother of the living. With her he begets many children, his helpers, who make life bearable, as the story goes on to tell. For Old Testament man, death was no punishment. Hence we should not read Yahweh's prohibition against eating of the tree and the accompanying threat of death in the way that theologians have. Here, as in Genesis 1 (see I.1 (p. 133)) they have used the myth to spark reflections on obedience and disobedience, sin and blessedness, and so forth. The great model for that sort of mythic interpretation is provided by the fifth chapter of Paul's letter to the Romans. The story in Genesis 2–3 is susceptible to such readings, but to decide whether any such speculations are reasonable or absurd one has to measure them against – among other things – the demonstrated original function of the myth. And, in its biblical form, that myth reveals no concrete ties with other myths outside of those, already indicated, from the coastal cities of Canaan. As we now have it, it is a thoroughly sound link in the chain of ancient Middle Eastern creation myths and a testimony to the creative achievements of biblical mythology.

III.2. *The Beginnings of Civilization*

The first child born to Adam and Eve was Cain. And Cain begot on his wife Enoch, for whom he built a city, named after his son. A son was born to Enoch named Irad, and Irad begot Mehujael, the father of Methusael. Methusael was the father of Lamech, who had two wives, Adah and Zillah.

Adah bore him Jabal, who became the father of those who dwell in tents and have cattle. His brother Jubal became the father of those who play the lyre and the pipe.

Zillah bore Lamech to Tubal-cain, the forger of all instruments of bronze and iron. And Tubal-cain had a sister, Naamah.

[Genesis 4:1, 17–22]

(i) The second half of verse 1 and the excerpt that follows belong to the myth of Cain's murder of Abel (see II.5.d (p. 56)), which is substantially later than the story of Cain's family tree. The earlier text is unacquainted with the murder episode and views Cain as a hero worthy of veneration. It belongs to the old Lay Source, which reflects the Kenite traditions of the nomadic tribes from southern Judah. These tribes, especially the Calebites, had a defence treaty with Judah, fighting as its auxiliary troops. In exchange for their help, they were given grazing rights. They were not subjects of the kingdom of Judah, but a sovereign people.

(ii) As in all Middle Eastern myths, the origin of civilization is described with remarkable brevity and terseness, which is not the case with Greek mythology. The biblical myth of the origins of culture is comparable to the lists of the kings of Kish. These too enumerate the mythical kings before the Flood, whose names clearly point out their different vocations: Gaur (he who lays the rafters), Gulla-Ni-da-ba-anna- ... sikal (who grinds the corn of the gods), Pala-kina-tim (administration of the law), Nangish-lishma (gladly may he listen, i.e. a reference to music). The fifth and sixth names are hard to decipher, but the seventh king is called Kalibum (dog), an allusion to the hunt, and the eighth king's name Kalumum (lamb) refers to the raising of livestock.

For the biblical myth, the patriarchs mentioned in this text are likewise kings, since they come from a royal race. Cain builds his son Enoch a city, which in the ancient Near East was a visible symbol of royalty. The legend of the origin of civilization is presented in the form of a family tree, as in the Babylonian king lists, because the family tree expresses a continual social development that attributes a positive function to the monarchy.

(iii) Cain and Lamech must have been famous desert dwellers. The practice of the vendetta is traced back to them, when in this passage the narrator quotes an ancient song:

> I have slain a man for wounding me,
> A young man for striking me.
> If Cain is avenged sevenfold,
> Truly Lamech seventy-sevenfold.

This saying, which the women must learn in order to pass it on to their children, is rooted in the nomadic situation. It clearly doesn't fit into the context of the story, because it presupposes the taking of revenge for wrongs suffered. The narrator considers vengeance important, but practising it signifies opposition to the law promulgated by the king.

(iv) The name Cain, which also means 'lance', is not explained here. This part of the Cain myth surely belongs to Kenite traditions, which are also mentioned elsewhere in the Old Testament. The Kenites were independent bedouin tribes with their own cities and kings. Like almost all Palestinian cities, those of the Kenites were only fortresses for refuge in time of war and places to stockpile supplies. The Rechabites of Jeremiah 35 and II Kings 10:15–16:23 followed Kenite tradition.

III.3. *The Worship of the Gods*

a. And Adam knew his wife again, and she bore a son and called his name Seth, for she said, 'Elohim has given me another child instead of Abel, for Cain slew him.' To Seth also a son was born, and he called his name Enosh. At that time men began to call upon the name of Yahweh.

[Genesis 4:25–6]

(i) The Hebraic word *Elohim* in this passage must be equivalent to the generic term, 'god'.

We may assume that Seth was an eponymous hero, whose descendants might be the same as the Suti people known to us from the Amarna letters, where they are described as nomads. From the myth as we have it here, we can only infer that the Yahweh cult was already of great antiquity. That is the point of the closing remark by the Yahwist narrator, for whom the idea that the murderer Cain had founded true divine worship was unthinkable. Cain's sacrificial practices were not to be the point of departure for the tradition on the origin of worship. The founders would be the new race of the Sethians, of which the Israelites thought themselves members. As a representative of the royal-military party of Judah, the Yahwist was interested in anchoring Jerusalem's claims to power as much as possible in ancient times, precisely to counter the ancestral local shrines in Canaan. It was well known in Canaan that the old gods were still alive, and in comparison with them the history of Israel and its god Yahweh seemed a petty affair. Hence the Yahweh cult is traced back to Seth, the second son. And as far as this myth is concerned, Adam and Eve never had more than two sons, Cain and Seth, while Abel was the son of Yahweh and Eve (see II.5.**d** (p. 56)).

b. Yahweh saw that the wickedness of man was great in the earth, and that every imagination of the thoughts of his heart was only evil continually. And Yahweh was sorry that he had made man on the earth, and it grieved him to his heart. So Yahweh said: I will blot out men whom I have created from the face of the ground, for I am sorry that I have made them. But Noah found favour in his eyes.

And Yahweh said to Noah: Go into the ark, you and all your household, for I have seen that you are righteous before me in this generation. Take with you seven pairs of all clean animals, and a pair of the animals that are not clean. For in seven days I will send rain upon the earth forty days and forty nights; and every living thing that I have made I will blot out from the face of the ground. And Noah went with all his household into the ark, as Yahweh had commanded. The flood continued forty days upon the earth; and the waters increased, and bore up the ark, but everything on the dry land in whose nostrils was the breath of life died. At the end of forty days Noah sent forth a raven from the ark, and it went to and fro until the waters were dried up from the earth. Then he sent forth a dove to see if the waters had subsided, but she returned to him, for the waters were still on the face of the whole earth. He waited seven days and again he sent forth the dove out of the ark; and the dove came back to him in the evening, and lo, in her mouth a freshly plucked olive leaf. So Noah knew that the waters had subsided from the earth. Then he waited another seven days, and sent forth the dove; and she did not return to him any more. Then Noah went forth from the ark and built an altar to Yahweh, and took of every clean animal and of every clean bird, and offered burnt offerings on the altar. And when Yahweh smelled the pleasing odour, he said in his heart: I will never again curse the ground because of man, for the imagination of man's heart is evil from his youth. Neither will I ever again destroy every living creature as I have done. While the earth remains, seed-time and harvest, cold and heat, summer and winter, day and night, shall not cease.

[Genesis 6:5–8; 7:1–5, 17, 22; 8:6–12, 20–23]

(i) The myth of Noah's miraculous rescue from the catastrophic Flood comes from the Yahwist tradition (ninth century B.C.). The story validates the custom of burnt offerings practised by the nomads. Both the reasons for the Flood and its consequences are important to the narrator. Thanks to the Flood, Yahweh's anger at men is soothed, and Noah's burnt offering reconciles him with them. Henceforth no such deluges will interrupt the regular course of the seasons or the farmer's labours, so dependent on the weather.

'The wickedness of man' which enrages Yahweh is not described in any detail. The marriage of the sons of the gods to the daughters of men was certainly not the original reason for this wrath, for that passage stems from another source (see II.1 (p. 41)). The more likely assumption is that, as was the case with Enlil in *The Epic of Gilgamesh*, Yahweh was 'moved to let loose the deluge'.

There are many similarities between the flood in *The Epic of Gilgamesh* and the biblical one. Both stories are adaptations (independently elaborated) of old Sumerian myths. The greatest similarity occurs in their use of birds as omens, the difference being that the biblical writer reverses the order of *Gilgamesh*, and also sends the dove forth twice, whereas Utnapishtim also releases a swallow: 'When the seventh day dawned I loosed a dove and let her go. She flew away, but finding no resting place she returned. Then I loosed a swallow, and she flew away but finding no resting place she returned. I loosed a raven, she saw that the waters had retreated, she ate, she flew around, she cawed, and she did not come back. Then I threw everything open to the four winds ...'

Likewise, in the scene of the burnt offering, the anthropomorphic image of the god Yahweh smelling the pleasant odour of sacrifice is demonstrably a common theme in Near Eastern mythology. In *The Epic of Gilgamesh* we read: 'When the gods smelled the sweet savour, they gathered like flies over the sacrifice.'*

*The Epic of Gilgamesh, translated by N. K. Sandars, Penguin Books (Penguin Classics), Harmondsworth, 1960, p. 111.

But as they now stand, the two traditional accounts differ broadly: the god Enlil, to expiate his criminal annihilation of living creatures, makes Utnapishtim and his wife divine, while Noah and his family become farmers. Furthermore, the biblical narrator has attempted to twist the myth into an historical aetiology to explain why erstwhile nomads are to become farmers. For the central government in Jerusalem was keenly interested in having the free nomadic tribes settle down to farming life. A sedentary existence was equivalent to dependency upon the temple and the monarchy. This is because the king now had his fighting done for him by a mercenary army, paid for by taxing the farmers, and because all land was the property of the gods, thus guaranteeing that the farmer would remain in a state of economic dependence. In contrast, the Babylonian *Epic of Atrachasis*, like *The Epic of Gilgamesh*, ends hopefully. After the heaven-sent plagues have culminated in the Flood, the hero escapes in the ark, warned by Ea. (See III.4.ii (p. 73).)

III.4. *The Flood: Yahweh's Revenge on Humanity*

Noah, the son of Lamech, was a just man. He had three sons, Shem, Ham, and Japheth. Now the earth was corrupt in Elohim's sight, and the earth was filled with violence. Then he said to Noah: Make yourself an ark of gopher wood (that is, a kind of stone pine). Its length is to be three hundred cubits, its breadth fifty cubits, and its height thirty cubits, with a roof and a door in its side, three decks and rooms. Cover it inside and out with pitch. Then you shall take with you into the ark your sons, your wife and the wives of your sons, and a male and a female of all animals, as well of all birds, cattle and creeping things. Also take with you every sort of food for you and for them. At this time Noah was six hundred years old. In the six hundredth year of Noah's life, in the second month, Noah and his sons, Shem and Ham and Japheth, their wives and the chosen animals, went into the ark, for all the fountains of the great deep burst forth, and the windows of the heavens were opened, and the mighty waters flooded the earth. The Flood lasted one hundred and fifty days and destroyed all life on earth. Then it slowly ebbed. After a year, on the twenty-seventh day of the first month in the six hundred and first year of Noah's life, Noah, his sons, their wives, and the animals went forth from the ark. They found the earth unpeopled, for all humanity had been killed, and all birds and animals. But Elohim blessed Noah and his sons, and said: Be fruitful and multiply, and fill the earth. You shall have power over all beasts of the earth, all the birds of the air, and all the fish in the sea.

You may eat of them as well as of the green plants. Only you shall not eat flesh that has not been bled. For your life-blood I will surely require a reckoning; of every beast I will require it and of man. Whoever sheds the blood of man, by man shall his blood be shed; for Elohim made man in his own image.

[Genesis 6:9–22; 7:6,11,13–16a,17a,18–21,24; 8:1–2a,3b,4–5,13a,15–19; 9:1–7]

(i) The Jerusalem priestly text from the post-exilic period views the disaster of the Flood as a prophetic sign. The descendants of Noah, particularly his son Shem, are spared the judgement that strikes the nations. They are to inaugurate a new humanity.

(ii) The Mesopotamian model for the legend of the Flood (see III.3.b.i (p. 71)) likewise speaks of the devastation of the earth and the annihilation of all living things except for Utnapishtim, who takes every sort of animal, as well as labourers, on board with him for himself and his family, as the god Ea had advised. But the gods regret the Flood when they see the disaster it causes. 'Even the gods were terrified at the flood, they fled to the highest heaven, the firmament of Anu; they crouched against the walls, cowering like curs. Then Ishtar the sweet-voiced Queen of Heaven cried out like a woman in travail: "Alas, ... why did I command this evil in the council of all the gods? I commanded wars to destroy the people, but are they not my people, for I brought them forth?"'

(iii) As in *The Epic of Gilgamesh*, the priestly narrator gives a precise description of the ship, including its measurements and layout. The anthropomorphic traits of the Babylonian myth are lacking in the priestly account. The god of the priests acts with reason and foresight, while in the Babylonian epic the Flood is a capricious stroke by some of the gods. The audience of the biblical epic is not supposed to feel terror, but to learn that the God of Israel saves his people from catastrophe (meaning the Babylonian captivity). The hideousness of wiping out all life on earth should impress the audience as less important than Elohim's kindness in presenting the world afresh to Noah and his family, as he once did to Adam and Eve. And Elohim explicitly assures humanity that he will protect their lives.

(iv) In Christian mythology, e.g. in the New Testament (I Peter 3), the myth of the Flood is equated with the waters of baptism. The Flood is seen as a purifying bath for the entire world.

(v) The old Near Eastern legend of the Flood is also a traditional part of Greek mythology. There it is an act of revenge by Zeus, and the rescued hero is called Deucalion. But, in the earliest versions, Themis (who corresponds to Ishtar) will have been the one who started the Flood. In its original form, the myth reflects the struggle between matriarchy and patriarchy. Ishtar, Themis and Selene fall victim to Marduk, Zeus and Dionysus. And Atlantis, the symbol of matriarchal society, sinks forever beneath the waves.

(vi) The Old Testament version, with its description of a new beginning in human history, has correctly understood and interpreted the myth. But priestly tradition strongly emphasizes that man after the Flood is the same as man newly created. That is why it recounts the origin of the Noachian line in practically the same language that it uses for the story of creation (cf. I.1 (p. 33)). This is an attempt to counteract the tendency to look upon the downfall of the kingdoms of Judah and Israel as the fault of the Jews. Such was the charge loudly proclaimed, especially by the schools of prophets among the northern tribes, men from the old priestly castes of the various local sanctuaries. These people rejected the visions of empire advanced by the priests of Jerusalem.

III.5. *The Scattering of the Human Race*

a. As men migrated from the east, they found a plain in the land of Shinar and settled there. And they said to one another: Come let us make bricks, and burn them thoroughly. And they had brick for stone and bitumen for mortar. Then they said: Come, let us build ourselves a city, and a tower with its top in the heavens, and let us make a name for ourselves, lest we be scattered abroad upon the face of the whole earth. And Yahweh came down to see the tower which the sons of men had built. And Yahweh said: Behold, they are one people, and they have all one language, and this is only the beginning of what they will do; and nothing that they propose to do will now be impossible for them. Come, let us go down, and there confuse their language, that they may not understand one another's speech. So Yahweh scattered them abroad from there over the face of all the earth, and they left off building the city.

[Genesis 11:2–8]

(i) The biblical myth of the building of the tower of Babel has been transformed into an aetiological legend by means of two learned observations which do not belong to the original body of the myth. The first is found in verse 1 of the biblical story: 'Now the whole earth had one language and few words'. The second appears in verse 9: 'Therefore its name was called Babel'. The word resembles the Hebrew verb for 'confuse' (*balal*). At Babel, Yahweh confused the languages of all nations and scattered the people all over the earth. The origins of the myth are obscure, but they surely go back to the Lay Source with its nomadic traditions. The myth was initially a positive one, even though many pious commentators attribute the building of the tower to human arrogance, with the subsequent dispersal of the race seen as God's punishment.

(ii) But that is not what the myth itself is about. For Yahweh merely states that men can do anything with the help of technology. He decides to confuse their speech with his heavenly hosts, and to scatter humanity, now broken up into language groups, all over the earth. This explains and interprets world history for the nomad passing through the various regions. People do not live in one city and master a single language, but everyone lives in his own part of the earth with his own language. There can be no doubt that the biblical narrator had in mind the ziggurat of Babylon, that is, the step-temple with its tower and the city itself, when he told this story. In the middle of the second millennium B.C., Babylon was the great metropolis, buzzing with all the languages of the world. But this cosmopolitan symbol, according to the narrator, was not to have any power of attraction, for he expressly states that Yahweh drives out the population of the city, surely thinking of the destruction of Babylon by the armies of Tiglath-Pileser I (1112–1074 B.C.).

(iii) The myth explains the fact that the nations of the earth are different. It is Yahweh's will that they live apart from each other. Hence this story also voices opposition to the merging central government in Jerusalem and the whole imperialist mentality of kings and priests since the time of David and Solomon. The myth, which presumably existed independently of the drama of the Flood, proceeds on the assumption that the nomads come out of the East, from the interior of the Arabian peninsula. The East is a metaphor suggesting the harmonious extended family of the nomads: once in the West, the nomads come into conflict with the despotic theocracies that keep their empires intact through oppression and exploitation.

b. All of humanity is descended from the three sons of Noah, Japheth, Ham and Shem, who were also in the ark, and their wives. After the Flood, children were born to them. Cush, the son of Ham, begot Nimrod, the first great king on earth. He was a mighty hunter, whence the proverb: like Nimrod, a mighty hunter before the Lord. And the capital of his kingdom of Babylon was the great city of Nineveh, which he had built. He also ruled over Uruk, Akkad and Calah.

Mizraim, Ham's second son, counted among his descendants the Ludim, Anamim, Casluhim and Caphtorim, whence came the Philistines. Descendants of Canaan, another son of Ham, lived between Sidon, Gaza, Sodom and

Lasha. Shem was the father of all the Hebrews, and his descendants lived in the eastern mountains.

[Genesis 10:8–19,21,24–30]

(i) The Yahwist catalogue of the nations, from the ninth century B.C., assumes that Canaan and Shem have long lived together in a well-ordered relationship, hence nothing further is said on the subject. The only one dealt with in detail is Nimrod, the legendary founder of Uruk and Nineveh. For, in the eyes of the ninth-century B.C. narrator, Babylon is a world power that must be taken seriously, and he seems to be familiar with Babylonian tradition. The suggestion has often been made that Nimrod is Amenophis III (1411–1375 B.C.), but this is less than certain. The latter's Egyptian name, Neb-me-re, does show a kind of similarity, but it can hardly have had the same connotations and local colour.

(ii) This myth is an independent creation of the Yahwist narrator. That is, he is informing his contemporaries that Yahweh placed the descendants of Shem between Ham and Japheth, between the land of the Nile and Mesopotamia. The myth is supposed to validate the Israelite claim to the territory that both those empires had always coveted.

c. The sons of Noah were Shem, Ham and Japheth. They each dwelt in separate lands, in accordance with their language and race. The peoples who came after the Flood were their descendants. The sons of Japheth were Gomer, Magog, Madai, Javan, Tubal, Meshech and Tiras. The dwellers in the islands also belonged to this group. The sons of Ham were Cush (Ethiopia), Mizraim (Egypt), Put and Canaan. The sons of Shem were Elam (Persia), Assur, Arphaxad, Lud and Aram.

[Genesis 10:1a,2–7,20,22–3,31–2]

(i) This account, a priestly text from the fifth century B.C., is evidently an editorial correction. Shem, though not the eldest brother, is named first. But, in listing the nations, the narrator then follows the traditional order, Japheth, Ham, Shem. The peculiarity of the biblical catalogue – for both the older Yahwist and the priestly tradition – lies in the notion that after the Flood all peoples are covered by God's blessing, which came their way with the benediction on Noah. By giving Shem unusual prominence, the priestly tradition now claims a special place for the people of Israel, precisely at a time when, as subjects of Babylon or Persia, their sense of political identity was at a very low ebb.

d. Noah was the first farmer, and was the first to plant a vineyard. Once he became drunk from the new wine and slept naked in his tent. His son Ham, the father of Canaan, happened to come in and saw him. He went out and told his brothers Shem and Japheth. But they walked backwards into the tent and covered up their father without looking at him. When Noah awoke from his drunkenness, he learned what his youngest son had done to him. Then he cursed him and ordered him to be the slave of his brothers Shem and Japheth. But Noah preferred Shem and gave him the blessing of Yahweh. For Japheth would be granted a broad domain, but he was to dwell in the tent of his brother Shem.

[Genesis 9:20–27]

(i) In contrast to the Yahwist and priestly myths about the allotment of men to different parts of the earth, the myth from the Lay Source attaches no importance to the Flood or to a detailed catalogue of the nations. If it tells the story of Noah's drunkenness, it does so because it believes there is a different principle that distinguishes the nations one from another. Canaan definitely belongs among the wine-growers, but Shem dwells in a tent, and Japheth (whose name is explained in connection with the verb 'to enlarge', which has the same consonantal stem) is to receive his hospitality. For the Lay author, the world is made up of farmers (here wine-growers) and herdsmen, the narrator considering himself one of the latter. The farmer's calling is described pejoratively, while the nomad enjoys Yahweh's special blessing. The 'tillers of the soil' are no better than the nomads' servants.

(ii) The historical root of this ancient myth is the fact that the Israelites (Shem) and the Philistines (Canaan), who came from Crete, divided up the land of Canaan between them. But the Israelite narrator claims that his people are the chief heirs. We know for sure that the Philistines, thrust forth from their homeland by the Dorian invasion, made their way from the shores of Asia Minor into the interior of Canaan *c.* 1200 B.C. In the process they ran into the nomadic Israelites, who around this time were trickling in from the East. The myth assumes that both immigrant groups joined forces at the expense of the native inhabitants. It makes no mention of Yahweh's readiness to bless all peoples equally. Rather it affirms the uniqueness and special status of Shem (used only in this context to designate Israel).

(iii) This myth, in its earliest form, was surely at ease with the world of polytheism. We know from Greek mythology that Iapetus was the father of Prometheus. This episode – which, as the Bible tells it, sounds like a rustic idyll with a tragic ending – may have once been an unedifying scene from the life of the gods. The text disavows Canaan, the ancient coastal people who were driven by the Dorian invasion to the Eastern shores of the Mediterranean Sea. To the pious Jew, Canaan, with its customs and practices, was a source of horror – although there was male cult prostitution even in the temple at Jerusalem (I Kings 15:12, II Kings 23:7). This was connected with the worship of the goddess Cybele from Asia Minor. Men would castrate themselves and put on women's clothing, in order to be like the great mother goddess. The myth attacks these customs and thereby takes a stand against King Solomon's policy of using religion to promote political ends. The text's praise for nomadic life shows us the opposition to the central government on the part of people dwelling on Judah's southern frontier.

The government was anxious to reduce the farmers to dependence on the king and the temple at Jerusalem, and through marriages between the kings and non-Jewish women it allowed foreign cults to enter Jerusalem.

IV. The Emergence of the People of God

IV.1. *The Abraham Stories*

a. Abraham was a son of Terah, who set out with him and his second son Nahor from Ur in Babylonia, heading for the land of Canaan. They came to Haran and settled down there. After that Yahweh appeared to Abraham, who was still called Abram, and commanded him: Go from your country and your kindred and your father's house to the land that I will show you. And I will make of you a great nation. Thereupon Abram passed through the land and came to the sacred tree at Shechem. There Yahweh appeared to him once more, and told him: I will give this land to your descendants. So Abram built an altar there, and another in the mountainous country near Bethel.

But when a famine threatened the land, Abram went down to Egypt. From there he returned in prosperity to Canaan with an escort provided by the Pharaoh. He had great wealth in cattle and gold. But as the grazing areas were too small for the whole clan, Abram and his nephew Lot divided the land between them. Abram dwelt at Hebron, near the sacred tree of Mamre. Here too Yahweh appeared to Abram and promised him that he would give this land to his descendants. And the promise was confirmed to Abram by a miracle.

Sarah, Abram's wife, had long been childless. She feared that Abram would die without issue, and so she gave him her Egyptian slave Hagar to be his concubine. Hagar bore Abram a son, whom she named Ishmael, as the angel of Yahweh commanded her. For Yahweh had appointed Ishmael to be a 'wild ass of a man, his hand against every man and every man's hand against him'.

Once, when Abram sat at the entrance to his tent beneath the sacred trees of Mamre, Yahweh appeared to him with two companions. Abram gave them hospitality and learned from Yahweh that Sarah would soon bear him a son. Sarah heard this and laughed at such a promise, for she was already very old, as was Abram. But Yahweh reaffirmed the promise. Then he went off to destroy Sodom and Gomorrah, because much evil had been reported concerning these cities. When Abram heard that, he tried to save the cities. And Yahweh promised him that if there were only ten righteous men in them, he would spare those places. But the ten could not be found, the cities were completely depraved. For pederasty was in common practice there, and Yahweh's companions had great difficulty in escaping the men of Sodom, who hounded them. Yahweh destroyed Sodom and Gomorrah and the near-by region by raining down fire and brimstone. Only Lot and his daughters survived. Lot's wife was turned into a pillar of salt during their flight, when she turned around to look back at their old home. Lot's daughters were impregnated by their father and became the ancestors of the Moabites and Ammonites.

Much later, after Sarah had died, Abram married Keturah and had many sons with her, before he finally died.

[Genesis 12:1–4,6–19; 13,14,16,18,19; 22:20–21; 25:1–5]

(i) According to the Yahwist tradition, Abraham, the ancestor of Israel, gave up his nomadic existence and settled down in the land that Yahweh gave him. As a symbolic act of seisin he erected the altars to Yahweh. Yahweh was the lord of the land, and obedience was his due.

The myth as we find it in the Bible dates from the ninth century B.C. Central government has been established in Jerusalem. King and priests rule the land in the name of Yahweh, to whom it must have belonged from time immemorial. The frontiers with neighbouring states have been closed off. For Yahweh has already ordered Abraham to break with his kin. The desert tribes from adjoining regions, the sons of Keturah, are made half-brothers of Isaac. This masks the formation of a social and economic dependency. The inhabitants of the wilderness are united with those living on cultivated land by a defensive alliance. In exchange for pasture rights and participation in the economic life of the little city-kingdoms, the nomads provide military protection. The Yahwist's genealogy describes conditions in the southern part of the country around the middle of the ninth century.

(ii) Abraham is a mythical character like Isaac and Jacob, even if these are genuine clan names. Their stories are the stories of the tribe. The figure of Abraham is a mythical creation that links the beginning of the old tribal tales with the so-called 'primeval history'. Abraham is the 'exalted father', the Aeneas of biblical mythology. Like Aeneas, he founds sanctuaries, i.e. he usurps ancient holy places. Aeneas rides on the heels of various Aphrodite cults into the arena of Roman mythology. Abraham claims the sacred trees – surely at one time cult sites of fertility goddesses – for himself. The name of Abraham's wife, Sara'i, is one further clear indication of the fact that the myths of Abraham and Aeneas have the same function. Sara'i is the name of the great goddess found in the Nabataean inscriptions. Only in the sixth century B.C. did the priests alter the name to Sarah, princess. Upon the advice of a god (Venus), Aeneas leaves Troy as it goes up in flames, and Abraham leaves his homeland of Ur. In mythical terms, the victory of the great hero from a foreign land signifies the beginning of a new historical epoch. The Julians used the Aeneas legend to substantiate their claims to rule the Roman Empire. The Jerusalem theocracy used the legend of Abraham to justify its claim to supremacy over all the tribes in the land of Canaan.

b. Abraham sojourned in Gerar in the land of the Philistines, whose king was Abimelech. Abimelech found Sarah pleasing, and had her taken to his harem. He did not know that Sarah was Abraham's wife, because out of fear of the Philistines Abraham had passed her off as his sister. But Abimelech became incapable of having children, as did all his wives, and he was unable to have intercourse with Sarah. In the night, Elohim appeared to the king and threatened him with death for having taken away Abraham's wife. Elohim ordered the king to give Sarah back, because Abraham was a prophet. Abimelech obeyed and gave Abraham a thousand silver pieces besides. He showered him with presents and allowed him grazing rights wherever he wished in the country. Thereupon Abraham prayed to Elohim, who healed Abimelech and his harem, so that once more they could have children.

In Gerar, Sarah gave birth to Isaac. But when she saw Isaac playing with Ishmael, the son of Hagar the Egyptian concubine, she demanded that Abraham drive out Hagar and Ishmael. She wanted her son to be the only heir. Abraham obeyed her, for Elohim told him that he would make Ishmael into a great people, but that only Isaac was to be Abraham's rightful heir. Hagar was cast out into the steppe of Beersheba along with the child. There she wished to take her life. But Elohim saved her and the child from dying of thirst. Ishmael grew up, took an Egyptian wife, and became the ancestor of a great nation.

Abraham remained a long time in the land of the Philistines. In Beersheba he entered into a formal treaty with Abimelech, making over Beersheba to him as his fief. After this Elohim laid a snare for Abraham and said to him: Abraham, take your only son Isaac and sacrifice him on a mountain that I will show you. Abraham obeyed and went off with the boy and two servants to the cult site that Elohim showed him. For the last part of the trip father and son travelled alone together. When they came to the place that Elohim had showed him, Abraham set up an altar and arranged the logs upon it and took the knife to slay his son. Afterwards he went back to the servants and returned home to Beersheba, where he dwelt.

[Genesis 20; 21:6–30; 22:19]

(i) The Elohist story of Abraham displays the typical features of the Elohist tradition. Abraham is viewed as a man living in the land of Canaan. The narrator knows nothing of his more remote origins. Abraham is familiar with many gods but reserves his obedience for Elohim. He gets along with the indigenous Philistines and makes treaties with them. There are no hostile words for the Philistines, and the king of Gerar is actually honoured.

(ii) The Egyptian woman Hagar is Abraham's concubine. She is manifestly under Elohim's protection. Her son Ishmael likewise marries an Egyptian and becomes the ancestor of a splendid nation, which also enjoys Elohim's protection.

(iii) Isaac, however, was sacrificed. This must have been stated in the Elohist text, because Genesis 22:19 explicitly says, 'So Abraham returned to his young men, and they arose and went together to Beersheba, and Abraham dwelt at Beersheba'. The Elohist text makes no further mention of Isaac, and the Elohist tradition continues its narrative with the story of Jacob.

The ancient local traditions of the pre-Israelite period survived in the hostile attitude towards Jerusalem of the various older parts of the population, who maintained peaceful relations with the Philistines and the Egyptians. For such people, Abraham was the supreme witness for the ideal of a quiet, healthy coexistence between nomads and farmers. Elohim rules over Abraham and Abimelech, Jew and Philistine. He is not a jealous rival but a friendly lord. His demand that Abraham sacrifice Isaac is something that would have been taken for granted in ancient matriarchal Canaan, as would the fact that the Great Mother Sarah ('the princess') expels her rival Hagar, along with her offspring, from the tranquil life of the clan and banishes her into the wilderness. For Elohim looks after the age-old Maternal Law. We know from the Babylonian Code of Hammurabi that concubines were legally separated from their children. They had no control over them – that was the prerogative of the lady of the house. But Elohim was overcome by Yahweh, as is shown by the Yahwist shaping of the Elohist myth about the sacrifice of Isaac: the angel of Yahweh intervenes and stops the sacrifice (see II.5.b (p. 54)).

c. After the death of his father, Abraham set out from Haran for the land of Canaan. There Lot had settled in the cities of the Jordan valley, while Abraham dwelt in the land of Canaan. Then Yahweh appeared to Abraham and told him: I am the one who has made a covenant with you, so as to make you the father of a multitude of nations. Therefore no longer shall your name be Abram (exalted father), but Abraham (father of a great people). And I will be your God and the God of your descendants. And I will give to you, and to your descendants after you, all the land of Canaan, for an everlasting possession, and you shall keep my covenant. And this is to be the sign of the covenant between me and you: every man among you shall be circumcised.

He that is eight days old shall be circumcised, and not only those born in the house but also slaves who have been bought. An uncircumcised male shall be cut off from his people; he has broken my covenant. Your wife shall henceforth be called Sarah. She will bear you a son who will have many descendants. In a year's time I shall make my covenant with him. Ishmael too will have numerous descendants. – Then Abraham circumcised himself, his son and all his household. Then after a year Sarah bore a son to Abraham. And Abraham circumcised his son Isaac when he was eight days old, as Yahweh had commanded him.

And Sarah died at Hebron in the land of Canaan at the age of 127 years. Thereupon Abraham bought a burial chamber from Ephron the Hittite in the Machpelah region, and laid his wife to rest in it. So the field of Ephron at Mamre with all the trees and the burial chamber were legally purchased by Abraham and became his property. Witnesses to this were the Hittites who, when the transaction was finished, went through the city's gate. Abraham died at the ripe old age of 175 years, when he was old and full of days. And his sons Isaac and Ishmael buried him in the cave at Mamre in the field that Abraham had bought from Ephron. Both Abraham and Sarah were now buried there.

Others tell of a raid by a group of allied kings from the country east of the Jordan against the kings in west Jordan and the south of Canaan. The kings of Sodom and Gomorrah were defeated and their cities plundered. Among the spoils of war were the family of Lot and their belongings. When Abraham heard of this, he mustered his troop of 318 men and pursued the brigand kings as far as Dan in the north of Canaan. There he attacked them at night and routed them beyond Damascus. He brought all the booty back with him. As he was returning with the prisoners and the spoils, he was met by Melchizedek, the king of Salem. Melchizedek brought Abraham bread and wine. He was a priest of El Elyon, the highest god, and blessed him: Blessed be you, Abraham, by the most high god, who created heaven and earth. – And Abraham gave him a tenth of the booty and all the rest he returned to the king of Sodom, agreeing only to accept the costs of the campaign from the king.

[Genesis 12:5; 13:11–12; 16:15; 17; 21:3–5; 23; 25:7–10; 14]

(i) The priestly account says nothing at all about the expulsion of Hagar and Ishmael. Ishmael and Isaac bury their father together. An important item for the priestly narrator is the introduction of circumcision, which is bound up with the promise of the land. But he is more interested in circumcision than in the promise, because after the Exile the priests were more concerned with maintaining the old religious customs than in stories of the promised land.

Abraham's burial was also important to the priestly tradition. The repeated stress on Abraham's purchase of the field makes it clear that Abraham was buried in his own soil, that is, in a ritually pure manner. The mourning for the dead and the burial by the sons were also part of the ritual.

Circumcision was not the usual practice in Mesopotamia, but it was customary in Egypt. During the early historical period in Israel it was performed on pubertal youths, while the priestly tradition introduced it for infants. Circumcision was once a part of the ceremonies initiating new clan members. It signified a man's submission to the rule of the Great Mother. During the later historical period, the tribal god (for the Israelites, Yahweh) replaced the Great Mother and sacred queen. Thereafter circumcision merely integrated one into the society of the god's worshippers; it symbolized the covenant between god and man.

(ii) Priestly interests were also behind the inclusion of the raid episode from Genesis 14, which has an archaic flavour. The story is important because it tells of Abraham's subjection to the priest-king of Jerusalem (Salem). And after the Exile the high priests of Jerusalem were the actual rulers in the country. Melchizedek of Salem was their model. If Abraham, the great general and progenitor of Israel, voluntarily submitted to Melchizedek, then the individual post-exilic patriarchs had to do so as well.

Both in Psalm 110:4 and in chapter 7 of the Letter to the Hebrews in the New Testament, Melchizedek is interpreted as a prototype of the salvific king and messiah.

IV.2. *The Isaac Stories*

a. After the death of Sarah, when Abraham wished to put his house in order, he commissioned the oldest servant he had to look for a wife for his son Isaac among Abraham's kindred in Aram. And the servant laid his hand on Abraham's sexual organ and swore to carry out this charge faithfully.

Together with many gifts and ten camels the servant journeyed to Mesopotamia, to the city of Nahor. At the well outside the city he ordered the caravan to halt. He waited there for the daughters of the city, who came every evening to draw water from the well, to discover the one whom Yahweh had chosen. This was Rebekah, the daughter of Bethuel, a niece of Abraham's. The servant presented her with a nose ring and bracelet for her arms, and when she told the people of her household about it, Laban, the girl's brother, went out to invite the caravan in. Then the servant carried out his assignment and requested Rebekah's hand for Isaac. For he had told himself that 'the girl who gives me to drink when I ask her, and who waters my camels, must be the one whom Yahweh wills to be Isaac's bride'. Because it all came about in just this way, Laban and Bethuel had no objection to raise against the marriage. Then the servant handed over the gifts, and a great banquet sealed the marriage contract. On the very next day the servant journeyed back with Rebekah. On the way they met up with Isaac. When Rebekah saw him, she veiled her face. But Isaac led her into his tent, he made her his wife, and he loved her.

Rebekah bore him twins, Jacob and Esau. Even before their birth Yahweh had told her: Two nations are in your womb, and two peoples, born of you, shall be divided. One shall be stronger than the other, the elder shall serve the younger.

– The first to be born was Esau, who was very hairy. After him came Jacob, grasping Esau tightly by the heel. When the boys grew older, Esau, much to Isaac's joy, stayed out on the steppe with the herds and went hunting, while Jacob stayed more at home, which pleased Rebekah. He was a good cook, and for a dish of lentils he tricked Esau out of his birthright, when Esau once came home hungry from the outdoors.

But when a famine came, Isaac went with his clan to Gerar, where Abimelech was king. Isaac passed Rebekah off as his sister, because he feared the Philistines might kill him to get possession of his wife. But King Abimelech noticed this, and took Isaac under his personal protection. That was very much to Isaac's advantage and he became so rich that the Philistines envied him. Then Abimelech told him: Leave my country, for you have become too mighty for us. Thus Isaac withdrew from the city into the valley below Gerar and dug himself wells, but these were taken from him by the other herdsmen. He retreated before them all the way to Beersheba. Thither came the king himself and made a defensive alliance with him, in order to be safe from him in the future.

When Isaac had grown old and could no longer see, he called Esau to give him the blessing of the first-born. But Esau was first supposed to hunt him some wild game and prepare it. Rebekah heard this, and she deceived Isaac by sending Jacob. She roasted two young kids as if they were game, and Jacob put their skins on his arms, so that his father would think he was touching Esau's hairy limbs. And Isaac ate the roast and blessed Jacob: Peoples will serve you, and nations bow down before you. You shall be a lord over your brothers, and before you the sons of your mother will bow down. Let him be cursed who curses you, but let him be blessed who blesses you.

Shortly thereafter Esau came in from the hunt. Then it became clear that Jacob had received the blessing before him. And Esau cried aloud and begged: Bless me too, father. But Isaac could only give him a different blessing: You shall live by your sword, and you shall serve your brother. –

But Isaac lived on long years after this in Hebron, near the gravesite of his father.

[Genesis 24; 25:21–6; 26:9–10; 27:2–27; 29:1–32; 35:1, 27–9]

(i) The story of Isaac as the Yahwist tradition tells it rides on a wave of national euphoria from the early monarchical period. Isaac is the glorious hero, blessed with riches, who fetches his wife from the non-Israelite stock of his homeland – a wife who cannot be refused him. The king of the Philistines comes to him and begs him for a defence treaty. Isaac's blessing descends upon Jacob, the man of sedentary civilization, while Esau, with his nomadic way of life, must bow down before him.

Isaac is a mythical person with no well-defined basis in history. His name means 'he laughs'. His laughter is that of the conqueror. His mother laughs, his father laughs: they triumph because they have overcome the curse of childlessness. His mythical importance derives from his being the father of Jacob-Israel and Esau-Edom.

The circumstantial description of nomadic life in the story of the wooing of Rebekah and the tale of Abimelech of Gerar are peculiar to the Yahwist narrator.

(ii) Genealogies belong among the earliest forms of myth. The mythological function of the Abraham-Isaac-Jacob-Edom bloodline is to explain the facts of political power: Jacob-Israel and Esau-Edom, two hostile nations, are supposed to have common parents, who decide that the younger Jacob should rule over the elder Esau. Isaac's blessing and Yahweh's prophecy are identical. They were dictated by the requirements of the early monarchy. They show that the original double kingdom of Beersheba has come to an end. Esau-Edom and Jacob-Israel had once shared this kingdom of the ancient local deity of Isaac, who was the sole husband of the great influential mother Rebekah. In this the function of the Bible's mythical twins, Jacob and Esau, resembles that of the mythical Greek twins, Acrisius and Proetus of Argos. After their father's death, Acrisius and Proetus were joint heirs of the kingdom. They were supposed to take turns ruling, but when his time had expired, Acrisius refused to hand over the power to Proetus. The latter had also begun a love affair with Danaë, Acrisius' daughter. This led to a conflict between the two brothers, which ended with the division of the kingdom.

b. Isaac was born as Elohim had predicted to Abraham. Abraham raised him and was ready to sacrifice him on orders of Elohim, until an angel prevented it (see II.5.**b** (p. 54)). Isaac married Rebekah, who bore him two sons, Jacob and Esau. And Isaac blessed Jacob who had tricked him into believing he was Esau by putting kid-skins on his neck and arms, and into giving him the blessing due to the first-born: May Elohim give you the dew from heaven and the fatness of the earth and plenty of grain and wine – and Esau he blessed with this word: Your dwelling shall be away from the fatness of the earth, and the dew of heaven will not moisten your land.

[Genesis 21:6–22, 19; 27:11–12, 27–9, 39]

(i) The Elohist source has contributed less to the traditional Isaac material than has the Yahwist. The only essential difference between the two is to be found in the formulas of blessing used by Isaac. The old Canaanite god, still recalled in the ninth century B.C. by the remnant of the Canaanite population as a sort of dream image, is a gardener, not a warlike commander lusting for power, as the Yahwist narrator describes him. The Canaanite remnant in the countryside rejected Jerusalem's ambitious, bellicose policies, which were promoted in the name of Yahweh. The name Jacob was surely once Jacobel (see the Akkadian name Ja'qub-ilu = God outwits, overreaches or rewards). In blessing him, Isaac can only be blessing a Canaanite farmer. One is reminded of Hesiod:

> Perses, lay up these things in your heart, and do not let that Strife who delights in mischief hold your heart back from work, while you peep and peer and listen to the wrangles of the court-house. Little concern has he with quarrels and courts who has not a year's victuals laid up betimes, even that which the earth bears, Demeter's grain. When you have got plenty of that, you can raise disputes and strive to get another's goods. But you shall have no second chance to deal so again: nay, let us settle our dispute here with true judgement which is of Zeus and is perfect. For we had already divided our inheritance, but you seized the greater share and carried it off, greatly swelling the glory of our bribe-swallowing lords who love to judge such a cause as this.*

c. This is the story of Isaac, the son of Abraham. Isaac was forty years old when he took to wife Rebekah, daughter of the Aramaean Bethuel from Mesopotamia and sister of Laban.

Isaac was sixty years old when Jacob and Esau were born. When Esau was forty years old, he married Judith and Bashemath, daughters of the Hittites Beeri and Elon. This was a source of great sorrow to Isaac and Rebekah. Then Isaac called Jacob and blessed him and said: You shall not marry one of the Canaanite women, but go to Mesopotamia to the house of your fathers and get yourself a wife from there. And Jacob obeyed Isaac. But when Esau observed that his wives displeased Isaac, he took yet another wife, Mahalath, the daughter of Ishmael, who was a son of Abraham just as Isaac was.

And Jacob, together with his wives, came to his father Isaac at Mamre near

* Hesiod, *Works and Days*, vv. 27–39, from Hesiod, *The Homeric Hymns, and Homerica*, Heinemann (Loeb Classical Library), London, 1974, p.5.

Hebron, where Abraham too had once sojourned. Isaac was 180 years old when he died and was gathered to his people, old and full of days, and his sons Esau and Jacob buried him.

[Genesis 25:19–20, 26b; 26:34–5; 28:1–9; 35:27–9]

(i) This priestly text is really interested only in Isaac's marriage. It affirms that Jacob remains ritually pure: he marries within the family. Jacob is the example from the heroic age of priestly interference in post-exilic marriages, as reported by the Book of Nehemiah, when all non-Jewish wives were repudiated.

Just as important for the priestly tradition is the ritual on the occasion of Isaac's death: it must be performed without error. Apart from this, the fifth-century B.C. Jerusalem priests were indifferent to the heroes of the early period. They were primarily concerned with the order from the Persian royal council allowing them only to re-establish a cultic community. For this reason they attached little importance to detailed accounts from the heroic past of the patriarchs. Isaac faithfully complies with all the ritual laws, but the priestly text ignores him as an independent figure.

IV.3. *The Jacob Stories*

a. After Jacob had stolen the blessing of the first-born, he fled on the advice of his mother Rebekah to Haran, to his uncle Laban, in order to escape the pursuit of Esau. On the way Yahweh appeared to him and promised him: I will give the land on which you lie to you and to your descendants, and I will always be with you and with them.

When Jacob was already near where Laban dwelt he saw a well out on the steppe. He came up to it and there with the herds he met Rachel, who was just going to water her father Laban's sheep. Jacob did this work for her, then kissed Rachel, and began to weep aloud. He said that he was her father's kinsman, the son of Rebekah. Laban received him cordially and gave him Rachel to be his wife, but he also gave him her sister Leah, because it was not the custom to marry the younger daughter before the elder. But when Yahweh saw that Jacob preferred Rachel to Leah, he made Leah fruitful, while Rachel remained barren. Leah bore four sons: Reuben, Simeon, Levi and Judah. Then when Leah saw that she had ceased to bear children, she gave Jacob her maid Zilpah to be his concubine. She bore him Gad and Asher. Once Leah's son Reuben brought home mandrakes from the field, and the childless Rachel entreated some for herself. In payment for the mandrakes Rachel allowed Leah to spend the night with Jacob. And Leah bore him two more sons, Issachar and Zebulun, and a daughter Dinah. But Rachel bore him only one son in Haran. She named him Joseph ['let him (the god) add'] in hope that Yahweh would give her yet another son. After Joseph was born, Jacob wished to return home with his wives and children to the land of his fathers. As payment for his work he asked his father-in-law Laban for all the spotted and striped sheep in the herd. Laban granted his request. And Jacob knew how to arrange things so that all the stronger animals in the flock brought forth spotted lambs, but those of a single colour were all weak. Thus he became exceedingly rich and soon had many sheep, camels, asses, servants and maids. Then, when Jacob heard that Laban's sons wished to dispute his right to his possessions, he went away with his wives, children and herds. But he made a covenant with Laban to mark off the borders of their respective grazing lands. To witness the covenant they set up a heap of stones on the spot, which at the same time served to draw the line between them. After that Jacob was reconciled with his brother Esau and settled down in Succoth, in the country east of the Jordan, near Shechem.

When famine came over Canaan, Jacob sent his people to Egypt to buy corn. They were led by the sons of Leah. But in Egypt Rachel's son Joseph gained power and influence and managed to get permission for the whole house of Jacob with all its herds to immigrate to the land of Goshen. Jacob lived there for another seventeen years. He was 147 years old when he felt his death drawing near. He summoned Joseph and made him swear to bury him in the homeland of his fathers.

And so it was. With the solemn escort of his children and a delegation from the Pharaoh, Jacob was conveyed to his father's grave in the region of Machpelah near Mamre. But Joseph and his brothers returned to Egypt. [See also IV.4.a (p. 96).]

[Genesis 27:41–5; 28:10;29:2, 31–30:9; 46:28–34; 50:1–14]

(i) The Yahwist narrator describes Jacob as a hero who succeeds in everything. Nothing can stop him. He receives the help of the god Yahweh and asserts himself with no regard for justice. He is blessed with children, wives and wealth. The whole country is promised to him and his descendants (see also IV.3.c (p. 92)) by Yahweh.

A clear distinction is drawn between Jacob and the neighbouring peoples. The family of Jacob's wives has its rights taken away. The matriarchy is gone. The last lingering memory of maternal law is the mother's privilege of naming the children. Jacob still performs sacrifices by himself, as both king of the tribe and its priest. On this score he resembles other Near Eastern princes.

(ii) Hence, for the Yahwist tradition, Jacob is a model for the kings of Judah.

His actions are the virtues of a royal despot on the throne of Jerusalem. Treachery, deception, theft, and even the murder of the Shechemites (see IV.3.f (p. 95)) have both his knowledge and approval. But the myth does not pass moral judgements, not even on this point. It looks forward to the arrival of David's empire. That is why Jacob (as father of the twelve tribes, he has twelve sons) is such a significant figure in the Bible, the patriarch and great founding father.

(iii) The original meaning of the tales may be found in the mythic, prehistorical time, when the alliance of the six tribes (the sons of Leah) was forged, and that Great Mother, the sacred queen, obtained a husband. (All this was part of the transition from matriarchy to patriarchy.) The tribe of Reuben surely played a leading role when the six tribes from the steppe-like land east of the Jordan invaded the agricultural regions west of the Jordan and conquered the ancient Canaanite sanctuaries of Bethel and Shechem. These were maintained by two groups of three tribes as joint cult sites. Leah means 'ibex', and Zilpah 'the angry one'. Rachel means 'the lamb', and Bilhah 'the terrible one' (cf. IV.3.c (p. 92)). Jacob was the progenitor of the Reubenites, who usurped these sanctuaries and combined their father god with the indigenous traditions. But by having Jacob buried in Hebron, David's first royal city, the Yahwist narrator is trying to do away with the old traditions and make Jacob a son of Isaac. Jacob's mythological function is comparable to that of Heracles. Heracles and his twin brother Iphicles undergo the same destiny as Jacob and Esau. The elder brothers Iphicles and Edom (the sacred kings) have to give way to their deputies, their younger brothers. Like Heracles, Jacob takes over the functions and privileges of his twin brother, who is driven out into the steppe.

b. Once Jacob came to Luz, where he stayed overnight. He took a stone and put it under his head and lay down to sleep. And he dreamed that there was a ladder set up on the earth, and the top of it reached to heaven, and the angels of Elohim were ascending and descending on it. Jacob was afraid, for he thought: How dangerous this place is! Surely it is Elohim's dwelling and the gate of heaven. – Early the next day he took the stone and set it up for a pillar and poured oil on top of it. He named the place Bethel (house of God). Then Jacob made a vow to Elohim: If Elohim will keep me in the way that I go, so that I come again to my father's house in peace, then this stone will be a house of God, and I will give a tenth of everything. When he came to Laban, who was of the family of Abraham, Laban gave him his daughters Leah and Rachel to wed. Rachel had no children except for Joseph. After Jacob had grown rich in Laban's service, he stole away from Laban, taking all his belongings with him. When Laban wished to pursue him, Elohim appeared to him and warned him against doing harm to Jacob. Once Laban caught up with Jacob, he spoke to him about this in a friendly manner. But he asked for the return of his household gods, which had been missing since Jacob took flight. With Jacob's consent he searched everywhere in the camp, but could not find them. For Rachel, unbeknown to her husband, had stolen them, and sat on her camel saddle, in which she had hidden the teraphim. Thereupon Laban turned back, after he had made a peace treaty with Jacob.

God was with Jacob and blessed him when he wrestled with him one night in Pniel [cf. IV.3.d (p. 93)]. And Jacob went on southwards and met his brother Esau, with whom he exchanged presents. He settled down near Shechem, where he also built an altar for El, the god of Israel, next to a stone marker, like the one he had built in Bethel.

From Shechem he went over to Bethel, to fulfil his vow and also to erect an altar, next to the stone marker, the *mazzebah* (pillar). First, however, they purified themselves and left all the household gods and amulets back in Shechem. From Bethel they moved south. At Ephrath, Jacob had to stop, because Rachel was in labour and bore a son, whom she named Benoni, son of my sorrow. She died in childbed and was buried there, on the highway from Ephrath to Ramah. But Jacob changed the name Benoni to Benjamin, son of the right or southerly side, that is, the side of good fortune.

And Jacob went on wandering through the country and came down to Egypt, when a famine drove him and his family from Canaan. In Egypt his son Joseph had become powerful through the favour of Elohim, and he made them at home in their new country. There Jacob made ready to die, after he had blessed Joseph's sons Ephraim and Manasseh.

[Genesis 28:11, 12, 17–22; 29:15–28; 30:1–8, 17–18; 31:4–45; 35:1–5; 46:1–5]

(i) The Elohist narrator does not mention many of Jacob's deeds that the Yahwist informs us of. His flourishing herds are a gift from Elohim, not a great achievement of the patriarch himself. Jacob behaves as a faithful follower of Elohim, setting up altars and 'pillars' in Bethel and Shechem. Jacob is blamelessly pious. And so Laban does not even grudge him his wealth. When he pursues Jacob, he is only looking for his household gods. Elohim is more tolerant than Yahweh. He allows the great progenetrix of the house of Joseph to steal the teraphim and take them with her in the baggage. Elohim blesses Jacob, who erects many altars to him. The Elohist narrator is unaware of any quarrel between Jacob and Esau; for him the two peoples are amicable brothers.

The anti-Jerusalem sentiment of the nothern tribes, among whom ancient Canaanite piety was still very much alive, comes through in the description of the various sanctuaries. Shechem and Bethel are looked upon as shrines founded by Jacob, which is why they enjoy such a high reputation.

(ii) The Elohist narrator has no knowledge of the change of Jacob's name to 'Israel', which was also not originally part of the priestly tradition. For this name change supports the Jerusalem hierarchy's claims upon the northern tribes. But the latter were deeply attached to the particularist ways of the clan and rejected the imperial ideology of the monarchical period. The mythological significance of the Elohist Jacob is analogous to that of the Greek hero Amphictyon, one of the sons of Deucalion. In the name of his wife, the goddess Amphictyonis, he created the first alliance of the northern Greek states, for which Acrisius of Argos, one of the famous twin brothers of Greek mythology, provided the constitution. The Greeks credit him with introducing the custom of mixing wine with water, to prevent drunken brawls (see also IV.3.c.ii (p. 93)).

c. At the bidding of his father Isaac, Jacob journeyed to Haran and there married Leah, Rachel and their maids Zilpah and Bilhah. With them and all his possessions he returned to Canaan and remained in Shechem. Once, when Jacob came to Luz, Elohim appeared to him and said: Your name is Jacob. No longer shall your name be called Jacob, but Israel shall be your name. (So his name was called Israel.) The land which I gave to Abraham and Isaac I will give to you, to you and to your descendants. – And Jacob had twelve sons: with Leah he had his first-born Reuben, then Simeon, Levi, Judah, Issachar and Zebulun. With Rachel he had Joseph and Benjamin. Rachel's maid Bilhah had borne him Dan and Naphtali, Leah's maid Zilpah bore Gad and Asher. And with them Jacob came to Mamre near Hebron, to his father Isaac. But when the great famine occurred, Jacob went with all his family, his herds and goods to Egypt. Before his death he adopted Joseph's sons, Ephraim and Manasseh, who were born to him in Egypt, and said: They shall be to me as Reuben and Simeon. But the children whom you beget after them shall be yours, and they shall be called by the name of their brothers in their inheritance. Then he blessed every one of his sons with a particular blessing and bade them lay him to rest in the grave of his fathers in Machpelah near Mamre. His sons obeyed him and buried him there near his wife Leah.

[Genesis 30:22; 31:18; 33:18; 35:6, 9–13, 22b–26; 46:6; 48:5; 50:12]

(i) The priestly story of Jacob is chiefly concerned with two themes. First, Jacob marries in a ritually irreproachable fashion and is buried in the same way. And secondly, it is the divine will that Jacob be called Israel and become a great nation. In conjunction with this, Jacob must have exactly twelve sons, and so he adopts Joseph's sons Ephraim and Manasseh. For his first-born, Reuben, had tried to overthrow his father by sleeping with his father's concubine (Genesis 35:22). The plan failed and Reuben was cast out. Simeon, the second son, was presumably wiped out (as a tribe) by the Shechemites during his clash with them. The ritual concerns of the priestly caste of Jerusalem, however, called for twelve tribes to tend the shrine in Jerusalem month by month. Jacob's act of adoption projects the circumstances of the early monarchy, when Ephraim and Manasseh were already inhabiting the country, back into the age of the patriarchs. The Bible often uses the name Jacob for the nation of Israel.

(ii) The elaborate presentation of his name change reveals Jacob's mythological function, which he shares with his Greek equivalent, Hellen, father of all the Greeks and son of Amphictyon. Hellen was the royal deputy of the moon goddess Selene, and his sons were the progenitors of the most important peoples of Greece, the patriarchally structured groups who invaded and settled in that country.

The name Israel means 'God (El) rules' or 'God shines'. It is probably of Canaanite origin. The Yahwist interpretation in Genesis 32:29 ('you have striven with God and with men, and have prevailed') is a folk etymology rather than an explanation of the original religious import of the name, which may have designated the tribal alliance from the conquest of Canaan onward. After the division of the nation in 932 B.C., the name was used as a secular term for the northern kingdom. But, after the fall of that kingdom, prophetic circles wished to limit the name to its cultic sense, as a title of the 'true people of God'. The New Testament also applies it in this way, for example, in Matthew 8:10; 10:6; 15:24, 15:31; or in Luke 1:68 and 1:80. In his Letter to the Romans, Paul devotes chapters 9–11 to a discussion of this problem.

(iii) Within the broad framework of the Priestly Source, the traditions concerning Jacob-Israel have no special prominence. The post-exilic age was not greatly interested in the historic political achievements of the tribal alliance. Since Jacob was in no way connected with the temple of Jerusalem, but rather with the dubious (as this later period viewed it) sanctuaries of Bethel, Shechem and Hebron, he is given marginal treatment.

d. On the evening before his encounter with Esau, Jacob had stayed behind all by himself on the bank of the Jabbok. And a man wrestled with him until the break of day. When the man saw that he did not prevail against Jacob, he touched the hollow of his thigh and put it out of joint. Then his attacker said: Let me go, for the day is breaking. Jacob answered: I will not let you go, unless you bless me. Then his opponent said to him: You shall be called Israel, for you have striven with God and man, and have prevailed. But you are not to ask my name. And he blessed him. Jacob called the place Pniel, because he had seen God face to face and yet come away with his life.

[Genesis 32:24b–32]

(i) This archaic tale derives from the southern Palestinian Lay Source. The etymology of the place name, Pniel (I have seen God), was surely not related to the person of Jacob, but rather to another hero. But connecting it to the patriarch Jacob-Israel allows the spokesman for the nomadic peoples from southern Judah the opportunity to observe that human beings can see Yahweh face to face without dying. Yahweh is a man who agrees to a wrestling match, not the sort of figure enthroned, like the kings of Jerusalem, in unapproachable majesty.

(ii) The name of the god remains unknown, but we have reason to believe that this was originally a moon god. The battle begins at dusk and ends with the break of day. Jacob fights Elohim as Yahweh's representative. We still have the original form of the myth, for instance in the Baal story from Ugarit: 'Death (M't) was strong, Baal was strong. They gored each other like wild oxen. Death was strong, Baal was strong. They bit each other like serpents – Death was strong, Baal was strong. They kicked each other like stallions. Death fell, Baal fell.'* But then Shapash (the sun god; in Hebrew, Shamash) cried out, awarding the victory to Baal.

e. While Jacob was encamped in the territory of Hamor, Hamor's son Shechem saw Jacob's daughter Dinah, seized her, and raped her. Jacob learned of this and told it to his sons, when they returned from the pastures with their herds. The sons became angry, and although Shechem, who had come to love the girl, offered to pay any bride-price, howsoever high, they refused him. Instead, three days later Simeon and Levi overran the unsuspecting town, slew all the men including Shechem, took Dinah out of his house, and went off. Jacob was horrified at this, for he feared that the inhabitants of the area would now take revenge upon them. But Simeon and Levi could only reply: Should he treat our sister as a harlot?

[Genesis 34:2–3, 5, 7, 11–14, 25–6, 30–31]

(i) The story of the murder of the Shechemites, in contrast to the Elohist version (IV.3.f (p. 95)) gives Shechem's rape of Dinah as the motive for the bloody deed. Simeon and Levi have to be the villains, because by the time the

---

* *Stories from Ancient Canaan*, translated by Michael David Coogan, Westminster Press, Philadelphia, 1978, p. 114.

myth was composed they no longer had any pasture land or place of
residence in the country.

The background of this story was surely the conflicts between the Shechemites and two of Jacob's sons, the tribes of Simeon and Levi. In mythology,
rape generally reflects a struggle between rival gods: the battle over the
woman is the battle over the sacred queen, the reigning goddess, who may
not be simply swept away. Shechem loses the struggle. Out of this old myth
the Lay Source has fashioned a moral fable on the inviolability of marriage,
as the nomads understood it. The narrator approves of Simeon and Levi's
behaviour. For the Lay Source, kings and priests are insignificant marginal
figures, law and power are vested in the clan. Tribal interests still determine
what is just and unjust.

f. When Shechem, the son of Hamor, a prince in Shechem, saw Jacob's
daughter Dinah, he fell in love with her and wished to marry her. And he
begged his father to ask for the girl's hand. Hamor conferred with Jacob: I
pray you, give her to my son Shechem in marriage. Make marriages with us.
Give your daughters to us, and take our daughters for yourselves. You shall
dwell with us, and the land shall be open to you. But the sons of Jacob
answered: We will accept your offer only on condition that you have yourselves circumcised as we are circumcised. Then we will dwell with you and
become one people. But if you will not listen to us, then we will take Dinah
and be gone. Hamor and the people of Shechem agreed, and all the men had
themselves circumcised on one day. But on the third day, when the
Shechemites were sore from their wounds, the sons of Jacob fell upon them
and slew all the men with the sword. They plundered the town and took all
the movable goods and the herds with them. They led away the women and
children as prisoners.

[Genesis 34:1–2, 4, 6, 8–10, 13a, 15–18, 20–25a, 25c–29. In v. 27, the
conjectural 'because their sister had been defiled' should be deleted.]

(i) This Elohist tale belongs to the local tradition of Shechem. All the sons
of Jacob are here clearly named as criminals, but not the patriarch himself:
Jacob and the people of Shechem are seen as peaceable folk. The old
Canaanites were, in fact, ready to come to peaceful terms with the immigrants. But the latter broke their word and caused a grisly bloodbath. At first
no motive is given – evidently such brutal zeal must have been as incompre-
hensible to the ancient narrator as it was foreign to Elohim. The Elohist
version of the surprise attack on Shechem casts no lustre on the Israelites,
the sons of Jacob. This story was passed by the priestly censor in the final
edition of the text (though only when conflated with the version from the Lay

Source; see IV.3.e (p. 94)); but this was simply to further the purpose of forbidding all intermarriage of Jews with non-believers, to preserve the cultic community.

IV.4. *The Joseph Stories*

a. Joseph was a son of Rachel, and Israel loved him more than his other sons. Once, when his brothers were herding their sheep near Shechem, Israel sent Joseph to them to ask if all was well with his brothers and their herds. But the brothers hated Joseph because he was their father's favourite, and when they saw him from afar, they conceived a plan to do away with him. But Judah would not hear of their killing Joseph and proposed to sell him to a passing caravan. They sold Joseph to the Ishmaelites for twenty silver pieces. After smearing Joseph's robe with goat blood, they sent it back to the house. And when he saw the robe, Jacob mourned greatly for his son.

The Ishmaelites went on to Egypt and sold Joseph there to an Egyptian, who soon made him overseer of his house. Now Joseph was handsome and good-looking. And the wife of the Egyptian tried to seduce him, but Joseph refused her. One day she caught him by his cloak, and he left it in her hand, and fled. But the garment served as an excuse for having Joseph thrown into prison: she now accused him of attempting to ravish her. In the prison among the royal prisoners he soon managed by his cleverness to become the supreme overseer. Then, once he was released, he rose to be the highest official in Egypt. Now, when a famine broke out in Canaan, the sons of Israel came to Egypt to buy corn, for Joseph sold it to everyone. They also got corn from him and returned home. And Joseph had the purchase money put back in their sacks, for he had recognized his brothers, but they had not recognized him. When once again they ran out of corn, they wished to set out for Egypt a second time. But Joseph had told them that on their next journey they would have to bring their brother Benjamin along with them. They had had to leave Simeon in Egypt as a pledge of their return. And, driven by necessity, Israel let them go with Benjamin, taking along presents and the purchase money for the corn from the last journey. In Egypt, Joseph gave them a warm reception and invited them into his house, where he ate with them. Then they were allowed to head back with their newly bought corn. Again he had the purchase money placed in their sacks, and in Benjamin's sack his own silver cup besides. Just as they left the city, Joseph had them stopped and their baggage searched for the cup. He accused them of theft and said he would keep Benjamin, in whose sack the cup was found, as a slave. Judah, the brothers' spokesman, tried to get Joseph to change his sentence, and offered himself as a hostage, to spare old Jacob the grief of losing the second son of his favourite wife Rachel, having already lost the first. For Judah had vouched for Benjamin to his father.

Then Joseph made himself known to his brothers and said: I am your brother Joseph, whom you sold into Egypt. I have fared well. Go back to my father and tell him of all my splendour in Egypt and of everything that you have heard, and make haste to bring my father here.

They went home, and when Israel had listened to their account, he said: I will go and see my son Joseph before I die. He sent Judah ahead of him on the way to Goshen. Joseph went up to meet his father, and fell on his neck, and wept on his neck a good while. Joseph settled his family in Goshen, because they were experienced shepherds and Pharaoh needed herdsmen there. Israel died in Goshen. Before his death he adopted the sons of Joseph, Ephraim and Manasseh, in place of Reuben and Simeon, who were cast out. He blessed the younger, Ephraim, with the blessing of the first-born, and said: Manasseh shall become a people, and a mighty one, but his younger brother shall become mightier than he, and his descendants shall be a great multitude of peoples.

And he died. Then Joseph fell on his father's face and wept over him. He had his father embalmed in the Egyptian manner and buried him in Machpelah by Mamre near Hebron. Then he returned to his brothers. He died in Egypt at the age of 110 years and was also embalmed and laid in a coffin.

[Genesis 30:24; 37:3–4, 14, 21, 25–7, 31–3; 39:1–3, 6–23; 42:5; 43; 44; 45:4, 13, 28; 46:28–47:5; 48:9, 13–14, 17–19; 50]

(i) The whole story of Joseph is much less a myth than a novella about the legendary fate of a shepherd boy from Canaan who becomes the supreme vizir of the Egyptian Pharaoh. This story was presumably admitted to the traditional corpus of the Bible simply to find a place in the historical schema for the eponymous hero of a central Palestinian tribal pair, Ephraim and Manasseh, which were latecomers to the twelve tribe amphictyony. Joseph's grave in Shechem (his body was conveyed there according to Joshua 24:32) was surely the starting point of his legend.

(ii) The story of Joseph must have been very tightly woven together, for the previous Yahwist version and the Elohist version given below are quite similar. There are differences, however, as, for example, in the betrayal scene. For the Yahwist narrator it is Judah who pleads with the brothers to spare Joseph's life; for the Elohist it is Reuben who speaks up. Here we find a clash between the northern and southern tribes, both labouring to win the sympathy of the powerful central tribes of Ephraim and Manasseh. The Yahwist narrator is less graphic and circumstantial than the Elohist. The fact that there are no theophanies or speeches by God must indicate that Joseph originally had no connection with the Yahweh cult.

b. When Joseph was a young man, he shepherded the flock with his brothers, and he told them his dreams. At one time he told them the following dream: He was with his brothers in the field binding sheaves. Then suddenly his sheaf stood upright, and his brothers' sheaves gathered around and bowed down before his. – Thereupon his brothers said to him: Are you indeed to reign or have dominion over us? – After that he told them another dream: He saw the sun and the moon and eleven stars bowing down before him. – His father rebuked him for this and said: Shall I and your mother and your brothers bow ourselves to the ground before you? – His father could not forget the dreams, and his brothers hated him for it. And one day when he came out to them in the field, they decided to kill him. But Reuben said to them: Let us not take his life, but cast him into this empty pit. He intended to pull him out again and bring him back to his father. Then Midianite traders passed by, they drew him up out of the pit and took him with them to Egypt. When Reuben came back, Joseph was no longer there. Then Reuben cried out in desperation: The lad is gone, and I, where shall I go? And Jacob long mourned Joseph.

The Midianites sold Joseph in Egypt to Potiphar, the captain of Pharaoh's bodyguard. Potiphar entrusted all his property to Joseph, leaving everything to his discretion. Some time later the Pharaoh's chief butler and chief baker were thrown into the prison in the house of Potiphar, and Joseph had to look after them, for he was the head of Potiphar's servants. One morning when Joseph came to them, they were greatly troubled, because they had dreamt but could not interpret their dreams. Joseph interpreted the dreams to them, and it all came true.

Two years later the Pharaoh dreamt of seven lean cows, which came up out of the Nile after seven fat cows and ate them. Then he dreamt that seven withered ears on one stalk swallowed up the seven good ears on another stalk. When no one could interpret the dream for the Pharaoh, the butler remembered Joseph, and Joseph came and interpreted the dream: First there will be seven years of great plenty, and then seven years of famine. And he counselled the Pharaoh that a large reserve should be gathered up during the years of plenty, and that a fifth part of the produce should be set aside for the years of famine. The Pharaoh heeded him and named him supreme vizir with unlimited authority. And he gave him in marriage Asenath, the daughter of the priest Potipherah. And Asenath bore him two sons, Ephraim and Manasseh.

Joseph ruled the land with wisdom. He gathered food betimes and copious provisions for Egypt and for all the world, and sold them when the famine became severe. And Joseph's brothers came from Canaan. Joseph recognized them at once. He could only think of the dreams he once had, and he sharply abused them. He accused them of being spies and had them locked up. But three days later they were allowed to go back, after they had promised to bring Benjamin, who had stayed home. Joseph held Simeon as a hostage. They also received corn, as much as they could pay for. But Joseph had given orders that the money should be put back in their sacks.

When the sons told their father Jacob of Joseph's demand, he at first refused to let Benjamin make the journey. But hunger forced him to give in. Reuben offered his sons to his father as a guarantee for Benjamin's life, and so Jacob let him go. In Egypt, Joseph made himself known to them and invited them to stay with him, and to live in the land of Goshen, whither Jacob would follow them. And Pharaoh heard that Joseph's brothers had come. He showered them with gifts, and gave them wagons and beasts of burden in order to fetch Jacob, and their wives and children and all their belongings, and bring them to Goshen. Thus Jacob came to Egypt, and Joseph supplied his father and his brothers and his father's whole family with corn and bread.

By clever husbanding of provisions, Joseph, acting in the Pharaoh's name, was the only one who had corn to sell. After the third year of the famine all the money was in the Pharaoh's coffers. In the fourth year, the farmers had to sell their herds to the Pharaoh for bread; in the fifth year, they sold their land; in the sixth their freedom, and they became serfs. But Joseph did not touch the priests, for they lived at the Pharaoh's expense. And so they kept their lands and herds. But everything else belonged henceforth to the Pharaoh. And the farmers ever after were strictly required to pay the Pharaoh a fifth of their harvest.

After Jacob's death, Joseph's brothers feared that he might pay them back for their sins, and they threw themselves at his feet. But he made them free men, for he did not wish his brothers to be serfs, and he provided for them in Egypt for as long as he lived. But he had his brothers swear an oath to take his mortal remains with them when they left the country.

[Genesis 37:2, 5–11, 19–20, 28, 34; 39:6; 40:1, 6–23; 41; 42; 45:1, 3, 5–9, 10b–26; 47:12–13; 50:15–25]

(i) The Elohist story of Joseph, in contrast to the Yahwist version, mentions only one test for Jacob's sons. Here, furthermore, it is Reuben who takes pains on Joseph's behalf and who leads the group. Finally, the Elohist narrator is very pro-Egyptian and very well informed about Egyptian life. The story of the origins of Pharaonic rule and its social structure in unsparing exploitation of economically weaker individuals at a time of crisis offers an exemplary account, classic in its brevity, of the character of the Middle Eastern despot. The Elohist narrator describes all this in detail, thereby revealing his hostility to Jerusalem. For, on the throne in that city, was a king from the tribe of Benjamin, Joseph's favourite, with similar ambitions.

(ii) One of the peculiar features of the Elohist version is the pattern of prediction through dreams and fulfilment in reality. The narrator uses this formal tool to move the heroic novella towards the realm of myth. Now it is Elohim who directs everything so marvellously, who pulls all the strings, and Joseph who is a willing instrument. Joseph does get sold into slavery, but soon becomes the chief servant of his lord. In this version Joseph never goes to prison on suspicion of adultery; he is, instead, the overseer of the prison, and no suspicions arise against him. Joseph is a thoroughly good man, the model of a royal officer.

(iii) The Elohist narrator comes from the northern regions of Palestine, where old local traditions were more alive than in the south. That is why he gives the name of Joseph's wife, which also provides us with the mythological setting of the Joseph stories. Joseph's wife is called Asenath, i.e. belonging to the goddess Neith. Neith was the goddess of Sais in Lower Egypt, originally a goddess of war and the dead, who protected the dead on their journey to the other world. Plato and Plutarch equated her with Athena. Neith is the primeval goddess of the Egyptian New Kingdom, similar to the goddess Anatha of Asia Minor, known from Ugaritic mythology as Anat, who brings the murdered Baal back to life.

(iv) In these stories the Elohist narrator takes up one of his favourite themes: the world as a scene of harmonious order. The ancient Canaanite peoples, the Egyptians, and the house of Joseph can live together in prosperity and peace. They can trade with and help one another. The Elohist narrator loathes war. He is a pacifist, and here, too, he runs counter to the militarism of Jerusalem, which did not quite know what to make of the figure of Joseph.

(v) The priestly tradition merely adds a few statements on Joseph's age. Under priestly influence, however, 'house of Joseph' came into use as a term for the rebellious northern kingdom (e.g. Amos 6:6; Psalms 80:2; Ezekiel 37:6; Zechariah 10:6,8). Only rarely does the name mean all of Israel (as in Psalms 77:16;81:6), to avoid using the sacred name Israel, which the northern kingdom had claimed for itself.

c. Esau, Jacob's twin brother, had numerous descendants, fulfilling the prophecy that his father Isaac had made over him. Jacob likewise had many descendants when he set off for Egypt. But he blessed his sons with a special blessing for each one:

Reuben, you are my first-born, pre-eminent in pride and power, you shall not have pre-eminence because you went up to your father's bed, and you defiled it [see IV.3.c.i (p. 92)].

Simeon and Levi are brothers. O my soul, come not into their council; O my spirit, be not joined to their company. For in their anger they slay men, and in their wantonness they hamstring oxen.

Judah, your brothers shall praise you and bow down before you. The sceptre shall not depart from you, nor the ruler's staff from between your feet, until he comes, whom all the peoples shall obey.

Zebulun shall dwell at the shore of the sea, and **Issachar** bends his shoulder to bear, and becomes a slave at forced labour. **Dan** shall judge his people, but he shall be a serpent in the way, a viper by the path. **Gad** shall struggle bravely. **Asher** shall be a good farmer, and **Naphtali** a good poet.

Joseph is showered with the fullness of blessings from heaven above, he is invulnerable, unconquerable. God almighty blesses him with the blessings of the deep that lies below, with the blessings of the breasts and of the womb. But **Benjamin** is a ravenous wolf.

[Genesis 36; 46; 49]

(i) The individual pronouncements in Jacob's blessing come from different eras and sources. The sayings about Reuben, Simeon and Levi derive from the nomadic Lay Source. Reuben is blamed for trying to overthrow his father by sleeping with his concubine. Simeon and Levi are rebuked for slaughtering the citizens of Shechem. The author has no notion of Levi's special role as a priest at the shrines of Yahweh.

The sayings about Judah, Benjamin, Issachar, Zebulun, Dan, Gad, Asher and Naphtali surely derive from Yahwist traditions. Judah is the great hero, and victory is his due. The royal maxim, 'The sceptre shall not depart from you ...', is undoubtedly based on the formula for anointing the king in the ritual of accession to the throne. Later readers have seen in this passage the proclamation of a redeemer from the house of Judah to come in the 'last days'. It reveals in fact the bid for power by the royal theocracy of Jerusalem. But the benediction over Joseph comes from a tradition that does not view Judah, the upstart from the south, as the prince among the children of Jacob, but gives that role to Joseph. That is why Joseph receives the 'blessings of the breasts and of the womb'. In these formulas we can see ancient pre-Israelite religious ideas, just as in the passage about Simeon and Levi who, as the source angrily notes, have not only murdered men, but have hamstrung oxen. This is a clear allusion to the old bull god of Shechem. These sayings, which correspond to Moses' blessings in Deuteronomy 33, have a structure modelled on the gathering at a sacred site, where the herald calls upon the subjects of his king by name and office.

IV.5. *The Moses Stories*

a. After Joseph's death, the people of Israel multiplied and grew exceedingly strong in Egypt. The Egyptians were troubled by this, and tried to enslave the sons of Joseph by the harshest forced labour. The Israelites had lost their old privileges. Now Moses was a shepherd and the son-in-law of the Midianite priest Reuel. Once, when he was out pasturing sheep, Yahweh appeared to him as a flame of fire in a thorn bush, which burned but was not consumed. When Yahweh saw that Moses was drawing near to have a look at this wonder, he said to him: Do not come near; put off your shoes from your feet, for this is holy ground. – Moses veiled his head, for he was afraid to look at God. And Yahweh said to him: I will bring my people out of Egypt. You shall go down to the Israelites and say, Yahweh, the god of your fathers, has sent me, he will bring you out of Egypt into a land flowing with milk and honey. And they will listen to you, and you shall go with the elders to Pharaoh and say: We wish to go on a three days' journey into the wilderness, that we may sacrifice to our god Yahweh.

And Moses said: What if they do not believe me and will not heed me? – But Yahweh taught him to do miracles. He could change a staff into a snake, make his hand turn leprous, and turn water into blood. And Jethro let Moses go, after he had told him all this.

In Egypt they delivered Yahweh's command to Pharaoh to let his people go, but Pharaoh did not let them go. Instead, he laid heavier work upon them by no longer giving them straw to make bricks. He made them gather stubble for straw from the fields, but he did not lower their quota of bricks. But Yahweh wished to force Pharaoh to let the sons of Joseph go, and he bade Moses change the waters of the Nile into blood. And so it came to pass, all the fish died and the water could not be used. After seven days, Yahweh sent a plague of frogs. But even after this plague, Pharaoh would not let the Israelites go, as he had first promised Moses, in order to be freed from the infestation. Then Yahweh sent a plague of gnats and a plague of flies that, like all the plagues, spared the land of the sons of Joseph. And even after that Pharaoh would not let them go. Then Yahweh sent a cattle plague, that struck all the livestock of the Egyptians, and after that the sixth plague, pestilent boils. There followed thunderstorms and hail, which struck down every living creature out in the fields. The eighth plague was a swarm of locusts that destroyed every plant in the country. But Pharaoh still would not let them go. Then Yahweh made darkness come over Egypt for three days, so that no one could rise from his place. Only the Israelites had light in their dwellings. When Pharaoh still would not let them go, Moses told him: Thus says Yahweh: Around midnight I will fall upon Egypt and kill the first-born of every man and beast, and I shall spare no one, neither Pharaoh nor the lowest of his slaves. Only after that happened did Pharaoh let them go and actually drove them out of the country. The departure was so hurried that they did not have time to get the dough ready to make bread, and carried it away in kneading bowls on their shoulders.

And Yahweh marched before them, by day in a pillar of cloud to show them the way, by night in a pillar of fire, so they could travel day and night. And he brought his people safely through a ford in the water by driving the water back with a strong east wind. But in the form of a pillar of cloud and fire he confused the army of the Egyptians. And when the pursuers fled, Yahweh drove them straight into the sea. Thus Yahweh rescued the Israelites. Afterwards Moses told Jethro that Yahweh had led Israel out of Egypt, and Jethro offered a sacrifice of thanksgiving. As they marched further on, they passed by Mount Sinai. Then Yahweh came down to Sinai and called Moses up to him on the mountain. But the people were not to break through to Yahweh and gaze, lest many of them perish. Moses and sixty of the elders climbed the mountain, and they looked upon their God. But they could only see under his feet as it were a pavement of sapphire stone, like the very heaven for brightness. They ate and drank in his presence.

But when Moses delayed coming down, the people became restless and said to his priest Aaron: Up, make us a god, who shall go before us. For Moses, the man who brought us out of Egypt, has disappeared. Then Aaron had them gather gold ornaments and made a golden calf, and said: This is your god, Israel, who freed you from Egypt, and he gave a great feast. In the meantime, Moses came down from the mountain, and when he saw what they were doing, he broke in pieces the tables of the law that he had received from Yahweh. He also broke the calf in pieces and purified the people. But Yahweh struck his people with a plague on account of the calf that Aaron had made.

And Yahweh gave Moses two new tables and had him write on them: I am your God, you shall bow down to none other. You shall make for yourself no molten gods. You shall observe the Passover meal [see VI.1.b (p. 125)]. Every first-born belongs to me. You shall celebrate the feast of weeks and the harvest festival. You shall not offer the blood of sacrifice with leaven. You shall bring the first fruits of the ground to me, and you shall not boil a kid in its mother's milk. – And Yahweh said to Moses: In accordance with these words I have made a covenant with you and with Israel.

Moses persuaded his Midianite father-in-law Hobab to go along with the Israelites as a guide through the wilderness. On the way, Yahweh fed his people with manna and, when they craved meat, with quails. At Kibroth-hattavah, that is the 'graves of craving', Yahweh struck many who had murmured against him. And Moses led the people up to the east bank of the Jordan. Then Yahweh told him: Now you will soon die. So Moses gave Joshua the authority to rule over the people. And Moses climbed Mount Nebo, where Yahweh showed him the whole country and said: This is the land that I promised Abraham, Isaac and Jacob I would give to their descendants. I have let you see it, but you shall not go over into the country. And Moses died there and was buried, but no one knows the place of his burial.

[Exodus 3; 5; 7–11; 12:29–34; 13:21–2; 14:10, 21b, 24, 25b, 27, 30; 18:8–12; 19; 20; 24:1, 9–11; 32:1–6, 19–20, 35; 34:10c–27; Numbers 10:29–31; 11:31–5; Deuteronomy 31:14–23; 34:1–6]

(i) The Yahwist story of Moses, from the golden days of the Davidic monarchy, describes Moses as the great hero and wonder-worker in Israel's early history. Yahweh is an aggressive god. He deals harshly with the Egyptians, and even with his own people he behaves like a Near Eastern potentate. Refractory and disobedient individuals are banished or wiped out. Moses is his servant, just as all Middle Eastern kings liked to view themselves as the servants of a god – and in the legal usage of the time that was equivalent to being the god's son. Moses is a mythical figure. He emerges from the obscurity of traditions passed down by nomadic herdsmen from southern Palestine, and he dies in foreign territory. He is the chief leader of the army until they get to the border of their new land, but Yahweh is the king and supreme ruler. The Yahwist tradition is greatly interested in stressing Yahweh's dominant role, whereas it says little about Moses' priestly functions. The Yahwist Moses is the model of the southern tribes' royalist ideology.

(ii) Moses' roles as lawgiver and priest stem from different interest groups. The Yahwist narrator takes a negative view of Aaron, who succumbs to temptation when he is egged on by the people. The narrator makes no mention of any positive role for Aaron as a mediator. Yahweh speaks only to Moses, who is the leader of the army and the king. Priests and people are presented as ingrates, with whom the sacred king can cope only by stern discipline. Without his laws and leadership they simply fall into the hands of their enemies, cannot survive and so forth. The Yahwist tradition uses the name Reuel for Moses' father-in-law only once. Elsewhere, the priestly editors have inserted the Elohist name Jethro (see IV.5.b.vii (p. 108)).

(iii) Judaism honours Moses as the mediator through whom the law was given. In addition, Jewish messianic expectations have understood the king of salvation, who will come in the last time, as a Moses *redivivus*. There are many apocryphal writings of Moses from the centuries just before and after the beginning of the Christian era. Christianity also views Moses as a prophet and mediator of the New Law. (See also II.4.**a** (p. 52) and II.5.**c** (p. 55).)

b. When the tribes of Jacob had greatly multiplied and a new Pharaoh had ascended the throne, he ordered the midwives of the Hebrews (as the sons of Jacob were also called) to kill all the boys as soon as they were born. But the midwives did not do this. Then Pharaoh commanded his people: Take all the boys born to the Hebrews and throw them into the Nile, but let the girls live. Because of this a mother from the house of Levi, to save her son, put him in a tightly caulked basket of papyrus and placed it among the reeds on the shore of the Nile. When the daughter of Pharaoh came down to the river to bathe and discovered the basket, she had pity for the child. The sister of the new-born baby, who had observed this, immediately went and fetched the child's own mother to be its nurse. Pharaoh's daughter named the child Moses. Later, when the boy grew up, in an outburst of anger he slew an Egyptian who was beating a Hebrew labourer. He feared he would be punished for this murder and so he fled to Midian. There Elohim appeared to him and said: I am the God of your father, the God of Abraham, Isaac and Jacob. And I have seen the affliction of my people in Egypt. Come, I will send you to Pharaoh that you may bring forth my people out of Egypt. Yet I know that Pharaoh will not willingly let you go, therefore I shall work wonders so that he will have to let you go. And you shall go forth from the country laden with the Egyptians' gold and silver ornaments. Now Moses was unwilling to accept this charge, for he was not an eloquent man. But Elohim said: Because you cannot speak well, your brother Aaron shall speak to the people. He shall be as a mouth for you, and you shall be to him as a god.

And Elohim's ten plagues [see IV.5.**a** (p. 102)] compelled Pharaoh to let Israel go. Now the Israelites had asked the Egyptians for gold and silver jewellery and costly garments, which were given to them, because the Egyptians looked favourably upon them. And so they despoiled the Egyptians by taking all these precious possessions.

Elohim did not let the people go by the direct way into the promised land, because the Philistines were dwelling there, and they had a mighty army. He made them go a roundabout way, and brought the remains of Joseph with them. After the Israelites had left, the Egyptians changed their minds, since they had lost such a large labour force, and Pharaoh had a group of six hundred warriors fighting from chariots set off to bring them back. But Elohim clogged their chariot wheels so that they drove heavily.

And during the march the Israelites wrangled with Moses, because they did not have enough to eat and drink, and always got the same thing. Still Elohim led them safely on. They happened to meet Jethro, Moses' father-in-law, with his wives and sons. Jethro saw how much trouble Moses had managing the people, because he thought he had to do everything by himself, and he counselled him: What you are doing is not good. You should represent the people before God and then teach them what they should do. Moreover, choose able men from all the people, such as fear God, men who are trustworthy and who hate a bribe; and place such men over the people as rulers of thousands, of hundreds, of fifties and of tens.

Moses heeded his father-in-law. He appointed such men of trust everywhere as judges and leaders.

And after they had made these arrangements, their god led them further on their way to the promised land until they came to Horeb, his mountain, where he made a covenant with them. Moses remained on the mountain for forty days and forty nights and there he received from his god the two stone tables of the Law, written by the finger of the god. Meanwhile, however, Aaron had had the image of a golden bull set up, and the Israelites worshipped it and danced wildly around it, because Aaron had said: This is your god, Israel. When Moses came down from Mount Horeb, he was violently angry with Aaron and the people. As a punishment for their crime they had to strip themselves of all their ornaments, from Mount Horeb onward. Now Moses had a tent which he entered, when he intended to speak with Elohim. Every time Moses was in the tent, the pillar of cloud came down and stood at the tent door and spoke with him.

Again Moses had trouble with the people, because they murmured and complained about the food sent from God, the manna and quails. Therefore Yahweh had Moses summon to his tent seventy of the elders whom he had appointed. And he said to Moses: I will come there and speak with you. But then I shall take away from you some of the divine spirit that rests upon you and share it with the seventy, so that they may be more of a help to you. And Moses acted accordingly. But Miriam and Aaron rebelled against Moses, because they did not belong to the seventy, and they rebuked him for having a Cushite wife. The god Yahweh punished them for this. Miriam was stricken with leprosy for seven days, but Aaron had to continue as Moses' interpreter.

Miriam died in Kadesh, where the nation dwelt for a long time and made a code of laws for itself. On the way to the land of Edom the people grew still more dissatisfied and murmured against Yahweh and Moses. Then the god Yahweh sent fiery serpents that bit the people, and many died. To save the people, at Yahweh's command Moses made a bronze serpent and set it upon a pole and raised it high over the camp. If a serpent bit any man, he would look at the bronze serpent and live, as the god Yahweh had promised.

And they continued on their way, even through the territory of Sihon of Heshbon, an Ammonite kingdom, and they conquered it. Now when Balak, the king of Moab, saw that, he had the seer Balaam brought to him from Pethor, in order to drive away the sons of Jacob. After a long delay Balaam came, but the angel of Yahweh three times stood in the way of Balaam's ass, so that he could go no further, because the ass refused to move on, even though he beat it. Finally the seer understood that he would not be allowed to utter a curse over Israel but only blessings. Thus the king of Moab was cheated of many costly sacrificial animals and the curse he had planned on. But Balaam foresaw the days of greatness God's people would enjoy. [See also V.5 (p. 122).]

At the border of the promised land the pillar of cloud appeared and called Moses and Joshua into the tent. And Moses gave Joshua, the son of Nun, his orders and told him: You shall bring the people into the land that I promised them, and I shall be with you. – This was on Mount Pisgah opposite from Jericho. There Moses died.

[Exodus 1:15–2:15; 3:6, 19–22; 4:10–16; 12:35; 13:17; 14:5–7, 25; 17:1b–7; 18:13–27; 24:18b; 31:18b; 32; Numbers 11; 20; 21:4b–9; 22; Deuteronomy 31:14,23; 34:1]

(i) The Elohist story of Moses describes him as a great military leader, but still more as the man who fashioned a wise democratic order through the institution of the tribal elders. By Moses' command, smaller individual groups of Israelites were to be independent. On this point Elohist tradition opposed the centralism of Jerusalem.

The second peculiarity of the Elohist account is its detailed description of how the heroic people of the Jerusalem kings lost heart during the years of wandering the wilderness. This feature may be explained by the past history of the carriers of the Elohist tradition: the farmer accustomed to land under cultivation boasts of his superiority over the nomad.

Yet another peculiar feature of this account is its devaluation of the priest Aaron, seen as the quintessence of apostasy. Moses himself is called a god, and Aaron is actually his spokesman, but he seduces the people into bull-worship and revolts against Moses. This is clearly a polemical thrust against the Jerusalem priesthood, which laboured in the king's service.

(ii) The Elohist tradition also reveals the mythological setting of the Moses story. The name Mosis is of Egyptian origin. When used in Egyptian royal names it designates a man as 'born of a god'. Thus, for example, Ramses means born of Ra (the sun god), Thutmose means born of Thoth. This king, Mosis, belongs to Kadesh, an ancient shrine with religious jurisdiction at an oasis in the north-east Sinai peninsula. Kadesh seems to have always had close ties to the god of Sinai, who presided over mountains, storms and war. If Mount Sinai was the centre of an amphictyony for Levites, Kenites,

Calebites and Josephites in the summer, then Kadesh presumably was the winter rendezvous for these same nomadic peoples. The god Yahweh of Sinai was associated with the serpent of Kadesh, which Moses raises on high to save the life of his people. Moses is the deputy, the high priest of the god, but he ends by seizing all the power for himself. Yahweh's connection with the serpent makes him typologically akin to Apollo, who is also a god of oracles. Like Moses, he utters wise sayings and heals people. (See V.3 (p. 119).)

(iii) It is likely that nomadic Hebrew tribes overran the sanctuary at Kadesh and killed the indigenous goddess, who had the form of a snake. This points up her function as a chthonic divinity, such as Hera, Persephone or the Egyptian Lady of Buto. The Pythia of Delphi, a dispenser of oracles, was also a snake goddess. And as the Greek priest of Apollo exercised Apollo's function in Delphi, after Apollo had killed the Python, so Moses took over the oracular function at Kadesh.

In Egyptian, the uraeus as a symbol of the sacred queen of Buto ultimately became the hieroglyph for all goddess names and then for 'goddess' *tout court*. At any rate, the Elohist tradition is aware of the archaic feud between the serpent Apophis and the sun god Ra, as shown by the way it divides the power between Sinai and Kadesh.

(iv) The nomadic invaders – the Hebrews, as the Elohist source calls them – are plainly presented as thieving and treacherous, while the Egyptians are judged favourably. The reader sympathizes with them and can understand them, even if he, like Balaam's ass, cannot help recognizing the fact that there is no resisting the sons of Jacob and their god Yahweh. The Elohist tradition always represents Yahweh as the god of Abraham, Isaac and Jacob, the god of the great heroes and sacred kings of olden times.

(v) In the gospel according to John (ch. 4), the serpent lifted up by Moses in the wilderness is interpreted as referring to Christ. This is how the staff of Aesculapius, even in the Christian Middle Ages, could become the symbol of doctors.

(vi) According to Exodus 2:4, Miriam is Moses' elder sister, while Aaron is Moses' brother (Exodus 7:7) and younger than Miriam. Her importance as a prophetess (Exodus 15:20) surely derives from her role as a long-serving priestess at Kadesh. In this role she is linked to the person of Moses.

Aaron was presumably a high priest at Kadesh. The myth associates him with Moses (Exodus 4:14–16; 7:1–6). He is the first priest before Yahweh (Exodus 28:29; Leviticus 8). The Aaronic blessing (Numbers 6:24–6), in use today among Jews and Christians, is named after him. In Hebrews 7, the New Testament compares his priesthood with that of Christ.

(vii) The Elohist tradition calls Moses' father-in-law Jethro, a Midianite high priest (Exodus 3:1), thereby shifting the cult of Yahweh away from a foreign land inhabited by nomads and closer to the farming country of Canaan.

c. When the Israelites were forced to do hard labour in Egypt, a god spoke to Moses and said to him: I am Yahweh. I appeared to Abraham, to Isaac and to Jacob, but by my name Yahweh I did not make myself known to them. Say therefore to the people of Israel: Yahweh will take you for his people and will be your god. He will lead you out of Egypt into the land that he promised to Abraham, Isaac and Jacob.

Moses told that to the Israelites, but they paid him no heed. And so Moses said to Yahweh: I cannot speak well. How then shall Pharaoh listen to me? Then Yahweh answered him: See, I make you as a god to Pharaoh, and Aaron shall be your prophet. And I shall multiply my signs and wonders, so that they let you go.

And Yahweh had Aaron do great wonders before Pharaoh. Aaron turned his staff into a serpent, turned the water of the Nile into blood by striking it with his staff. Aaron did these great wonders in Egypt, and he also made the plague of frogs come over Egypt. Then Yahweh said to Moses and Aaron: Go and have every Israelite family slaughter an unblemished male lamb or a goat at eventide on the 14th of Abib. With their blood you shall streak the lintel and the two doorposts, and you shall completely consume the animal that same night. But as you do this, you shall be dressed for a journey. On that night, Yahweh will slay every first-born male in Egypt. But the angel of death will not cross the threshold of the houses that are streaked with blood. And henceforth you shall celebrate this day each year with such a Passover meal, because Yahweh freed you out of the land of Egypt, and the festival shall last seven days. On those days you shall eat unleavened bread, but strangers shall not eat of it.

When the first-born of Egypt had been slain, just as Yahweh had announced, the Israelites went forth from Egypt, marching by tribes. And they camped for the first time at Etham at the edge of the steppe. Now Yahweh made Pharaoh foolish so that he tried to bring the Israelites back. And the Egyptians who set out after them were all drowned. In the wilderness, Yahweh fed the Israelites with manna and quails, and Aaron kept a jar full of manna before the ark of the covenant. In the third month they came to the Sinai desert and camped there. Moses climbed the mountain, veiled in the cloud that accompanied them on their way. And the glory of Yahweh came down in the cloud, like a fire in appearance. On the seventh day Yahweh spoke with Moses and commanded him: Take from among you an offering to me. Whoever is of a generous heart, let him bring me an offering, and from the gifts build me a sanctuary, as I will show you. It shall be a tent, with a table, a candlestick with seven branches, curtains, and a tabernacle of acacia wood for the Law that I will give you. Aaron and his sons shall serve as priests.

But when Moses came down from the mountain, the tables of the Law in his hand, then Aaron and all the Israelites saw that the face of Moses shone, for he had spoken with Yahweh. And Moses made known to them the will of Yahweh. After he had spoken to them, he put a veil over his face. He took it off only while he spoke with them and when he stayed in the tent, which was the home of the ark of the covenant. And every time that he spoke with the Israelites, they saw that the skin of his face shone.

The Israelites prepared everything very carefully, as Yahweh had commanded, speaking through Moses. When the work on the tent was concluded, the cloud covered the tent of meeting, and the glory of Yahweh filled the tabernacle. During this time Moses could not come into the tent. But whenever the cloud was taken up from over the tabernacle, and the glory of Yahweh went out of it, the people would march onward. But if the cloud was not taken up, they stayed in the camp. Aaron performed the sacrifices in the forecourt of the tent.

And Moses appointed the heads of families as counsellors. All able-bodied males over twenty years of age were mustered for military service. The Levites were excused from bearing arms, and they did not have to pay the war tax. While the Israelites were at Sinai, regulations were laid down for the army and for life in camp. The war tax, the charge for redeeming first-born sons, and the head tax were to go to the priests in perpetuity, and the Levites were to be their servants.

And the princes of the tribes gave lavish sacrificial offerings when the new ritual laws were introduced.

And Yahweh said to Moses, when the Israelites were camped at Paran: Send men to spy out the land of Canaan, which I will give to the people of Israel. And Moses sent a representative from every tribe to spy out the land from north to south. After forty days they returned to Moses and Aaron at Paran, and they murmured about the land, and rebelled against Aaron and Moses. Only Joshua the son of Nun and Caleb the son of Jephunneh advised the people to go on into Canaan. Yahweh became angry at this and decided that not one of the able-bodied men would come into the country except Caleb and Joshua: For forty years, he said, you shall go on through the wilderness, before you come into the country. During that time all the able-bodied men, who have rebelled against me, will die. – And the spies, except for Joshua and Caleb, were also very soon dead.

Now there were men among the people, who rose up against Moses and Aaron, and said: You have gone too far! For all the congregation are holy, every one of them, and Yahweh is among them. Why then do you exalt yourselves above the assembly of Yahweh? Most of the rebels were from the Levitic clan of the Korahites, who were no longer satisfied with their cultic functions. Yahweh punished the uprising: all 250 men burned to death. Then the whole community rebelled against Moses and Aaron and rebuked them for being the murderers of the 250 men. Again Yahweh punished the people, and killed 14,700 men, until Aaron stopped the plague with an offering of incense. After that the whole people went on to the wilderness of Sin, where there was no water. Then, once again, the community banded together against Moses and Aaron, and shouted: Why have you brought us here so that we and our cattle should die? Would we had died with our brothers whom Yahweh slew. But Yahweh said to Moses and Aaron: Have the people assemble, and tell the rock before their eyes to yield its water. But Moses and Aaron did not speak to the rock, they struck it with Aaron's priestly staff. The rock gave forth water abundantly for the people and all their cattle. But Yahweh was angry at Moses and Aaron, because they had not believed him that the rock would give forth water at their word, but they had struck it. This is why Moses and Aaron were not allowed to lead the people into the promised land. And Aaron died on Mount Hor. Thereafter the Israelites set off to the steppes of Moab across from Jericho. The number of those men required to pay the army and priest tax was regularly recorded, and in the last census before the entrance into Canaan the total was 601,730 men.

They also defeated the Midianites and pillaged everything, leaving only the young girls alive.

And Moses wrote down their whole time of wandering, with all the places and events, and also set down the people who were to attend to a fair distribution of the land when the Israelites came there. The Levites were to be assigned forty-eight cities with their pasture land throughout the country as their portion. Six places were to be cities of refuge for manslayers or those who unintentionally killed someone. There they would be given asylum until they were judged or until the death of the current high priest. For every new high priest declared an amnesty.

Moses died on Mount Nebo, after seeing the land that he himself would never enter. He died at the age of 120 years, and the Israelites mourned him for thirty days.

[Exodus 6–9; 12; 14:4; 16:1–4; 24:15–18; 25; 34:29; 35–40; Numbers 1; 7; 13; 14; 16; 17:6–7; 20; 26; 31; 33:2–3; 35; Deuteronomy 32:48–52; 34:7–8]

(i) The priestly version of the Moses story limits Moses' activity to leading the people. All priestly functions are attributed to Aaron, who is both priest and prophet. Moses is the supreme mediator of Yahweh's will. He is only considered divine vis-à-vis Pharaoh.

(ii) The mythology of the priestly source is chiefly orientated towards cultic aetiology. The emigration from Egypt is the basis for the Passover festival. The arrangement of the tribes in the army and the camp is the model for the priestly taxation system. The description of the tent of testimony and all the sacrificial ceremonies serves to justify the expenses involved in running the temple after the return from exile in Babylon. The priestly hierarchy is a divinely ordained institution, for Yahweh kills all those who rebel against it.

(iii) This priestly view of Moses had to come to terms with the living traditions about Moses still flourishing in the individual tribes. Such traditions could not be altered, and hence the Priestly Source did not insert any new mythologems into the story, but tried everywhere to dilute the old ones. Only in its judgement of the people does the Priestly Source take a harsher line. Its usual formula is: the whole community rebels or murmurs against Moses and Aaron, but then Aaron always saves the people from Yahweh's curse. The priest is assigned the role of saviour. Here we can see the post-exilic situation, where the only important force left was that of the priests serving the rebuilt temple of Jerusalem.

(iv) The priestly text provides no biographical information about Moses and Aaron. This lack of interest is understandable, for the source was mainly concerned with the historical undergirding of their claims to power. For this reason, it hands down many tax lists and the whole system of imposts, which aimed above all at contributions to Yahweh through the hands of the priests, and it describes in great detail the appearance of the sanctuary.

(v) The numbers cited by the priestly text are figures of fantasy, unrelated to the real data, which we can infer from archaeological evidence. In telling stories, the Oriental loved to exaggerate. But the partisan stance of the priestly tradition becomes evident in its anti-Midianite polemic. This suggests the conclusion that Moses had roots in Midianite tradition.

(vi) The priestly text's hostility to the Levites was presumably based on the fact that they took advantage of their right to maintain cities of refuge (Numbers 35) and gradually built up a position of resistance to the Jerusalem priesthood. This tendency was only heightened by the way they were more and more thrust into the role of minor clergy.

V. The Conquest of Canaan

V.1. *The Sea Miracle*

a. The people of Israel, ready for battle, journeyed from Rameses to Succoth, to escape slavery in Egypt. And Yahweh went before them by day in a pillar of cloud to lead them along the way, and by night in a pillar of fire to give them light. But when Pharaoh came after them with his troops, the Israelites were seized by great fear. Then the pillar of cloud changed its position. It came between the host of Egypt and the host of Israel, and at night the pillar of fire separated the armies. And in the morning watch, Yahweh, in the pillar of fire and of cloud, looked down upon the host of the Egyptians, and discomfited them, so that they tried to flee. But day soon dawned, and the sea rushed back and overwhelmed the Egyptians. Thus on that day Yahweh rescued Israel from the might of the Egyptians, and Israel saw the Egyptians lying dead on the seashore. And Israel saw the great miracle that Yahweh did against the Egyptians.

[Exodus 12:3; 13:21; 14:19b, 21b, 24, 30]

(i) The Yahwist tradition concerning the crossing of the sea places the myth on the eastern edge of the Nile delta. Yahweh uses the east wind to make the edge of the sea passable for the Israelites, while, as the day dawns, the winds change and drive back the waters, which sweep away the army of the Egyptians.

Yahweh is lord over the cosmic powers. Winds and waters obey him, and he is the storm god (see II.2 (p. 44)). The people who first heard the myth were not concerned with rational explanations of phenomena. The myth's task is to show the omnipotence of Yahweh, who stands by his battle-ready people. Yahweh combines the functions of Zeus and Poseidon: like those two gods, he overcomes the moon goddess, who was once the mistress of heaven and earth, the sea and the underworld. For an example of this triform divinity, consider the Greek goddesses Eurynome, Eurybia and Eurydice.

(ii) Yahweh is invincible, and sunrise seals the fate of the Egyptians. We can see a polemical thrust at Egypt here. For the Pharaoh was like Ra, 'when he goes up on the horizon to pour forth light on him who is in darkness, who inundates both lands with his brilliance, like the sun-disc in the morning', to quote a fifteenth-century B.C. Egyptian text dealing with Osiris. And now Yahweh strikes down the Egyptians in the symbol of the sun god Ra.

The story is not an aetiological legend, but a component part of Yahwist mythology and a tradition stemming from an Israelite tribe that had laboured in Egypt. (Egyptian documents make it clear that the Pharaohs employed "pr people', which corresponds to the Old Testament Hebrews.) And so the myth passed from the repertoire of a single tribe into the history of the whole nation. The myth describes the political conflict of a nomadic people with pharaonic Egypt in the form of a battle between gods: Yahweh strikes down the chosen one of Ra, that is Rameses, Ra himself.

b. When Pharaoh let the people go (for Yahweh had given the people favour in the sight of the Egyptians), they did not take the direct route to the land that had been promised them, because it was too difficult. The many kingdoms along this way were powerful obstacles. But the Egyptians changed their minds, and said: What is this we have done, that we have let Israel go from serving us? And they wished to bring them back. Then the angel of Elohim, who went before the host of Israel, moved and went behind them, between the host of Egypt and the host of Israel. And he made the wheels fall off the Egyptian chariots, so that they had difficulty advancing, and they perished miserably in the Reed Sea of the Nile delta.

[Exodus 13:17; 14:5b–6, 19, 25a]

(i) The Elohist tradition recounts the downfall of Egyptian troops and the victorious exodus of the Israelites from Egypt in a very restrained manner. With his partiality for Egypt, the Elohist narrator presents the miracle in a less dramatic light. His god Elohim wishes to avoid war, and so he chooses for his people a route that does not lead to military conflicts with the inhabitants of the country. The angel of Elohim also prevents a confrontation between the two armies in which, it is the unspoken assumption, Israel could only lose. (For a mythological reading of this episode, see V.1.a (p. 113).)

c. When the sons of Israel moved on from Succoth, Moses told them to camp by the sea near Pihahiroth. There a division of Pharaoh's war chariots overtook them. The sons of Israel were terrified and cried aloud. But Moses obeyed Yahweh's command, and lifted up his rod, stretched out his hand, and divided the sea. The Israelites went through the waters heaped on both sides of them like walls, and the Egyptians followed after. Then Yahweh said to Moses: Stretch out your hand and make the waters flow back. And the waters returned and covered the chariots and horsemen of Pharaoh so that they all perished. Then Moses and the Israelites intoned a song of thanks-giving for this miracle.

[Exodus 13:20; 14:1, 2, 6, 21, 22, 26, 28]

(i) In contrast to the Yahwist and Elohist narrators, the priestly narrator is interested in showing that Moses uses his power to destroy the pursuing Egyptians. And Yahweh is praised for this in a great hymn (Exodus 15). The hymn is a much more recent composition than the rest of the account. It presupposes that the land has been completely conquered and the temple erected. In all probability, it was originally sung at the dedication of the temple.

The story of the sea miracle, as the priestly narrator tells it, is less mythical than the other two versions. It is chiefly concerned with establishing Moses' claim to primacy.

V.2. *Wandering in the Wilderness*

a. Leaving the sea, the Israelites set out and came to the wilderness. There Yahweh nourished them with bread that he rained down from heaven. But at first the Israelites did not know what it was. It was white and tasted like cake with honey. They ate it until they arrived at the border of Canaan.

On Mount Sinai the god Yahweh gave them a Law that was to govern relations between him and the sons of Israel [cf. VI.1 (p. 125)]. And Yahweh promised them: I will send my terror before you, and drive off your enemies or make them fall into your hands, till you come into the land that I have promised you. And they were led by Hobab, Moses' father-in-law, who was a Midianite.

On the way Yahweh also gave the sons of Israel flesh to eat when they cried out for it, and he made quails come, until they arrived at the border of the land which they had spied out. But Yahweh caused all those who rose up or murmured against him, such as Korahites, to die along the way. They never got to the border alive. And Miriam and Aaron, Moses' sister and brother, also died in the wilderness.

But the rest of the nation went on through the wilderness to the east of the land until they came to the Jordan. There Reuben, Gad and part of Manasseh settled down, while the others crossed the Jordan near Jericho.

[Exodus 15:27; 16:4, 15, 31b; 23:30–32; 34:1–28; Numbers 10:29–32; 16; 20; 25:1–5; 32:1–5, 16, 24; 33:38; Joshua 1–2]

(i) The Yahwist narrator gives a brief, brisk account of the journey in the wilderness, describing it as a victorious raid, in the Near Eastern fashion.

Enemies retreat or fall into the hands of the Israelites. Everyone who disobeys or mutinies must die. Even Aaron the priest and his sister Miriam are subject to this rule (see also IV.5.b.vi (p. 108)).

For the representative of the Jerusalem military aristocracy during David's reign, the wanderings in the wilderness are the prototype of the planned wars of conquest. Yahweh is the god of storms and war (see II.2 (p. 44) and II.3 (p. 47)).

b. When the Israelites had come from the Sea of Reeds as far as Marah, they murmured because the springs there gave only bitter water. Moses cried out to Yahweh, and he gave him a tree, which he threw into the water, and it became sweet and drinkable.

Moses also made water gush from the rock on Mount Horeb, when he struck the rock with his staff at Yahweh's command. This was at Meribah (contention) and Massah (temptation). For the people were thirsty and they had rebelled against Moses and said: Why have you led us out of Egypt, to have us die here?

Near Rephidim, Israel had to fight the Amalekites. Joshua, Moses' servant, led the Israelite troops. But Moses stood on a hill behind the battle line. In his hands he held up the staff of God, and as long as he held up his hands in blessing, Joshua's men prevailed. Whenever he lowered them, the tide of the battle turned against them. Then Aaron and Hur supported Moses' arms till evening, when the Amalekites were defeated.

On Sinai the people were so frightened by the thunder-claps, the lightning and the smoking mountain top that they begged Moses to go up to the mountain for them all by himself. And Moses went alone to receive the Law of Yahweh, who promised him: I will send my angel before you to guard you on the way and to bring you into the land that I have prepared. Remain true to me and I will bless your food and water, and keep sickness far from you. No woman shall miscarry, and you shall live to old age. But I will not drive out all your enemies at once, lest the land become desolate and the wild beasts multiply against you. Little by little I will drive them out until you are increased and possess the land.

Moses came down to the people and passed on to them all these words of Yahweh. Thereupon they made a covenant with Yahweh and sealed it with a sacrifice of twelve bulls. And after forty days and nights Moses received tablets of stone from Yahweh, on which Yahweh himself wrote the law of his covenant. And Moses kept the tablets in the tent of the testimony.

But despite all Yahweh's help and promises, the wanderers were dissatisfied. They had nothing to eat but manna, and longed to be back in Egypt, remembering the fish, the cucumbers, melons, onions and leeks. Their groans moved Yahweh to send them quails to eat. Yet Moses grieved because all the people had not been seized by the prophetic spirit of God, but only a few. For God had said on Horeb: If you obey my voice and keep my covenant, you shall be my own possession among all peoples; and you shall be to me a kingdom of priests and a holy nation.

On their way through the land east of the Jordan the Israelites went around Edom and marched to the Jordan near Jericho.

[Exodus 15:22–5; 17:1–15; 19:5–6; 20:18–19; 23:20, 29–30; 24:4–8; 33:7–11; Numbers 7:1–3; 11:4–30]

(i) The Elohist narrator does not characterize the Israelites as heroes. He strongly emphasizes their inability to cope with the situation in the wilderness. Without Moses and his kindly god, the great champion of the people's welfare and the country's, they would never have arrived in the land. The pro-Egyptian narrator, familiar with the theme of nostalgia for Egypt, belonged to the people that originally possessed the land.

(ii) His negative attitude towards Jerusalem is also evident in his belief that the whole nation should have a royal priestly office. Like Moses, he grieves that not everyone has been supplied with the prophetic spirit, as was Moses the wonder-worker. (See IV.5.b (p. 105).)

(iii) The final edition of the priestly text has consistently deleted the name of Elohim and inserted Yahweh even in the Elohist texts after the theophany in Exodus 3.

c. On the march away from the sea, the Israelites arrived in the wilderness of Sin. There Yahweh fed them with manna that he rained down from heaven at the beginning of each day. And each day everyone gathered as much as he needed. But on Friday they gathered a double portion, for the Sabbath, the seventh day, was a day of rest for Yahweh. On these two days, the manna did not spoil, although otherwise it was edible only for one day.

And Aaron filled a jar with manna and kept it in the tent of the testimony for an eternal reminder of the miraculous nourishment of the people in the wilderness.

In the third month after the exodus they camped on Sinai. There Yahweh commanded Moses, whom he had called to him, to tell the Israelites to build him a sanctuary. And Yahweh stipulated very precisely how the ark of the covenant, the show-bread table, the golden candelabrum and the tabernacle were to be constructed. And he likewise described in great detail the vestments for the priests, the ritual for their ordination, and the whole process of worship, including the cultic laws that the whole people had to submit to.

Yahweh also ordered Moses and Aaron to take a census of all Israel, to muster the able-bodied men and draw up regulations for the camp. The Levites were only to carry out their duties at the sanctuary; they were to be free from all other obligations. All Israel was to provide for the support of the priests and to make rich sacrificial offerings. On the twentieth day of the second month in the second year after the exodus, they left Sinai and went off into the steppe of Paran.

When the Korahites rose up against the priests Moses and Aaron, they had to die, as all those had to die who approached the sanctuary improperly. Only Moses, Aaron and his sons were permitted to set foot in it.

Aaron died on Mount Hor. He was not allowed to enter the promised land because he had not believed Yahweh. From there the Israelites went on farther to the steppes of Moab across from Jericho.

There the Israelites played the harlot with the daughters of the Moabites. Therefore Yahweh caused a great plague to come over the camp, which only subsided when all the foreign women were removed from the camp, and Yahweh once again gave many laws which the Israelites were to obey.

They were not to marry foreign women. For this reason, after the victory over the Midianites, Moses had all the women who had first been spared put to death, so that of all the Midianites only the young girls survived.

And at Yahweh's command Moses put down in writing the exact course of the people's wandering. He likewise wrote that Yahweh had ordered the land to be apportioned by lot. After that, Moses died on Mount Nebo, east of Jericho, after he had seen the land.

[Exodus 16:15, 22–31; Leviticus 25:16; Numbers 1–10; 15:1; 16; 17–19; 20:1–13, 22–9; 25:6–32; Deuteronomy 33:2, 33–6]

(i) The priestly narrator tells this story from a contemporary point of view. He wishes to prove that the cultic community, which had arisen after the exile with Persian approval, had already been founded by Yahweh on Sinai. That is why the years of wandering are described very cursorily, while the laws promulgated by Yahweh are reported at great length.

The whole way of life of the cultic community gathered around the temple, with sacrificial regulations and a body of civil law, is projected back to the migratory camp. Thus, with the isolation of this tradition concerning the god Yahweh, the remarkable notion arises that while his people wandered about in the wilderness, he was concerned only with vestments for his priests and furnishings for his residence, and that his greatest anxiety was that his people would associate with foreign women.

Such thinking is presumably a mask for the puritanical approach of the rigorist group that restored the cultic community of Jerusalem after the Babylonian exile, specifically the policies of Ezra and Nehemiah, as described in the books of the same name. The myth of wandering through the wilderness under Yahweh's guidance becomes an aetiological legend explaining the structure of the Jerusalem cultic community. The myth transcends its own boundaries and becomes an aetiological account of the Law.

V.3. *The Miraculous Serpent of Kadesh*

On the way east the people of Israel became impatient, and they spoke against Yahweh and against Moses: Why have you brought us up out of Egypt to die in the wilderness? For there is no bread and no water, and we loathe this worthless food. And Yahweh sent fiery serpents, and they bit the people, so that many of the people of Israel died. And the people came to Moses and said: We have sinned, for we have spoken against Yahweh and against you. Pray to Yahweh, that he take away the serpents from us. So Moses prayed for the people. And Yahweh said to Moses: Make a fiery serpent, and set it on a pole; and everyone who is bitten, when he sees it, shall live. So Moses made a bronze serpent, and set it on a pole; and if a serpent bit any man, he would look at the bronze serpent and live.
[Numbers 21:4b–9]

(i) This Elohist tale is deeply rooted in mythological thought. Yahweh appears as the lord of serpents, the *Saraphs*. Mythologically, the serpent is always a female divinity. In Egypt, the uraeus, symbol of the sacred queen of Buto, became the hieroglyph for all the names of goddesses and finally the hieroglyph for 'goddess' pure and simple. The Greek serpent goddesses, Hera and Persephone, were chthonic deities. The Pythia of Delphi was also a serpent goddess. In Delphi, Apollo had killed the Python and usurped the place of the Pythia, just as Yahweh superseded the serpent goddess of Kadesh, assuming there was one. Kadesh is one of the mythical place names on the route of the wandering Israelites. The name means, equivalently, 'sanctified' (see also IV.5.b.iii (p. 108) and vi (p. 108)). And even as the Greek priest took over Apollo's oracular function, so Moses takes over this function of Kadesh. Evidently Moses and Yahweh had to placate the angry serpent goddess of Kadesh, now deposed, by erecting her brazen image. Gazing at it cures those who have been made sick by the enraged goddess. In the course of their wanderings, the Israelites had presumably violated the ancient sanctuary and raped its priestesses.

(ii) The myth is older than the prohibition against graven images and the law that only one god was to be worshipped. It was handed down by people who secretly denied Jerusalem's teachings. Sinai and Kadesh stand side by side, equally privileged (see also IV.5.b (p. 105) and IV.5.b.ii (p. 107)). The fact that Hebrew makes the word for 'snake' a masculine noun is just another clear indication that Yahweh has usurped the function of the serpent goddess. According to II Kings 18:4, Moses' bronze serpent was still in use as a cult object in Jerusalem as late as the reign of King Hezekiah, *c.* 720 B.C. People were still burning incense to it as 'Nehushtah', when Hezekiah had it smashed in pieces along with all the other images of the gods. Nehushtah was a woman's name, suggesting that this deity was feminine (II Kings 24:8).

(iii) On the positive role of the snake in the myth of man's origins, see III.1.viii.

V.4. *Stories of the Spies*

a. When the Israelites were in the steppe of Paran near Kadesh, Moses sent spies to reconnoitre the land that lay before them. He told them to find out what the land and the people in it were like. They went out as far as Hebron, where they met the Anakim. Upon returning they told him: The land is rich. But the people who dwell in it are strong, and the cities are fortified and very large. And besides, we saw the descendants of Anak there. When Caleb the son of Jephunneh heard this, he wished to set out immediately, and said: If Yahweh is gracious to us, the land will soon be ours. For Caleb went out with them, and by order of Yahweh he was to dwell in that land.

[Numbers 13:17, 22, 27–8, 30; 14:8]

(i) The myth of the great hero Caleb derives from the ancient southern tradition which has been labelled the Lay Source, and which was handed on down by the clan of the Calebites. The latter was a nomadic tribe whose chief camp sites lay around Hebron. It maintained a sort of defensive alliance with the tribe of Judah, its troops securing Judah's southern border. Its tribal traditions were predominantly military, as we can see from Joshua 14:6–14. Hence the myth says nothing about any defeat suffered by the spies.

b. When the Israelites had drawn near to the land from the south, Moses directed men to spy it out, to see whether it was fertile. And since just then it was the time when the grapes first ripen, in the valley of Eshkol they cut down a branch with a single cluster of grapes, and they carried it on a pole between two of them. They also brought some pomegranates and figs, because Moses had ordered them to bring fruit as well. Then they reported to Moses and Aaron and the whole assembled community. But some of the spies said: Let us not enter the country, for the men are all of great stature, and compared with them we seemed like grasshoppers.

Then the people began to moan and wished to return to Egypt. But Yahweh said to Moses: Go and say to the people that because of their unbelief none of them shall set foot in the land, except for their children and Caleb. All the others shall die before then.

When Moses told the people, they mourned greatly. They would not listen to him and went, as Yahweh had first commanded, to take the field against the Amalekites and the Canaanites. But they were defeated and scattered through the wilderness. And all the spies died, except for Caleb.

[Numbers 13:20, 23, 26b, 31, 33; 14:3-4, 30, 39-44]

(i) In characteristic Elóhist fashion, the myth presents Canaan as fruitful and well settled, and its inhabitants as fearsome. On the other hand, the Israelites in this description do not come off very creditably. Yahweh consigns his murmuring people to defeat.

The Elohist narrator is undoubtedly working with memories of an attempted conquest of his homeland, which he aims to explain. But he obscures the aetiological element in the story by making Yahweh responsible for the failure. Here we can see the latent opposition to the Israelite immigrants on the part of the old Canaanites. The sacred king and god is not assailed, but it is still possible to mock his followers.

The myth could get past the priestly censors in its present form in the fourth century B.C. By the Babylonian exile, if not sooner, it had become apparent that the person of God could be saved if people had to die for him.

c. When the Israelites had drawn near to the southern part of the country, Yahweh said to Moses: Take one man from every tribe, every one of them a leader of men, and send them to spy out the land. And Moses appointed them by name. The spies went through the country from south to north. After forty days they returned and reported bad news to the Israelites. The land, they said, devours its inhabitants. Then the Israelites rebelled against Moses and Aaron, who fell on their faces before the assembled community. But Joshua the son of Nun and Caleb the son of Jephunneh said: The land that we have spied out is a very good one. – When the people wanted to stone them to death for this, the glory suddenly appeared at the tent of God and spoke with Moses and Aaron: Your dead bodies shall fall in this wilderness, all of you who are older than twenty years. And because you have taken forty days to spy out the land, you shall now go about in the wilderness for forty years, until everyone has died who murmured against me. Only Joshua and Caleb shall remain alive. And so it came to pass.

[Numbers 13:1-17, 21, 25, 32; 14:2, 5-7, 10, 26, 29, 34-8]

(i) The priestly narrator gives the tradition a still harsher turn. In his eyes, the community, the pious folk, are utterly disobedient and rebellious, and so Yahweh must punish them with death. Only Joshua and Caleb survive. The figure of Joshua will have been modelled on that of his namesake, the first great high priest after the exile, for whom the narrator creates a parallel life. During the exile, the Calebites evidently remained in the country, that is, were spared deportation. The whole complex of spy accounts was moulded into its present shape under pressure from the priestly question of how to find a historical legitimization for the new beginnings after the Babylonian exile. The present (the years after 537 B.C.) is interpreted in the guise of the past as a divinely ordained process.

(ii) The great discussion between Moses and Yahweh in Numbers 14:11–24 has been adapted from an older Yahwist source, because it gave the priestly editors an opportunity to explain Yahweh's promptness to wrath. Formally speaking, within the overall framework of the priestly vision, the myth of the spies is a historical parable.

(iii) The proverbial remark, 'the land devours its inhabitants', is based on the ancient Near Eastern idea that the land and its sacred queen are synonymous. Hence the expression means that the land just reconnoitred is ruled and exploited by a harsh queen.

V.5. *Balaam's Ass*

When the Israelites came to the borders of Moab, Balak the son of Zippor, king of Moab, sent to Balaam, a prophet from Ammon, so that he might curse the Israelites. Balaam set out on his way. Yahweh grew angry at this, and placed his angel in Balaam's path. Now Balaam was riding on a she-ass. And the ass saw the angel of Yahweh standing in the road with a drawn sword in his hand, and she turned aside into the field. Then Balaam struck the ass, to turn her into the road. A little later the angel of Yahweh stood in a narrow path between the vineyards, with a wall on either side. The ass pushed against the wall so that she crushed Balaam's foot. And the prophet beat her once again. A third time the angel of Yahweh blocked his way, so that there was no way for the ass to turn, so she lay down under Balaam. And when he struck her with his staff, she opened her mouth and spoke with Balaam. Then he, too, saw Yahweh's angel standing before him with a drawn sword. The angel said: If the ass had not turned aside from me, I would have killed you. Balaam wanted to go back, but the angel forbade him, and so the prophet went on to Balak of Moab, who called upon him to curse the army of Israel from three places. But three times Balaam said only what Yahweh gave him to say. And that was not words of cursing but of blessing. Balak's anger was kindled against Balaam, and he sent him back. But before he returned home, Balaam prophesied one more time and predicted the downfall of Moab.

Others say that Balaam refused to follow the two groups of messengers that Balak sent, because while he was still at home the god Yahweh had appeared to him in a dream at night and had forbidden him to go along with the messengers and to accept Balak's reward. But when Balaam had gone along anyway, he tried to appease Yahweh with many sacrifices of bulls and rams. Yahweh accepted the sacrifices for the benefit of Israel and through Balaam's mouth he poured out rich blessings over Israel, as is recorded in beautiful songs:

> Behold, a people! (Israel) As a lioness it rises up
>   and as a lion it lifts itself.
> Behold, a star shall come forth out of Jacob,
>   and a sceptre shall rise out of Israel;
>   it shall crush the princes of Moab.

[Numbers 22–4]

(i) The story of the prophet Balaam is one of the legends that sprang up after the Israelites migrated into the land of Canaan. The Elohist narrator uses Balaam's she-ass to give the story shape and vividness. The Yahwist inserts the dream as a device to avoid any direct participation in the story by Yahweh. In the period when both narrative traditions arose, the ancient pre-Israelite office of prophet had not been so well integrated into Israel's cultic institutions as it would be 200 years later, around the time when the monarchy collapsed. The Elohist narrator's god wishes to avoid mass slaughter by means of Balaam, but the Yahwist takes the opportunity to infuse Balaam's sayings with the militarism of the royal party in Jerusalem.

(ii) The story received priestly approbation after the exile thanks to the Yahwist expansion of Balaam's sayings through references to a mighty tribe of Jacob-Israel, symbolized by a lion. In the post-exilic period, people were looking forward to a miraculous restoration of the ancient glory.

(iii) The mythological setting of this sort of heroic tale is like that of the Greek story of Teiresias: the conflict between two eras, two worlds, in fact between two divine kingdoms. Teiresias became a woman and then was changed back into a man again. In the case of Balaam, the mythical images have been shunted from the body of the story to the prophet's sayings, but they portray him as a true replica of the god, who is still intrinsically biform, representing two different populations still struggling for supremacy.

Balaam's sacrifices, like those of Teiresias, reveal at once the true position of both men: they are not lords of fate, but its servants. The god makes use of each of them as he wishes. The prophets are hybrids, half god and half man, belonging half to the future, half to the ancient past.

VI. God Gives the Law

VI.1. *On Sinai*

a. When the Israelites were camped in the wilderness before Mount Sinai, Yahweh came down to the mountain [cf. II.2.a (p. 44)] and said: I am your God Yahweh, who brought you out of the land of Egypt, out of the house of bondage. You shall have no other gods before me. You shall not make for yourself a graven image, or any likeness of anything that is in heaven above, or that is in the earth beneath, or that is in the water under the earth. You shall not bow down to them or serve them; for I, your god Yahweh, am a jealous god, visiting the iniquity of the fathers upon the children to the third and the fourth generation of those who hate me, but showing steadfast love to the thousandth generation of those who love me and keep my commandments. You shall not take the name of your god Yahweh in vain, for Yahweh will not hold him guiltless who takes his name in vain. Remember the sabbath day, to keep it holy. Six days you shall labour and do all your work, but the seventh day is the sabbath of Yahweh your god. On it you shall not do any work, nor shall your son, nor your daughter, your manservant, your maidservant, nor your cattle, nor the stranger within your gates. For in six days Yahweh made heaven and earth, the sea and all that is in them, and rested the seventh day. Therefore Yahweh blessed the seventh day and hallowed it.

Honour your father and mother, that your days may be long upon the land that Yahweh your god gives you. You shall not kill. You shall not commit adultery. You shall not steal. You shall not bear false witness against your neighbour. You shall not covet your neighbour's house. You shall not covet your neighbour's wife nor his servants nor anything that belongs to him.

When the people heard this, they cried out their willingness to observe this Law faithfully.

[Exodus 20:1–17]

b. Others say that the god Yahweh gave Moses another law, which was: You shall worship no other god. You shall make no molten gods for yourself. You shall keep the feast of unleavened bread. The first-born of cattle and men belongs to me. You shall observe the feast of weeks, and the harvest feast at the year's end. You shall not offer the blood of sacrifice with leaven, nor shall the sacrifice of the feast of Passover be left until the morning. You shall not boil a kid in its mother's milk. You shall bring the first fruits of your land to the house of your god Yahweh.

[Exodus 34:1–26]

(i) The ten commandments (the Greek term decalogue was introduced by the Church) has come to be viewed as the quintessence of God's law. The various traditions concerning this law stem from different parts of the population, and have survived centuries of disruption only because such groups held on so long to their peculiar characteristics. The basic structure of the decalogue as we find it in the Lay Source, judging from Exodus 34, mirrors the ancient institutions of tribal worship. The eldest in the family is responsible for the observance of sacrificial rites. This decalogue is pure cultic law, with no provisions dealing with the state of the family. The extended family or clan still has no need for such regulations, because it has no notion of private ownership of the means of production (which include women). The social function of parents is still insignificant.

(ii) In contrast, the somewhat later Elohist decalogue in Exodus 20, which comes from an old, previously Canaanite group, has a much more pronounced orientation towards civil law. Here only the first three commandments are concerned with worship. They lay down the claims of the god-sacred king. They presuppose both marriage and private ownership of the means of production. The original wording of the tenth commandment, 'You shall not covet your neighbour's house', has been expanded into a detailed statement of what goes with the house.

The similarities linking the decalogue to the ancient Babylonian Code of Hammurabi and the Hittite or Assyrian-Babylonian codes may be traced back to comparatively similar socio-economic conditions prevalent in Canaan before the Israelite conquest. Thus, for example, in a collection of Hittite laws, it says:

> If a man rapes his own mother, he is to be punished.
> If a man rapes his daughter, he is to be punished ... If a man rapes his stepmother, he is to be punished only if his father is still alive.
> If a man steals an ox, let him cancel his guilt by paying fifteen oxen, five two-year-old, five one-year-old, and five under a year old oxen. ⬎

(iii) The decalogue from the Elohist tradition differs from the more recent Deuteronomic decalogue (see VI.2 (p. 127)) of the late monarchy. The Elohist decalogue connects the introduction of the sabbath with the theology of Creation, and in the tenth commandment it mentions the neighbour's house as the first thing that the Israelites should not covet. We have here a silent reproach for the usurpers who were doing just that – seizing the homes of the former inhabitants. But the Deuteronomic decalogue explains the sabbath rest by referring to the erstwhile bondage in Egypt, and it expressly notes that everyone in the house is to rest, just as 'you' do. The 'you' in both the later decalogues is no longer the head of the clan, but the individual resident of the country. (See IV.5.c (p. 109).)

The second different feature of the Deuteronomic decalogue is the way it formulates the tenth commandment, where the wife is mentioned first, while the house, symbolizing ownership of the means of production, is relegated to second place. Between the Elohist and the Deuteronomic decalogue there lies a significant legal-historical development: the married woman becomes a sort of correlative to masculine office, power and wealth. When, for example, Absalom sleeps with his father David's concubines, he is thereby formally arrogating to himself the dignity of king and the kingdom itself. For this reason, the Deuteronomic tradition words the tenth commandment differently.

The Elohist tradition has none of the pessimistic, disaster-ridden atmosphere of the Deuteronomic. By locating the transmission of the Law on Mount Sinai, it takes Jerusalem's leading idea and transforms it. From the history of religion we know that the cue for the 'divine legislation' was provided by the growth of the monarchy. For as the king's orbit of power widens through annexation of more territory, he has a dwindling opportunity to make personal decisions on all matters as he could in the old, small-scale communities. The king now needs the state and law, the generalized expression of his autocratic will (see also II.6.c.i (p. 58)).

VI.2. *On Horeb*

When the sons of Israel on their way from Egypt came to Mount Horeb, Moses bade them camp there. Moses had already formed a council of the elders and wise men from each tribe to attend to matters of law and order. And Yahweh spoke out of the midst of the fire to the assembled people. He caused his voice to be heard from heaven and a great fire to be seen on earth. Out of the fire he spoke to them and proclaimed his Law:

I am Yahweh, your god, who brought you out of Egypt, the land of slavery. You shall have no other gods before me. You shall not make yourself any graven image or any likeness of anything in heaven above or in the earth beneath or in the waters beneath the earth. You shall not bow down before them, nor serve them, for I, your god Yahweh, am a jealous god, avenging the iniquity of the fathers upon the children unto the third and fourth generation of those who hate me, but showing mercy to the thousandth generation of those who love me and keep my commandments.

You shall not take the name of Yahweh, your god, in vain, for Yahweh will not hold him guiltless who takes his name in vain.

Remember to keep the sabbath holy, as your god Yahweh commanded. Six days you shall labour and do all your work. But the seventh day is the sabbath of Yahweh your god; on it you shall do no work, nor your son, nor your daughter, nor your manservant, nor your maidservant, nor your ox nor your ass, nor any of your cattle, nor the stranger within your gates, that your manservant and your maidservant may rest as well as you. And remember that you were a servant in the land of Egypt, whence Yahweh set you free. Therefore you shall keep the sabbath. Honour your father and your mother, as your god Yahweh has commanded you, that you may live long, and that it may go well with you in the land which Yahweh your god will give you.

You shall not kill. You shall not commit adultery. You shall not steal. You shall not bear false witness against your neighbour.

You shall not desire your neighbour's wife, neither shall you covet your neighbour's house, his field, or his manservant or his maidservant, his ox, or his ass, or anything that belongs to him.

Yahweh spoke these words and no more with a loud voice to all the people from atop the mountain in fire, cloud and thick darkness. But at Yahweh's command Moses taught the sons of Israel many more commandments and statutes, which they were to obey.

[Deuteronomy 5–6:3]

(i) The Deuteronomic tradition goes back to the Jerusalem temple priesthood, which in the seventh century B.C. tried to save the Davidic dynasty, no longer capable of properly ruling and administering the country. The old social and economic structures had broken down completely. The little kingdoms located on the edge of the wilderness and sealed off to the outside world were no match for the new empires on the Euphrates and Nile with their political and economic centralization.

And so, once again, with the scene of the promulgation of the law on Horeb the jealous god is conjured up, the god who takes the fiercest revenge on rebels. The ancient idealized image of the harmonious social order of the clan is invoked to halt the process leading to the imperial state. Just as the law represents the will of the absent king, so the law of Yahweh is now supposed to replace a ruined central government. The myth of the law takes on the function of heroic legend. As the hero Moses once overcame all obstacles, so now the law is to bring salvation, and hence the whole nation must be obedient and bear their responsibilities. The Jerusalem temple caste would like to see the barriers between the classes removed – without really removing them. Hence apodictic law (characterized by the formula 'you shall') serves as the escape clause from responsibility for the crisis that has arisen.

(ii) Apart from the question of its historical origins, the Deuteronomic decalogue is a monumental *locus classicus* for students of religion, illustrating the emergence of monolatry. In monolatry, only one god is worshipped, but the believer is perfectly well aware that there are other gods, other kings as well. As for monotheism, i.e. the doctrine that only one god exists, Jerusalem in the sixth century B.C. was the worst sort of environment for such an idea.

To explain the markedly social character of the entire body of Deuteronomic law, one need only recall the shattered condition of social and economic life in the southern kingdom of Judah around this time.

VI.3. *On Ebal*

When Joshua had crossed the Jordan with the Israelites, they came to Mount Ebal. Now Moses had told them: When you have crossed the Jordan, Simeon, Levi, Judah, Issachar, Joseph and Benjamin are to station themselves on Mount Gerizim, to bless the people. But the others, Reuben, Gad, Asher, Zebulun, Dan and Naphtali, are to stand on Mount Ebal, to curse. The curse was to fall upon all those who worshipped the image of a strange god or did not honour their parents or removed their neighbour's landmark, who led the blind astray, perverted the justice owed to widows, orphans and strangers, slept with their mother, sister, sister-in-law, mother-in-law, or copulated with an animal; upon those who were murderers, defamed their neighbour or did not observe the law. And all the people were to say: Amen.

But the blessing was to extend to work in the city and in the fields, to children and the fruits of the earth, to animals and tools, to coming in and going out.

And on Mount Ebal, Joshua wrote the law of Moses upon stones in the presence of the children of Israel. All Israel, and their elders, officers and judges, stood before the ark of the covenant across from the Levites who bore the ark with the law of Yahweh. Half of them looked up to Ebal, and half looked up to Gerizim, as Moses had commanded. And Joshua proclaimed the whole law of Moses to the people.

Others say that Joshua built an altar on Mount Ebal for Yahweh, as Moses had commanded, and that he offered sacrifice there.

[Deuteronomy 27:11–13, 15–26; 28; Joshua 8:30–35]

(i) The promulgation of the decalogue on Ebal (actually a duodecalogue, a list of twelve commandments) is made in the language of theocratic law, with the characteristic formulas, 'Cursed be he who . . .' or 'Blessed be he who . . .' Twelve times we hear the resounding formulaic line: 'Cursed be . . . And all the people shall say, Amen'. The number twelve is obviously connected with the twelve tribes, for each of which a speaker is called upon to respond.

(ii) Deuteronomy divides past history into sections, each of which is marked off by a transmission of the Law. For this source, the Law and only the Law is the highest form of divine revelation.

What gives the story its specifically Deuteronomic shape is the attempt to suppress the ancient cultic importance of the northern Israelite sanctuary of Ebal/Gerizim. (It was on this site, as the Elohist narrator is aware, that Joshua built an altar.) That is why a decalogue has to be linked up with this mountain. The Deuteronomic narrator wants the notion of a single, central place of worship in Jerusalem to prevail, and sites where laws are revealed are less dangerous than places of worship scattered throughout the country. Hence the narrator deliberately locates this archaic law code on Ebal-Gerizim.

That fiction has been kept alive by the Samaritans after their break with Jerusalem. To this day they look upon Mount Gerizim as the place where Yahweh's Law originated.

VI.4. *At Shechem*

When Joshua had conquered the land, he thought of Moses' command to remind the people of Israel of his Law, so that the Israelites might dwell tranquilly in the land that Yahweh would give them. For it was a land flowing with milk and honey. And when he knew that his time had come to die, he summoned the whole nation to Shechem, gathering together the elders, heads of families, judges and officers, and told them: Now I am going the way of all the earth, and you know that all of Yahweh's promises have so far been fulfilled. But Yahweh will also make good on all his threats, and even drive you out from this fair land, if you are not faithful to his Law. So now fear the god Yahweh and do away with your gods, the ones you had in Egypt, in Mesopotamia, and before that. Choose this day whom you will serve, either those gods or the gods of this country. But as for me and my house, we will serve Yahweh.

Then all the people answered: We too wish to serve Yahweh. Then Joshua proclaimed the covenant of the people with Yahweh, and gave the people statutes and ordinances in Shechem. Now there already was a sanctuary in

Shechem, with an oak tree. And Joshua set up a great stone there and said: This stone has heard all of Yahweh's words. Let it therefore be a witness for the covenant.

And after that Joshua the son of Nun died at the age of 110 years.
[Deuteronomy 27:7; Joshua 23–4]

(i) There is no doubt that Shechem was a pre-Israelite sanctuary, which was captured by some of the northern tribes and taken over as a place of worship. The Deuteronomic narrator suppresses the ancient cultic significance of the site and assigns it a niche only in the legend of Joshua, not in that of Moses. Because the sanctuary at Shechem became a royal residence after Jeroboam led the northern kingdom to break away from Jerusalem (I Kings 12:5), the Jerusalem narrator reports that at Shechem Joshua simply reminded the people of the Law of Moses and got them to renew their commitment to it. But we can be sure that Shechem was more important than that. The covenant agreed to at Shechem under Joshua's guidance established a defence treaty linking the tribes that had settled in Canaan. The Deuteronomic narrator tells us nothing more about this, because he is interested only in proving the uniqueness and distinctiveness of Jerusalem.

The description of Canaan as a 'land flowing with milk and honey' is a widespread theme in the history of religion. Thus, for example, in Greek mythology the golden race of humanity lives without work or cares during the age of Cronus. People feed upon honey dripping from the trees (i.e. nectar), and drink the milk of wild sheep and goats. This motif alludes to the matriarchal form of society: the queen bee is the symbol of the sacred Great Mother and Queen.

For the nomadic Israelite tribes, the arable land of Canaan genuinely *was* the Promised Land flowing with milk and honey. In this mythic image from later centuries the nostalgia for the lost 'Golden Age' – which was always a retrospective utopia – is vividly evoked.

VI.5. *In Jerusalem*

When King Josiah of Jerusalem and Judah had reigned for eighteen years, he ordered the temple to be restored. While this was going on, it happened that the priest Hilkiah found a book in the temple containing the Law of Yahweh. The priest gave it to the chief scribe Shaphan, who told the king about it. Josiah had the book read to him. When he heard it, he tore his clothes for grief, because the prescriptions of the Law were a far cry from the way people really lived. For this reason the king asked the priest for an oracle of Yahweh concerning the future. Hilkiah turned to the prophetess Huldah, who lived in the second district of Jerusalem and was married to the keeper of the royal wardrobe. She prophesied the downfall of the land and the city, because they had fallen away from Yahweh; Yet, because of his repentance, Josiah would not live to see the downfall, but die before then. Josiah heard this, and gathered the elders of Judah and Jerusalem, and together they renewed the covenant with Yahweh, as it was described in the book they had found.

After that he commanded that all the strange gods and their cult sites in Jerusalem and in the high places throughout the land were to be destroyed. Only the temple in Jerusalem was to be left, and even there Baal and the goddess Asherah and their images were banned and destroyed. Josiah drove out the priests who served the stars, the host of heaven, the gods of the sun and moon. And he banished the harlots and male cult prostitutes of Ishtar and destroyed the shrine of Molech in the valley of Hinnom. He desecrated all the sanctuaries of the gods of the countryside, and did the same to the gods Chemosh and Milcom. In his zeal he pressed across the borders of the country as far as Bethel and Samaria, and there he tore down the shrines and altars on which the priests slaughtered victims, in order to defile these places of worship for ever. And furthermore King Josiah directed that henceforth the feast of Passover should be kept in accordance with the book of the Law. This was the first time that such a Passover was celebrated in Jerusalem in honour of Yahweh. He likewise commanded that all the conjurors of the dead and wizards, all the household gods, the gods of the tribes, and all other images of the gods be rooted out of the country.

Neither before or afterwards was there such a godfearing king in Israel. He was slain in the war against Necho of Egypt.

[II Kings 22–3]

(i) The legend of the great King Josiah and his cultic reforms (622 B.C.) stems from the Deuteronomic tradition of Jerusalem. The legend explains why a law code should be marked by such a rigorous monolatry. Other parts of Deuteronomy doubtlessly come from this period as well. They reflect the desire of the newly strengthened central government and its priests to limit all legal cultic activities – which were quite profitable – to Jerusalem. This goal was served by the 'new Law', which was suddenly discovered during the restoration of the temple. It contained, as Deuteronomy shows, a complete legal code. Until this cultic reform, Jerusalem had no obligatory (for all the tribes) festive calendar with a uniform ritual. This matter was now settled by royal decree. In the same way, prior to this reform, foreign gods and cults, as well as vestiges of the old popular piety (mediums and wizards) were still going strong. Their extirpation meant that the coffers of the central government now received the donations which had once been lost to cultic organizations that were not only foreign to Yahweh but foreign to Canaan. This economic bloodletting – for the cultic organizations were at the same time independent economic units, with each temple having its own lands and workshops – now was staunched. With the new Law the people of Jerusalem and the royal priests obtained an absolute commercial monopoly. This measure was an important step towards the stabilization of Josiah's central authority, but it none the less drove the country closer to disaster. For the parts of the population that had been deprived of their rights and power fell into the welcoming arms of the Egyptian and Babylonian empires, whence the losers hoped to see the restitution of their former privileges.

(ii) The individual items in this account are a reliable indication of how complex the mythological environment was in Israel and Judah. Asherah and her husband Baal are the Near Eastern fertility gods Ishtar and Tammuz (in the myths of Ugarit Astarta and Aleyin Baal). Chemosh and Milcom are Syro-Phoenician and Moabite deities, at once gods of cities and of war. It is fairly certain that when the text speaks of sun gods and horses of the sun it means the Middle Eastern sun god Shamash, while the 'moon god' refers to the Babylonian Sin. These gods presumably came to Jerusalem in the wake of lively contacts between the empires on the Euphrates and the Nile, passing through Palestine and leaving permanent traces there. Foreign traders and artisans also brought their gods with them. Add to this the ancient indigenous fertility cults of Canaan, and II Kings 23 provides a true picture of the situation. The harlots and male cult prostitutes are the devotees of Ishtar and Tammuz. The women served Ishtar. The votaries of Tammuz were castrated men who wore women's clothing.

(iii) It is likely that the Molech mentioned as being in the valley of Hinnom originally referred to a kind of sacrifice rather than a god, as Punic inscriptions lead us to believe. Still, in many Semitic religions, 'Malk' appears as the name of a god, although the context is always one of child sacrifice. From this practice we may conclude that he must have been a god of death.

(iv) The 'host of heaven' is presumably a euphemism for spirits and demons, fabulous creatures from above and below the earth, such as the Assyrian Igigi and Anunaki. The whole chapter clearly reveals the religious syncretism prevalent in Israel-Judah during the seventh century B.C.

VII. The Great Sanctuaries and Heroes of the Early Period

VII.1. *The Ark of the Covenant*

When Moses was on Mount Sinai, Yahweh gave him directions for building a chest of acacia wood, to be covered with gold inside and out. It was to be carried on two gilded poles, which were put through golden rings running along the length of the chest. Inside it was kept the Law. The cover ('mercy seat') of the ark was of pure gold. It was crowned with two cherubim, throned at opposite ends, whose wings spread over the chest. From there, between the two cherubim, Yahweh wished to speak with Moses, when he had commands for the Israelites.

The ark accompanied the people on their journey through the wilderness, and when the Israelites crossed the Jordan, the waters of the river were dammed up above the ford, because the ark went ahead of the march. The waters gave way before it. As a memorial of this, Joshua set up twelve stones in the Jordan at the spot where the priests carrying the ark had stood, when the people marched over the river-bed. This was in Gilgal.

At the siege of Jericho [see II.3.c (p. 48)], the ark went about the city at the head of the army. After the conquest of the land, it stood in the temple of Shiloh, where it was looked after by the house of Eli. But it was lost to the Philistines when the Israelites took it with them into the battle at Aphek.

Yet the Philistines were not able to keep it very long, for it caused great mischief in their land. The Philistines had placed it in the temple of their god Dagon. The next day they found their god overturned in front of the ark. They took him and righted him again, but on the next morning he was again overturned, and this time his head and arms were broken. At the same time bubonic plague broke out in the region of Ashdod. So the people of Ashdod sent the ark to Gath, and from Gath it was sent on to Ekron, but the plague followed everywhere. Then the priests and soothsayers of the Philistines met together and said: Give the ark back with an offering of atonement in the form of five golden plague boils and five golden mice, for you have been visited by that plague as well. They must be five in number on account of the five Philistine kings. Then take a new wagon, harness two milch cows to it that have never borne the yoke, and place the ark and the offerings on the wagon, but leave the cows' calves in the stable. And if the cows at once head directly for Beth-shemesh, then we know that Yahweh, the god of Israel, is tormenting us because of the ark. The Philistines did this, and the cows went straightaway to Beth-shemesh without anyone's showing them the way. There the people greatly rejoiced that the ark had returned, but the sons of Jeconiah did not rejoice: And for this reason, Yahweh struck seventy men of them, so that they died. But after a great sacrifice was celebrated, the ark was brought to Eleazar the son of Abinadab at Kiriath-jearim, where it remained from then on. From Kiriath-jearim, King David transferred it to his new residence in Jerusalem. The journey took a long time, and on the way the oxen pulling it stumbled. A man named Uzzah took hold of the ark to prevent it from overturning, and he died. Then David grew frightened of the ark, and had it stored in the house of Obed-edom. After three months he observed that great blessings came forth from the ark, and he fetched it to his city in a festive procession. But Solomon was the first to take the ark out of the royal palace and install it in the inner sanctum of the temple he had built. It remained there until the destruction of the temple by the Babylonians. After this it was no more to be found.

[Exodus 25:10–25; Joshua 3:6–17; 4; 6; I Samuel 3–6; II Samuel 6; I Kings 3–6; 8:1–9; 25:8–17]

(i) The origin of the ark is uncertain. Perhaps it was an ancient Canaanite cult object belonging to the sanctuary of Shiloh, a cultic centre for a group of tribes. The ark seems to have been the palladium or war talisman of this religious alliance.

(ii) The only information we have about its appearance is the detailed report of the priestly tradition in Exodus 25. The 'mercy seat' was surely invented by this tradition, which views the ark as the throne of God by analogy with the throne of Solomon. In the early period, this 'mercy seat' was undoubtedly not part of the ark, and is not mentioned in any of the older accounts (Joshua 3:4; Judges 2:1–5; II Samuel 11:11). The idea of interpreting the ark as God's throne only made sense later, when Solomon transferred it from the city of David to the temple.

The remarks about the contents of the ark date from a later period. The Deuteronomic and priestly traditions state that the ark contained the tables of the Law (Deuteronomy 10:1–5; Exodus 25:16). That is why it is called 'the ark of the covenant of God' or 'the ark of the testimony'.

(iii) The history of the ark clearly shows the development of Israelite religion. In the end, the law, which once was a matter that anyone could pronounce on for anyone, was now hidden away in a chest, on whose lid the king was enthroned. His word, which only the priests could hear anyway, now replaced ancient tribal law.

(iv) The oldest characterization of the ark as 'the ark of Elohim' (I Samuel 4:11) suggests a connection with ancient Canaanite cult utensils. The literal meaning 'chest' (Heb. *aron*) excludes any possibility that the ark was originally a throne or the footstool of a throne. It may conceivably have been a container for the tribal badges of the cultic alliance. Beyond that, the note in II Samuel 6:2 indicates that Yahweh's association with the ark is of a later date.

(v) The powerful effects of the ark, as we see in the story of the plague and the infestation by mice, and above all in the incident with Uzzah, are supposed to demonstrate that no one is to touch the ark. This is why it is best hidden away in the adytum of the temple of Jerusalem.

VII.2. *The Cities of Refuge*

When Moses received the Law from Yahweh, Yahweh ordered him to single out three cities in the land, which were to be declared sacred. The whole country was to be divided up in such a way that each city should have its own specified district. These places were to be sanctuaries for all those who had accidentally killed someone. Once the manslayers had reached these sites, they could no longer be handed over to those seeking vengeance. Only murderers, that is, those who wilfully sought a person's life, were to be handed over and condemned to death.

Afterwards Moses selected three cities in the country east of the Jordan, namely Bezer, Ramoth and Golan.

But when the Israelites had conquered Canaan, they added three cities west of the Jordan to the three eastern ones, as Moses had taught them. The rule in force was that the individual villages could also bring in the fugitive, under a safe-conduct, for a regular trial. But he enjoyed the right of asylum until the death of the high priest, during whose reign he had become a fugitive. When the high priest died, the right to take blood revenge was extinguished. The cities of refuge west of the Jordan were Kedesh, Shechem and Hebron.

[Deuteronomy 19:1–7; 4:41–3; 19:8–10; Numbers 35:1–15; Joshua 20]

(i) It can be shown that the establishment of the cities of refuge was not connected to the great Israelite immigration, but should be attributed instead to the cultic reform under King Josiah of Jerusalem. Such cities became necessary after the reform abolished all the local sanctuaries that had previously served as places of refuge for involuntary lawbreakers.

(ii) Jerusalem is deliberately not mentioned. The sacred temple must not be desecrated by the presence of murderers. This cultic pretext, however, chiefly guaranteed that in Jerusalem, the seat of government, the number of notorious malcontents would remain small. Meanwhile, to take one example, Hebron was politically precarious and the scene of rebellion, as were the other five cities that practised this widespread religious custom of allowing fugitives to take refuge at the altar of a god.

(iii) The cities of refuge had been ancient Canaanite shrines. According to Joshua 12:2, Kedesh was the residence of a Canaanite king, who surely had a special shrine for his royal headquarters. Shechem was an old Canaanite sanctuary, a sacred grove, which tradition associated with Abraham, and with the patriarchs Jacob and Joseph (see IV.1, IV.3 and IV.4 (pp. 79, 88 and 96)). Shechem was also the location of the sanctuary frequented by the tribal alliance of the invading Israelites (see VII.3.d (p. 139)). Hebron was the abode of an ancient tree goddess, but Israelite tradition expunged all memories of her by locating stories about Abraham and Isaac there (see IV.1 and IV.2 (pp. 79 and 84)). In the early period of Israel's history, Hebron was the heart of the territory of the Calebites, a tribe which helped David to subjugate the other tribes.

The cities of refuge east of the Jordan, Bezer, Golan and Ramoth, were similar cult sites. They were often the scene of commotions because the men living within their walls had severed their family ties and were ready to join up with political adventurers at a moment's notice.

VII.3. *Gilgal, Bethel, Dan and Shechem*

a. When Joshua and the tribes of Israel had crossed the Jordan, they first camped at Gilgal. And Joshua stayed in Gilgal, in order to lead the conquest of the land from there. The angel of Yahweh also dwelt there, until he withdrew to Bethel, but Gilgal remained a sanctuary. And it was in Gilgal that King David waited for the elders of his nation, to be led back in solemn triumph to his palace, from which he had fled before his son Absalom. For Gilgal was the place where monarchy had been established in Israel. Saul had been the first king who went forth from Gilgal.

Others say that not only was there a Gilgal north of Jericho on the Jordan, but there was also one east of Shechem. That was where Samuel passed judgement; and after him Elijah and Elisha, the great prophets and miracle workers, also stayed there. Still others say that there was a Gilgal, also called Geliloth, on the sea-coast. Joshua slew its king and occupied the land.

[Joshua 4:19–20; 9:6; 10:6–7; 14:6; Judges 2:1; II Samuel 19:16; I Samuel 10:8; 11:14–15; 13; I Samuel 7:16; II Kings 2:1; 4:38–9; Joshua 12:23; 15:7; 18:17]

(i) The name Gilgal comes from a term which originally meant circle of stones. The stone columns, arranged to form a circle, symbolized the cultic associations which met in this place. Each stone represented a tribe and its calendrically regulated duties at the sanctuary. The Gilgal north of Jericho as well as the others were older than the religion of Israel: along with the land the Israelite immigrants also usurped its culture and places of worship, to which they later attached different cultic legends. The Israelite cultic legend concerning the Gilgal north of Jerusalem is the story of how the twelve tribes crossed the Jordan; the shrine's earlier legend has been lost beyond recovery. Given the use of Gilgal as the setting for the coronation ritual of Israelite kings, we can only assume that this Gilgal was a former cultic site. One argument in favour of this may be that the other places named Gilgal always appear in connection with ancient Canaanite sacrificial sites (see also VII.1 (p. 134)).

b. When Jacob was searching for a bride, he came to Luz, and there his god appeared to him in a dream. After that he named this place Bethel, that is, 'house of God'. Jacob also built an altar there.

Later, when the Israelites were already in the country, the ark of Yahweh was kept in the sanctuary at Bethel, where Pinchas, Aaron's grandson, was priest. For this reason the judge Samuel often came to Bethel, to pronounce judgement.

After Solomon's kingdom was broken up, Jeroboam, the king of the northern kingdom of Israel, made Bethel into a state sanctuary, where he had the golden image of a bull set up, with services conducted in front of it. But Josiah of Judah invaded the country as far as Bethel and destroyed the altar that Jeroboam had erected.

Bethel was also where the prophet Amos lived and worked. He tried in the name of Yahweh to win the northern kingdom to conversion, to get it to submit to Jerusalem.

[Genesis 28:19; Judges 20:26–8; I Samuel 7:16; I Kings 12:24–32; II Kings 23:15; Amos 3:14; 5:5; 7:10]

(i) Bethel, the house of God, was presumably the place sixteen miles north of Jerusalem that already lodged an ancient sanctuary (see also IV.3.b (p. 90)). It must have been so important that Israelite mythology could appropriate it only by incorporating it into the history of Israel and dislodging its original significance.

c. When Rachel, Jacob's second wife, bore him no children, she gave Jacob her maid Bilhah as a concubine. Bilhah gave birth to a son, whom Rachel called Dan, for she said: God has judged me. Dan became a valiant people among the sons of Jacob, and when they were hard pressed by the Canaanites, the men of Dan conquered the city of Laish, whose name they changed to Dan. The Danites were brave and became famous for their sense of justice. The great hero Samson came from the tribe of Dan. In the reign of Jeroboam, the city of Dan became a state sanctuary.

[Genesis 30:6; 49:16–17; Joshua 19:47; Judges 18:29; 13–16]

(i) Like Bethel, Gilgal and Shechem, Dan was an ancient Canaanite sanctuary. Its local hero is forgotten, because his cult was destroyed root and branch. Since Jeroboam had two bull statues erected in Dan, we may assume that Dan was (perhaps) a bull-god shrine, and that of a fertility goddess associated with him (see II.4.**b** (p. 52)).

d. Hamor, the son and heir of Shechem, sold Jacob a piece of land outside the city of Shechem, when Jacob returned from Haran. But this was near the place (the grove of Mamre), where Abram had already built an altar to Yahweh, when Yahweh promised him there that one day the entire land would belong to the descendants of Abram (as Abraham was called, when the Canaanites were still in the land). Others say that Jacob sacrificed all his household gods and amulets to Yahweh in Mamre near Shechem. Later Joseph's coffin was interred there too. The presence of the sanctuary was the reason why Shechem later became an asylum for manslayers. There were no limits to the law of blood vengeance. When the Israelites had conquered the land of Canaan, the tribes assembled in Shechem to hear the law from Yahweh and to swear fidelity to him. Joshua also gathered the tribes together in Shechem to inculcate obedience to God in them one more time before he died. He ended his exhortation with the words, 'But as for me and my house, we will serve Yahweh.'

Joshua also set up a stele in the grove of Mamre as a memorial to the oath of fidelity that Israel had taken. The cult site of Shechem was the central shrine for the ten northern tribes. For this reason Rehoboam, after the death of his father Solomon, came to Shechem, to receive the royal crown of Israel. But the people of Shechem refused it to him, because he would make no concessions to them, and so they broke away from Judah and Jerusalem with the words: What portion have we in David? We have no inheritance in the son of Jesse. To your tents, O Israel! Now see to your own house, David. – Then they chose Jeroboam for king, in place of Rehoboam. And Jeroboam made Shechem his royal residence.

[Genesis 33:19; 12:6–8; 35:4; Joshua 8:30–35; 24:1, 26–7; I Kings 12; Joshua 20:7]

(i) The role of Shechem as a cultic site and city of refuge predates Israelite traditions. The grove of Mamre, with its oracular terebinths (a kind of oak), suggests that such places must have originally belonged to a goddess, since all sacred trees, especially oaks, belonged to goddesses of love and fertility. For example, the Greek goddess Dione was the threefold divinity of the dove and oak-tree cult, and her daughter was Aphrodite. Zeus, the god of the invading Greeks, became Zeus of Dodona, the giver of oracles, after the Greeks had captured the sanctuary of Diana or Dione of Dodona. The biblical Yahweh becomes the divine dispenser of oracles at Shechem, once the invading Israelites have displaced the shrine's former owners. At such shrines, by listening to the rustling of the leaves or to the clinking of copper tubes hung in the tree branches, the priestesses and priests could hear and interpret the voice of their mistress.

(ii) Assuming that this was part of Shechem's ancient past, we have only echoes of it in the choice of the city as a place for listening to Yahweh the lawgiver and Joshua his deputy. The mythical anecdotes in the tales of the patriarchs witness to the unbroken cultic tradition of the place, which is still considered sacred by the Samaritan community.

VII.4. *Joshua*

When Moses was encamped with the people in the wilderness of Paran, at Yahweh's command he sent twelve spies out into the land of Canaan. Among them was Hosea the son of Nun, who had been chosen from the house of Joseph for the tribe of Ephraim. But Moses named the son of Nun Joshua (that is, Yahweh helps).

Even before this, Joshua had been a confidant and servant of Moses and had accompanied him up to the mountain, where Moses received the Law. Later, some believe, he was constantly in Yahweh's tent of the testimony. But others say that on the contrary he was always fighting in the front line in the battles against the Amalekites and the inhabitants of Canaan.

Joshua was also the only one of the spies, along with Caleb, who after they returned urged the people to conquer the land after all. Yahweh rewarded him for this: he let him conquer and apportion the land, after Moses had died. For when Moses asked Yahweh for a successor, Yahweh had said: Take Joshua the son of Nun, a man gifted with the spirit, and lay your hand upon him in the presence of the priest Eleazar and the whole congregation, so that you may install him in office. And Eleazar shall consult the oracle of the Urim and Thummim. Then Moses did as Yahweh had ordered.

And Joshua led the people into the land of Canaan, conquered it, and divided it among the tribes. Yahweh was with him and blessed him. He died at the age of 110 years, and he was buried in the region of his inheritance, Timrath-serah on Mount Ephraim. He had requested this place for himself, when he and the priest Eleazar apportioned the whole country by lot among the tribes. They had taken up the work of apportionment in Shiloh, before the door of the tent of Yahweh.

Joshua was a faithful servant of Yahweh and he admonished his people to remain faithful to Yahweh. To this end he held a great assembly in Shechem just before his death. [See also IV.5 (p. 102); V.4.c (p. 121); VI.3–4 (pp. 129–30); VII.3.d (p. 139).]

[Exodus 24:13; 33:11; 17:8–13; Numbers 13; 14; 27:15–23; Joshua 19:50–51; 23–4]

(i) The biblical figure of Joshua was shaped most decisively by the hand of the priestly tradition, which wanted a heroic prototype for Joshua, the first high priest after the Exile. This becomes quite clear in Numbers 27:23, where the narrator says of Moses that he installed Joshua in the precise manner that 'Yahweh had commanded him'.

(ii) Joshua's original role was surely much more modest. Under his old name Hosea (i.e. salvation) he will have been simply a general, up to the point of the priestly revision. Then the mythic process of legend formation connected him with Moses' servant Joshua.

We can be sure that in the beginning he had only a tenuous part in the stories of the spies and the account of the conquest of Canaan. He was presumably one of the first priests of the oracular sanctuary at Shechem who declared for the Israelite invaders. As such, his mythological function is that of an eponymous hero.

(iii) The second Joshua, to whom the mythical Joshua the son of Nun owes his biography, was the first high priest after the Exile (Ezra 2–3; Haggai 1:1, 12; 2:2, 4 and elsewhere). After the monarchy was eliminated, he was faced with the task of combining his priestly functions with royal ones.

VII.5. *Deborah*

Deborah was a prophetess who dispensed justice in Israel after the people had lived for twenty years under Canaanite rule. Her place was under the palm of Deborah between Ramah and Bethel on Mount Ephraim, and the Israelites came up to her for judgement. She sent for Barak, who dwelt in Kedesh in Naphtali, and she instructed him to assemble an army to strike down the Philistine king Jabin. But Barak said to her: If you will go with me, then I will risk it. But if you will not go with me, then I will stay home. And Deborah said to him: Good, I will go with you. But the glory of the victory over Sisera, the captain of King Jabin, will not go to you, but to a woman.

And Deborah went forth with Barak and his troops from Zebulun and Naphtali to Mount Tabor. There they defeated Sisera and his band of chariots. And Sisera fled away on foot. In his flight he came to the tent of Heber the Kenite, who lived in peace with his king Jabin. Jael, Heber's wife, invited the fugitive into the tent, gave him refreshment, and covered him with a blanket. But when in his exhaustion he fell asleep, she murdered him by hammering a tent peg through his temples. Then Barak, who had been pursuing the fugitive, came up, and Jael led him to the corpse of the slain man in her tent.

After the victory over Jabin, Deborah and Barak sang a song:

> Yahweh, when you went forth from Seir,
> when you marched from the fields of Edom,
> the earth trembled, the heavens streamed,
> the clouds streamed with water.
> Mountains melted before Yahweh,
> before Yahweh, the Elohim of Israel . . .
> Awake, awake, Deborah, awake, awake, sing a song!
> Arise, Barak, lead your captors captive, son
> of Abinoam! . . .
>
> The kings came and fought,
> then fought the kings of Canaan
> in Taanach by the waters of Megiddo,
> but they had no rich booty.
>
> The stars fought from heaven,
> they fought in their courses against Sisera.
> The brook of Kishon swept them away,
> the brook of Kishon, the brook of Kedumim . . .
>
> Then the horsehooves pounded,
> from the hunting, from the hunting of the heroes.
> Curse upon Meroz, said the angel of Yahweh.
> A curse upon its inhabitants,
> for they hastened not to Yahweh's aid,
> to the aid of Yahweh against the mighty.
> But praised be Jael among women,
> the wife of Heber, the Kenite,
> let her be praised above all women in the tent.
> He asked for water, and she gave him milk,
> she brought him milk in a splendid dish.
> But her hand reached out for the tent peg,
> her right hand for the workman's hammer,
> and with the hammer she smote Sisera,
> she shattered his head,

and pierced through his temples.
Sisera collapsed at her feet,
and where he fell, he lay there slain ...

So let all your enemies perish, Yahweh,
but let your friends be as the rising sun.

[Judges 4–5]

(i) In this version of the Song of Deborah, all details concerning the individual sons of Jacob have been omitted, along with the verses mocking Sisera's mother. Chapter 4 is considerably more recent than chapter 5. It is an anecdotal introduction, designed to clarify what follows – presumably the oldest piece of poetry in the Bible. It is quite probable that the Song of Deborah (i.e. the bee) is the song of a great queen who belongs to the prehistory of biblical mythology.

(ii) The battle against King Jabin was undoubtedly a battle fought by Deborah alone, and only later did it become a contest between the Israelites and the Canaanites. Jael kills the king as the bees kill the drones. Without a mythological background, it would be unthinkable to present the murder of a stranger seeking asylum in one's tent as a praiseworthy act of heroism on the part of a woman, instead of loudly condemning it as a crime.

(iii) The poem about Deborah's heroic deed was, we may assume, handed down by the southern nomadic tribes of Judah, which also preserved the texts that make up the Lay Source. For here the monarchy and farming life are unmistakably rejected, while the nomads are addressed as follows: 'You who ride on tawny she-asses, who sit on carpets, and who live on the roads' (5:10). But the ancient narrator has already transformed Deborah's battle into Yahweh's and Israel's battle.

(iv) Rebekah's nurse in Genesis 35:8 is not the same person as the prophetess. The term 'prophetess' is obviously a poetic way of concealing Deborah's original function, that of sacred queen.

(v) The Song of Deborah and Barak is one of the most impressive examples of Hebrew poetry. It is a triumphant song of victory. Its rhythm is hardly comparable to the sorts we are familiar with, but it might be said to resemble anapestic metre. The use of parallelism displays great formal beauty.

VII.6. *Gideon*

When the Israelites had immigrated into the land of Canaan and settled there, the kings often attacked their territories to plunder them. Thus the Israelites were once obliged to pay tribute to the Midianites for seven years.

During this time they tried to conceal their corn from the Midianites. For this reason, Jerubbaal, the son of Joash, threshed his corn not out on the barn floor but in the wine press. There the angel of Yahweh appeared to him once and commanded him: Go in your might and strike the Midianites. I will be with you in the battle. You need have no doubts of my victory.

Then Jerubbaal went into the house and brought out a sacrifice for Yahweh. The angel had kindly promised to wait for it. And the angel of Yahweh accepted the sacrifice: he touched it with his staff, and fire rushed out from the rock and consumed it. When Jerubbaal started in fear, Yahweh himself called out to him: Peace be unto you, fear not, you will not die. – Thereupon Jerubbaal built an altar to him on the same spot and called the shrine 'Yahweh is peace'.

Now when the Midianites had gathered once more for a raid, Jerubbaal raised an army from Asher, Manasseh, Zebulun and Naphtali; and the army of their enemies were encamped below them on the plain. But at night Yahweh appeared to Jerubbaal and ordered him to storm the Midianite camp. Jerubbaal obeyed, after learning from a night-time reconnaissance mission how dispirited the Midianites were. In the middle of the night, he made his troops blow trumpets and smash clay jars, making such a deafening noise that he confused his opponents. Then he attacked the enemy with his little band. After he had captured and killed their kings, he returned and asked them only for the golden rings they had taken as booty. From them he made an ephod, a household god, which he set up in his native city of Ophrah. There Jerubbaal remained until he died in old age. He left behind seventy sons, for his harem was large. His concubine in Shechem bore him Abimelech [see IX.1 (p. 173)].

Others say that Yahweh appeared to Jerubbaal one night and commanded him to destroy his father's Baal altar and Asherah, to erect an altar to Yahweh instead and to sacrifice a bull on it. Jerubbaal obeyed. He overturned the altar to Baal and the Asherah. This is why Jerubbaal was also called Gideon (i.e. the one who fells or hews down). Yahweh was always with Gideon. Before the battle with the Midianites, he ordered him to let most of the people go. And 22,000 men from the army went home. Of the 10,000 men who remained, Yahweh chose for the battle the 300 men who, when they were drinking from the brook, did not waste time in putting aside their weapons but lapped up the water like dogs.

And so Yahweh struck down the 138,000 men of the Midianites by means of Gideon and his 300 men.

Then, when he returned home in triumph, the Israelites wished to make him king. But Gideon turned them down: Neither will I rule over you, nor my son, but Yahweh shall be your king. But when Gideon was dead, the

Israelites carried on the old idolatry with the Baals once again and even chose Baal-berith (the covenant Baal) of Shechem for their god, and they forgot all the good things that Yahweh had done for Gideon and for Israel.

Still others say that Gideon was a great temporizer who had strongly balked against going off to war. And so he twice asked Elohim for a sign. On the first night he requested that a fleece of wool he had placed on the threshing floor be moistened with dew, while all the floor around it was dry.

When Elohim gave him this sign, Gideon asked for another the following night: that the fleece might be dry while the threshing floor was damp with dew. And Elohim granted him this request as well.

[Judges 6:1,4–6,11–24,33–4; 7:9–8:1; 8:24–27a, 29–32; 6:25–32; 7:2–7; 8:22–3, 33–5; 6:36–40]

(i) During the Peasants' War, Thomas Müntzer was compared to Gideon. The legend of Gideon is given a striking presentation. It set the standard for generals – who, as this tradition saw it, were more important than kings. The story of Gideon was presumably handed down by the nomads who roamed the frontiers of Judah, whence the Lay Source was derived.

(ii) The hero's original name was surely Jerubbaal (i.e. 'Baal contends'). This name carries us back to the early period of Israelite history. We can be more or less positive that Jerubbaal was a Canaanite king, whose significance for the Israelites lay in the fact that, in avenging his brothers (Judges 8:13–21), he killed the Midianite kings Zebah and Zalmunna, who were also two powerful opponents of Israel. By so doing he entered the ranks of the heroes cherished by the Israelite tribes, without being an Israelite himself. The old myth goes on to tell how, after the battle, he returned home with his oracular household god, which he ordered to be made from the spoils of war.

(iii) The ancient Hebrew narrator took it for granted that Jerubbaal-Gideon should build an altar to Yahweh. The narrator connects the great hero with a cultic legend, and thereby conceals the fact that, for the Israelite, Gideon once was a royal divinity.

(iv) The later Deuteronomic tradition was uncomfortable with the name Jerubbaal, and so it created the myth of the obedient Gideon who tears down the sanctuary of the Baal and the Asherah, and who, for the sake of Yahweh (that is, of the priests), renounces the throne. The Deuteronomist tries to explain the name Jerubbaal in a way that contradicts its real meaning. But we have the Deuteronomic tradition to thank for the consistent insertion of the name Gideon throughout the story. Gideon means 'the feller', that is, one who slays men. This term, originally descriptive of a general, is now made to refer to attacks against idols. Gideon is now less the great hero than the obedient servant of Yahweh.

(v) The Elohist narrator of the ancient collection of tales celebrating the great heroes cannot help dealing much more cautiously with war than does the Lay Source. The latter describes Yahweh's battles with gusto, because it speaks for the old nomadic tribes on Judah's border that did military service for Judah. In contrast, the Elohist narrator has Gideon take up the sword only after twice consulting Elohim. It is obvious to him that Gideon was not a king of Israel, but the lord of Ophrah.

VII.7. *Jotham*

Jotham was Gideon's youngest son; he managed to escape the assassination attempt by his brother Abimelech, who slew all his other brothers [see IX.1 (p. 173)]. When Jotham heard that Abimelech wished to make himself king, he went up to the top of Mount Gerizim across from Shechem and cried out: Hear me, men of Shechem. Once the trees went forth to anoint a king. And they first went to the olive tree and said: Reign over us. But the olive tree said: Shall I cease to pour forth the oil for which men and gods praise me, only to rule over you? And the fig tree said when they made the same request of it: Shall I cease to bring forth my delicious fruit, only to rule over you? And the vine also refused: Shall I leave my wine which gives cheer to gods and men, only to rule over you? – Then all the trees said to the bramble: Reign over us. But the bramble said: If in truth you anoint me king over you, then come to me and bow down beneath my shade. And if you do not, then a fire will come forth from me and devour the cedars of Lebanon.

After that Jotham fled to the south and dwelt there.

[Judges 9:7–15, 21]

(i) Jotham is known to us only through this fable, which he delivers to the citizens of Shechem to warn them that kingly rule will bring nothing but evil consequences for people who once were free. He should not be confused with King Jotham who ruled over Judah, first as the deputy of his father Uzziah, who was stricken with leprosy, and then as sovereign, *c.* 730 B.C. (see, e.g., II Kings 15:2, 32–8; II Chronicles 27).

The legend makes the author of this fable a son of Gideon, but we may assume that he was a wandering bard.

(ii) The fable is one of the finest instances of ancient biblical poetry. It is unambiguous. The historical novella that follows it, dealing with the despotic reign of Abimelech, turns the fable into an allegory, which in the beginning it surely was not. Fables need no historical examples to be understood. The narrator, from the highlands of central Palestine, presumably found this fable ready to hand and used it in this context. Jotham shows himself to be a spokesman for the old nomadic way of life which sees no need for a strong central government or monarchy. Hence he pays homage to a romantically envisioned social order, which no longer corresponded to the needs of the day. In the face of the justifiably angry people, he flees south into the steppe.

(iii) Shechem was the site of an ancient Canaanite sanctuary. Its local god was the 'lord of the covenant' (Baal-berith), who lent many of his traits to the covenant god of the Israelites. He stood for social and economic progress as opposed to nomadic life and its dream of the Golden Age (see VII.3.d (p. 139)).

(iv) The anti-royalist novella of Abimelech was handed down to strengthen the priests' insistence on submission to King Yahweh. To their mind, Yahweh was the king, and they were his representatives.

VII.8. *Jephthah*

Soon after the immigration of the Israelite tribes into Canaan, conflicts arose with the individual kings whose territory they had invaded. Among their bitterest enemies were the Ammonites, who used to send raiding parties into the country east of the Jordan. And the sons of Gilead, who dwelt there, fought back against them.

Jephthah, a son of Gilead who had been banished from their midst, was now chosen to lead their army. While in exile, Jephthah had gathered together a band of scoundrels, with whom he went forth from his base in the land of Tob and hired himself out for military service. And now, when the Ammonites were taking the field against Gilead, the elders of Gilead asked Jephthah to help them. They promised to make him their prince, and under this condition he agreed. And the spirit of Yahweh came over him, and Jephthah routed the Ammonites.

Jephthah also defeated the Ephraimites, who had rebelled against him; and after this battle he had the fords of the Jordan occupied and the Ephraimites killed when they tried to cross. For the Ephraimites, when challenged to say 'shibboleth' – that is, 'ear of corn' – could only say 'sibboleth', and so they were found out.

Now before the battle Jephthah had made a vow: If I come back safe and victorious, I shall offer up to Yahweh as a burnt offering whatever comes out from the door of my house to meet me. But when Jephthah came home, his daughter, an only child, came out to meet him. He was deeply afflicted, but his daughter admonished him to keep his vow. After she had mourned for two months, she returned to Jephthah, and he fulfilled his vow on her which he made to Yahweh. Since then every year the daughters of Israel mourn Jephthah's daughter for four days.

But Jephthah ruled another six years in Mizpah.

[Judges 10:17–18; 11:1–11, 29, 33; 12:1–6; 11:12–28, 30–32, 34–40]

(i) The heroic tale of Jephthah was originally, like the stories of the other so-called 'major judges', a Canaanite legend. Jephthah was a king residing in Tob and then was made elective monarch of Gilead after he freed that land from the pressure of attacks from the Ammonites, Moabites and Ephraimites.

Although Gilead was a place name, here it is traced back to a mythical ancestor. Consequently it is also more or less certain that Jephthah was originally *not* a 'judge in Israel'. That institutional function undoubtedly played a part in the creation of the Shechem covenant. Presumably the judges were the administrators of covenantal law, as sworn to in Shechem. The so-called 'lesser judges' (Judges 10:1–5; 12:8–9) were surely such magistrates. The figures given for their years of service sound reliable. In Assyria, the *limus* were officials who performed comparable tasks.

The so-called 'major judges', as can be seen in the case of Jephthah, Gideon and Samson, were all, without exception, Canaanite heroes.

(ii) The story of Jephthah reveals certain similarities to the story of David. Jephthah and David were both leaders of armed bands with whose help they captured the throne. Both men were exiles. Common to both heroes is a well-defined *topos*: the hero makes his way to power with rebels and outlaws, who have had to flee into the wilderness to escape the bloodhounds of the courts.

(iii) The historicity of Jephthah is uncertain. The name rather suggests that he was a mythical character, since Jephthah means 'he sets free'. The tale of Yahweh's gift of his spirit to Jephthah, by means of which he wins all his victories, is presumably just the attempt by pious eighth-century Israelites to integrate this ancient Canaanite hero into the tradition of the tribes. In this way Jephthah lost his original historical-aetiological function of liberator. His heroic deed was undoubtedly the liberation of a small Canaanite city-state, Mizpah, say, or Gilead, from servitude to a larger kingdom, such as Moab.

(iv) Once again, in contrast to the southern Judaean narrator, the Elohist stresses how Jephthah tries to settle the conflict amicably through negotiations. He also tells the aetiological anecdote of the father's sacrifice of his daughter, a practice in which the Elohist finds nothing out of the ordinary. Jephthah completes the sacrifice, and this time Yahweh does not intervene as he did in the sacrifice by Abraham (Genesis 22) or in the sacrifice of Iphigeneia at Aulis. Iphigeneia was supposed to be sacrificed to win Poseidon's favour towards the Greek fleet; Jephthah's daughter dies to win her father success in battle. The key to understanding such stories is mythological analogy: the sacrifice of a maiden brings liberation from the predominance of the Great Mother and sacred queen. Jephthah flees his native land – and the ancient matrilineal law of succession (Judges 11:2). He returns as a conqueror with a new kind of law. Matrilineal succession is done away with by the sacrifice of his only daughter. The old law lives on only in the ritual form of a (misunderstood) festival, as shown by the note on the mourning by the daughters of Israel.

VII.9. *Samson*

In the days when the Philistines were still very powerful in the country, there lived in Zorah a man named Manoah from the house of Dan. After his wife had long been barren, she bore him a son whom she named Samson.

For an angel of Yahweh had appeared to her and foretold to her that she would bear a son. At the same time he had ordered her to drink no more wine henceforth and to eat no impure foods, and also never to cut her son's hair, for he was to be dedicated to God. The woman had told this to her husband, and Manoah had heard the same oracle yet one more time from the angel of Yahweh. Then they sacrificed a kid as a burnt offering, and the angel of Yahweh ascended in the flame from the altar.

Samson grew up blessed by Yahweh in the camp of Dan. But he sought and found a wife among the Philistines at Timnah. On the way to woo his bride he slew a young lion with his bare hands. When, after a while, he returned to marry her, he found a wild swarm of bees in the carcass of the lion. He tore out the honey and gave some to his parents. At the wedding Samson made up a riddle out of this, which he posed to the wedding guests: Out of the eater came meat, and out of the strong came sweetness.

But the guests could not solve the riddle, and so they pressed Samson's wife to draw the answer out of him. And he betrayed his secret to her because she was so persistent. Then, when the wedding guests gave him the right answer, he replied in anger: If you had not ploughed with my heifer, you would not have solved my riddle. But Samson's wife was given to his companion, a member of the wedding party.

After some time Samson returned and took bitter revenge on the Philistines by capturing foxes and tying burning torches to their tails, then letting them go through the fields and orchards, which they destroyed. In reprisal, the Philistines burnt down his wife's house with all the people in it.

At this Samson became so furious that, when his country unleashed him upon the Philistines, he slew around a thousand men with the jawbone of an ass that he had happened upon. From there he went on to Gaza. There he spent the night with a harlot, and when they tried to capture him, around midnight he ripped out the gate of the city, hinges and all, and carried it up to the top of a hill near Hebron.

Samson was invincibly strong. But his next mistress was the Philistine Delilah, and she tried to worm the secret of his strength and invulnerability out of him. Several times he misled her with false information, and each time Delilah was forced to send the hired murderers away. But finally he did betray his secret to her: it was that Samson would be invincible and invulnerable so long as his hair was not cut. The next night she cut off the hair of his head, the Philistines rushed in, overpowered him and gouged his eyes out. Then they kept him as a slave in prison. Apart from the work he had to do, they also brought him out at feasts to amuse the guests. At one such entertainment Samson avenged his disgrace: His strength had come back, because his hair had not been cut for a long time. And so at a feast for the high princes of the Philistines he had himself led to the middle pillars of the hall, and he knocked them over. The roof collapsed and crushed all the guests in the hall to death. The three thousand people on the roof who had watched Samson make sport were also killed. Samson, too, died beneath the wreckage. His tribal brothers brought him from there and buried him in the tomb of his father Manoah.

[Judges 13–16]

(i) The story of Samson is self-contained. The biblical narrator's efforts to include him among the judges of Israel are feeble. The evidence is everywhere that the hero, whose name means 'born of the sun', can never have been a judge in Israel, because he did not spend his whole life there.

(ii) Various details in the story have led some to see an analogy between the myths of Samson and Heracles, and to assume that both are based on the same Middle Eastern pattern. This theory is probably not altogether false. Whether or not it holds water depends upon whether it can prove its presupposition that both myths arise out of comparatively similar socio-economic conditions. In the biblical tale, the setting is Philistia, the society a smoothly functioning Philistine despotism (see IV.4.**b**.i (p. 91)). Delilah is presented as a whore. But the socio-economic foundation of the myth of the sun hero – who is sacrificed by the moon goddess when she cuts off his hair – is the extended family, ruled by the sacred queen and Great Mother.

(iii) Hence we can only assume that the ancient myth as the Bible has it is further removed from its point of departure than the Greek version. The Bible still keeps the structural feature of the hero's always needing help from his divine father. As Heracles continually needs Zeus, and in the ancient Tyrian myth the god of the city needs Shamash, so Samson needs his god and father Yahweh. For, in the language of myth, the angel of Yahweh's prediction to Manoah's wife, 'You shall conceive and bear a son' (Judges 13:3c, 5) is equivalent to impregnation. Even pious readers of myth have never been able to understand the angel's message to Mary, the mother of Jesus (Luke 1:31), in any other way except that the god himself impregnated the woman.

(iv) The story of Samson's birth shares similarities with the story of Samuel's birth (I Samuel 1, cf. VIII.1 (p. 153)). Such similarities do not mean that one of the myths depends on the other, but simply reveal a common theme: the hero is not a true god but a godlike man. Heracles was never one of the twelve full-blooded Olympians, Samson was never a god like Shamash or Sin, Samuel was never Elohim.

(v) The statements in the biblical text connecting specific geographical points with the Samson legend are historical-aetiological attempts to give the hero cultic and ritual roots. They are parts of the myth.

(vi) In the Christian tradition, Samson becomes the classic example of the man who succumbs to lust, and is therefore shamefully punished. But such a reduction of the myth to the level of moral fable misses the Bible's intention. For the biblical version celebrates Samson's death as a noble and marvellous achievement: 'So the dead whom he slew at his death were more than those whom he slew in his life.'

VII.10. *Ruth*

In the old days when Israel still had no king, Elimelech went from Bethlehem to the land of the Moabites with his wife Naomi and his two sons. The sons married Moabite women, but soon all three men died. Naomi was left with her childless daughters-in-law, Orpah and Ruth. Naomi went back to Bethlehem. Ruth insisted upon going along with her mother-in-law, and said: Whither you go, I will go; and where you lodge, I will lodge. Your people shall be my people, and your god shall be my god.

And so they both returned to Bethlehem. Ruth hired herself out to work in the fields for the farmer Boaz, who was also related to her father, and who was pleased with her. On the advice of her mother-in-law she kept close to him and followed him at night into the barn, where he slept near the winnowed barley. So it came about that he got her with child. Thereupon Boaz married Ruth in accordance with the law of Bethlehem in the presence of many witnesses. And all the people at the gate, together with the elders, said: May Yahweh make your wife fruitful, like Rachel, and Leah, who built up the house of Israel. May she thrive in Ephratah, and be praised in Bethlehem.

Ruth gave birth to Obed and laid him in the bosom of her mother-in-law Naomi, as was the custom. And the women congratulated Naomi, because she had not been left quite childless. And Obed became the father of Jesse, who begot David.

[Ruth 1–4]

(i) The Book of Ruth is structurally a classic novella. Its mythic nature is almost lost in the detailed depiction that shows how well informed the narrator was about conditions in the country during a pre-exilic era (the seventh century B.C.). The mythic character of the book is still recognizable, but only in the plot. It tells how, by Yahweh's wonderful dispensation, the childless Naomi (i.e. 'the sweet one') gets a child. When she takes Ruth's child to her bosom, it becomes her own, just as Heracles only became an Olympian when he crawled through Hera's spread legs.

(ii) This mythological form of the act of adoption belongs to the stories about kings that were common in antiquity. Against all expectations a god provides an heir for a childless woman, who then becomes mother of a great line. Such a mythic gesture was surely required before biblical history could fully accept David's family tree. The act of adoption is a radical one. It makes men into gods, and Moabites, Israel's arch-enemies, into Israelites. For Obed, according to the then law in force, would have been a Moabite – until the act of adoption wiped out this blemish in David's genealogy.

(iii) In Judaism, the Book of Ruth is listed among 'the Writings', which are of lesser importance, while the Christians include it in the 'Former Prophets'. Because its action takes place in the pre-monarchic period, it has to be placed between Judges and I Samuel. This brief book is only in the Bible at all because it became attached at an early date to the Davidic genealogy, with which it became part of biblical tradition.

VIII. Miracles and Other Incidents from the Lives of the Prophets

VIII.1. *Samuel*

Elkanah the Ephraimite lived in Ramah. He had two wives, one of whom, Hannah, was long childless. During the annual pilgrimage to Shiloh, Hannah stole into the sanctuary and asked Yahweh for a child. She promised: Yahweh Sabaoth, if you give your maidservant a son, I will dedicate him to Yahweh. The old priest Eli, who was sitting at the door of the temple and watching her, thought at first that she was drunk, and took her to task for it. But when she told him her trouble, he promised her that Yahweh would hear her vow and grant her request.

After a year Hannah bore her first son and named him Samuel, that is, 'granted by God'. And when his mother had weaned him, she brought Samuel to Eli at Shiloh, so that he could take him in, as the vow had provided for. Every year she came with her husband Elkanah and brought clothing for Samuel. Eli blessed her, and Hannah bore Elkanah three sons more and two daughters. Samuel grew up with Eli and slept in the temple, where the ark was kept. There Yahweh appeared to him at night and revealed to him the coming downfall of the house of Eli, for his sons, Hophni and Pinchas, were evil priests, who cheated the people offering sacrifices and took their pleasure with the temple prostitutes. But others say that a man of Elohim had already told Eli the same thing and that he did not hear it first from Samuel.

Samuel's reputation as a good prophet quickly spread throughout the country, and he was indisputably the greatest prophet and judge in all Israel his whole life long. This was after Eli and his sons had perished when the ark of the covenant was lost to the Philistines in a battle.

But Samuel later rescued Israel from the hand of the Philistines, and there was peace between Israel and the Philistines and Amorites as long as he was alive. During the year he went from temple to temple, in Bethel, Gilgal, Mizpah and Shechem-Ramah, back and forth, to sit in judgement. When he had grown old, and his sons had made themselves disliked by the people, the elders came to him and asked him to appoint a king over them. Samuel did not want to, but Yahweh told him to give in to their demands. And so Samuel anointed

Saul king, after giving a speech to the people that described all the vices of kings. But he was soon dissatisfied with Saul and his behaviour, and so with Yahweh's help he anointed David, while Saul was still living. When Samuel died, all of Israel gathered together and mourned him. He was buried at Ramah.

[I Samuel 1; 2:18–21; 3:1–18; 2:27–36; 3:19–21; 4; 7:1–17; 8; 10:1–8; 15:10–30; 16; 25:1]

(i) Samuel is a mythical figure. The miraculous story of his birth marks him as a hero. His towering importance as a righteous judge, prophet and priest caused his name to be put at the head of stories about the kings Saul and David, even though he is dealt with extensively only in the opening chapters of I Samuel.

(ii) It is certain that Samuel's mythological significance derives from his connection with the cult site of Shechem, where the ark of the covenant, the palladium of the twelve tribes, must have been stationed (see VII.1 (p. 134)). Shechem was also the source of Samuel's role as the founder of Saul's military-style kingship, whose traditions openly clashed with the interests of Davidic Jerusalem.

(iii) This is the reason why, on the one hand, Samuel is considered a spokesman for a party hostile to kings (e.g. I Samuel 8, 10:19–27), while, on the other, some accounts (I Samuel 9:1–10, 16) make him sound like a vigorous supporter of kings. But the speeches favouring the monarchy do not contradict the speeches opposing it. Both sorts make it clear that Samuel is the star witness for elective monarchy, especially as practised by the northern tribes, a system which naturally ran counter to the hereditary despotism of the Davidic dynasty in Jerusalem.

(iv) This tradition concerning Samuel managed to pass the final stage of priestly editing only because in the fifth and fourth century B.C. Judaism was chiefly interested, not in presenting itself as a national political power to be reckoned with, but in earning the reputation as a pious cultic community, in keeping with the norms of the Persian empire. The northern Israelite tradition of Samuel as an opponent of King Saul (who subordinated the old cultic regulations to political interests) corresponded to those norms

(v) Mythologically, Samuel is a hero somewhat comparable to the Greek Theseus. (The name means approximately 'divine pledge'.) Theseus, who united the twelve cultic communities of Attica, was considered a law-abiding ruler. While he promised them to do away with the monarchy, in fact he accomplished this, if we may believe Plutarch, by naming himself commander-in-chief. Like Samuel, Theseus stands on the threshold separating mythical and historical consciousness, and like Samuel the hero, his nature is both human and divine.

VIII.2. *Elijah*

When Ahab son of Omri was king over Israel, along with his other wives he also married Jezebel, daughter of the king of Sidon, and he had an altar built to her god Baal in his capital city of Samaria. At this Elijah from Tishbe in Gilead grew infuriated and prophesied to Ahab the coming of a drought. After that Elijah hid away, on orders from Yahweh, in the country east of the Jordan, by the brook Cherith. There the ravens of Yahweh brought him bread to eat in the morning and meat in the evening. Then, when the brook dried up in the drought, Yahweh commanded Elijah to go to Zarephath in the kingdom of Sidon, where a widow would take care of him. Elijah obeyed and went to Zarephath, and a widow shared her last flour and oil with him. But Yahweh made her supply of oil and flour last all during the time of drought. And Elijah brought the widow's son, who had fallen ill around then and died, back to life again.

When three years had passed, Yahweh ordered Elijah to return to Samaria and to show himself to Ahab, who had long sought for him in vain, hoping to kill him. Elijah appeared before the king at the height of the famine, and this time the king obeyed him. On Elijah's orders he had all the priests of Baal and Asherah gather on Mount Carmel. Here Elijah challenged them to an ordeal. He proposed to the people to arrange two burnt offerings. He would prepare one, the priests of Baal the other. Neither should use fire, but the true God would be the one, either Yahweh or the god Baal of Sidon, who would send down fire in response to an appeal. The assembled people agreed. And after Elijah had called upon Yahweh, Yahweh's fire fell from heaven and consumed the burnt offering, although Elijah had ordered much water to be poured over it. But the priests of Baal prayed and danced all day long, without their sacrifice catching fire.

When the people saw that, they all cried aloud: Yahweh is God! Yahweh is God! Elijah bade the people seize the priests of Baal, and he brought them down to the brook Kishon and had them killed there. In the evening the rain came up that ended the drought.

Jezebel heard what Elijah had done to her priests, and wanted to have him murdered. But he fled into the wilderness, where the angel of Yahweh led him to Mount Horeb. There Yahweh appeared to him in a soft breeze and ordered him to anoint Hazael king of Aram, Jehu king of Israel, and Elisha his own successor. And Elijah prophesied their downfall to King Ahab and his wife Jezebel, because Ahab had made a treaty with the king of Aram, whom he had allowed to get away, and had perverted justice in other ways as well.

When the time arrived for Elijah to journey to heaven, he went with his servant and successor Elisha from Gilgal to Jericho, and from there to the other side of the Jordan. The prophets of Jericho already knew that Yahweh would come to take Elijah. On the far side of the river the fiery chariot of Yahweh with its horses of fire suddenly came and separated Elijah from Elisha, and Elijah went up to heaven in a thunderstorm. Elisha cried aloud: My father, my father! Israel's chariots and horsemen!

[I Kings 16:29–34; 17–19; 21:17–20, 27–9; II Kings 2:1–12]

(i) The stories of Elijah presumably date from the middle of the eighth century B.C. Elijah is considered a prophet of Yahweh. The office of prophet was widespread in antiquity, not only in Greece but also in Egypt. The prophet emerged from priestly traditions, and he exercised both priestly and judicial functions. The historical setting for the rise of non-cultic prophetic activity was the final phase of the monarchy. When royal power – which includes priests and temple – dwindled, individual spokesmen arose from the oppressed class of the former local tribal priests (who also joined together in groups).

(ii) Such spokesmen, who always look to the legal norms and social traditions of the past, became the focal point not only for their disciples but also for mythological motifs and materials. All this serves to give the otherwise insignificant spokesman outstanding importance.

(iii) The mythologems peculiar to Elijah in these stories are the sojourn in the wilderness with the feeding by the ravens, Yahweh's theophany on Mount Horeb, and the ascension into heaven. The nurturing of the poor widow, the resurrection of her son, the curse upon the king and his house, and the zeal for Yahweh's commandment are familiar mythologems found in other sources.

The desert wilderness is considered a kind of space both hostile to civilization and close to God. The raven is a symbol of the god of battle and light, who shows man the way. Ravens accompany Apollo, the god of death, of wisdom, the earth and the sun. The raven is also the symbol for the intercalary month in the Babylonian leap year. Mythologically speaking, to be fed by ravens means to be of godlike nature, and hence Elijah's activities have a special significance. The ascent into heaven only confirms his divinity, also attested to by the lack of any story concerning his birth.

(iv) The fact that the prophet Elijah is given a historical basis by locating him in the reign of actual kings in no way alters his mythological significance: representatives of the ancient priestly traditions of the tribes attempted to use the myths of Elijah to promote their interests, after they had been suppressed for almost a century. The archaic character of the Elijah stories is more an index of the fundamental conservatism of the bearers of this tradition than a sign that the text itself is an ancient one.

(v) The ordeal of 'judgement of God' on Mount Carmel has no foundation in history. This scene attributes a role to the prophet Elijah (the name Eliyahu means 'my god is Yahweh') similar to that once played by Moses and Joshua: all three men wished to convince the assembled people of Yahweh's uniqueness by means of a miracle.

(vi) As with all the other prophets, we find in Elijah an opponent of the monarchy, the central government, the royal priesthood serving the temple at the king's residence, and the court prophets. Yahweh appears to Elijah not in Jerusalem but on Mount Horeb.

(vii) Because of the similarity between Moses' function and his own, Elijah became extremely important to biblical piety. The book named after its supposed author, the prophet Malachi, which comes at the end of the Old Testament, has God declare that the prophet Elijah will appear before the coming great and terrible day of Yahweh, in order to call men to repentance. This is why the author of Matthew's gospel mentions Elijah along with John the Baptist as a precursor of Jesus of Nazareth (Matthew 11:14; 17:10–13), just as, according to the myth of the Transfiguration, Moses and Elijah appeared to Jesus and spoke with him. But the evangelist Luke, who had a different bias, has Jesus warn his disciples about Elijah (Luke 9:54). In his narrative of the Passion, Matthew reports (27:46–9) that even when Jesus was on the point of death people thought that Elijah might come to help him.

Elijah's ascent into heaven, like the rapture of Enoch, was the reason why, in the centuries immediately before and after the beginning of the Christian era, many apocryphal works – 'Apocalypses' of Elijah and supposed writings of Enoch – were composed, whose main theme was the battle between Elijah or Enoch and God's evil counterpart. The prophet's honorary title, 'Israel's chariots and horsemen', which is also applied to Elisha at his death, was presumably an ancient attribute reserved for kings. The term stems from military technology: war chariots and cavalry were the most powerful weapons. Applying it to the prophet is thus a way of ascribing to him high dignity and importance.

The graphic presentation of Elijah's miracles led the New Testament to make frequent use of him as an example (Luke 4:25–6; 9:54; Romans 11:2–5; James 5:17).

VIII.3. *Elisha*

In Abel-meholah, Elisha, the son of Sharphat, was once out ploughing when Elijah passed by and threw his mantle over him. Thereupon Elisha left his work and his homeland and followed Elijah and served him. When Elijah was about to ascend to heaven, he went with Elisha to the Jordan and asked him: What more can I do for you before I am taken away from you? I will grant your request. Then Elisha asked for two thirds of Elijah's spirit. Elijah answered: You have asked a hard thing. Nevertheless you will get it, if you can see how I am carried off. And Elisha saw how Elijah ascended to heaven in a thunderstorm. Left by himself, he took up the mantle of Elijah, and walked across the Jordan without wetting his feet, for the river was parted before him, when he touched it with the mantle. And he betook himself to the prophets of Jericho, who acknowledged him as Elijah's successor. He performed his first miracle when he made Jericho's water supply drinkable again. Then he procured drinking water in the desert for the troops of Israel, Judah and Edom when they joined forces against Moab. He also helped a widow become rich, by making her oil jar inexhaustible for a time, so that she could fill many vessels with oil and sell them. And he helped a woman from Shunem who had long been childless to bear a son. And when the boy died in the bloom of his youth, Elisha brought him back to life. He also helped the woman regain her property that had been taken from her.

Once he sat down to table with his hundred disciples, and he had only twenty flat cakes of barley for all of them, for there was a famine just then in the land. Still they ate, and there was some left over, as Yahweh had promised through Elisha.

Elisha also cured the Aramaean commander-in-chief, Naaman, of leprosy, ordering him to bathe seven times in the Jordan. Despite all these miracles, and many more, he remained a modest man and accepted no money. He interceded to prevent unnecessary bloodshed in war. Thus he caused the armies of the Aramaean king Ben-hadad to lose their way, and when they were besieging Samaria, the capital of Israel, Elisha made them flee before Yahweh's mighty sound of an army, so that the sons of Israel plundered the rich camp without a battle. But when little children mocked him and called him 'bald head', he had forty-two of them torn to pieces by bears. Elisha also carried out Yahweh's charge to Elijah, to make Hazael king in Damascus, even though he knew that one day Hazael would burn Israel's cities, defeat its armies and put its women and children to death. Elisha also carried out Yahweh's command to Elijah to anoint captain Jehu king of Israel.

When Elisha lay dying, King Joash of Israel came up to his bed in tears, and said: My father, my father! Israel's chariots and horsemen! – And while yet on his deathbed Elisha consented to promise a victory for Israel over the Aramaeans. Even after he was dead, Elisha did a miracle. For when yet another dead body was being hastily buried in Elisha's grave on account of a foray by a band of enemy raiders, the dead man was revived because he had touched the bones of the prophet.

[I Kings 19:19–21; II Kings 2:1–22; 3; 4:1–37; 8:1–16; 4:38–42; 5; 6; 2:23–5; 8:71–5; 9:1–10; 13:14–21]

(i) Elisha, like Elijah, is a mythological figure. His relationship with kings in Israel and Aram-Syria changes nothing in this regard. The narrator of the Elisha stories makes use of a pattern that is also applicable to the Elijah tradition. The wonder-worker makes it rain, has all sorts of political success, raises the dead, miraculously feeds people and enables childless women to become fertile. As in the case of Moses, so with Elisha, the narrator wishes to stress that the prophet has been filled with the spirit of Yahweh. The analogies between remarks about Elisha and those about Moses and Elijah force us to conclude that Elisha has a function comparable to theirs: he is the antithesis to the centralized spiritual and political power of temple and palace.

(ii) The name Elisha (meaning roughly 'God helps') is a symbol of those parts of the population which had to suffer under the despotic political structures that were going up even in the northern kingdom, that is, the country folk. For such people, the prophet (the quintessential non-priest) stood for the observance of the old land laws, which forbade, among other things, any arbitrary seizure of farms by the king. The prophet as non-priest, then, had deep roots in the rural masses. That is why he was also an anti-war spokesman.

(iii) The individual miracle stories are indicative above all of the basic religious position of the people who handed them down. The rural population was still attached to the old Canaanite religious traditions, more so than in the economically better developed southern kingdom of Judah. The anecdote told in II Kings 1 about King Ahaziah, who sends messengers to a Philistine god, Baal-Zebul of Ekron, to ask if he will recover from a disease, makes clear that the old Canaanite ideas were still alive. In the myths of Ugarit, Zebul is the name of the sea god, and in a city as involved with navigation as Ugarit, the sea god was an altogether respectable person. And so the Baal-Zebul of Ekron originally meant 'lord of the prince', that is, a supreme god. Only later does the Bible repudiate him, call him 'lord of the flies' (Beelzebub), and make him an anti-god (Matthew 10:25; Mark 3:22, etc.).

(iv) Biblical piety has made more of the character of Elijah (see VIII.2 (p. 155)) than of Elisha. The myth of Elijah's ascent to heaven played a large part in this, together with the importance that Elijah acquired in Jewish thought in the last few centuries before Christ.

VIII.4. *Isaiah*

In the year that King Uzziah died, the prophet Isaiah saw Yahweh. He was sitting on a splendid lofty throne, and the hem of his mantle filled the temple.

Seraphim hovered in front of him, each with six wings. With two wings they covered their faces, with two they covered their feet, and with two they flew. The seraphim took turns singing: Holy, holy is Yahweh Sabaoth, the whole world is full of his glory. – And the house shook and filled with smoke.

Isaiah was greatly frightened and thought that he would have to die now because he had seen Yahweh Sabaoth with his own eyes. But one of the seraphim came and touched the mouth of Isaiah with a glowing coal from the altar and cleansed him with it, so that he could hear Yahweh's intention of foretelling to Israel its downfall.

And Yahweh charged him to take a clay tablet and write on it, 'The spoil speeds, the prey hastes.' Soon afterwards, when Isaiah's wife bore a son, Isaiah named him 'the spoil speeds, the prey hastes' (Maher-shalal-hash-baz), because Yahweh had said: Before the boy can say 'father' and 'mother', Damascus and Samaria will have fallen to the king of Assyria. Isaiah had already named his first son Shear-jashub ('a remnant will return'). Isaiah kept these revelations and initiated his disciples into their secrets, and said: I will wait for Yahweh and I will hope in him, for I and my sons, whom Yahweh has given me, are a sign from Yahweh to Israel. The same was also true for his son Immanuel ('God with us').

From that time on, the hope that Yahweh would send help never failed. As the song puts it: A child is born to us, a son is given to us, and the government will be upon his shoulder. And he shall be called: Wonderful Counsellor, God-Hero, Eternal Father, the Prince of Peace. His reign of peace on the throne of David will endure for ever. On that day, a remnant of the house of Jacob will turn to Yahweh, the God-Hero, on the day when Yahweh sits in judgement on the nations.

From the stump of Jesse a sprig shall come forth, and the spirit of Yahweh, a spirit of understanding, of wisdom, of counsel, of might, of knowledge and fear, will come over this scion, who will be just, kind and peaceable. Then the wolves will dwell with the lambs, the leopards lie down with the goats. A little child will pasture calves and young lions and fatlings together. Cows and bears shall feed together, their young will lie down together. Sucklings and little children will play with adders and serpents.

On that day when he judges the nations Yahweh will chastise Leviathan with his great merciless sword, he will chastise the coiling serpent, and kill the dragon that dwells in the sea.

And Isaiah wrote down the verdict against the people of God on a tablet so that it should bear witness for ever to the falseness and rebelliousness of the sons of Israel.

But when misfortune stood at the gates of Jerusalem, and when the king of Judah, Hezekiah, did penance, Isaiah persuaded Yahweh to put king

Sennacherib of Assyria to flight by means of an angel, so that he could not invade the city. And Isaiah also caused Hezekiah to be cured of a serious illness. As a sign that the king would get well, on that day Yahweh made the shadow on the sundial go back ten hours. Isaiah healed the king's boils with a fig poultice.

[Isaiah 6; 7:3; 8:1–6, 16–18; 9:1–7; 10:20–27; 11:1–10; 27:1; 30:8–9; 36:10–37, 1; 38:1–8, 21]

(i) It is generally admitted that Isaiah was a historical person, but his life story has certainly picked up some mythological embellishment. There is no doubt that he was active in the years from around 740 to 690 B.C. We know nothing about his birth and death except for post-biblical legends. His theophoric name means 'Yahweh helps'.

(ii) Only certain parts of the book named after him can be traced back to the period assumed to be Isaiah's lifetime. Chief among these are chapters 1–23 and 28–32, while chapters 36–7 are of slightly later provenience, and chapters 24–7 much later than that. The remaining chapters of the Book of Isaiah come from still more recent times. The reader is well advised to accept the scholarly division of chapters 40–66 into 'Second Isaiah' (40–55) and 'Third Isaiah' (56–66). Second Isaiah reflects the situation of the Babylonian exile, while Third Isaiah deals with the period after it. On the mythological significance of Second and Third Isaiah, see XIV.2.e.iv (p. 242); XIV.3.c.i (p. 246); XIV.3.c.vii (p. 247).

(iii) Isaiah, son of Amoz (not the same person as Amos the prophet), was presumably a teacher of wisdom at the temple in Jerusalem. He did not come from a family of priests or royal officials, but apparently from well-to-do country folk who had a clearly defined sense of identity vis-à-vis the throne and the temple. Isaiah attacks not only social abuses but the priests themselves and their teachings about divine worship (e.g. in 10:1–4). This is due less to his vision of Yahweh, where the seraphim cry out to him, 'Holy, holy, holy is Yahweh Sabaoth', and to Yahweh's revelations, than to his roots in the rural population, which was not only more conservative than the city dwellers, but above all was more closely connected to the original inhabitants of the country, who kept up certain religious customs. Almost all the prophets came from this rural environment.

(iv) Isaiah's vision of his calling is the mythologem that gives his words their divine authority. During this scene, Yahweh is invisible, veiled by the seraphim. The introduction of the seraphim into his vision surely derives from the prophet's familiarity with older, non-Israelite ways of thinking. The seraphim were originally serpents (see IV.5.b (p. 106) and V.3 (p. 119)). They represent the mother goddesses, now banished. The graphic fashion in which they spread their wings to cover their faces completely is an attempt to repress still more deeply their original significance – which the contemporary audience was well aware of.

Sharply contrasted with the seraphim are the Leviathan, serpent and dragon in Isaiah's discourse on the world empires. In this context, the beasts are obviously symbols of the great kingdoms on the Euphrates and the Nile: the Medes, Babylonians and Egyptians. Isaiah has Yahweh himself fight this battle, for only thus can he counsel the king of Judah to show a readiness for peace and neutrality towards all sides.

(v) There is mythological significance, too, in the names of Isaiah's sons, which are certainly legendary inventions. Like the sons of Heracles born of Omphale, they represent certain epochs. The number three is important here, because as a geometric expression of fullness it stands for the transcendental realm in the history of religion. Hence it is more than just a hypothesis to argue that in the 'Servant Songs' on the judgement of the nations and the reign of peace Isaiah is thinking less of a divine person than of the prophet's son Immanuel. One can scarcely imagine that the prophet had a member of David's dynasty in mind, after such a negative verdict on the house of David. His son Immanuel is to be the symbol of the truly pious man, who relies only on Yahweh.

(vi) Furthermore, we can be sure that the prophet Isaiah expected to see weal and woe, salvation and catastrophe in his own lifetime. Hence he stays within the bounds of his role as a teacher of wisdom. Late Jewish tradition, along with Christianity, made him (and the authors of the other sections of the book) into the originator of the Messianic genre.

(vii) The custom of describing the people of God with the image of the vineyard (5:1–7) goes back to Isaiah, the first one to use this motif. It is widespread in the New Testament (Matthew 20:1; 21:28–41) and in Christian mythology. In John's Gospel, for example, Jesus is called the true vine and God is called the vinedresser.

VIII.5. *Jeremiah*

In the days before the kingdom of Judah was destroyed by Babylon and a part of the nation was forced into exile, lived a prophet named Jeremiah, the son of Hilkiah from Anathoth. He dwelt in Jerusalem and served in the temple. There Yahweh appeared to him, touched Jeremiah's mouth with his hand and said: See, I place my words in your mouth, that you may proclaim my will to Judah and Jerusalem. I will bring their downfall upon them from the north because of all their wickedness and their godlessness. For the priests do not ask: Where is Yahweh? And the judges do not trouble themselves over my law, and the kings have become rebellious. Israel has already perished because it did not obey me, and the same will now happen to you. The temple of Yahweh will not save you, but only a good life and fair dealing with strangers, widows and orphans, the poor and the innocent.

And Yahweh said to Jeremiah: Buy yourself a linen waistcloth and place it around your hips, but protect it from water. Shortly afterwards he spoke again to Jeremiah: Go and hide the waistcloth in a cleft in the earth on the Euphrates. Jeremiah did as Yahweh had commanded him. After some time Yahweh ordered Jeremiah to go and fetch the waistcloth. But in the damp cleft it had become worn out and rotten. And Yahweh used the waistcloth to explain Judah's fate to Jeremiah: Just as Jeremiah had adorned himself with the waistcloth, so Yahweh had made Judah his adornment, but now it would rot.

Jeremiah despaired over his mission, and over the difficulties that the people in Jerusalem threw in his way, when he gave threatening sermons to them. He cursed himself and the day of his birth. But Yahweh spoke with him and comforted him. Nevertheless Yahweh forbade him to take a wife and beget children, for Yahweh intended to put an end to all shouts of joy, to all the rejoicing of bride and bridegroom.

Because of his seditious and menacing sermons, Jeremiah was put in the stocks and cast into prison. But Yahweh saved him from death. Meanwhile, however, the prophet Urijah, who like Jeremiah had prophesied against Judah, but then had fled in fear to Egypt, had been abducted by King Jehoiakim and murdered.

Jeremiah bore a wooden yoke on his neck: Yahweh had ordered him to do this, to show what a burden would hang over Jerusalem. This outraged priests and prophets alike. One of the prophets, Hananiah, smashed Jeremiah's yoke, and predicted that within two years Yahweh would lift the yoke of Nebuchadnezzar from the nations in just the same way. Jeremiah countered by proclaiming the word of Yahweh: You, Hananiah, have indeed smashed a wooden yoke, but now I, Yahweh, will lay an iron yoke upon all of you. You will become the subjects of the king of Babylon. And as for you, Hananiah, you will die this year because you have lied to the people.

When the Jews had been carried off to Babylon, Jeremiah still did not stop saying and writing that they should adapt to life there. Yahweh himself would bring them back home to Jerusalem, when he wished to.

And when Jerusalem was destroyed, Jeremiah remained in the city to help those who were compelled to remain in the country.

But the people rebelled against the Babylonian governor and murdered him. Then they fled to Egypt and forced Jeremiah and his companion Baruch to come along with them. Nothing further is reported about his life.

Even before this, Baruch had written down Jeremiah's sermons. One time the king of Judah burnt the scroll on which they were all recorded, for fear they would be made public. Thereupon Baruch had been instructed by Jeremiah, on orders from Yahweh, to write everything down once more. And Baruch did this, but in addition many other sermons of the same kind were added to the book, especially on the subject of the neighbouring peoples.

[Jeremiah 1:1–9; 2:8; 3:1–11; 7:1–7; 13:1–4; 15:10–21; 16:1–2; 27:1–11; 28:1–17; 29; 36:1–2, 32–3; 41–4]

(i) Jeremiah – the name means something like 'Yahweh raises up' – was probably a historical person. The book named after him contains so many historical reminiscences that this seems a reasonable assumption. He was active from *c.* 626 to 580 B.C. His father was in all likelihood a priest in Anathoth, and after Josiah's cultic reform in 624 B.C. he must have been thrown out of work. The family's means must have been considerable, enabling Jeremiah to live off them.

(ii) Jeremiah's priestly origins explain, presumably, his agreement with the cultic reform and the new legislation by the priests of Jerusalem. For all his attacks on the priests, Jeremiah surely must have been one of their number. He does not assault the temples, priests or the monarchy as such, but only their dishonourable and spineless representatives, who, as he sees it, are the chief cause of the (divinely intended) ruin of the country.

(iii) Jeremiah sides unequivocally with the king of Babylon. He calls Nebuchadnezzar the 'servant of Yahweh'. His efforts to rid Jerusalem and Judah of their perverse political resistance to Babylon and to get them to adopt instead an attitude of good will and non-militant neutrality may most likely be explained by his origins. Country people saw the kings of Judah as a greater threat to their interests than the king of Babylon.

(iv) The language of the Book of Jeremiah reveals not only the author's literary talent but also his characteristic kind of piety. Quite differently from the Jerusalem theologians, he describes how Yahweh acts and talks immediately and directly with *him*, Jeremiah the man. Yahweh often appears in these stories as an active character speaking a language crammed with imagery, in the Near Eastern fashion: Yahweh is the creator of the world and its ruler, but also a smith, a farmer, a potter, a father, mother, judge, priest and physician. The mythologems Jeremiah uses are graphic and readily understood.

(v) Yahweh is the husband and lord of his bride Israel (chs. 2–3), and Israel is at once his son, heir and beloved child (3:4, 9; 31:20). A point not to be overlooked here is that these terms are not just images of another sphere of reality, but mythologems, of the sort familiar to anyone versed in ancient

Near Eastern religion. When Gudea of Lagash addresses the goddess Ninlil as mother, when Enlil is called the father of the king of Sumer or the moon god Sin is invoked in Babylon as the 'father of gods and men', such titles are a dim recollection of the sacred kings of yore who walked the earth and ruled and were called gods. Israel was no exception to this.

The anthropomorphic use of Yahweh as an image of the sacred king also explains the motif of the wedding between Yahweh and Israel. Some have argued that the collection of love poems in 'The Song of Solomon' should be viewed as the ritual text for the sacred marriage between king and priestess, with the priestess standing for the land and its inhabitants. This idea is not present in the Song of Songs in the guise of a marriage between Yahweh and Israel, but it was a widespread theme of popular piety. The most extensive body of material reflecting this notion is to be found in the poems about Tammuz and Ishtar. The image of the marriage of Yahweh and Israel is also the leading motif or mythologem of Hosea (see VIII.7 (p. 169); XIV.2.e.i–iii (p. 241)).

VIII.6. *Ezekiel*

When the priest Ezekiel, the son of Buzi, sat by the river Chebar in Babylon with the exiles from Jerusalem, he had a vision [see II.6.h (p. 61)]: he saw a whirlwind come out of the north, and a great cloud within it, out of which streamed light and flaming fire. Out of the midst of the fire four figures became visible, and they had the likeness of man, but each had four faces and four wings. Beneath the wings they had human hands. Their faces did not turn when they went. In each case, the face looking straight ahead was that of a man. The face on the right was of a lion, on the left of a bull, and at the back that of an eagle.

With two of their wings each of the four figures moved about, with the other two wings they covered themselves. In the midst of the four figures was a blazing fire, with lightning bolts flashing out of it. Near the figures were wheels, whose rims were full of eyes, and which could move in all directions when the figures beat their wings. And over the wings of the four was something like a throne of sapphires, on which a human figure was sitting, wrapped in gleaming light and fire. This was the appearance of the likeness of the glory of Yahweh. And the rustling of the wings was like the roaring of mighty waters. Ezekiel fell down, but heard a voice ordering him to stand up, to speak to the house of Israel. And a hand reached out, gave him a scroll, closely written on both sides, for him to eat, and said: Son of man, consume this and fill your innards with it. And it tasted like honey. But the words that Ezekiel had to swallow were a harsh message for Israel.

After this the glory of Yahweh rose with a thunderous noise like an earthquake and disappeared. And Ezekiel found himself among the exiles at Tel-abib in Babylon.

And every time the glory of Yahweh appeared again, Ezekiel received a charge for the house of Israel, which Yahweh had determined to bring to ruin, because it was unfaithful to him. Yahweh ordered Ezekiel to perform signs to let the people see what awaited them:

First he was commanded to take a brick and to carve on it a picture of the city of Jerusalem. He was to put mounds and towers against it, as at a siege, and to set up an iron pan against the city.

Thereafter Yahweh commanded Ezekiel to lie on the ground tied up, 390 days on his left side for the sins of Israel, and 40 days more on his right side for the sins of Judah.

Another time Yahweh ordered Ezekiel to eat unclean bread, baked on cow dung, and to drink only a little water, for Yahweh wished to show that he would spoil the bread in Jerusalem and make the people drink the water with dismay.

Ezekiel was also bidden to take a sharp knife and to shave the hair of his head and beard with it, to burn a third of the hairs, cut a third in little pieces, and scatter the last third into the wind, so as to tell Jerusalem: A third of your inhabitants shall die of the plague, a third shall perish by the sword, and a third shall be scattered and persecuted. All this was to happen, because the people had turned away from Yahweh and his Law.

After Yahweh had gone on to let Ezekiel see the horrible idolatries that the elders and aristocrats who had stayed behind in Jerusalem were committing in the temple and in the city, he made Ezekiel boil a pot of meat over the fire, to show how Jerusalem was to come to its end. But the people in Babylon to whom Ezekiel spoke were unwilling to listen to him. Then Ezekiel was given a further assignment, to take his luggage and to leave his house with everyone looking on. And he was to go out through a hole that he had to break in the wall. Thus would Jerusalem be unpeopled, and its prince taken captive and brought to Babylon.

And the hand of Yahweh came over Ezekiel and led him in the spirit into a valley full of dead bones. There Yahweh said to him: Prophesy my word to these bones, that I will make them live again. And Ezekiel prophesied, as he had been ordered. And it came to pass, that with a tremendous clatter the bones came together. They took on sinews, flesh grew on them, and they were covered with skin. And the spirit came from the four winds, breathed on the slain, and they came to life once more, a vast army. And this was Yahweh's sign through Ezekiel that Yahweh would bring his people back from their graves and lead them, full of life, into the land of Israel.

And Yahweh gave the prophet yet another task, to take two wooden sticks, and to write on one, 'Judah and all the allied Israelites,' and on the other, 'Joseph and all the allied house of Israel,' and then to bind them closely together. Then the prophet was to say to the people that Yahweh would soon gather the children of Israel from among the nations, to make them one people, under one king and one shepherd, under David's servant, and then there should be an eternal reign of peace. And in the middle of this kingdom Yahweh would erect his dwelling, in the rebuilt temple, which he revealed to Ezekiel in all its particulars.

All this would come about once Jerusalem was destroyed by the Babylonians. And Yahweh had Ezekiel deliver a blistering rebuke to the nations who were Israel's neighbours, Edom, Sidon, Ammon, Moab, the Philistines and the Egyptians.

Concerning the king of Tyre, Yahweh told the prophet to say: You have said, I am a god, and I sit on the sacred mountain of the gods in the middle of the sea, and I have been called by you to the holy mountain of the gods. But now that you have sinned, I will cast you down from the mountain of the gods and give you up to the kings, and you shall be lost for ever.

But Yahweh would allow no blame to be laid on Nebuchadnezzar of Babylon.

[Ezekiel 1; 10; 3:1–18, 22; 4:1–17; 5:1–12; 8:1–17; 11:7–12; 12:1–12; 37:1–14, 17–28; 40–48; 25–32; 28:1–19; 29:17–21]

(i) The Book of Ezekiel is surely the most dramatic in the Old Testament. It is a poetic work, presumably composed over a long span of time, at least from 592 to 530 B.C., if not an even longer period. The name of the prophet (Ezekiel means 'may God strengthen') and the skimpy biographical information in the book compel us to assume that behind its first-person narrator stands a mythical rather than a historical figure.

(ii) The language of the book is by no means easy. Numerous corruptions in the text often leave us guessing what its original meaning must have been. By comparison, the Greek and Latin translations provide a simpler text, but they are just as strangely graphic. The linguistic problems are also connected to the fact that the book has more than one author. It is reasonably certain that the dates frequently assigned to the prophet's visions aim less at guaranteeing the book's historical reliability than at creating its literary structure.

(iii) The book obliges us to compare it with the works of Homer and the solution of the Homeric question. That is, we must assume that a great poet and mythographer laid its foundation, which later bards (who must have come from various regions, from Jerusalem, Babylon and exile in Egypt) took over and built upon. That is why certain terms not found elsewhere appear in several sections of the book: we need not assume that Ezekiel actually worked in Jerusalem and Babylon.

(iv) Ezekiel is the poet of the great biblical metaphors. His address to the 'shepherds of Israel' (ch. 34) has exerted a stronger influence than the shepherd parables of the other prophets. The obscure, menacing sermon on Gog and Magog (ch. 38) stimulated both Jewish and Christian mythology. Ezekiel launches violent abuse at Israel (Samaria) and Judah (Jerusalem), calling them Oholah and Oholibah, and accusing them of the uttermost lasciviousness with vivid imagery unmatched elsewhere in the Bible. These passages, as well as Ezekiel's consoling sermons on the new spirit (36:25–30), are more impressive than Isaiah's lyrical poems or Jeremiah's sermons and letters.

(v) The prophet is unequivocably anti-Egyptian, and manifestly sympathetic to Nebuchadnezzar of Babylon, 'who works for Yahweh' (29:18). His hostility to Jerusalem, as with the other prophets, is based on his social position. Ezekiel did not belong to the group of prophets and priests at the court, but to the rural population. Chapters 40–48 do give a detailed description of the new temple of Jerusalem, and they do contain regulations governing cultic practice. But this is not inconsistent with the poet's great vision; it is rather the only possible conclusion his followers could append to the book without running into conflict with the order from the Persian cabinet concerning the establishment of the cultic community in Jerusalem. Christian mythology has interpreted the closed eastern door of Ezekiel's temple, which only the new prince can use, as referring to Mary, the mother of the Jesus, the 'door' through whom Jesus came into the world.

(vi) The description of the chariot-throne was frequently used by the early Church as a source of representations of God. The *quadrigae Domini* (the four-horse chariot of the Lord) was the most favoured motif, because it recalled the ancient images of the chariots of Helios, Poseidon and other gods.

The four faces of the Cherubim became symbols for the four evangelists in the early Church. Chapter 4 of Revelation began this process. Since the days of the church father St Jerome, the lion has been read as the symbol for Mark, the bull for Luke, the eagle for John and the man for Matthew.

Originally, however (and Daniel 2 and 7 still point to this), the living creatures were symbols for the four parts of the world, or the four elements of sun, moon, heaven and earth, as they appear in ancient Babylonian and Assyrian inscriptions. The lion is the animal of the goddess Ishtar, the bull is the icon of Marduk, the eagle-headed dragon is the animal of Nergal, the manlike creature is the god Enlil – 'the Marduk of empire and the government', as it says in a Babylonian hymn, in which Marduk is placed on an equal footing with all the great gods. The image of the chariot-throne is therefore unambiguous: Yahweh is the great king, the sole lord, and hence Nergal, Enlil, Ninurta and Marduk, all in one.

(vii) As a mythographer and poet, Ezekiel also attests to the historical origins of the term 'god'. Gods are actually kings, and kings are gods. In the prophecy directed at the king of Tyre (ch. 28), Ezekiel cites the Tyrian and general Middle Eastern formula, 'I am a god,' and makes Yahweh say that he (Yahweh) has called the king to the holy mountain of the gods. But in his characteristic zeal for the great king Yahweh, Ezekiel has Yahweh casting out the king and god of Tyre from his council and annihilating him. A distinctive feature of the poet is that, like Homer with Zeus, he presents Yahweh in a completely anthropomorphic manner. Yahweh loves the virgin Israel, somewhat as Zeus loves Europa.

(viii) The poet has to perform twelve symbolic tasks, which are to make clear the fate of Jerusalem and Israel. Although the number twelve appears nowhere else in the book, it points to closure and consummation. Everything Ezekiel does has to be done to warn Judah and Jerusalem lest they become even more corrupt. Through his image of the tightly bound sticks with Judah and Joseph written on them, the prophet wishes to demonstrate the indestructibility of unified alliances, while an individual stick is easily broken. At the same time the twelve tasks, like the twelve labours of Heracles, are a symbolic pattern for the redemption and liberation of the godlike hero.

(ix) As in no other book of the Bible, the aesthetic value of Ezekiel's central myth – the downfall of Jerusalem and its resurrection – is fully independent of any religious sentiment. In this the prophet resembles Homer. But Homer presents the downfall of Troy as the result of a whimsical decree of the Olympians, whereas Ezekiel never stops insisting that the downfall of Jerusalem is caused by the crimes of its inhabitants. More than any other biblical writer, Ezekiel individualizes guilt and atonement, ethics and morality. This clearly identifies his historical standpoint as the epoch when uniform social mores and customs went to ruin, when the kingdom was destroyed.

VIII.7. *Hosea*

Yahweh spoke to Hosea, the son of Beeri, at the time when Jeroboam, the son of Joash, was king of Israel: Go and marry a harlot, and let her bear you a harlot's children. And her three children shall be named 'Israel', 'Not-loved', and 'Not-my-people'. And this is so that all may recognize that I am devoted to the nation and love it. Take yet another wife, and then make her sit alone, for Israel will sit all by itself like that, without God, without a king, without worship. When Israel was a child, I came to love her, and brought her out of Egypt. But the more I wooed her, the more she gave herself to other gods.

But I will not destroy her completely. I will forget the consequences of her apostasy, and love her. I will be like the dew to Israel, I alone will hear her requests, I alone am like a verdant cypress.

[Hosea 1:1–8; 3:1–5; 11:1–4; 14:5–9]

(i) The Book of Hosea is a collection of poems and allegories; there is no reason to postulate a historical person behind the protagonist. Formally speaking, some of the poems in this book (ranked among the 'minor prophets') are quite similar to love songs. Psychologizing interpreters of the collection have tried to make its author out to be an unhappy husband, but that is surely wide of the mark. The mythological content of the book runs counter to this notion.

(ii) As we have already seen in the case of Jeremiah (see VIII.5 (p. 162)), the poet employs the metaphor of a marriage between king and land, god and human, which is based on concrete historical traditions. In ancient Sumer (*c.* 2000 B.C.), the country's king celebrated a sacred marriage with the goddess, whose part was played by the high priestess of Innana-Ishtar. The goddess represented the land and chose her husband and king. In Sumer, it was the shepherd Dumuzi, whom the goddess preferred to the farmer Enkimdu. But Dumuzi soon ousted Innana-Ishtar.

(iii) Like Jeremiah and Ezekiel (see VIII.5–6 (pp. 162–9)), the poet turns to this myth of a divine marriage to explain the downfall of the northern kingdom of Israel (which he calls Ephraim) in terms of whoredom with strange gods. This is a metaphor for political alliances with neighbouring kings. The author's notion that Israel's fate should be a warning for Judah reveals him as a partisan of the southern state.

VIII.8. *Jonah*

One day the word of Yahweh came to Jonah, the son of Amittai: Arise and go to the city of Nineveh, and announce its downfall, for I have heard about their wickedness. Jonah fled from this charge. He embarked on a ship going from Joppa to Tarshish. But during the voyage Yahweh made a great storm come up, so that it seemed the ship would capsize. The sailors first threw all the gear overboard to lighten the ship. Jonah meanwhile had been sleeping below deck, until he was awakened by the captain so that he might invoke his god. When the danger kept increasing, the sailors cast lots to find out who was to blame for this misfortune. The lot fell upon Jonah. Then they asked him: Why has this evil come upon us? He told them that he was a Hebrew and worshipped the god who made heaven and earth. Nor did he conceal from them that he was running away from this god. Then the sailors were even more afraid and told him: What shall we do with you so that we may have a quiet sea again? And he told them: Throw me overboard, then the sea will become calm, for the great tempest has only come over you on my account. Then they threw him overboard, after vainly trying to bring the ship to land. And the sea became calm. But Yahweh made a great fish come to swallow Jonah. For three days and three nights, Jonah was in the belly of the fish and prayed for his rescue and promised to do the will of Yahweh. Then Yahweh spoke with the fish, and it spat up Jonah on land. And Jonah went to Nineveh and preached successfully about the city's downfall. Nineveh was converted from its evil ways, and Yahweh abandoned his plan of destroying the city. Now Jonah was truly vexed and angry over this, so that he preferred to die rather than having to see his prophecy unfulfilled. But instead of letting him die, Yahweh tried to explain to him that he could not simply destroy a city like that, where more than 120,000 people lived and many animals besides.

[Jonah 1–4]

(i) We know from II Kings 14:25 that there was a prophet named Jonah, son of Amittai from Gath-hepher. He is supposed to have reconciled the country with Yahweh during the reign of the godless king Jeroboam II of Israel (784–744). But the connection between this person and the above story is fictional. The tale was presumably conceived in the third century B.C. and ascribed to the prophet Jonah because of his merits.

(ii) The fairy-tale style of the story makes it sound like a sailor's yarn, all the more so because the swallowing by the fish is described in only three short sentences. Babylonians, Egyptians, Assyrians and Phoenicians told it more circumstantially: in those accounts the man swallowed by the fish enters upon a new kind of existence. But Jonah remains as sceptical as ever. Among the Babylonians, three days was also the period of time of no gods, just before the New Year's festival. This grudging treatment of mythological elements is characteristic of Hebrew poetry. The Middle Eastern myth is sharply downgraded in the story of Jonah: the fish simply has the function of bringing Jonah back to the coast of Palestine.

(iii) The story aims to teach third century B.C. Israel, through the example of the great prophet Jonah, long since dead, that Yahweh does not exterminate his enemies. Nineveh is a code word for Persia and perhaps also for the empire of Alexander of Macedon. Israel's belief in a vengeful god is corrected. Forgiveness should take the place of retaliation, because even people from a foreign world can do penance and win Yahweh's favour.

Christian iconography has seen Jonah, who spends three days in the belly of the fish, as an Old Testament anticipation of Christ's descent into hell.

IX. The Legends of the Kings

IX.1. *Abimelech*

After the death of the judge Gideon-Jerubbaal, one of his seventy sons, named Abimelech, went to Shechem, where his mother's brothers lived. There he got the help he needed to murder all his brothers and to become sole king of Israel. His plot succeeded, and he ruled over the country for three years. But the inhabitants of Shechem proceeded to hire footpads to ambush the king, and they made the king's highways unsafe. Among these men the most esteemed were Gaal and his comrades. Gaal also stirred up the Shechemites to resist Abimelech. The royal governor of Shechem, Zebul, informed Abimelech of this, and the king attacked Gaal and the citizens of Shechem, who had all taken refuge in the temple of the covenant god. Abimelech had all the inhabitants killed, and the city was levelled and sown with salt. Thereafter he set out against the fortress of Thebez. But he could not capture it, because in the middle of the city was a stout tower, to which the inhabitants had fled. Now when Abimelech came up to the tower, to set the gate on fire, a woman on the roof threw down a millstone that crushed his skull. He had just enough strength left to order his servant to kill him, lest it should be said that a woman had killed him. When the Israelites heard that Abimelech was dead, his troops scattered, and they all went home. Thus Elohim requited the crimes of Abimelech and the Shechemites.

[Judges 9:1–6, 25–57]

(i) This text comes from the early monarchical period. It is assuredly not a Jerusalem tradition, but rather from the northern part of the country. As evidence of this we have the thoroughly anti-royal bias of the legend, and the fact that Elohim takes responsibility for the downfall of Abimelech and the city of Shechem. To the members of the northern tribes, Solomon's kingly rule was as suspect as that of Abimelech.

(ii) Furthermore, the destruction of the god of Shechem, who is a *baal berith*, i.e. a covenant god, is an infallible sign of this tradition's hostility to Judah. The Israelites had brought with them into Canaan the notion of a covenant between themselves and their god, something similar to the alliance between them and their chosen leader. In Shechem and its sanctuary, Israelites and Canaanites now joined in venerating the city god of Shechem, who resembled their god Yahweh. This pious symbiosis draws the narrator's fire. Elohim asserts his territorial rights against the Baal of the covenant. Abimelech tries to assert himself, in league with the long-term inhabitants of the land, against the invading newcomers, the Israelites.

(iii) For further discussion of the importance of Shechem, see VII.3.d (p. 139). Jotham's fable (VII.7 (p. 146)) is also embedded in the story of Abimelech. This story was included in the historical corpus of the Bible undoubtedly because it could be used to bolster the post-exilic priestly argument for Yahweh's absolute supremacy. But the unintentional adoption of the name Elohim for the god allows us to see clearly the legend's original meaning.

IX.2. *Saul*

a. There was a man from Gibeah in Benjamin, whose name was Kish. He had a son named Saul, who was extraordinarily handsome. No one among the Israelites was better looking than he, and he towered over all of them, for he was a head taller than his fellows. Now at one time his father's she-asses had gone astray, and Saul set out with a servant to look for them. In their search they came to the land of Zuph, to the prophet Samuel, and they wanted to ask him which way they should go. But Samuel had received a revelation from Yahweh that he should anoint Saul prince over Israel. So Samuel welcomed Saul and entertained him splendidly. Early the next day he left the city together with Saul, anointed him prince over Israel, and ordered him to tell no one about it just yet. He also told Saul three things that would happen to him that very day, as a sign that this anointing would have full force. And the predictions came true. He met three men, who told him that the asses had been found. At the oak of Tabor three men gave him two loaves of bread. And last of all he met a band of prophets in ecstasy. He joined them, for the spirit had come over him as well. The people who knew him marvelled at this, and asked: Is Saul, too, one of the prophets?

After this Saul went home once again to his work. Once he was coming back from the fields with the oxen after ploughing, when the people from Jabesh in Gibeah begged for help against the Ammonites, who were pressing them hard. Then Saul cut the oxen in pieces, which he sent all over Israel, and had his messengers say: So shall it be done to the oxen of every man who does not march forth behind Saul to battle with the Ammonites.

Then, when Saul had conquered the Ammonites, the whole nation went to Gilgal and installed him as king in the presence of Yahweh. Saul also defeated the Philistines, with the help of his son Jonathan. But Samuel had already turned away from him, because in Samuel's absence Saul had made a burnt offering on his own, in order to win Yahweh's favour in the battle against the Philistines. Samuel also rejected him because, against Yahweh's will, Saul had not strictly observed the ban in the war against King Agag of Amalek, but had taken the defeated king, the best of the livestock and the most valuable possessions of the Amalekites as booty. Also on one occasion, by the casting of lots, the oracle of the Urim and Thummim had condemned Saul's son Jonathan to death for disregarding the command to fast, but this sentence was lifted when the people protested against it. Samuel did not forgive Saul the crime of sparing Agag, and told him: Because you have rejected the command of Yahweh, he has rejected you from being king over Israel.

And so Samuel anointed David the new king. He had already served Saul at court as his armour bearer. And when the evil spirit of Elohim tormented the king, David played for him on the zither, so that the evil spirit left him. But Saul soon became jealous over David's success in winning over everyone. So David fled from Saul, and the king hounded him and his friends terribly. Meanwhile the Philistines were growing noticeably stronger and arming for war against Saul. Since Samuel was dead and neither the prophets nor the Urim and Thummim gave him any information, Saul did not know what to do. And so the superior forces of the Philistines caught him unprepared at Gilboa. When he saw that his sons had fallen, Saul fell upon his own sword. After this the Philistines conquered the country and entrenched themselves in it.

[I Samuel 9:1–10, 16; 11:1–15; 13:10–15; 15:1–23; 16:13–23; 22:6–23; 31:1–13]

b. Others say that Samuel summoned the people to Yahweh at Mizpah and told them: You wish to have a king. Then present yourselves by tribes and by thousands. Then Samuel made the choice by casting lots. First the tribe of Benjamin was taken, and from among them the family of the Matrites. And out of this family the lot fell upon Saul, who at first had hid among the baggage. They ran and fetched him, and he towered over everyone by a head. All the people cried: God save the king! Then Samuel set forth the laws of kingship, wrote them down, and presented them before Yahweh.

Shortly before his death, Saul went to Endor to see a woman who could conjure up the spirits of the dead. He wished to ask Samuel, who had died, for advice, because a battle with the Philistines was imminent. And Samuel prophesied to Saul his downfall and the ruin of the nation. Yahweh had decided on the destruction of Saul and the nation because they had become disobedient to him.

[I Samuel 10:17–24; 28:3–25]

(i) The stories about King Saul come from the traditions of the southern tribes. These tales undoubtedly took on their final shape during the early monarchy, during the reign of Solomon. That explains why this tradition prefers to characterize Saul not as a king but as a prince. The difference between *nagid* (prince) and *melek* (king) is that the first is an honorary function associated with the role of military leader, while the second attends to political, cultural and economic matters. The priestly chroniclers of Solomon's court were most interested in describing Saul's position so that it contrasted sharply with that of David and Solomon. – Only the Elohist narrator relates that Saul was a duly appointed king, chosen by lot and properly installed with the acclamation, 'God save the king!' This description gives a fairly accurate account of the ritual of electing a military king. All males bearing arms – that is, all free inhabitants of the country – were entitled to vote and take part in the election. Women, children, servants and maids were excluded from public life.

(ii) The economic basis of the various independent tribal alliances was, in the first instance, privately owned herds put out to graze on the commons. Secondly, there was privately owned land, farmed with the help of servants, maids and women. At this time the cities were still, for the most part, populated by the former country folk of Canaan, and they took no part in the election of the king. But they were assigned the task of defending the nomadic rural population, which lived predominantly in tent villages. The cities were built as commercial centres and fortresses of refuge, that is, for herds and people in times of danger. In so far as there were large temples near or inside the cities, there would also be artisans living there, most of them temple servants. The urban kingships that replaced military kingship were always connected to a temple. The local god represented the great king, to whom city, land and people all belonged. The ancient Near Eastern kingdoms have therefore been accurately called theocratic despotisms. Sociologically speaking, this period marks the transitional phase from a society based on the clan to one based on slave-holding.

(iii) There can be no doubt that Saul (the name means 'the desired one') was a historical figure, even if there is no clear extra-biblical evidence of this. His campaigns against neighbouring peoples obviously provide us with some clues, but, since such raids were so common, any attempt to find an exact date for Saul is doomed to failure. We do know that he must have lived *c.* 1000 B.C.

(iv) Apart from its local colour, which has made Saul familiar to generations of readers, the story of Saul is an instructive prototype of the mythological notion of the great divine king Yahweh. For when the subordinate king Saul transgresses Yahweh's commandment, he is punished. The prophet Samuel (see VIII.1 (p. 153)) carries on the functions of the god's deputy. The office of prophet developed out of the old Canaanite priesthood, as is still apparent in the theophoric names of the great prophets Samuel, Elijah and Elisha, where the syllable 'El' points to Elohim, the representative of the old Canaanite gods.

The band of ecstatic prophets, therefore, whom Samuel knows and Saul happens upon, is surely descended from similar groups indigenous to Canaan and Asia Minor, such as, for example, Dionysian bacchantes, worshippers in the mysteries of Ishtar, and later on, Islamic dervishes.

(v) It is certainly no accident, then, that according to the legend Saul is looking for his father's she-asses. The ears of an ass on a reed sceptre were the symbol of the ruling gods of Egypt. The Egyptian god Set had the form of an ass. Asses were also sacred to Dionysus, who, the legends say, placed two asses among the stars. Dionysus, the son of Semele, won a place for himself at the table of the gods by callously ousting the modest Hestia. Participation in his cult was supposed to bring perfect bliss. His followers were transformed into new men and women. This is also what Samuel predicts to Saul, expressly advising him to join the band of ecstatic prophets.

(vi) From the Jerusalem narrator's point of view, this account undoubtedly explained Saul's downfall. The narrator presents Samuel as a man of God who is a prophet, priest and seer. The tasks he performs in Zuph are still those of a pre-Israelite cultic official. The tradition is aware of this, as we see in I Samuel 9:9: 'For in earlier days in Israel, when a man wished to inquire of Elohim, he said: Come, let us go to the seer. For the men who are now called prophets were formerly called seers.'

Saul's illness ('an evil spirit from Elohim') is presumably a polemical touch by the Judah party against Saul, who consistently adhered to the practices of the ecstatic prophets.

(vii) The Elohist narrator, who was the spokesman for the erstwhile inhabitants of the country, also recounts the episode with the woman from Endor. He finds nothing extraordinary in the king's visit to a medium. The only significant point here is that he presents Yahweh as a fanatical lord and king, whose displeasure can be calmed only by the sacrifice of Saul, his family, and a large portion of the army.

IX.3. *David*

a. When the spirit of Yahweh had departed from King Saul and the evil spirit from Elohim tormented the king, his servants found in David, a handsome youth and a powerful fighter, the man who could drive away the evil spirit by playing the harp and so ease Saul's anguish. And Saul took David into his service.

David fought worthily as Saul's general and was given Saul's daughter Michal in marriage. But when Saul observed that David soon became more popular with everyone than he himself was, he tried to have him killed. But David was warned by his friend Jonathan, Saul's son, and fled. Before long he was joined by many people who had been banned from their tent villages because of conflicts with the law. David went with these men on raids. In those days he had two wives travelling with him, namely Ahinoam from Jezreel and Abigail, the widow of the rich man Nabal from Maon.

Later David went into service with the Philistine king Achish of Gath, and robbed and murdered from Ziklag out into the territory of the Amalekites. But he did not take part in the Philistine campaign against Israel, because the other Philistine princes did not trust him. So David fought against the Amalekites, who had attacked his headquarters at Ziklag. From the booty he won he sent presents to the inhabitants of the southern regions around Hebron. When David heard of the death of Saul and Jonathan in the battle against the Philistines, he put the messenger who had brought the news to death for reporting that he had given Saul his death-blow, at the king's request. David composed a lamentation on the death of Saul and Jonathan. After this he set out to Hebron at Yahweh's command. There the people of Judah anointed him king over the house of Judah, while, in the north, Saul's son Esh-baal ruled over Israel. A long war broke out between the two kings, with David's strength continually increasing and the house of Saul getting weaker and weaker. Finally Esh-baal was betrayed to David by his own people and murdered. David punished the murderers with death, and then had himself anointed 'prince over Israel' by the nobles of Israel. After this he captured the stronghold of Zion, fronting Jerusalem, from the Jebusites, called it the city of David, and had a splendid palace built for himself with the aid of the king of Tyre. In Jerusalem he took possession of Bathsheba, the wife of the Hittite Uriah. For while Uriah was away with the army, David had impregnated her and, in order to conceal this, he had at first ordered the man to be sent home from the campaign so that he would sleep with his wife. But when Uriah, in keeping with the rules of war, refused to visit Bathsheba, David had sent Uriah back with a letter to the captain in the field, ordering him to see that Uriah did not come back alive from the battle. And Uriah was killed. But Yahweh made Bathsheba's child die, as the prophet Nathan had foretold. After this Bathsheba bore another son, Solomon, who was brought up by the prophet Nathan.

David also had more sons from his other wives. Of these, Amnon fell by the hand of his half-brother Absalom, because he had raped Absalom's sister Tamar and would not marry her. But Absalom regained his father's trust after spending three years at Geshur in Aram. He was a tall, handsome man with a fine head of hair. Because he refused to wait for his father to die and bequeath the throne to him, he tried to overthrow David. But the uprising failed. David's friends thwarted Absalom's plan, which even David's adviser Ahithophel had supported; and Joab, David's military chief, killed Absalom, who had been caught by his hair in the undergrowth beneath an oak tree. Some thought that Yahweh had made all this happen because David had committed adultery with Uriah's wife.

David himself was deeply disturbed, and only pleas and threats could make him go back to ruling the country once more. And then there was the unrest among the northern tribes, which were feuding with the southern tribes and wished to break away from David. But Joab waged war against them until the people of Abel-beth-maacah delivered to him the head of Sheba, the leader of the rebellious northern tribes. On this campaign, Joab also treacherously murdered Amasa, the leader of the troops levied from Judah. Now all that David had gathered around him was a single band of brave champions.

When David had become old, and could no longer get warm in bed, his servants provided him with a young girl, Abishag from Shunem, who stayed with him constantly. Before his death, David named Solomon as his successor, and had him anointed at the spring of Gihom by the priest Zadok and the prophet Nathan, who prevented David's other son Adonijah from ascending the throne with the help of Joab. Before David died, he charged Solomon to have Joab murdered. David had ruled over Israel for forty years.

[I Samuel 16:14–22; 18:17–28; 25; 27:1–12; 29; II Samuel 1–2; 4; 5:1–14; 11; 12:15–25; 13–16; 12:11–12; 17–20; I Kings 1–2]

b. Others say that David was anointed king by Samuel. When Saul had already been king in Israel for a year, he had so little regard for Yahweh that Yahweh decided to place a new king over his land. He ordered Samuel, who had long since retired from public life, to anoint a new king from among the sons of Jesse, a man from Bethlehem. Yahweh's choice fell upon Jesse's youngest son David, who was still watching over sheep then, but was a handsome lad.

David kept his anointing secret. And so it came about that Saul first noticed this brave and capable soldier in a battle with the Philistines. Then Saul took David in, because his son Jonathan greatly loved him. But Saul soon grew jealous of David and persecuted him, so that David fled to Samuel in Ramah and remained in the house of the prophets. Saul sent messengers to look for him there, but they were all seized with prophetic ecstasy. When Saul finally went forth himself to capture David, he, too, was seized by the spirit of Elohim, so that he rolled naked on the ground for a day and night. This is why the saying arose: Is Saul, too, one of the prophets?

And Saul could never lay a hand on David, because his son Jonathan loved David so dearly that he conspired with him and always warned him of his father's plans. But David always respected Saul's life and spared him.

[I Samuel 16:1–13; 17:55–18:24; 20]

c. Others again say that David, the son of Jesse from Bethlehem, was a brave soldier who as a young lad in a battle against the Philistines had killed the giant Goliath of Gath with only a shepherd's sling and so had decided the battle. Then, when the Israelites came home from the battle, the cry spread over the land: Saul has slain thousands, but David tens of thousands. Saul flew into such a rage over this that he wished to have David killed. But Yahweh was with David, while he had abandoned Saul. David fled from Saul to Keilah, and then to Maon, and with him were 600 men. They were all hard-pressed, people who were fleeing from their creditors, and other malcontents. David never attempted to take Saul's life, although he had many opportunities to kill him.

On the other hand, once he became king, David did not spare the Philistines, but smote them and their guard of giants. And Yahweh fought on his side. After Yahweh had won him peace from his enemies, David thought of building a temple for the ark of the covenant, which he had brought to Jerusalem. But Yahweh told him through the prophet Nathan: When your time is fulfilled and you are laid to rest with your fathers, then will I establish the kingdom of the offspring of your body. He shall build a house to my name, and I will establish his kingly throne for ever. I will be a father to him, and he shall be a son to me. So David built no house for the name of Yahweh, but he did gather a great treasure for Solomon to build with.

In his own lifetime, David had all Saul's descendants killed. He spared only Meribbaal, the son of Jonathan, because he was sworn to him.

His last great work was a census of the nation, which Yahweh himself moved him to take. But that same year Yahweh sent the prophet Gad to David and had him announce to the king three possible punishments, bidding him decide which one the land should be struck with, for Yahweh's anger had blazed out anew. And David chose the plague, which raged for three days, until Yahweh bade the angel of destruction stop, when the angel was already at the threshing floor of the Jebusite Araunah outside Jerusalem. Then David bought this place and erected an altar there and offered burnt sacrifice, with which he appeased Yahweh. This was the site where Solomon built the temple.

[I Samuel 17:1–54; 18:28–19:17; 23–4; II Samuel 5:17–18; 21; 24]

(i) David was without any doubt a historical person (he ruled presumably *c.* 1000 B.C.), but the way tradition has dealt with this first king in Israel has mythological significance. Biblical tradition sees David not only as a handsome man and a great hero, but also as a poet. Some of the songs in the books of Samuel and Kings ascribed to him are perhaps really his, but most of the Psalms bearing his name cannot be.

(ii) The origins of David's kingship most likely followed the course described by the Priestly Source. David was a freebooter who built up a troop of escaped law-breakers and won so great a name for himself with them that the men of Judah chose him to be their king. In this he resembled Jephthah (see VII.8 (p. 147)). This must have been the usual pattern of development for ancient Near Eastern despotisms.

(iii) The narrator does not find it shocking that David loved men as well as women (as we see in the chapter on his love for Jonathan). After all, there were, as we know, both male and female cult prostitutes in Jerusalem, and the custom may not have been eradicated until the reform of King Josiah (see VI.5.i (p. 132)). Polygamy at this time was taken for granted. The disputes between the various wives in David's harem were fought out by their children. David's first wives were not bought by him, and were as yet no mere merchandise, but much-sought-after symbols of power and influence. Not until the story of Bathsheba do we see that the established king is a despot with no bounds to his authority.

(iv) A typical feature of the story is that David does more than a little to ensure the murder of all Saul's descendants. The legend stresses that David never went to war against Saul, although his many confrontations with Saul suggest the opposite. In any case, there is no doubt that in the battle with the Philistines David was not fighting on Saul's side.

At the same time, the fate of David's various sons shows him looking on passively at their intrigues, which end with Solomon as the sole successor to the throne. The tradition also shows very clearly how, under David's rule, the old social structures of the tribes were broken down. For, by the end of David's reign, Joab, once he has murdered Amasa, is the most powerful man in the country. With the death of Amasa, Judah's custom of raising armies by the voluntary enlistment of men subject to conscription was done away with. Also destroyed was the power of the various family alliances to assert their rights against the increasingly powerful central government. But this historical advance stopped at the borders of the northern states, who could take the risk of refusing to follow David.

(v) The story of the royal succession accurately recounts how, instead of a free election by the tribal elders, the priests take over and decide who shall be king. Ancient Near Eastern despotisms were actually more or less theocratic, like kingship in the Old Testament. The priests trained the heirs to the throne and determined who would be king. David spent time with Samuel in Ramah; Solomon was raised by the prophet Nathan and put on the throne with the help of the priest Abiathar. David and all the kings in Judah and Israel had their 'seers', their prophet-advisers. Whatever the god Yahweh willed took place.

(vi) The narrators from the northern tribes (see b) tell us that David was anointed king by Samuel, and did not make himself king by his own accomplishments. Furthermore, according to this source, Saul possessed the spirit of Elohim even in the latter part of his career, as is clear from the episode in Ramah, when, while searching for David, he fell into ecstasy. For the descendants of the ancient Canaanites it could not be otherwise. They also relate that David escaped Saul's efforts to hunt him down only because his beloved Jonathan warned him each time. They do not ascribe to David any deeds of military heroism, because they want a peaceable king, who has the time and a feeling for love and religion, who spares his rivals and lets them live. Hence their ideal image of David is fundamentally different from that of the people living in the southern borderlands of Judah and Jerusalem.

(vii) For the latter (see c), the story of David can only begin and end with a great battle. And so they take the heroic deed of Elhanan, who slew the giant Goliath of Gath in the battle at Gob (II Samuel 21:19), transfer it to David, and considerably embellish the feat besides. The shepherd boy puts an army to flight with his slingshot. For this source, David is the great hero who does not spare his opponents inside or outside the country. The treacherous murders of Saul's descendants, of Amasa and Absalom, are made to seem justified. Yahweh himself advises David to take a census of the nation, which will serve as the basis for the introduction of a new military system. As the southerners view it, the continued survival of the Davidic dynasty is not at all problematic: for them there can be no doubting Yahweh's revelation that the throne of David will stand for ever. They are partisans of the new social order built around a theocratic despotism with hereditary succession to the throne. The future temple-state casts its shadows backwards. Booty taken in war is no longer divided up among the army, but brought to the treasury of the royal temple. Henceforth the name of Yahweh, as represented by priests and prophets, counts for more than the will of the assembled elders of the people. The glorious deeds of the tribe are no longer recounted, only those of David's champions, i.e. his royal mercenaries.

(viii) The historical texts concerning David were presumably composed during the reign of his successor, Solomon. They follow a fixed pattern: the blameless young lad is led by the hand of God to the summit of glory. The divine king Yahweh helps him to the utmost of his power. He is a father to the king, and the king is a son to him, as Yahweh promises the successor to the throne. David's greatness is seen as coming from Yahweh's strength. Criticism of the king would instantly become criticism of his divine father Yahweh. It is no longer for the people to judge the king, but for Yahweh alone. Only the supreme king can censure, condemn and pass sentence on the subordinate king, and only he in turn can judge the viceroy. And so, when the northern tribes, failing to understand that the historical situation had changed, try to break away from David, they are forcibly brought back to obedience.

Hence passages promising that the royal house of David will endure forever are simply pious rhetoric, not the expression of eschatological or messianic thinking. Only later did Jewish and Christian theologians feel obliged to turn this prediction into an allegory for future ages, and to make the transcendent bearer of salvation 'the son of David', as Matthew's genealogy of Jesus puts it.

(ix) Historically speaking, the royal mythologies that portray the king as the son of a god mark an end to the era which saw the completion of the process centralizing the economy, cultural activity and national defence around the temple and palace in Jerusalem. The people, both in the cities and the countryside, were now subjected to social and political oppression. They found they were now the property of a temple-king, but they could no longer give vent to their distress. Finding fault with the king and his policies was a sin against God. Only criticism from the prophets was not punished, because it was uttered in the name of the great king Yahweh.

The gulf separating the image of God from institutionalized worship was the basic reason for the incomparable development of the Old Testament myths concerning Yahweh. In his image of God, the pious Israelite fashions for himself a world in which the king too is subservient to a higher lord. Thus he subjectively overcomes the actual world around him; and by negating the king as the supreme authority, he creates the subjective prerequisite for providing history with a way out, a future dimension with a character different from the present. This is the key to both the permanence and transitoriness of this human idea of comprehending the total dialectic of reality.

IX.4. *Solomon*

a. Solomon ascended the throne while David was still alive. After David's death he sought and found reasons and pretexts for doing away with his father's enemies. Thus he had his half-brother Adonijah killed, as well as Joab the military commander and the rich man Shimei of Bahurim. He exiled the priest Abiathar to Anathoth. After Solomon had secured his throne in this way, he married the daughter of the Pharaoh of Egypt.

Solomon still offered sacrifices in Gibeon, because it was the foremost place for this in the country. There in Gibeon, Yahweh appeared to him in a dream one night and told him to choose whatever he wished. Solomon said to Yahweh: Give your servant an understanding heart to rule your people, that I may discern between good and evil. This greatly pleased Yahweh, and he said to him: Because you have asked for this, and not for long life or riches or the death of your enemies, I will give you a wise and understanding heart. But that which you did not ask for, namely riches, honour, and that none of the other kings should be equal to you your whole life long, that you shall receive. And Solomon's wisdom increased.

Thus, two harlots once came to him for judgement. Both had borne a son at about the same time and lived in the same house. The son of one of the women had died three days later, and that same night his mother secretly exchanged her child for the other. But the mother of the living child had noticed this in the morning and now desired justice from the king, while the other woman challenged her claim. Solomon had a sword brought, and ordered the living child to be cut in two so that each woman would have a half. Then the mother of the living child cried out: Give her the child, don't kill it. – The other insisted that the child be divided. Thereupon Solomon gave the child to the right mother, who had begged that the child be allowed to live.

The size of his kingdom forced Solomon to divide it into twelve regions, each managed by a royal officer. Solomon ran a lavish court. Thus he had four thousand horses for his chariots and twelve thousand horsemen. And each of the officers had to provide for the court and the garrisons for one month out of the year. And Solomon ruled over all the kingdoms between the Euphrates, Philistia and Egypt. He lived in peace with all his neighbours and received rich presents from them all. Everyone in his kingdom could dwell in safety beneath his vine and his fig trees. Elohim gave Solomon very great wisdom and understanding and a rich intelligence. His wisdom excelled the wisdom of all those from the East and Egypt. And he spoke three thousand proverbs, and his songs were a thousand and five. He spoke of all the trees, of beasts, of birds, and of the other living creatures. People came from all lands to hear his wisdom.

After a time, Solomon also built the temple, as he had promised David he would do. The king of Tyre helped him. Solomon paid for the cedar wood from Lebanon and the other building materials with corn and oil. He had the work done by conscripting labourers. For seven years he was building the temple, while his own palace took thirteen years. When the temple was finished, Solomon gathered all the heads of the tribes, to accompany the ark of the covenant, along with the tent and the sacred vessels, in solemn procession to the temple. And Solomon composed the words of consecration:

> Yahweh, you have said you would dwell in thick darkness,
> Now I have built you a house to dwell in,
> a place for you to abide for ever.

Then Solomon made over twenty cities to the king of Tyre to pay for building the temple (but the king was not pleased with them). He had received from the Pharaoh the lands around Gezer as a dowry for the latter's daughter. Solomon had this city enlarged into a fortress, as he did with other cities. Around that time he also received the visit of the queen of Sheba, who had heard of his wisdom and riches. Solomon answered all her riddles and questions, and he showered her with gifts just as she, too, had brought the king rich presents. Solomon amassed these riches in his temple.

But Yahweh let a strong adversary arise against Solomon in Hadad the Edomite, who had grown up in Egypt and, against the Pharaoh's will, went back to his homeland, which David had once conquered.

Elohim made Rezon of Zobah grow strong, the man who usurped the kingship of Damascus and became an opponent of Solomon. He also supported Hadad in Edom. Jeroboam was yet another enemy who conspired against Solomon. Jeroboam was the supreme overseer of the forced labourers from the northern tribes in Solomon's service, and he rebelled against the king. He escaped the threat of arrest by fleeing to Egypt. Solomon ruled over Israel for forty years, then he died and was buried in the city of his father David.

[Kings 2–7; 8:1–13; 9:10–18; 10:1–20; 11:14–29, 41–3]

b. Others say that Solomon consecrated the temple with a great dedicatory prayer and many sacrifices, and that he offered sacrifices only at this site. When Solomon had thus completed the temple, Yahweh appeared to him and said: I have chosen this temple, which you have built, as a dwelling for my name, and my eyes and heart shall be there for ever. But if you and your children do not keep my commandments and statutes, and serve other gods, then I will cause Israel and the temple to be destroyed.

At first Solomon walked in the laws of Yahweh. He built many cities. For the construction work he made use of forced labour, not recruiting Israelites, but only people belonging to subject nations. But his soldiers and highest officials were Israelites. Later he transgressed Yahweh's laws, for he loved many foreign women, apart from the Pharaoh's daughter. Thus he had seven hundred wives who were princesses, and three hundred concubines. And they seduced him into following other gods and sacrificing to them, to the goddess Ishtar and the god Milcom. He also had high places built for sacrifices to the Moabite god Chemosh and Molech of the Ammonites.

Yahweh became very angry at this, and told Solomon: Because you have disobeyed me, after your death I will give your kingdom to your servant. I will leave only a single tribe to your son, for the sake of my servant David and for Jerusalem.

[I Kings 8:14–66; 9:1–9; 10:22–4; 11:1–13]

(i) The name Solomon (actually Shalomo, meaning approximately 'the peaceful one') was, we may assume, a coronation name, given to its bearer to attest that, after David's ceaseless wars, the god Yahweh wanted peace. Solomon's original name may actually have been Jedidiah, as appears from the note in 2 Samuel 12:25. He was certainly a historical figure, and his reign occurred during the second third of the tenth century B.C.

(ii) The first account of Solomon's life was composed in Jerusalem sometime about the eighth century B.C. For this reason, it pays scarcely any attention to events going on among the northern tribes. To this source the most important thing is the description of the king's buildings, riches and wisdom. Solomon is obviously viewed as a figurehead acting on orders from Yahweh, who is lord of the temple. Yahweh does not need war, but an era of commerce and prosperity. Hence all the officials of his father David who adhere to the old policies are put to death.

(iii) Solomon's political system is that of an oriental despot. Workers are forced to do the jobs necessary for the upkeep of the state and the temple. The Jerusalem narrator reports that Solomon conscripted workers from Israel. This is a way of stating Jerusalem and Judah's claim on the northern tribes, which, after Solomon's death, broke away from the south as the kingdom of Israel under Jeroboam. This claim is dropped by the second, later narrator from the sixth century B.C., when he expressly declares that Solomon conscripted workers only from the subject nations, while the Israelites looked after the army and the civil service.

(iv) The wisdom of Solomon (a favourite topic with the first narrator) as well as his great poetic and rhetorical achievements are essential for depicting him as the good and righteous king. This theme reveals how great a distance separates the king from his people, and it aims at substantiating the dignity, necessity and unique qualities of the king. This *topos* may be found in all royal mythologies, and tells us nothing about the real Solomon and his talents.

(v) The older narrator is still aware that Elohim and Yahweh are different gods. Elohim strengthens one opponent of Solomon, Yahweh another. On Yahweh's side are Jeroboam and Hadad of Edom, while Rezon of Damascus fights on Elohim's side. The language of myth translates rival gods into political opponents.

The much later narrator, who belongs to the Deuteronomic tradition, attributes Solomon's downfall to his apostasy from Yahweh, the god of Israel, and to his involvement with the gods of his innumerable wives. The attack on polytheism in Jerusalem at the time of Solomon was no idle polemic: such cults had undoubtedly flourished until the last third of the seventh century B.C., till the reform of King Josiah.

(On the story of Solomon's birth, see also IX.3.a (p. 179) and IX.3.c.v (p. 182). On the building of the temple, see X.2.ii (p. 200).)

IX.5. *Jeroboam and Rehoboam*

Jeroboam was the son of Nebat from Zereda in Ephraim. His father was already dead when, because of his industriousness, Jeroboam was appointed by Solomon supreme overseer of the conscript workers from the northern tribes.

But Jeroboam revolted against Solomon. Once he met the prophet Ahijah of Shiloh out on the open road. Ahijah tore his cloak into twelve pieces and gave ten of them to Jeroboam, prophesying to him that, after Solomon's death, Yahweh would give him ten tribes of the kingdom and make him king over Israel. And Jeroboam fled from Solomon to Egypt and remained there till he heard the news of the king's death. Then he returned and came to Shechem, where the assembly had gathered to make Solomon's son Rehoboam king over Israel, after he had already become king in Jerusalem and Judah. Jeroboam and the whole assembly spoke with Rehoboam and said: We will be subject to you if you promise not to impose any more heavy burdens and forced labour upon us, as your father did. Rehoboam asked for three days to think it over and consulted his royal advisers. The older ones, who had already served under his father, advised him to agree to the demand, but the younger ones, whose advice he took, told him to give the following answer: My little finger is thicker than my father's loins. And if my father laid a heavy yoke upon you, I will make it even heavier. If my father chastised you with whips, I will chastise you with scorpions. – Now when Rehoboam gave this answer to Jeroboam on the third day, all Israel cried out:

> What portion have we in David?
> We have no inheritance in the son of Jesse!
> To your tents, O Israel,
> now see to your own house, David!

And they chose Jeroboam to be their king. But Rehoboam was compelled to flee, when he tried, with Adoram his supreme taskmaster, to bring the rebels to heel. Adoram himself was stoned to death. Yahweh sent his command to Rehoboam through the prophet Shemaiah: You shall not fight against your brothers in Israel, for this has come about because of me. – And so Judah did not fight against Israel.

After this, Jeroboam fortified Shechem and made it his city. But so as not to endanger his people by the attractive power of the temple in Jerusalem, he set up two golden bulls in Bethel and Dan, and he had the word proclaimed: This is your god, O Israel, who brought you out of Egypt. He also erected small sanctuaries on the high places, and permitted non-Levites to be made priests. And Yahweh sent a prophet from Judah to Bethel, to warn Jeroboam against such worship, and threatened Israel with ruin because of this.

After a reign of twenty-two years, Jeroboam died. He was followed by his only son Nadab, after another had died in childhood. While the child lay sick, Ahijah, a prophet from Shiloh in Judah, on orders from Yahweh, had foretold the downfall of the house of Jeroboam and of the kingdom of Israel.

Rehoboam was king in Jerusalem and Judah for only seventeen years, and did everything that was evil in Yahweh's eyes. He brought back the cults practised by the people who had lived in the land before. His son Abijam followed him on the throne of David.

[I Kings 11:26–12:33; 13:1–14, 21; 15:1–2]

(i) The stories of Jeroboam and Rehoboam belong to the Jerusalem tradition; they date from a period after the fall of the northern kingdom. Writing in the last third of the sixth century B.C., the narrator presents the facts as they were viewed from Jerusalem.

(ii) In the narrator's opinion, the break-up of the kingdom took place with Yahweh's approval. The picture of the split between the two halves of the kingdom is undoubtedly accurate. The northern tribes – henceforth the name for the tribal confederation centred around Bethel and Shechem would be 'Israel' – were more conservative than Judah. The influence of the Jerusalem court was not strong enough in the north to dissolve the old tribal arrangements. In particular, the system for levying troops continued as before. Socio-economically, the divided kingdoms were two different worlds, the south being much more advanced than the north.

(iii) The wrath of the priestly narrator from Judah is directed chiefly at the revival of the ancient sanctuaries in Bethel and Dan. For the measures Jeroboam took against pilgrimages by northerners to Jerusalem cost the temple there a drastic loss of income. At the same time, the priests of Jerusalem thought it would endanger the doctrinal structure, so painfully and ingeniously elaborated, of the one and only God of Israel, if they conceded that the same god could be worshipped under an altogether different form in Bethel and Dan. Jeroboam's proclamation that the bulls of Bethel and Dan were the god who had brought Israel out of Egypt may refer to contemporary beliefs about Yahweh as a bull-god, for such an announcement would have been unthinkable without traditions to back it up (see II.4 (p. 52)).

(iv) The prophecy by Ahijah of Shiloh on the end of Jeroboam's dynasty and the downfall of Israel is a projection by Jerusalem of subsequent history back into the past. The myth of Yahweh as the lord who makes history happen is the explanation for the short duration of the northern kingdom (from 932 to 722 B.C.). The narrator does not blame the disintegration of Israel on its socio-economic structure and its unstable, incompetent government, but rather ascribes it to the will of Yahweh. The gulf between the key religious symbol and social reality now yawns so wide that the narrator no longer centres his attention on human beings (the obvious actors and sufferers in his story), but on the divine king Yahweh, upon whose good pleasure history depends. In his fable, 'How Treachery Came to Russia', Rilke once wrote: 'In primitive languages many things have the same name. And so there is a country called God, and the one who rules it is also called God. Simple peoples often cannot tell their country and their emperor apart. Both are great and kind, frightful and great.' We must not assume that the narrator of the Bible's royal mythologies speaks with such archaic naïvety, which has, quite to the contrary, been left behind. For classical biblical prophecy, a genre unique in history, overcomes the primitive dialectic of country-as-people and country-as-God by claiming that the catastrophic history of the erstwhile people of God is God's punishment for the misdeeds of his nation's kings and princes. In this way, the prophets extend Yahweh's jurisdiction beyond the borders of his land into the universal; they make him king of the world, 'lord of the four parts of the world', to cite one of the titles given the king of Assyria.

(v) The large number of kings following Jeroboam in the northern kingdom reveals a grave problem: the northern tribes stuck with the outdated elective monarchy, as they had known it from the time of Saul and David. This meant that, at every election, the rival parties engaged in great battles, which persisted during the reign that followed. Accordingly, *coups d'état* and royal assassinations were no rarity in the history of the northern kingdom. In addition, successors to the throne who had been designated as such by one prophet or other knew well – once they had managed to get anointed, often in curious ways – how to make illusory promises and procure enough followers to overthrow the king. All this contributed significantly to the northern kingdom's continuing weakness.

IX.6. *Jehu*

The prophet Elisha had witnessed all the horrors set afoot by Queen Jezebel in Israel [cf. VIII.2 (p. 155)]. And so he charged one of his disciples to go to Ramoth in Gilead and by order of Yahweh to anoint Jehu, the son of Nimshi, king over Israel. At this same time Joram, Jezebel's son, was still king over Israel.

After his companions had learned of Jehu's anointing, they paid him homage and set out for Jezreel, where the king was recovering from the battle against the king of the Syrians. Ahaziah, king of Judah, was also staying with him. Jehu was Joram's field commander, and hence both kings went out to meet him when the guard announced his name. But Jehu shot them both with arrows. When he arrived at the palace, Queen Jezebel was hurled out of the window in all her finery by her own stewards, and trampled by Jehu's cavalry. The dogs came and devoured her flesh, as the prophet Elijah had once foretold.

After this Jehu had all the king's living relatives in Samaria put to death, along with all his priests and counsellors. When he was on the road and met the brothers of the king of Judah, he had them all slain. Then he organized a great Baal festival, to which all believers in Baal had to come. Jehu had them all put to the sword and the temple of Baal destroyed and desecrated. On account of this, Yahweh told Jehu: I am well pleased with you because of your deeds, and so your throne will remain in your family through four generations.

But Jehu did not cease worshipping before the golden bulls which Jeroboam, the first king in Israel after the break-up of David's kingdom, had introduced. He died after reigning twenty-eight years. In his lifetime, Israel had already become smaller and weaker, for the king of Syria had conquered great portions of the country.

[II Kings 9–10]

(i) The story of Jehu shows clearly how a military commander usurps royal power. He overthrows the king with the help of a loyal band of daring soldiers, and has the king and all his adherents put to death. The narrator explicitly makes Yahweh bless Jehu for his display of zeal in murdering all the servants of Baal. The details of this palace revolution sound convincing: presumably this is just the way Jehu came to power.

(ii) From a mythological point of view, it is noteworthy that the narrator (who must have been a resident of Judah in the middle of the seventh century B.C.) can depict a ghastly zealot in this fashion. Even if the numbers cited in the story are less than those usually found in ancient Near Eastern royal inscriptions, they are surely not accurate. Apart from this, it is significant that the prophet Elisha evidently sees nothing objectionable in what Jehu does. The narrator, too, inured to the proverbial cruelty of the ancient Near East, simply wishes to give an example to deter anyone who might toy with the idea of infidelity to the great king Yahweh.

IX.7. *Hezekiah*

In the days of the last king of Israel, Hezekiah was king of Judah and Jerusalem, where he reigned for twenty-nine years. He did only what was right in Yahweh's eyes. He got rid of the sanctuaries on the high places and cleansed Jerusalem of all foreign cults. He defeated the Philistines and managed to shake off the sovereign authority of the Assyrians by paying them tribute. At this same time, the Assyrians were conquering the northern kingdom of Israel and deporting parts of the population. Hezekiah soon attempted to recover his complete independence, and he succeeded: when the Assyrians tried to subdue rebellious Judah once again by besieging Jerusalem, they were forced into a premature retreat, because Yahweh's angel slew thousands in the camp one night. Before this, the Assyrian general had sought by means of negotiations outside the walls to get the city to capitulate, and he had warned against trusting the Egyptians or even the help of Yahweh. But Hezekiah listened to the prophet Isaiah's [cf. VII.4 (p. 140)] advice and made no response to a letter from the Assyrian king Sennacherib. For Isaiah had foretold to him, announcing the word of Yahweh, that Sennacherib would be punished for his blasphemy: I will put my ring in your nose and my bridle in your lips, and I will turn you back by the way you came. And I, Yahweh, will defend this city, to save it.

In those days Hezekiah fell gravely ill. Then Isaiah came to him and told him that he would die. When the king greatly bemoaned his fate, Yahweh took pity on him and gave him fifteen more years of life. After this, Hezekiah received an embassy from the king of Babylon, to whom Hezekiah was evidently very well disposed. He showed the envoys all the treasures of his kingdom. But because of that Isaiah directed a message to Hezekiah from Yahweh: The time will come when everything in your palace will be brought to Babylon. And some of your sons will be made eunuchs in the palace of the king of Babylon.

[II Kings 18–20. There is an almost verbatim parallel to these texts in Isaiah 36:1–22; 37; 38:1–8, 21–2; 39]

(i) This outline of the reign of King Hezekiah of Judah and Jerusalem can be shown to have some historical validity. In the Assyrian royal inscriptions, Sennacherib boasts: 'From the Judaean Hezekiah I captured after the siege forty-six fortresses [i.e. larger towns] and innumerable smaller cities [i.e. villages]. For booty, I carried away 200,150 people, young and old, men and women. And I locked Hezekiah like a bird in a cage in his capital city of Jerusalem.'

Furthermore, we can be reasonably sure that the envoys of the Babylonian king Merodach-baladan (Mardukapalidinna) took the trouble to visit Hezekiah of Jerusalem, because Mardukapalidinna tried several times to overthrow the Assyrian king and annex his throne. It took another century (604 B.C.) before King Nebuchadnezzar succeeded in doing this. He went on to conquer Jerusalem in 586 B.C. and to fulfil Yahweh's prophecy spoken by Isaiah (see VIII.4 (p. 159)), which, of course, must be ascribed to a later source.

(ii) Hezekiah was, along with Josiah (see VI.5 (p. 131)), the most important king of Judah. During his reign the prophet Isaiah appeared on the scene. The fact that the story of King Hezekiah occurs in Isaiah and II Kings with practically the same wording surely indicates that both texts had a common written source. This would have been the *Book of the History of the Kings of Judah*, now lost, which had a counterpart, likewise no longer extant, in Israel. Both these books are not to be confused with the biblical books of Chronicles, which originated in Judah and once formed a unit with the books of Ezra and Nehemiah. The books of Chronicles were designed as a history of the kingdom of Judah, which was understood as the kingdom of God. That is why they begin with the birth of Adam and end with the rebuilding of the temple by Nehemiah. The presentation draws upon older sources from the Pentateuch to the books of Kings. The books of Chronicles were composed around the middle of the fourth century B.C., the books of Kings and the story of Hezekiah toward the close of the sixth century B.C.

(iii) An important mythological point in the story of Hezekiah is that Yahweh can change his mind very quickly. First, he condemns the king to death, then he lets him live another fifteen years. The great king need not supply reasons to explain his turnabout. His favour and disfavour are beyond rational calculation. The under-king is at the mercy of the great king, for weal or woe. Yahweh may accept his act of submission or reject it. Hezekiah is under-king to Yahweh the great king. He pledges a change of heart and renewed obedience. Thereupon Yahweh graciously accepts him and gives him another fifteen years in his feudal office of prince in Judah. Thus, what was originally a ritual between vassal and lord, becomes for biblical piety the model for the merciful God's forgiveness of the repentant sinner.

X. Jerusalem: City and Temple

X.1. *The City*

In the days of Abraham there was already a king ruling in Jerusalem. When the Israelites began to settle the country, they also captured Jerusalem and reduced it to ashes.

But David was the first to conquer and occupy Jerusalem, which was still a Jebusite city at the time, along with the stronghold of Zion. He did this after being crowned king of Judah, and he named the stronghold David's city. He expanded it considerably, and there he had the ark of Elohim brought, which was given the title, 'The name of Yahweh Sabaoth abides upon it above the Cherubim'. David's successor Solomon built a splendid palace in the city, and above all he built the temple of Yahweh. Solomon made the walls around Jerusalem higher and strengthened them. They were torn down for the first time by Joash, king of Israel, when he fought King Amaziah of Judah and plundered the temple and the city, as the Egyptian Shishak had done before in the days of King Rehoboam. But King Hezekiah fortified Jerusalem again, so that it withstood the onslaught of the Assyrians. The city, however, could not hold out against the siege by Nebuchadnezzar, and surrendered to him. Nebuchadnezzar ordered the city and the temple to be pillaged, and the royal family, as well as all officials and artisans, carried off to Babylon. He installed Zedekiah as governor, an uncle of the last king, Jehoiachin. When Zedekiah rebelled against him, Nebuchadnezzar stormed the city and burned it to the ground. Zedekiah was blinded, after his children were murdered right before his eyes, and taken as a captive to Babylon. Only the farmers were allowed to remain in the land; all others were carried off.

Not until the fall of Babylon were the people of Jerusalem able to return, by command of the Persian king Cyrus, and to rebuild their temple and city. They were permitted to take from the temple treasury of Babylon all the sacred vessels that Nebuchadnezzar had looted from the temple of Jerusalem. In addition, Cyrus allocated to them – and his successor Darius confirmed the privilege – sufficient means from the royal revenues to carry on the rebuilding. The Jewish priest Ezra journeyed from Babylon to Jerusalem with a royal decree to arrange everything in accordance with the law of the 'God of heaven', lest the wrath of this god come upon the kingdom of Persia. And Ezra, as well as the Jewish governor Nehemiah, appointed by the king of Persia, faithfully arranged everything and built up the city and the temple, as Yahweh had once commanded their ancestors to do. They also got the citizens to commit themselves afresh to Yahweh's Law. The returnees decided that the tenth part of each tribe from the house of Israel should dwell in the city, and the other nine tenths should live in the country. They followed the old custom of drawing lots to see who should henceforth live in Jerusalem.

The city was not enlarged again until Herod the Great was king in Jerusalem under Roman rule. Herod had the temple renovated, endowed the city with splendid buildings and erected the third city wall. This was the magnificent city that Jesus knew. It collapsed in dust and ashes when the Romans came to crush the rebellious Jews.

And then there was nothing left of the city of David but a heap of rubble. Isaiah's prophecy that, in the last days, the mountain where the house of the Lord stood would be established, that it would be exalted above all mountains, that it would be a place of pilgrimage for all the nations, had not been fulfilled. There was weeping and lamentation to be heard in the ruins, not the promised 'exultation of those ransomed by Yahweh, returning home'.

And yet Yahweh had sworn to protect the city for David's sake and for his own. For he had loved Jerusalem, as a young man loves his bride, had wooed her and given her rich presents, adorned her with jewels and with a beauty whose fame was widespread among the nations. And he watched in sorrow how his bride did not return his love, but went after other gods. Still he loved the virgin Jerusalem so greatly that he wished to forgive her even these transgressions, remembering his vow of fidelity. And Yahweh swore that he would strike the shepherds who now fed his flock, his people, his city, and would care for his flock himself, which a new king David would serve as shepherd. For a small remnant of his people would always remain until the day when there would be a new heaven and a new earth, and the holy city, the new Jerusalem, would come down out of heaven like a bride adorned for her husband Yahweh.

[Genesis 14:18–20; Joshua 10:1; Judges 1:7; II Samuel 5:6–9; 6; I Kings 6–7; II Kings 14:12–14; I Kings 14:25–6; II Kings 18; 24:10–17; 25; Book of Ezra; Book of Nehemiah; Isaiah 2:2–4; 35:10; 37:35; Ezekiel 16; 34; Micah 4:1–3; Revelation 21:2–10]

(i) Jerusalem (i.e. 'the city of peace') is to this day the holy place *par excellence* for Jews and Christians. Even Muslims call the site *el quds* ('the holy'), meaning the entire city. Jerusalem acquired this importance by a long historical process. After Yahweh accepted Solomon's temple as his dwelling place, the city of David and residence of the kings of Judah – more so than the nation state of Judah – became a symbol and code word for the people of God (Yahweh, Elohim and Allah). The Persian title for God, 'the lord of heaven', enters the Bible's lexicon in II Chronicles 36:23, Ezra 1:2, and elsewhere. In this borrowing, we see one of the ways ancient Judaism assimilated foreign material. It shared this practice with other Near Eastern peoples, who often identified the supreme deity of their conqueror with their own highest god.

(ii) The historical information that the Bible provides here would seem to be accurate. We have evidence from the Amarna texts (which mention a King Abdihipa as ruling over 'Urusalim' in the fourteenth century B.C.) that Jerusalem is older than Israelite history. It may have been the city's strength that prevented the invading tribes of Israelites from capturing it until so late a date. One thing we do know, the fortified hill with the ancient name of Zion, which David made into his stronghold, originally lay outside the city and only merged with it as a result of the expansion under Solomon and the Herodians. For the time being, David brought the ark at first to his stronghold. The later biblical predilection for the name Zion to designate Jerusalem is linked with the prophets' plan of reviving, for the benefit of the temple, the old tribal piety of the nomadic patriarchs. When the prophet Zechariah (ch. 9) addresses the population of Jerusalem as the daughter of Zion, he is consciously referring to earlier sociological conditions, not to the cultic institutions of the later monarchy.

(iii) The city became more of an attractive force because of Solomon's temple than because of the royal palace. Beginning with the cultic reform of King Josiah, if not sooner, it grew perceptibly stronger, and it continually survived the various plunderings and pillagings until its final destruction by the Romans. The city's vitality was based on the unique status of the temple, which believing Jews were obliged to visit three times a year. The city lived on the business generated by the temple. Like every ancient temple in Greece, Rome or Babylon, it was protected by strong walls and contained storerooms, a bank, the state and temple treasuries. Eschatological prophecies had seized upon the city's vitality as an important motif expressing the prospects for survival of God's people, concluding that Yahweh would keep faith with his city, and at the end of time would inaugurate from Jerusalem the new age of peace and justice. This priestly teaching, it goes without saying, was warmly greeted and supported by the inhabitants of Jerusalem, because it ensured their existence, ideologically speaking, through all their political troubles and confusion.

(iv) At the time of Jesus, the Herodians' splendid Jerusalem was also a centre of pious reformers and zealots. But the city had not yet become an archetypically 'holy place', because pious Jews in those days did not think salvation would be had merely from being present in Jerusalem, but from the arrival and dominion of a divine king from the house of David. (In this, Jerusalem differed from, say, Olympia in Greece.) This is the only way to explain why, in the vision of the new Jerusalem in Revelation, the city no longer has a temple. The temple has become superfluous because God himself is now physically present as king, and rules like any other king. Post-biblical Judaism shared this notion.

(v) The Bible's habit of speaking of Jerusalem as God's beloved is rooted in the old way of thinking that saw cities and sanctuaries as having originally been the homes of sacred queens who had been conquered by patriarchal foreign invaders. But, by the time that biblical prophecy was flourishing, this concrete aspect of its past had already fallen into oblivion. Only the feminine gender of the Hebrew word for city ('*îr*) remained as the last vestige of that imaginative world where house, homeland and nation were enveloped by the symbol of the Great Mother, the many-breasted Magna Mater of late antiquity. The name of the first historically attested king of Urusalim, Abdihipa, that is, 'servant of Hiba', refers us back to this world, because Hiba is known from other sources as a Hittite goddess.

(vi) Jerusalem plays a major role in Christian mythology. It is in Jerusalem that the gospels place the most important incidents from the life of Jesus. To this day, the city is still crowded with Christian shrines, including the Church of the Holy Sepulchre, the sacred tomb of Jesus on the hill of Golgotha, the Katholikon, where the graves of Adam and Melchizedek, the legendary king of Jerusalem (see IV.1.c (p. 82)) are shown, the Stations of the Cross, and the garden of Gethsemane (see XIII.1 (p. 218)). All the leading branches of Christianity are represented at these sites. Early Christian mythology expected that, after his ascent to heaven, Jesus would very soon return to Jerusalem, to complete the kingdom of salvation (also called the kingdom of God or kingdom of heaven), which had already been inaugurated. The temple no longer had anything to do with this expectation, it was all a matter of the final, radical reversal of the existing situation in the world.

(vii) The image of the city of Jerusalem as a woman has been treated impressively in the hymns and poetical texts of the Bible, e.g. in the 'Lamentations of Jeremiah'. These, to be sure, were not written by the prophet; they were composed in different centuries (chs. 2 and 4 perhaps during the Babylonian exile, chs. 1 and 5 in post-exilic Jerusalem). Thus the poet writes, for instance, in the first Lamentation, v. 1:

> Ah, how lonely lies the city,
> that once was full of people,
> how is she become like a widow,
> she that was great among the nations.
> The princess among the cities,
> she must do slave's labour.

In the second Lamentation, v. 13:

> What shall I compare you to,
> O daughter of Jerusalem?
> What shall I liken you to, so as to comfort you,
> virgin daughter of Zion?

(viii) In the time of transition from the theocratic monarchy of antiquity to the classical epoch of Roman slavery the social tension between lord and servant raises the problem of grace and merit. This increasingly dominates religious thought, and is permanently lodged in the image of God as a lover. The grace bestowed by the despot turns into the love that the supreme god has for humanity. Love is supposed to grant what one's own achievement cannot, namely, admission to the divine kingdom of glory.

X.2. *The Temple*

After Solomon had ascended the throne of his father and had brought about order and tranquillity in the land, he remembered Yahweh's word to his father, that his son was to build a house for the name of Yahweh. And so he sent messengers to the king of Tyre and asked him for artisans and building materials, especially cedar from Lebanon. His wish was granted. Thousands of conscripted labourers busied themselves with the transport of building supplies and in the quarries. All the material was prepared before it came to the building site, so that no sound was heard there of hammer or axe or iron tool. The temple was built entirely of dressed stone and was a hundred cubits long, fifty cubits wide, and thirty cubits high. There were side-rooms running all around the building, on three storeys which were connected by stairways. On the east side was a great entrance hall. In the temple itself a transverse wall separated the Holy of Holies, where the ark was kept, from the outer sanctuary. The Holy of Holies was panelled with gilded cedar, the other room only with carved wood. The carvings were chiefly of cherubim, flowers and fruits. On the back wall of the Holy of Holies, two ten-cubit cherubim were set up, covering the entire wall. In front of the Holy of Holies, in the temple proper, Solomon erected a gilded altar. In front of the temple he had two bronze pillars, eighteen cubits high, set up to the right and left of the vestibule. Their lily-work capitals were decorated with pomegranates.

For sacrifice in the temple Solomon had a great bronze water basin cast, supported by twelve statues of bulls, with three bulls facing each of the cardinal points. Besides this he ordered ten bronze stands on wheels, embellished with cherubim, lions and palmettos. The workman, Hiram of Tyre, also made golden candlesticks, pots, shovels, basins, lamps, door hinges, the table for the showbread, and the altar. Construction went on for ten years until the temple was finished. And Solomon dedicated the temple with pomp and pageantry, after he had brought the ark into the Holy of Holies. And he sacrificed an enormous number of sheep and oxen. The festival of consecration lasted fourteen days. Others say that he let the people go home on the eighth day.

After this Yahweh appeared to Solomon and told him: I have hallowed this house and have put my name there for ever. But if you cease to observe my laws and commandments, and go after other gods, then I will uproot you from this land and I will have this house torn down, so that all who pass by will ask: How could Yahweh let this happen? In the temple chambers king and priests gathered together the treasure, which was first plundered by the Egyptian king Shishak during the reign of Rehoboam. Later, Joash of Israel also robbed the gold and silver temple vessels. After that Hezekiah of Judah took some of the temple treasure, as well as the gold foil from the temple walls, to meet Sennacherib's demands for tribute. Finally, Nebuchadnezzar of Babylon took whatever was left, before burning the temple down.

After the fall of Babylon the Jews returned to Jerusalem under their governor Zerubbabel, who had full authority from the Persian king. On the former site of the temple they rebuilt it just as it had been during Solomon's reign. The temple of Zerubbabel stood until King Herod renovated it. The Romans destroyed this temple when they took Jerusalem by storm.

Yahweh allowed all this destruction, in keeping with what he had already said through the prophet Jeremiah: I will give this city into the hands of Nebuchadnezzar, king of Babylon, and he will burn it down. For ever since this city was built, it has angered and enraged me, so that I must do away with it; and its people have polluted my house with strange idols. But later I will raise it up again and people it in peace and salvation.

Through Ezekiel [see VIII.6 (p. 165)], Yahweh gave the exiles in Babylon a view of the new temple and the new Jerusalem in a vision that spirited the prophet off to the inner court of the temple. The glory of Yahweh filled the entire house, and Ezekiel heard Yahweh saying to him: Son of man, this is the place of my throne and the place of the soles of my feet, where I will dwell for ever among the children of Israel. And now describe the house to the children of Israel, so that they may be ashamed of their sins and mend their ways, that I may bring them back to this city and to my mountain, on which my house shall stand, the Holy of Holies. And it shall also come to pass that, from my house, a rich stream of blessings will flow for the land and the city.

Then the prophet Haggai encouraged Zerubbabel and the people who were building the second temple, but had lost heart. He told them Yahweh's words: Only a little while longer, and I will shake the heavens and the earth and all nations, and then I will fill this house with glory, a glory greater than that of the former house, and in this place I will give peace.

Yahweh likewise showed Zechariah in visions at night the restoration of the temple, the city of Jerusalem and the high-priesthood, and said to him: I have returned to Jerusalem, and I will dwell in Jerusalem. Jerusalem shall be called a city of truth, the mountain of Yahweh Sabaoth, the mountain of holiness. And the streets of Jerusalem shall be filled with hale old men and women and also with children at play. They are to be a seed of peace. And then all nations will flock to the mountain of Yahweh.

[I Kings 5:15–6:37; 7:13–51; 8; 9:1–9; 14:25–8; II Kings 14:13–14; 18:14–16; 25; Jeremiah 52; 32; Ezra 2:64–70; 3; 6; Ezekiel 43:5–7; 40–48; Haggai 2:6–9; Zechariah 1–8:17]

(i) The historical traditions contained in accounts of the building of the temple are reliable. The temple of Jerusalem is comparable to those of the leading cities of Phoenicia, Tyre and Sidon, a type structurally closer to Egyptian models than Assyrian or Babylonian. The temple tradition is bound up with Jerusalem and its priesthood. If the temple none the less emerges as a theme in prophetic literature, that is only when the prophets in question come from priestly circles in Judah.

(ii) The detailed description of the temple and palace in Jerusalem, including the furnishings, and a report on Solomon's mercantile practices (see IX.4 (p. 184)), renders rather accurately the world of a Near Eastern theocratic king, and shows how much the cultures of the various kingdoms were all of a piece. The artists and craftsmen working in Tyre are the same as those working in Sidon and Jerusalem. They bring their own forms and pictorial elements with them. Bulls, lions, cherubim, lambs and fruits had no trouble gaining admission to the repertory of motifs of Israelite art. None of the narrators accuses Solomon of idolatry for any of this, because Yahweh himself accepted this splendid house. To get an idea of its size, recall that a cubit measures about forty-five centimetres.

The prohibition against graven images did not apply to the temple. But the narrator is anxious to point out that, while there were many other images in the temple, there were none of Yahweh. The narrator is evidently unaware of the evolutionary process leading from Yahweh the bull-god to the Yahweh with no shape or form.

The sacrificial ceremonies, the prescriptions for which are listed so exactly in Exodus and Leviticus, more or less correspond to the sacrifices offered elsewhere in the ancient Near East.

(iii) Nothing has been left standing of the temple except the site of Herod's temple (20 B.C.). The sacred rock beneath the Dome of the Rock, the mosque Qubbat as-Sakhra on this site, was presumably the mid-point of the temple. According to Islamic mythology, Muhammad is supposed to have ascended to heaven from this spot. Calif Abd al Malik (A.D. 637–91) erected the Dome of the Rock in honour of Muhammad's ascension.

(iv) The temple site is of importance only for Jewish and Islamic mythology. Christian mythology is more interested in the rest of Jerusalem, where important events of Christian mythology took place. In Christian eschatological expectation, the temple is no longer the centre of interest. In its stead comes the image of God or of his holy people, as, for example, in I Corinthians 3:16–17, where Christians are called God's temple.

(v) The Jerusalem priesthood's association of Yahweh with a single temple and the ethical legislation that the narrator views as bracketed with it is a unique phenomenon in the history of religion. Elsewhere in antiquity the gods possess several houses, but Yahweh insists on having only one house for all time, in Jerusalem. It is there that Yahweh will always return, even if he abandons his house temporarily and it becomes a pile of ruins. With this notion, the priests of Jerusalem usher in a development which will turn David's state into Yahweh's cultic community. Those who are 'redeemed' will be able to come to Jerusalem from all nations. Membership in the community of Yahweh's worshippers is no longer tied to residence in Yahweh's land. Various demands made by the prophets (such as Amos or Isaiah, see VIII.4 (p. 159)) are subsumed under this principle, which also guarantees the temple's economic survival: the temple tax is collected from all Jews, even if they live in Egypt or Rome.

(vi) An important feature of biblical mythology is that with the transformation of a state religion into a cultic one, Yahweh changes from a national to a universal god. As part of this topos, his dwelling place is declared to be the centre of the world (Ezekiel 5:5). For the Greeks, a stone in Delphi was the *omphalos* (navel) of the earth, the exact centre; in the Roman Forum there was the *umbilicus urbis Romae et orbis* ('navel of the city of Rome and the world'). Another element of this topos is the fertility that emanates from the temple. Not only the country (Malachi 3:11–12), but the city of Jerusalem too will be richly blessed. This is expressed in the image of the streets crowded with vigorous old people and playing children.

The picture of a happy Jerusalem is taken up again in apocalyptic literature. (See XIV.3.c (p. 244) and XIV.3.c.vii (p. 247).)

XI. The Wonderful Deeds and Adventures of Job, Esther and Daniel

XI.1. *Job*

In the land of Uz there once lived a man named Job, an upright, god-fearing, pious man. He had seven sons, three daughters, and such wealth in livestock that it won him the greatest esteem. His sons each took turns inviting him every day to a festive meal, to which their sisters also came. But Job offered burnt offerings every day for his children, for he wished to prevent Yahweh from getting angry with them.

One day when the sons of the Elohim gathered before Yahweh, Yahweh asked Satan how his pious and upright servant Job was faring. Satan replied to Yahweh: You have literally showered him with blessings. If you take away your hand from him, he will curse you to your face. Then Yahweh gave Satan permission to take everything away from Job, only he was not to touch Job himself. And Satan struck Job: the Sabeans robbed all his oxen and asses, lightning slew all the sheep, and the Chaldeans drove off all his camels. And, at the same time, all Job's children died, when the house collapsed on them during a banquet. Then Job stood up, tore his clothes, shaved his head, adored Yahweh, and said: Naked came I out of my mother's womb, and naked shall I return. Yahweh has given, and Yahweh has taken away, blessed be the name of Yahweh.

Yahweh heard this and at the next gathering before his throne he called Satan to account. Satan answered: But if you let me touch his bone and his flesh, then Job will curse you to your face. So Satan was permitted to strike Job with leprosy, but he had to spare his life. Job was disowned by his wife, and now sat on the ash heap in front of the village. With all this he said nothing against God.

And his three friends, Eliphaz, Bildad and Zophar, came to visit him and tried to comfort him, when in his agony he cursed the day he was born and the night he was conceived. In long speeches they explained to him that he alone was responsible for his misfortune. But Job was sure of his innocence and sinlessness; he said that only Yahweh could mete out such injustice to him. He quarrelled and disputed with Yahweh. His friends were horrified at this, but Job was sure that Yahweh was tormenting him and that Yahweh would one day free him from these torments.

And Yahweh did not abandon him, but when the wisdom of Job's friends was exhausted, he himself spoke with Job from out of the whirlwind. He showed him how full of wonders the earth was, how the universe was laid out and governed by Yahweh, and that Job was unable to penetrate all these mysteries or to control the great monsters, behemoth and leviathan. Then Job answered Yahweh and repented of his senseless talk. Up till then he had only known Yahweh by hearsay, but now he had seen him with his own eyes. But God rebuked Job's friends, because they had not spoken rightly of him. He ordered them to clear themselves of their guilt by means of burnt offerings and Job's intercession on their behalf. And when Job prayed for his friends, Yahweh reversed Job's fortunes. He gave him back his health and doubled his possessions, together with children, friends and acquaintances. Job died old and full of days, after he had lived to see four generations of his descendants.

[Job 1–32:1; 38–42]

(i) The Book of Job was presumably composed in the fourth century B.C. The many Aramaisms in the text suggest that the poet lived in an area of Persian influence, since Aramaic was the official language of the Persian empire. In 9:24, Job is undoubtedly referring to Alexander of Macedon, and 12:17–13:2 describes the events following Alexander's conquest of the Persians.

(ii) The Book of Job is a poem, an epic. The passage in Ezekiel (14:14 and 14:20) calling Job, along with Noah and Daniel, a model of righteousness, ranks him among the mythological heroes and indicates that Job was certainly not a historical figure. The prose portions of the book (1:1–2:13 and 42:7–17, i.e. the story framing the various speeches) constitute the novella of Job, which was probably the narrative Ezekiel was familiar with. Thus it would have been older than the Book of Ezekiel. The great achievement of the poet-author of Job is his transformation of this small-scale prototype into a mighty epic on the relations between God and man.

In the Septuagint there is a note at the end of the book declaring that Job is none other than King Johab of Edom. This statement is found elsewhere in tradition, but it is improbable, even though biblical authors do sometimes have recourse to non-Israelite narrative material. The Job poet, to be sure, may have drawn upon a legendary figure from such a source, because in 1:1 he situates Job in the land of Uz. According to priestly tradition, Uz was a son of Aram, who was Shem's son and Noah's grandson (Genesis 10:21–3), whereas the Yahwist tradition calls Uz a son of Nahor, Abraham's brother

(Genesis 22:21), who was considered the progenitor of the Aramaeans. Hence, the subject-matter of Job probably originated in the region east of the Jordan and entered the corpus of the legends of Judah when the Edomites invaded parts of that territory which had been depopulated by Nebuchadnezzar.

(iii) The text of Job gives evidence throughout of being the work of a single author, with the exception of chs. 32–7 and some shorter passages. One of these is ch. 28, on wisdom (only Yahweh knows the way to it), which disturbs the flow of the plot. The same is true of the speeches of Elihu (chs. 32–7), who enters the story out of nowhere, delivers four discourses, without letting Job have his say, and then vanishes without a trace. Elihu seeks to refute Job's charges against Yahweh. He argues that Yahweh sends suffering to men to test them and educate them. Yahweh is not unjust, for, as the supreme ruler of the world, he is righteousness itself. Since the reader is familiar with the frame story and knows how Job got into this plight, Elihu's speeches are evidently an attempt to rescue Yahweh's honour, which Job has called into question. They are evidently a learned tract by an eloquent priest who has set himself the task of neutralizing the subversive elements in the Book of Job.

(iv) The main problem raised by the book is the conflict between the just man and his unjust lord or god. The characters of Yahweh and Satan are traditional expressions for forces at work in the narrator's world of the third century B.C. That is to say, kings and despots and their viceroys make use of their right to rob other men of *their* rights, possessions, honour, children and health. Thus, just as the great king whimsically permits his viceroy to plunder a faithful province, so Yahweh lets Satan prove his contention about Job. Of course, the righteous king, otherwise invisible and known to his subjects only by word of mouth, does appear in the end to repair all the destruction caused by his viceroy. But the actual meaning of the epic is that Job has no idea beforehand that the man suffering injustice should not lose faith in his own innocence, but should rather trust that his good name will be restored. This is something that Job has to work out for himself. The Job story that the poet had at his disposal undoubtedly showed Yahweh rewarding Job handsomely for his faith and loyalty. Once Job has acknowledged that he will praise the name of King Yahweh even after everything has been taken away from him, then Yahweh can give everything back to him twice over. The difference between the original novella and the Book of Job lies in the poet's use of the arguments Job has with his friends and with Yahweh himself to depict the process of settling one's differences with the powers that be. The author openly assaults the simple concept of guilt and punishment which was then generally accepted, the theological dogma of retribution with which priests and prophets tried to explain the political realities of the third century B.C. Job's complaints against Yahweh are the poet's complaints against his world. The poet suffers and identifies with Job, not the Job of the frame story, which estranges us from the real world, but the Job of the great speeches, who wants the justice due to him. The frame story as we now have it, integrated into the entire book, shows that the world is subject to the council of the gods. It shows that a man like Job, who is in the dark about the agreements reached by Yahweh and Satan, can still discern the power structures that determine his lot in life, if only he exerts himself and does not lose faith in the justice of his cause. By the end of the story, Job has heard Yahweh himself, seen and understood him, when before he had only known him somewhat by hearsay.

(v) There is mythological significance, not in the two beasts, behemoth, that is, the hippopotamus (Job 40:15–24), and leviathan, the crocodile (Job 40:25–41:26), which are often interpreted mythically, but in the images derived from Wisdom literature. The function of the king or of God is made clear by means of examples from nature and society. Other instances of a similar literary character may be found in Proverbs and Ecclesiastes. The genre of Wisdom literature was widespread both in Egypt and in Babylon, and the biblical variety was akin to these. It differed only in its optimism, which is lacking, for example, in the Egyptian poem, 'Dialogue of an Old Man with his Soul', which rather resembles the pessimistic third chapter of the Lamentations of Jeremiah, another poetic work from about the third century B.C. (For the angels, see II.1.c (p. 42); for Satan, see XII.1 (p. 212).)

XI.2. *Esther*

In the third year of his reign the Persian king Ahasuerus gave a great feast in Susa. It ended with the king's repudiating his wife, because she had refused to appear before him at his command, for he was drunk. But the king divorced her above all on account of the advice of his highest officials, who said that such an example could have evil consequences for the country because all other wives would now no longer obey the commands of their husbands.

After this the king got his officials to search throughout the kingdom for beautiful virgins for the palace harem. The one who pleased him was to be queen. And the choice fell upon Esther, a Jewish orphan, who lived with her uncle Mordecai in Susa. She was very beautiful and very modest besides, and during the long waiting period in the harem she had found favour with everyone. In the seventh year of the king's reign the marriage and her coronation were celebrated.

Soon after this, Mordecai succeeded in uncovering a plot against the king, and he informed Esther of it. Thus she was able to save Ahasuerus' throne and life. Both of the eunuchs who had planned the insurrection were hanged. In their place the king named Haman the Agagite to be head chamberlain, who made it obligatory to bow down before him. Only Mordecai would not bend his knee to Haman, because he was a Jew. Haman flew into a rage over this and decided to have all the Jews in the country exterminated. He obtained the king's consent by telling him that he would confiscate all the wealth of the Jews for the crown. The great bloodbath was to take place all over the kingdom on the same day, the 13th of Adar. Couriers brought the order at once to all the provinces. When Mordecai heard this, he got Esther to intercede for the Jews with the king. Esther invited the king and Haman to a banquet on the following evening, at which the king offered to grant any request she made.

Haman had now, on the advice of his wife, planned to murder Mordecai even before the 13th of Adar. To this end he had a large gallows erected. Then, early the next day, he was summoned to the king. Ahasuerus had not been able to sleep that night, and so he ordered his servants to read to him from the chronicles of the kings of the Medes and Persians. He had been reminded of Mordecai's help in uncovering the conspiracy against him, and had decided to honour Mordecai for this. He asked Haman how a man who had deserved well of the king could be honoured. Thinking he himself was meant, Haman proposed that the man be led through the city, riding the king's horse and wearing royal apparel. Then the king ordered him to honour Mordecai in this way. That same evening at the banquet Haman was condemned to death on the gallows when the king learned from Esther what Haman was planning to do to Mordecai, and still more when he saw how indecently Haman pleaded with Esther for his life. Mordecai was placed over the house of Haman, and bore the king's signet ring, as Haman had done before him.

And now, to avert the disaster threatening the Jews, the king issued a new command throughout the kingdom, which allowed the Jews to defend themselves against their enemies on the 13th of Adar, and to kill all their adversaries, including the women and children. And so, on that day, the Jews held a dreadful reckoning for their enemies, and the Jews were supported by royal authority. In Susa they were also allowed to murder their enemies on the 14th of Adar, but they did not touch their property.

On the 14th and 15th of Adar, on Mordecai's advice, they celebrated the feast of Purim, as a sign of their victory over their enemies. Queen Esther made Mordecai's directive into a permanent law. And Mordecai, Ahasuerus and Esther stood in high esteem with the Jews and with all the inhabitants of the country.

[Esther 1:1–9:19; 10:1–3]

(i) The Book of Esther is a legend. The name of the Persian king Ahasuerus (Artaxerxes, in the Greek translation) is unhistorical, like those of Mordecai, Haman, Esther or Vashti. The Book of the Persian Royal Chronicles is a fiction. Naturally, there is nothing impossible in the king's seizing the opportunity to fill his coffers by means of a pogrom, or that he should have been indifferent to the question of who was to be killed. This sort of situation was common in the Middle East.

(ii) The story is a grim cult-legend for the feast of Purim, which is still celebrated today, but it has no historical credibility. The origins of the festival are still obscure. It is just possible that the story of the Syrian general Nicanor was combined with the tale of Mordecai because the anniversaries of these two men fell around the same time of the year. It may be that the feast of Purim was a tradition among some group of Jews who then introduced it into the biblical canon, although the name of God does not occur once in the entire narrative. Its adoption as a canonical work was possible only by way of the cultic calendar. It was presumably to explain the festival that an editor of the first century B.C. interpolated 9:20–53, on the origins of Purim.

(iii) The book as we now have it was probably composed in the first third of the first century B.C. By then the author could not have had more than a vague notion of the Persian empire, and certainly was unaware that the legend which he made use of concealed an ancient myth. This myth dealt with the battle between the Babylonian god Marduk (the Jew Mordecai) and the Elamite god Humman (the chamberlain Haman), in which Marduk was victorious, just as the Babylonian goddess Ishtar (Esther) ousted the Elamite goddess Vashti. King Ahasuerus must have been a symbol for the land of Babylonia-Assyria-Media, which Marduk had sought to win.

The narrator has turned this myth into a historical tale by adding contemporary colour, as in the exact description of the bridal ceremony, the carrying out of the royal commands, and court etiquette. When the author has Esther's membership in the community of Jewish exiles kept a secret, as Mordecai asks his niece to do, he may have been conscious of the connection to the Ishtar myth. If so, that is why he inserted Hadassah (perhaps meaning 'myrtle') into the story as a Jewish name for Esther.

(iv) The book undoubtedly maintained its place in the canon because, for Jews in the first century B.C., it opened up vistas, for once, of their taking brutal revenge on their enemies, who had been oppressing them for centuries.

XI.3. *Daniel*

Among the Jews deported to Babylon there was a man named Daniel, from an aristocratic family. Because he was handsome and clever, he was chosen to serve in the royal palace. But Daniel and his three companions from Judah were very careful, in accordance with Elohim's command, not to defile themselves with the food and drink offered them at the king's table. King Nebuchadnezzar observed that they were ten times wiser than all the soothsayers and magicians in his kingdom, for Elohim had taught Daniel and his companions the art of understanding every sort of writing and knowledge, and Daniel could even interpret dreams. And so on one occasion he saved his own life and the life of his companions and of all the soothsayers in Babylon, when King Nebuchadnezzar had ordered all the wise men to be killed because they could not tell him what his dream had been and what it meant. But Daniel could, because Elohim had let him know the dream. In it a vision of the future was represented by an image of a mighty hero made partly of gold and partly of silver, and of bronze and of clay, and it was shattered in pieces by a stone. Daniel interpreted the parts of the image to mean the kingdoms that would follow Nebuchadnezzar's.

After this the king elevated Daniel to chief superintendent of all the wise men in Babylon and paid him royal honours. A little later Nebuchadnezzar erected a new idol of gold and ordered everyone to worship the statue. But Daniel's companions refused, whereupon Nebuchadnezzar condemned them to death in the fiery furnace. But the flames did them no harm, for a messenger from heaven had joined them in the fiery furnace. Then Nebuchadnezzar gave orders that no one was to say anything amiss against their god. And he issued a decree to his subjects in which he described a wondrous thing that had happened to him: For a long time I was sick, driven out from the community of men, and I ate the grass of the field as oxen do. And after seven times passed over me I became well again, as Daniel had foretold to me from my dream vision. And now I, King Nebuchadnezzar, praise, honour and thank the king of heaven, for all his deeds are true, and his ways are righteous.

King Nebuchadnezzar was succeeded on the throne by his son Belshazzar. Once, when he was giving a great feast in Babylon and used the golden vessels from the temple of Jerusalem to drink to idols, a hand suddenly appeared on the wall, across from the candlestick, and wrote words that no one could read or interpret. The king was seized with fear, and his face went pale. Then the queen remembered Daniel, whom Nebuchadnezzar had appointed chief of the astrologers, soothsayers, Chaldeans and stargazers, and given him the name Belteshazzar. And Daniel appeared, read and interpreted the writing to the king: *mene, mene, tekel, parsin* – the God of heaven has numbered your kingdom, weighed it, divided it and given it to the Persians. And the king made Daniel the third ruler in the land, before he was murdered that very night and the Mede Darius seized power.

Under Darius, the men who envied Daniel tried to prevent him from worshipping his god by an insidious law. When Daniel continued to say his prayers with his face turned towards Jerusalem, he was thrown into the lions' den. But the lions did not touch him. From this, Darius realized that the god of Daniel was the living God, whose kingdom is indestructible and eternal, who does signs and wonders in heaven and on earth. And Daniel remained the highest official in the realm under both Darius and Cyrus the Persian, but his envious maligners were thrown into the lions' den and torn to pieces.

When Belshazzar was still king in Babylon, Daniel foresaw the future in a dream vision: First he recognized in an apparition of four fighting beasts that the Ancient of Days upon his throne of fire in the clouds would finally pass judgement on the kingdoms of the world and would give the rule to the saints of the Most High, who were represented by a son of man who came with the clouds of heaven.

Then, in the third year of Belshazzar's reign, Daniel saw a vision of the battle between a ram from Persia and a he-goat from the west. The goat's one horn became four, and one of these grew tremendously all the way up to heaven. And Daniel knew that the last days would bring about the end of a mighty and pernicious kingdom in the west.

Last of all, in the third year of Cyrus' reign, Daniel saw how in a great battle of angels the fate of the nations would be decided, and how the kings would fight out the same battle on earth. But the angel would not reveal to him the moment when Michael, the prince of angels, would save the children of Israel, whose names were entered in the book of life; for the words remained hidden and sealed up till the time of the end, and only the wise would understand them.

[Daniel 1–12]

(i) The Book of Daniel was composed in about the year 164 B.C. There is no doubt that it was originally written in Aramaic, and chapters 2:4b–7:28 are still in that language. The beginning and end of the book were translated into biblical Hebrew to win it admission to the sacred scriptures of the Old Testament. The book's origin in the mid second century B.C. also explains how the author could be so unversed in history as to confuse the order of the Babylonian and Persian kings. And there is no evidence that a King Belshazzar ever existed.

(ii) Beyond this, the historical allusions are simply designed to invest the author with a certain authority. We have no reason to believe that, during the exile in Babylon, there was ever a Jewish official with the sort of influence Daniel possessed. The person known to Ezekiel as Daniel was presumably a folkloric figure to whom, as with Noah and Job (Ezekiel 14:14), a particular kind of story naturally became attached. We may assume that Daniel was, like Job, a figure to whom people ascribed prudence, courage and piety (his name means 'God is judge'). Daniel, then, did not originally belong to the pre-exilic narrative tradition of Israel and Judah, but may have come from one of the Aramaean tribes which were thrown together with the deportees into the Babylonian melting pot. (See also XI.1.ii (p. 203).)

(iii) The author is well informed about the situation in Palestine during the reign of the Syrian king Antiochus IV Epiphanes, which suggests that he was a contemporary of the king. In Daniel's night visions, Antiochus is the one horn that became greater than the other three, together with which it emerged at the place of the horn belonging to the he-goat. (The he-goat refers to Alexander the Great, who strikes down the Persian ram.) For Antiochus IV Epiphanes had made an attempt to Hellenize divine worship in Jerusalem. Antiochus was a Seleucid, one of the successors of Seleucus on the throne of the kingdom of Syria. Together with Ptolemaic Egypt, Syria, which was also carved out of Alexander's empire after his death, was the leading force in the Near East in the last centuries before the Christian era. Antiochus forbade the celebration of the Sabbath, circumcision or possession of the Torah under penalty of death. In December 168 B.C., he set up an altar to Olympian Zeus in the temple of Jerusalem, and also dedicated the temple to Zeus. The author had personal experience of this period of persecution, and hence the wicked king Belshazzar must be seen as a portrayal of Antiochus IV.

(iv) The terms used for the god worshipped by Daniel and his companions, the god who appears in the dream visions, are barely comparable to older divine epithets used in the Bible. Most High, God of Heaven, Ancient of Days, God of Gods, Everlasting One are titles more evocative of Persian kings than biblical gods. The section of the book that refers to God as Yahweh (9:1–20) is considerably later than the rest of Daniel. Like other additions that have not been accepted into the canon but are contained in the Septuagint version of Daniel, this one was doubtlessly the work of a priest from Jerusalem who wished to assimilate the book, otherwise so alien to Yahweh, to the body of canonical writings. The additions found in the Greek translation include the stories of Susanna in the bath, of Baal at Babylon, the dragon of Babylon, the prayer of Azariah, and the Song of the Three Young Men in the fiery furnace. These anti-Babylonian motifs, expressed in a blunt and drastic manner, are foreign to the book's Hebrew-Aramaic text, which wages a far more subtle campaign against Babylon. Daniel's request that he and his companions be permitted to adopt a vegetarian diet (1:8–16) may strengthen the conjecture that the author came from a background steeped in Persian religion, since the followers of Zoroaster were intent on preserving the purity of body and soul and preferred vegetarianism. This Persian source would also provide a ready explanation for the unusual god-names.

(v) The doctrine of the succession of world empires and the future kingdom of salvation and happiness, symbolized by a human figure rather than the beasts that appear elsewhere, is typologically different from the rest of Old Testament prophecy, which has no such teaching. Again, this derives from Persian tradition. The Book of Daniel has an eschatological orientation. It deals with the coming of a final age, an after-time, which it cannot describe concretely, but whose approach is foreshadowed by vivid images.

These pictures of the last time are called apocalypses. The Book of Daniel provides some of the earliest evidence for the penetration of this genre into biblical piety. Resolution of the real historical crises in economic and social life is put off to an after-time, problems are transcended. The little theocratic kingdoms with their patriarchal social structures were distintegrating. In the wake of Alexander the Great and his successors, slavery was evidently becoming a permanent feature of life. And so the credibility of the wondrous future envisioned in the Book of Daniel is validated by the presentation of quasi-historical evidence of the power of the 'Most High', who has already shown himself to be the mightiest of gods.

XII. The Devil: Satan, Azazel, Beelzebul and Other Gods

XII.1. *Satan*

a. Satan was one of the sons of God, who occasionally appear before their father's throne to give an account of their doings. He accused Job to Yahweh of impure, because self-seeking, faith, and he accused the high priest Joshua of uncleanness, and Yahweh examined these charges. He was one of the sons of the gods like Gabriel and Michael, who along with their holy brothers cared for the human beings entrusted to them. [See also II.1.c.i (p. 43).]

But Satan was concerned for Yahweh's rights, lest they be diminished by men. He also tested God's people, when David, driven by the wrath of Yahweh, had a census taken of Israel. Satan also looked into whether human beings got their just due, whether, for example, married couples lived up to their conjugal obligations.

[Job 1:6–2:7; Zechariah 3:1–2; I Corinthians 7:1–5; Daniel 9:21; 10:13; 8:13; I Chronicles 21:1]

b. When Jesus was led by the spirit into the wilderness, Satan appeared to him there, too, to put him to the test and see if he was obedient to his father. Jesus passed the test and conjured him to depart, telling him: Begone, Satan, for it is written: You shall worship the Lord your God, and him only shall you serve. – For Satan had promised to Jesus might, miraculous powers and dominion over the world, if Jesus would acknowledge him as lord. But Satan did not give up so easily, and in the end he took possession of Judas Iscariot, in order to overcome Jesus [see XIII.1 (p. 218)].

[Matthew 4:1–11; Mark 1:12–13; Luke 4:1–13; John 13:2; Matthew 26:14–25; Luke 22:3]

c. Many demons and evil spirits in the heavenly regions were subject to Satan, for he was not only a prince in this world but ruled in heaven too. Sometimes he was disguised as an angel of light.

Others called him Belial and believed him to be the god of this world, because he ruled over men. Others say that Jesus fought with his disciples against the prince of this world, because the devil was the father of lies and a murderer of men. For this reason, the sinners among men are his children, while the children of God are free from sin. God and the devil struggle for the mastery of this world, as long as it lasts. As far back as Cain, there were sons of the devil. Wherever the word of God is proclaimed, Satan is busy at work to uproot it from the hearts of men. He even creates his own synagogues.

[Luke 10:17–20; Ephesians 6:11–12; II Corinthians 4:4; 6:15; 11:14; John 12:31; 14:30; 8:37–47; I John 3:8–15; Mark 4:14–15; Luke 8:12; Matthew 13:19; Revelation 2:9–10]

(i) In the Bible, Satan is the term for one of the sons of the gods, i.e. the gods in the entourage of Yahweh, who is the supreme god. In the New Testament, Yahweh is called only Lord (*Kyrios*) and God (*Theos*). (See XIII.1.vii (p. 225).) The texts cited above describe Satan's original role, which gave him his name, meaning 'the adversary'. He has the task of enforcing Yahweh's law among mankind and accusing lawbreakers of perverting justice. He is the prosecutor of men in the name of Yahweh, the adversary of mankind. In the account of David's census (I Chronicles 21), the term describing his behaviour becomes a proper name, recognizable by the absence of the definite article before the noun.

(ii) Even in New Testament tradition, Satan is not at first a completely negative and repulsive figure. For the story of Jesus' temptation shows the spirit of God leading Jesus to the devil, who is to test him. The narrator uses the Greek word for devil, *diabolos*, throughout. Only when Jesus addresses the devil does the narrator put the name Satan in Jesus' mouth. This is a harking back to the Old Testament idea of the devil as a son of God with the juridical function of tempter-tester-accuser.

(iii) In the language of the Bible, human beings are occasionally called Satan, e.g. David in I Samuel 29:4, the sons of Zeruiah in II Samuel 19:23, Solomon's opponents in I Kings 5:18, even Peter in Matthew 19:23 and the parallel passage in Mark 8:35. Here the term Satan quite clearly means an adversary, that is, one who takes the opposite side in a legal conflict, with no pejorative ethical or moral connotations. For biblical religion the monolatrous notion of the uniqueness of one's own god is a decisive factor: next to this god there can be no equal. Satan is man's opponent, appointed by God himself.

(iv) Unlike the ancient Persian religion of Zoroaster, biblical religion at first has no supreme dualism that views the world and its destiny as the result of an eternal battle between the powers of light and darkness. In the Bible this battle takes place in the here and now; it follows a dialectical pattern inherent in the nature of things.

As a living being, man always has an adversary, who has, and is the spokesman for, a different point of view and different interests, that is – in the image of his lord and king – his god. The fact that David and Jesus are described as having adversaries makes their significance relative. The adversary is a necessary component of the prophetic-priestly assault on all ambitions for autocratic rule. Neither the nation nor the king is all-powerful, for both have an adversary in the god who, through his angels, tests human obedience to his law and sees that it is executed (see, for instance, II Samuel 24:10–17; I Chronicles 21:15; Malachi 3:1). The angels can have names like Gabriel, Michael and even Satan.

(v) The myth of the expulsion of the bad angels from heaven and the rise of an antagonism between Satan (or Uriel) and the god Yahweh comes from outside the Bible and became important only in the formative process of Christian mythology, which was deeply influenced by the dualistic legacy of Hellenism. We can see this in the passages from the Second Letter to the Corinthians, the Gospel according to John (which has a close affinity to the Gnostic world view), the First Letter of John, and the Letter to the Ephesians from the end of the first century A.D. In later Christian mythology, the devil is presented either as the erstwhile angelic prince, i.e. the head of the angels and cherubim, or as the older or younger brother of Christ. In the first reading, Satan rebels against God because he wishes to become a god himself; in the second mythopoeic interpretation, according to Augustine, the devil is jealous of the obvious preference shown to Christ, and on account of this is banished for ever to the fiery pool of hell.

XII.2. *Azazel*

Azazel was a god who dwelt in the wilderness. During Israel's wanderings there, Yahweh ordered Aaron, the brother of Moses, to celebrate the day of atonement once every year. On that day Aaron was to sacrifice a bull to Yahweh, and a goat as well, chosen by lot from a pair of goats. The other goat was set aside for Azazel in the wilderness. And all the people were to cleanse themselves of sin and hallow themselves by offering a bull and a he-goat to Yahweh. Meanwhile the other goat was brought out to Azazel in the wilderness, and Aaron likewise laid on it the sins of the people.

In the days of the kings, the Israelites still sacrificed to goat gods and, to the great chagrin of Yahweh's prophets, held the priests of these gods in high honour. The Israelites also worshipped the Shedim and sacrificed their children to them. These were spirits who were not gods, and gods whom the patriarchs had not known, and who came from close by.

[Leviticus 16; Isaiah 13:21; 34:12, 14; II Chronicles 11:15; Leviticus 17:7; Deuteronomy 32:17; Psalms 106:37]

(i) Azazel was undoubtedly a god worshipped in the early days by one of the tribes of Israel. The name is otherwise unknown in the Bible: it has been eliminated from tradition. But we can conclude from Leviticus 16 that Azazel and Yahweh were equals, because only when sacrifices were offered to both were the people reconciled and ritually pure.

(ii) Hence Yahweh and Azazel must have been equally important for the lives of the people. It is a reasonable assumption that Yahweh was the divine king ruling at the gates of the tent village, while Azazel was the god who ruled over the pasture land. Both had to be put in a benevolent mood by sacrifice. But after the return from exile, when the bearers of the priestly tradition read aloud the old rules for feast days to the community, this custom had already been forgotten. The only thing left was a ritual, which had to be explained in a way that made Yahweh's uniqueness clear. Yahweh gets the burnt sacrifice of a bull and a he-goat, Azazel only the unslaughtered goat.

(iii) Before this priestly regulation was laid down, the cult of the goat-shaped god with its priests and altars was still tolerated in the country. Azazel was presumably Yahweh's half-brother or foster-brother, just as the goat-shaped Pan was Zeus's foster-brother. In the fertility cults of Arcadia, Pan was also considered to be a mythologem for the 'devil' or 'the upright man', who was clad in a goatskin and accompanied the maenads on their orgiastic processions. He was also considered a master of prophecy and flute-playing. Apollo acquired his proficiency in these two arts from Pan. Just as Pan was defeated by Zeus and took on the form of a goat, so Azazel was defeated by Yahweh.

(iv) The Shedim were probably black, bull-shaped gods similar to the Assyrian bull god Shedu. They were originally Canaanite fertility gods and were polemically called 'little gods' (idols) by the authors of the Bible. The diminutive form was supposed to show their insignificance, but they were no less important for popular piety than the Yahweh cult (see also II.4 (p. 52)). It must be an accident that the Shedim mentioned in II Kings 23 are not specified by name (see VI.5 (p. 131)).

XII.3. *Beelzebul, the Demons and the Dragon*

a. Baal-zebul was the name of the god of Ekron. He helped people in sickness and affliction, and ruled over all the powers of disease. He alone could grant or withhold a cure.

When Jesus, too, cured men and women of diseases, the people thought that Beelzebul was helping him, and they saw in him a servant of Beelzebul, because he could drive out evil spirits. Once he even made them enter into a herd of swine, which then plunged into the sea. Jesus resisted the idea of being connected with Beelzebul, and said that he worked cures through the spirit of his father and not through Beelzebul, the head of the demons. For Beelzebul was overcome by Jesus.

[II Kings 1; Matthew 12:24–32; Luke 11:15–23; Mark 3:22–30; 5:1–20]

b. In another passage we read that Beelzebul strove mightily against Jesus' followers; and deceiving spirits and demons spread doctrines which caused some to fall away from faith in Christ. For this reason, believers were to be vigilant, for the devil was prowling about like a roaring lion in search of someone to devour.

[Galatians 4:8–12; 1 Peter 5:8]

c. Others again say that the tempter, the great serpent, the old dragon, will not try to seize power until the last days. Michael and his angels will then do battle with the crowned, seven-headed dragon and his angels and cast them down upon the earth, for there will be no more place for them in heaven. But on the earth the dragon will fight yet a little while longer, until he is defeated, the great dragon, also called the devil, Satan, or the ancient serpent. On the great day of almighty God he will try once more to incite all the kings of earth to war. That is the short period for which the angels of heaven will release him from his chains in the underworld, after he has lain bound there for a thousand years, lest he harm the nations.

But after this the devil will be thrown into the sea of fire and brimstone, where he will be tormented through all eternity. To him will be sent all people who in the day of God's judgement do not pass the test.

[Revelation 12:1–17; 16:12–14; 20:1–3; Matthew 25:41]

(i) In the historical and religious development of New Testament thought Beelzebul was at first an independent figure. As a reincarnation of Baal-zebul of Ekron, the saviour of sick people, this god enjoyed high esteem even among the people of Jesus' time and later. In the Old Testament his name is read to mean 'god of the flies' (Beelzebub), to minimize his importance (see VIII.3.iii (p. 159)). To the unscientific mind, sickness often appears to be fate, an arbitrary decree by gods and demons. Accordingly, recovery from illness seems like the victory of one demon over another.

(ii) To this way of thinking, apostasy from Jesus could likewise only be explained as a sickness, and these demons had to be exorcized and burned. The Inquisition lived by this mythology as late as the eighteenth century (it was active in Spain till then).

(iii) The images of the great dragon, the ancient serpent, the devil and Satan were merged in the world of apocalyptic symbols. The descriptions of natural marvels in Isaiah 14:12 and Job 41 were used to represent the Evil One who is finally defeated by the combined force of Michael and his angels. This eschatological expansion is the consequence of the development of apocalyptic piety that had been going on in the Middle East since the fourth century B.C. The pious individual could no longer endure the conditions of slavery under the Diadochi of Alexander the Great and the Romans, and could also no longer explain the situation as his god's way of testing him. Under the influence of Persian dualism, he imagined an absolute antagonism between the power of the Evil One and the almighty power of the Good, and, judging from his own destiny, concluded that they were irreconcilable. Hence he placed his hopes for a change in that destiny in the hands of the heavenly powers, who would help him at whatever moment it pleased them.

(iv) In a parallel development, religious feeling was confined to cultic worship. Normal everyday human life remained untouched by piety. This deliberate, conservative ritualization was the point of departure for the moral degradation of the devil, the Evil One, seen now as the epitome of the new, of change, of the differences between the present and the days of the patriarchs. The petrifaction of the holy as the past, as history, opened the way for the demonization of the present. The fact that the forces of novelty are often nurtured by oppressed elements in the old order has led critics to view devils, witches and demons as simply old deities robbed of their power. But such beings remained dangerous for priests, apostles and prophets less on account of their former importance than because of their ability to become a symbol of something new – and hostile to the established order. Thus Ishtar and Marduk posed a threat to Christianity and Judaism, because after the second century B.C. they came back to life in a new and different form in the mystery religions as Isis and Osiris.

(v) Around the beginning of the Christian era there was such a triumphant burst of mythopoesis because the apocalyptic images of the dragon, the serpent or the woman on the crescent moon (Revelation 12) made possible a less perilous confrontation with the political authorities. Besides that, the eschatological mode of thought could be construed both in the strictest and the loosest way imaginable. This explains its widespread popularity.

XIII. The Myth of the Redemption

XIII.1. *Jesus of Nazareth*

After God had spoken in the past at various times and in various ways through the prophets, he spoke at last through his son, Jesus Christ, whom he appointed his one and only successor. This son was with him from the beginning, even when he created the world, and hence he was placed higher than the angels. For only to Jesus Christ did God say he was Father, when he said: You are my son, this day have I begotten you. But he had been with his Father from all eternity. When the Father sent him forth into the world, he commanded all the angels to serve Jesus, whose throne was to stand for ever beside the throne of God.

And God sent him to earth to redeem his people from the curse that had weighed down on humanity after Adam. Thus he was born as a man through Mary, the wife of Joseph from Nazareth, whom God had impregnated through the Holy Spirit.

This occurred at the same time that a decree of the Roman emperor Augustus required new tax lists to be drawn up everywhere in the empire. With this end in view, everyone was compelled to go to his birthplace. So Joseph set out with his pregnant wife to Bethlehem, his birthplace. And Jesus was born there. He was laid in a manger in the inn, because there was no room anywhere else. On that same night the heavenly hosts appeared to near-by shepherds, and the angel of the lord announced to them: The Christ, the Redeemer, is born in the city of David. Then the shepherds went to Bethlehem, and there they found Mary, her husband, and Jesus. The shepherds spread the news everywhere, telling what they had seen.

When Joseph and Mary went to Jerusalem, in accordance with the laws of their people, in order to offer sacrifice, there was in the temple an old man named Simeon. He had been told by an angel that he would not die before seeing the Christ. He came into the temple and announced that Jesus was the redeemer, and the old prophetess Hannah did the same.

While Jesus' parents were still staying in Bethlehem, Magi came out of the east to Jerusalem, to search for the new-born king of the Jews. They had seen the tidings of his birth written in the stars. King Herod was frightened by the news, but he helped them find the way to Bethlehem, where, according to tradition, the Christ would one day be born. And the Magi found their star; it stood over the place where the child was. And they worshipped Jesus and offered him rich presents of gold, frankincense and myrrh. Then, as a dream had bidden them, they secretly withdrew, without informing Herod which child was the new-born king of the Jews.

Then the angel of the Lord appeared to Joseph in a dream, and commanded him to flee with the child and his mother to Egypt, until the death of Herod. After that they returned home and dwelt in Nazareth, in Galilee, because they feared the Jews. Thus was the prophecy fulfilled, that the Messiah would be called a Nazarene. But Herod had given orders for all the boys under two years of age in Bethlehem and its surroundings to be put to death, to make sure that he had killed the new-born king.

Jesus grew up in Nazareth and, like many others in those days, he came to John the Preacher on the Jordan, and had himself baptised as a sign of purification and conversion. Then the heavens opened above him, and the Holy Spirit came upon him, as a dove flies out of the sky. And at the same time a voice rang out from the heavens: This is my son, whom I love and in whom I am well pleased.

In all things Jesus proved himself to be the true son of his divine father. He overcame Satan's temptations in the wilderness, whither the spirit of God had led him. And he preached all over the country that the people should have a change of heart and turn to the kingdom of heaven, the divine kingdom, which had drawn near. Many believed in him, and thus he soon had gathered twelve men about him as his followers. They were Simon, whom Jesus called Peter, and his brother Andrew, the sons of Zebedee, James and John, who left their father's fishing boat and went off with him. He was much sought after on all sides, and so among his disciples there was even a tax collector, Matthew. The others were Philip, Bartholomew, Thomas, Simon, Judas of Iscariot, James the son of Alphaeus, and Judas the son of James. He called these men apostles. And Jesus wandered through the country, preached to the people, healed the sick and brought the dead back to life. He also sent out his apostles and charged them to teach that the kingdom of heaven was near. They were to make the sick well, cleanse lepers, resurrect the dead and drive out devils. And he travelled on through the country. With him were not only the twelve apostles, but also women whom Jesus had cured. Among them were Mary Magdalen, Johanna and Susanna.

Jesus did not observe strictly the customs of his time. For he taught that all things had been given over to him by his heavenly father, and he invited everyone to submit to him. He promised them that his yoke was easy and his burden light. For this reason he disregarded many pious customs of the Jews and did not keep the Sabbath commandments strictly.

He taught people about the kingdom of God with many parables and similes. But he was not liked in his home town of Nazareth, and when he spoke in the synagogue there of the coming kingdom of God, the townsfolk did not believe him. They even tried to murder him. One of his miracles was the feeding of many people with bread and fish, when they were listening to his preaching and became hungry. With five loaves of bread and two fish he was able to satisfy five thousand people, and afterwards twelve baskets full of leftover scraps were gathered up. Another time he fed four thousand people with seven loaves, and there were still seven baskets of fragments left.

Once he saved his disciples' lives, when the boat they were out in threatened to capsize, by walking over the water to them.

Another time Moses and Elijah appeared to Jesus when he was staying with Peter, James and John on a high mountain; and both Moses and Elijah spoke with him. A cloud came down from heaven and overshadowed them, as a voice resounded from out of the cloud: This is my son, hear him. – And Jesus was completely transfigured. His appearance changed, and his garments became radiantly white. The apostles wanted to build huts at once for the three men, but Jesus forbade them. He repeatedly told his disciples that he would be sentenced to death in Jerusalem, and that he would have to suffer, die and rise again. When he entered Jerusalem, the people spread their clothes out on the street and cried aloud: Hosannah, hail to him who comes in the name of the Lord, to the son of David and to David's kingdom, which comes in the name of the Lord.

And Jesus saw the misery that would come to the city, and its destruction. He did not cease speaking in parables about the coming kingdom of God. He threatened Jerusalem: Your house shall become desolate, and you shall see me no more, until you say: Blessed be he who comes in the name of the Lord.

And he announced to them the coming of a dreadful time, full of persecutions, cruel treatment and temptations. But soon after that time the sun and moon would grow pale, and the stars fall from heaven. Then the Son of Man would appear in the clouds of heaven with great power and glory. And he would dispatch his angels to gather his chosen ones together from all over the world. But Jesus said nothing about the exact moment when his kingdom would begin. He admonished the people to be watchful and ready like wise virgins waiting for the bridegroom with a good supply of oil for their lamps. They would enter the kingdom of heaven, but the foolish virgins whose lamps went out for lack of oil would have to remain outside and go to damnation, like all those who in the coming judgement did not pass the test of the Son of Man.

Jesus' discourses and miracles threw the priests of Jerusalem and the council of elders into apprehension. They tried to do away with Jesus quietly, because they feared an uprising among the people on account of Jesus' large following. But among Jesus' disciples there was one, Judas of Iscariot, who declared his readiness to betray him for money. The opportunity presented itself when Jesus celebrated the feast of Passover [see IV.5.c (p. 109)] in Jerusalem with his friends.

At the Passover meal he spoke with the twelve over the bread and wine they were having, and gave them the bread and the cup, saying: Take, this is my body. – And after they had all drunk from the cup he had given them, he said: This is my blood, which will be shed for many. – After the supper Jesus went with his disciples to the Mount of Olives, near the farm of Gethsemane. There Judas came with the constables of the High Council – the Court of Justice – and they took Jesus prisoner, and led him to the high priest Caiphas. But the disciples fled.

Jesus was interrogated before Caiphas and beaten, to get a confession out of him. And he acknowledged that he was the Christ, the son of God. The next day the High Council sent him to the Roman procurator Pontius Pilate, to obtain the death sentence for Jesus. They accused him of high treason, declaring to Pilate that Jesus had said he was the king of the Jews. Pilate let himself be swayed by the unanimous desire of the people to condemn him to death on the cross. Before this he was led out for scourging.

The soldiers struck him and made sport of him. After that they brought him out to the place of execution on Golgotha. Together with Jesus two murderers were also crucified. On a sign over his head was written as his crime: Jesus of Nazareth, King of the Jews. As he hung on the cross, all those who passed by mocked him. But when he died uttering a great cry, the sun grew dark, the earth quaked and many dead bodies climbed out of their tombs, which had burst asunder. And the curtain of the temple was torn in two from top to bottom.

The Roman centurion who had watched all this said: This man was surely God's son.

That evening Jesus was buried in a tomb which his follower, Joseph of Arimathea, had had cut out of the rock. The tomb was sealed and guarded by Roman soldiers. But when the Sabbath was over, and the new week began, Mary Magdalen, Mary the mother of James, and Salome came to the grave to anoint the corpse. And the grave was already open and empty. An angel of the Lord sat there and told them to go and tell the disciples that Jesus had risen from the dead and gone before them to Galilee, where the disciples were to follow him. The women went immediately to the disciples, but no one believed them until Jesus himself appeared to them. Then they all went to

Galilee, to a mountain whither Jesus had summoned them. There he charged them to go and teach all nations and to baptise those who would believe.

After he had thus spoken with them, he was taken up to heaven and seated at the right hand of God. But the disciples went and spread the word that Jesus had died on the cross for the sinners in the world. He had come into the world to make sinners blessed. Soon he would return on the clouds of heaven for the final judgement, just as a cloud had taken him away after he spoke one more time with his disciples. But when he returned he would bring on a new heaven and a new earth.

[Hebrews 1:1–2; John 1:1–4; Philemon 2:6–11; Galations 4:4; Matthew 1:18–25; Luke 2:1–10; Matthew 2:1–23; Mark 1–16; Romans 5:8; Timothy 1:15; Revelation 1:7; Acts 1:9]

(i) The biblical Christ is not the historical Jesus, about whom scholars have known since Albert Schweitzer's *The Quest of the Historical Jesus* that they can approach him with the available sources, but never get a concrete hold on him. The biblical testimonies concerning Christ are mythical. This myth presents the life, death and resurrection of a son of the gods to whom the carpenter's son, Jesus of Nazareth, has lent some legendary, though significant, traits. On the strength of biblical and extra-biblical sources, only two facts can be considered historically certain: Jesus was active as a preacher in Galilee and died on the cross in Jerusalem. The narrative patterns (one is common to the first three gospels, the so-called synoptics, Matthew, Mark and Luke; the other is peculiar to John) that describe Jesus' travels through Palestine are a poetic framework designed to provide a historical context for the countless sayings and speeches of Jesus handed down by tradition. We may assume, however, that the statement in Mark 3:32 about Jesus' brothers and sisters belongs to history.

(ii) The above sketch of the myth of Jesus Christ, the Messiah, aims at presenting the most broadly acceptable version possible of the basic Christian myth. But this myth displays variations and special features in the work of the individual New Testament authors, with their contrasting socio-economic backgrounds and commitments – apart from the fact that they lived in different parts of the Roman Empire and at different times.

Thus, for example, the gospel according to Mark was undoubtedly composed in Jerusalem before the city's destruction. That is why the author fills half the pages of his work with an account of Jesus' activities in Jerusalem. Perhaps he was an eyewitness, as some readers have concluded from the information contained in 14:51–2. In any event, the gospel according to Mark does not yet presuppose any fully developed Christian mythology. Theologians have consequently interpreted Mark's umpromising reserve vis-à-vis theology as an indication that the gospel's theological programme was to present the 'mystery of the Lord', the supposed key to which is that Jesus does *not* reveal himself as the son of God.

On the other hand, the gospel of Matthew was unquestionably composed after the destruction of Jerusalem. It takes for granted a self-conscious community of Jesus' worshippers in conflict with Judaism. Jesus is viewed here as, incontrovertibly, the son of David. The author, we may assume, came from a group of prosperous Jews who thought salvation could be achieved by means of an interior transformation in the face of the coming eschatological judgement. Such people were interested, not in a world-wide missionary operation, but in the rescue of the 'lost sheep' from the house of Israel.

An altogether different point of view from Matthew's is taken by the non-Jewish author of the gospel according to Luke. This writer no longer understands Jesus' menacing words against Judah and Jerusalem simply as outbursts of prophetic rage but as a rejection of the narrow-mindedness of his audience. Luke thinks like a Roman: salvation is for the whole world. Luke's ethical standpoint, closely related to the stoic-cynic way of life, despises wealth and possessions. The poor man, the man without property, who trusts in God's power is nearer to the kingdom of God than the rich.

All the evangelists shared the expectation of an eschatological kingdom of heaven, a kingdom ruled by God. This expectation was the crucial point of departure for the myth of Jesus Christ. We find in Jesus a manifest hope for revolutionary change in his own lifetime. That is why the first three gospels open their account of Jesus' public life with the cry: Repent, for the kingdom of heaven is at hand!

There can be no doubt that this interpretation of the kingdom of God was already well established in the early days of Christianity, because the authors of the gospels are thoroughly familiar with it. By adopting it, they clearly disavow earlier apocalyptic thinking and the eschatological models that made the coming of Yahweh's kingdom dependent upon a great catastrophe.

(iii) The myth of Jesus Christ contains elements of older myths concerning kings and saviours. In the immediate neighbourhood of Palestine, in Asia Minor, the myth of the dying and rising god Attis still survived, as did the mystery religion of Mithra, in which the initiates acquired eternal blessedness and divinity through a baptism of blood. Sabazius and Asclepius were miracle-workers and saviours of this sort, and communities of their worshippers were spread all throughout the Roman Empire. As early as 40 B.C., Virgil's *Fourth Eclogue* described a son of god who descends from the heights of heaven, lives as a god, and brings peace to the world, ruling with his father's power. Jesus' birth from a virgin mother impregnated by the spirit of God, the adoration of the Magi from the east (*anatolē*), his triumphal progress through the country to Jerusalem, and his elevation to godhead – all these are mythologems found in other religions as well. They are designed to prove that Jesus is the Lord of all lords. A similar purpose is evident in the Christian adaptation of the traditional Jewish motifs of the 'son of man' and the 'servant of God'. Both these traditions were alive in Judaism around the time of Christ. The authors of the gospels and the first Christians identified Jesus with these messianic prototypes (see XI.3 (p. 208) and Revelation 1:13 and 14:14; see also XIV.2.c (p. 240)). The same holds true for the title, 'son of David' (see IX.3.c.viii (p. 183)). These traditions flourished at every level of society.

The historical Jesus apparently claimed none of these lofty messianic titles for himself, but, like the prophets, simply preached that the kingdom of God (plainly meaning the Judaic god Yahweh) had already begun. The New Testament narratives themselves lead to this conclusion, but by the same token it was also possible for representatives from every segment of the Jewish population to recognize Jesus as the Messiah. He never drew up a precise picture of the coming kingdom of God, and so members of conservative Jewish groups, who were looking for the son of David, as well as of the oppressed country populace, whose longings were reflected above all in the image of the son of man coming on the clouds of heaven, and of the priestly-prophetic circles, who pinned their hopes on the servant of God – all these could acknowledge Jesus as their Messiah and glorify him as such. These different points of view are the reason why the picture of Jesus in the Bible is so contradictory. Thus the New Testament Jesus pleads neither for slavery nor the liberation of the slaves. When he praises the poor as blessed, he does not mean that the rich cannot become blessed too, but simply that the rich put their trust less in the kingdom of God than in their own possessions. Hence the biblical Jesus is no revolutionary. He merely urges people to consider that humanity's current situation will be swept away with the coming of the kingdom, which he himself represents.

(iv) The peculiarity of the biblical image of Jesus does not lie in the myth of the resurrection, which it shares with the mystery religions and tales of other gods, such as Heracles (a human being who was not elevated to Olympus until after his death). In the history of religion, resurrection myths are always a mode of primitive dialectic that anticipates the philosophical law of the negation of negation. Easter as the date of Jesus' death signifies, historically speaking, the nullification of the most characteristic feature of his activity. That, according to the New Testament, was his life and work for the rule of the Old Testament Yahweh, considered as a this-worldly phenomenon. The uniqueness of the biblical Jesus is rooted in his sense of exclusiveness:

Jesus thinks that, only by following him, can man find salvation and admission to the kingdom of God. The first Christians expressed this claim to absoluteness through the image of divine sonship, as is shown by the stories of Jesus' birth.

(v) The crucifixion of Jesus was undoubtedly a historical event, but it remains unclear on what day and in which year the execution occurred. The synoptic gospels cite Friday, the 15th of Nisan, John gives Friday the 14th of Nisan. According to John's gospel, then, Jesus must have been executed on the first day of Passover, which is unlikely. We may assume that the date of Jesus' death was given as the 15th in order to identify the traditional Last Supper with the Jewish Seder. Jesus is supposed to be the true sacrificial lamb who bears the sins of the world and is sacrificed. Formally speaking, the account of the Last Supper is genuine cultic legend.

Jesus surely died in Jerusalem, just as surely as he was not born in Bethlehem, but Nazareth. From a mythological point of view, Bethlehem had to be Jesus' birthplace, so as to prove him a son of David (see Romans 1:3–4; II Timothy 2:8; Mark 10:48). With their stories of Jesus' birth and baptism, the synoptic gospels contradict the myth of Christ's eternal pre-existence, as taught by John's gospel and the New Testament epistles (II Philippians). The synoptics give a graphic presentation of the problems posed by the doctrine of two natures, which states that Jesus Christ, though a single person, united in himself two natures, one human and one divine.

(vi) But John's gospel and the Johannine letters controvert this teaching. For this source Jesus is the *Logos*, who was originally God and appears on earth as such. Thus John's gospel has no story of Jesus' temptation. And it also sets no great store by Jesus' family, but plainly downgrades it by not mentioning a single name (John 2:1–12; 19:25–7).

(vii) The New Testament has no name for Jesus' divine father. In dealing with Jesus' relation to the Old Testament god Yahweh, New Testament tradition speaks only of 'the God and Father of Jesus Christ'. In so doing it harks back to the Jewish custom of not pronouncing the name of Yahweh but paraphrasing it with 'Lord'. The first Greek translation of the Bible, the Septuagint, had already rendered the name of God with the Greek word for lord, *Kyrios*. For this reason the angel of Yahweh appears in the New Testament as the angel of the Lord (Matthew 7:20, etc.). Translations of the New Testament follow this usage, because New Testament authors operate under the assumption that there is only one god, the god of Abraham, Isaac and Jacob, who sent his son Jesus (e.g. Acts 3:12–26). When theological passages in the New Testament speak of God as 'Lord', the mythological resonance of the term is always 'Yahweh'.

In the New Testament, *Kyrios* is also applied to Jesus. In Peter's speech in

Acts 2:25 or Romans 10:9 and elsewhere in the Epistles the text speaks of Jesus Christ *Kyrios*, who has risen from the dead and ascended into heaven and now sits at the right hand of God. For Christians, the *Kyrios* is now Jesus Christ (Colossians 2:6). Jesus, *the Christ*, is he who died on the cross and was raised again (Romans 5:6, 8; 6:4, 9). He redeems humanity (Romans 8:35 and elsewhere), and the gospel of Christ sets us free, but Jesus *the Kyrios* is the one who will come (I Thessalonians 4:15–18; I Corinthians 4:5, etc.). He is the *Kyrios* who judges (e.g. I Corinthians 4:4; 11:32; II Corinthians 5:11), he is the Spirit (e.g. II Corinthians 3:17), and Paul can pray to him as well (II Corinthians 12:8). This brings to a close the development of the concept of Jesus as the son of God, which ends by making him God himself. And on this point the Christian community broke once and for all with Judaism. Out of a Jewish sect came the Christian Church.

(viii) This process follows the evolutionary pattern of sectarian growth, which scholars have also traced in other contexts. A group raises its partisan understanding of a doctrine to the level of the one and only truth. Then it splits with the parent body when a conflict of interests arises. In a second stage it takes up rejected and forgotten ideas and refashions them, drawing on old traditions and creating a new doctrine around the core of its original perception. Thus Jesus, the prophet from Nazareth, taught that the kingdom of God had arrived. Jesus Christ, the Son of God, then becomes the guarantor that his message is reliable and true. He is the heavenly helper and saviour, and then finally he must be the Lord and Creator himself.

XIII.2 *Mary the Mother of Jesus*

a. Mary came from Nazareth. She was of non-Jewish origin, like many of the women in her husband's family line (Joseph belonged to the house of David). Jesus was her first-born son, after him she bore another six children to Joseph. They lived in Jesus' neighbourhood.

Joseph observed that his wife was already pregnant when he was about to marry her. But an angel of the Lord appeared to him and told him that Mary was with child by the Holy Spirit and would bear a son, whom he was to call Jesus. Joseph obeyed the angel and married Mary. After the birth of the child they fled with him to Egypt, because King Herod put all the new-born children in Bethlehem to death. They did not return to Nazareth until after the king's death. Later Mary accompanied Jesus on his journeys and became one of the founders, in Jerusalem, of the first Christian community.

[Matthew 1–2; Galatians 4:4; Mark 6:3; Acts 1:14]

b. Others relate further that the angel Gabriel announced the birth of Jesus in advance, saying: He will be great, and will be called the son of the Most High. And he will be a king on the throne of David, ruling over the house of Jacob, and his reign will endure for ever. And he will be a son of God, for the Holy Spirit will come over you, and the power of the Most High will overshadow you. And thus the fruit of your womb will be called the son of God. – Mary surrendered to the Lord, and the angel left her. After this Mary went to Jerusalem to see her friend Elizabeth, who foretold to her the same thing as had the angel of the Lord. Then Mary returned to Joseph's house. But when the time came for her to give birth, they were in Bethlehem. And so Jesus was born in an inn in Bethlehem, where there was really no proper place for an infant, so that they had to lay the child in a feeding trough. But Mary stored up in her heart all the words she had heard from the angels and also from the shepherds who visited them in Bethlehem, as well as those of Simeon and Hannah in the temple of Jerusalem [see XIII.1. vi (p. 225)].

[Luke 1:26–45; 2:1–40]

(i) Mary (Maria) is the Greek form of the Hebrew name Miriam, meaning the bitter, or rebellious, one. Whereas her husband quickly disappears from the scene in the New Testament (after Jesus' birth the gospels speak only of his mother, brothers and sisters), Mary remains longer as an active figure. Her role is ambiguous. In the older tradition, found in Mark 3:33–5 or 3:21 and parallel passages in Matthew and Luke, she takes a distant, hostile stance towards her son's work. In the later tradition, which includes the accounts of Jesus' birth, she becomes the first to testify that he is the Messiah. This inconsistency is explained by the time separating the two sources.

(ii) The later passages on Mary as witness to Jesus' divine origin merged in biblical tradition with the image of the divine queen of heaven in Revelation 12:1. The glorification of Mary that begins in Luke 1 with the use of honorific titles comes directly from the mysteries of Isis. Isis was the typical Hellenistic Divine Mother, and her cult was widely celebrated. The transfer of parts of mythologems from Isis worship to Mary the mother of Jesus undoubtedly took place in the middle third of the first century A.D. In the older myth, Isis is impregnated by a falcon and gives birth to Horus, whom she has to rescue from persecution by Set. She becomes the pattern for the *mater dolorosa*, mourning her husband and her son. Thus other mythologems made their way into Mariology, which expanded beyond its originally modest biblical framework. Mary's importance as queen of heaven, co-redemptrix, archetype of the Church, helper in time of need and so forth, derives from the Church's mythology. It can be seen as early as the apocalyptic gospels, which also tell of her death and assumption into heaven. (See also II.2.**b.** ii (p. 45).)

XIII.3. *James the Brother of Jesus*

One of Jesus' brothers, the son of a carpenter and his wife Mary, was James. Apart from Jesus, his brothers were Joses, Simon and Judas. He first lived with his parents, brothers and sisters in Nazareth. After the death of Jesus, James, as the leader of the Jerusalem community, received word of the miraculous resurrection and spread the news. Then, when Simon Peter declared that God had chosen him to gather a congregation from among the Gentiles, James went among the Jews to proclaim the gospel. He was one of the first to experience a vision of the risen Christ. He was known as 'the just', because he was upright and faithful in caring for the people in Jerusalem who followed Jesus. Because of his apostasy from the synagogue, he was thrown from the pinnacle of the temple and stoned to death. The Lord himself often appeared to him and initiated him into the mysteries of true life. The revelations and sermons of James were widely disseminated.

[Matthew 13:55; Acts 12:17; 21:18; 15:21; Galatians 2:9; I Corinthians 15:7; Jerome, *De viris illustrissimis*, III,1; First and Second Epistle of James from Codex V of the Nag Hamadi MS.; Josephus, *Jewish Antiquities*, 200]

(i) The New Testament reports of James seem to have a solid historical core. After Jesus' death, his brother occupies a privileged position. The accounts of his visions were needed to legitimize him as a spiritual authority. They belong to the myth of James as it was subsequently taken up by Gnostic literature. In Christian iconography, the extra-canonical tradition of his martyrdom was especially popular. James was certainly not the author of the New Testament epistle that bears his name.

(ii) Early Catholicism tried to present him as Jesus' cousin rather than his brother, in order to justify the dogma of Mary's virginal purity (see, for example, the chapter on St James the Less in the *Golden Legend*).

XIII.4. *John the Baptist*

In the days of King Herod there lived a priest named Zacharias. His wife Elizabeth belonged to the house of Aaron. They had no children, because Elizabeth was barren. Once, when he was serving his turn in the temple, the angel Gabriel appeared to Zacharias and prophesied to him: Your wife will soon bear a son, and you shall call him John. From his mother's womb, the child will be filled with the Holy Spirit, and he shall taste neither wine nor strong drink. He will bring many people to God in the spirit and power of

Elijah. – Zacharias would not believe this, because he and his wife were already advanced in years, and so Gabriel told him: Because you do not believe, you will be struck dumb until the day the child is born. And everything came to pass, as Gabriel had foretold. On the eighth day after his birth, when the child was to be given a name, Zacharias was able to speak once more, and he praised God in a hymn in which he said that his son would be called a prophet of the Most High and would go before the Lord to prepare the way for him. The child grew up in secret, until a word from the Lord called him forth from the wilderness. And John preached with the words of the prophets about the coming of the divine redeemer, whose arrival he had already welcomed while he was yet in his mother's womb. For when Mary had visited his mother Elizabeth during her pregnancy, John had stirred in his mother's womb. Thereupon Elizabeth had intoned a song of praise to God's grace. [See also XIII.2.b (p. 227).]

After receiving God's call, John went down to the Jordan and preached there and baptised. He was dressed in a garment of camel's hair, and his food was grasshoppers and wild honey. He said that he was only baptising with water, but that after him would come a stronger man who would baptise with the Holy Spirit and with fire. He dealt harshly with Pharisees and Sadducees, but gently with the poor people, tax collectors and soldiers.

Jesus, too, came to him, to have himself baptised, and John did baptise him, although he knew that he ought to have been baptised by Jesus instead. And he proclaimed to all the people that Jesus was God's sacrificial lamb, who was to take away the sins of the world. He taught that Jesus baptised with the Holy Spirit, and testified that Jesus was the Son of God. John was compared to Elijah, by Jesus among others. After Jesus appeared, John continued to preach repentance and conversion. In so doing, he aroused the disfavour of Queen Herodias and King Herod, whom he accused of incest, and they had him thrown into prison. There he heard of Jesus' doings and sent some of his followers to ask whether he was the Promised One.

John was later beheaded in prison on orders from Herod. For Herodias' daughter Salome danced before the king during a banquet on his birthday, and so pleased Herod that he promised to grant her every wish. Prompted by her mother, she asked that the head of John be given to her at once on a platter.

After John's death, Jesus went on teaching that Elijah had already come, to proclaim the approach of God's kingdom.

[Luke 1:5–25, 58–80; 3:1–18; 1:39–55; Mark 1:4–8; Matthew 3:1–12; John 1:6–8, 15, 19–34; Mark 6:14–29; Matthew 11:1–15; Mark 9:11–13]

(i) Extra-biblical data lead us to conclude that John the Baptist was a historical person. The story of his birth, however, is legendary. It was obviously conceived in imitation of the story describing the birth of the Prophet Samuel (see VIII.1 (p. 153)) and aimed to establish a link between him and Jesus. Another of these mythical legends is the story of Jesus' baptism, which must have been a late addition to the picture of Jesus. This would account for the inconsistency between Matthew 11, where John inquires of Jesus whether he is the Promised One, and Matthew 3, where John acknowledges Jesus at his baptism as the son of God.

(ii) The relationship between Jesus and John is described in terms of the theological myth, based on the Old Testament, that the prophet Elijah (see VIII.2.vii (p. 157)) would come before the dawn of God's kingdom. But Jesus and John must originally have been equals. Both preached the coming of a divine kingdom, both attracted many disciples. After John's death, his disciples apparently went over to Jesus, bringing their experiences with them. This was Jesus' victory over John.

(iii) The discovery of the library of the Qumran community near the Dead Sea in 1947 has shed light on the background of the doctrines taught by Jesus and John. The library belonged to a Jewish sect called the Essenes, which had broken away from the temple in Jerusalem and lived in this monastery from 130 B.C. to A.D. 68. They followed a strict rule, holding all property in common and striving to lead a group life without any public worship but according to strict legal and ethical norms. They were looking forward to an early arrival of the Messiah, and thought of themselves as the sons of light doing battle with the sons of darkness, among whom they gave a prominent place to the priests of Jerusalem. Apocryphal literature was evidently treated as sacred scripture, as we see from the texts discovered there. It is quite possible that John was acquainted with this pious community. In any case, he unquestionably shared the practice of baptism with them and understood it as they did. Through baptism man was purified and sanctified for reception into the ranks of the sons of light.

(iv) While Jesus evidently never baptised anyone, the first generation of Christians, which included the disciples of John, integrated baptism into their doctrinal system. Baptism with the Holy Spirit, which according to John was reserved for Jesus alone to administer, had long been viewed by the Qumran community as a key part of the divine day of judgement and a sign of the New Age. For this reason, the conclusion of Matthew 28, with the command to baptise all nations, and the 'outpouring of the Holy Spirit' (Acts 2:1–13) is one of the ingredients of the myth of Jesus as the son of God who has already led humanity into the new kingdom. Hence the baptism with water is seen in combination with the baptism of the Holy Spirit (Acts 2:38). The hostility that John the Baptist and Jesus display towards religious ritual is attributable to the close links between Jewish sects (e.g. the Essenes, which some say includes Qumran) and the old prophets.

XIII.5. *Peter*

Simon the son of Jona was a fisherman in Capernaum on the lake of Gennesareth in Galilee. One day Jesus came to his house and stayed as a guest for the Sabbath. Just at that time, Simon's mother-in-law had fallen sick, and Jesus cured her. The next day Simon hastened after him and thenceforth remained with him. Later Jesus called him to be one of his twelve disciples, who were to accompany him and be his spokesmen. In calling him, Jesus gave Simon the name of Peter [Greek for 'the rock'], just as he named the sons of Zebedee, James and John, 'the sons of thunder'.

Others say that Jesus called Simon aside, together with his brother Andrew, and told them: Follow me, I will make you into fishers of men. (The brothers came from Bethsaida in Galilee and fished in the Sea of Galilee, which was also called Lake Gennesareth.) When Jesus said this, they left their nets and boats behind and followed him.

Others again say that Simon's brother Andrew led him to Jesus, for Simon had been the first to hear of Jesus. At their first meeting, Jesus said to Simon: You are Simon, the son of Jona; from now on you shall be called Cephas [Aramaic for 'the rock'].

Once when they were in the neighbourhood of Caesarea, Jesus asked his disciples who people said he was. Then they answered: Some think you are John the Baptist, others say Elijah, still others a prophet like Jeremiah. But Simon said: You are the Christ, the son of the living God. Then Jesus replied: Blessed are you, Simon son of Jona, for flesh and blood has not revealed this to you but my heavenly father. Therefore I say to you: You are Peter, and upon this rock I will build my church. You shall have the keys to the kingdom of heaven.

Peter was one of the most important disciples and often spoke with Jesus. He also tried to prevent Jesus from risking his life, and for that he had to endure Jesus' rebuking him as Satan. But Jesus did not cast Peter off. He let him see his transfiguration when he spoke on a high mountain with Moses and Elijah. And he let Peter hear when a voice from out of the clouds acknowledged Jesus as the son of God, whom the disciples were to obey.

In Jesus' time of trial Peter was with him. After the Last Supper when Jesus spoke of how the disciples would soon abandon him, Peter vowed to be true to him. But Jesus announced: This very night, before the cock crows, you will deny me three times. And so it came to pass. After Jesus was arrested, Simon Peter went along into the court of the high priest's palace, where he was recognized by various people as a follower of the prisoner. And Peter denied him three times. But after the resurrection, Jesus made himself known to Peter first of all.

After Jesus' death, Peter became the spokesman for the disciples and, as the risen Jesus had bidden him before ascending into heaven, he gathered together the community of Jesus' followers in Jerusalem and organized it. He proclaimed everywhere, especially after the miraculous outpouring of the Holy Spirit at Pentecost, that the kingdom of God had come in the name of Jesus. And Peter healed the sick in the temple, pronounced judgement for the community, raised the dead and travelled around the country to preach, even to Gentiles, much to the distress of the Jerusalem congregation, whose members were intent on keeping to themselves. But Peter did not cease to labour in this way. Even prison did not hold him back, for the angel of the Lord set him free. And he defended Paul when Paul went to the cities of Greece and baptised there. He died a martyr in Rome under the emperor Nero.

[Mark 1:29–36; I Corinthians 9:5; Mark 3:14–17; Matthew 4:18–20; 16:13–17:5; 26:30–40; Luke 24:34; I Corinthians 15:5; John 1:40–42; Acts 1:1–15:11. First Letter of Clement 5–7 (a patristic text from *c.* A.D. 100)]

(i) On the evidence of the sources, Peter is the cult name of Simon, the son of Jona (a shortened form of Yohanan or John, as in John 1:42). Simon is the Greek form of the Hebrew Simeon. From the first, the New Testament presents him as the Prince of the Apostles, which he only became after Jesus' death. Thus we can be certain that the passage (Matthew 16:13–20), which aims to show that Peter's name was coined by Jesus and that he was pre-eminent among the Apostles and specially blessed by God, did not become a part of Christian tradition till very late. Besides, this passage does not fit the context, for Jesus was not asking the disciples for their opinion but for that of other people. Also, apart from this instance, Jesus always addresses his apostle as Simon.

(ii) Peter's miracles, sermons and raisings of the dead are the typical motifs associated with a priestly cult hero with divine powers. New Testament mythology ascribes to Peter the role of founder of a religion. He establishes a community and gathers it together, and holds the keys of authority over heaven and earth. These *topoi* apply to every priest serving a mystery religion in the ancient world, who would decide whether to accept or reject novices seeking admission.

(iii) One cannot help being struck by the scenes where Peter denies Jesus and where Jesus reviles him. Their force is not cancelled by Jesus' charge, 'Feed my lambs', which is thrice repeated in the supplementary chapter 21 of John, because even those negative passages try to present Simon as a cult hero authorized by Jesus. They testify to the resistance of the conservative Jewish–Christian party in Jerusalem, which did not accept Peter's position as prince of the apostles and lord of the community.

(iv) The New Testament tells us nothing about Peter's martyrdom. The accounts of his death derive from the early patristic writers.

XIII.6. *Paul*

Saul was the son of a strict Jewish family from Tarsus in Cilicia, and was brought up and trained in the law of the Fathers. He was a zealot for the cause of God, as he had learnt it, and so he violently persecuted people whose beliefs differed from his. Once he was journeying to Damascus, to bring to trial the followers of Jesus of Nazareth, who had been executed. Around midday, when he was already in sight of the city, a great burst of light from heaven shone all around him, and he fell to the ground. Then he heard a voice saying: Saul, Saul, why do you persecute me? But Saul did not know whom this voice belonged to, and asked; Who are you, Lord? And he heard the answer: I am Jesus of Nazareth, whom you persecute. Arise and go to Damascus, then you will be told what to do.

Saul was blinded by the flash of fire, and so his companions led him into Damascus. He was visited by Ananias, who was, like Saul, one of the chosen people and had a good reputation among all observant Jews. Saul had been duly circumcised on the eighth day after his birth, he was a Benjaminite and a Pharisee. But, at the same time, he was a Roman citizen by birth, because his father before him had had Roman citizenship, and for this reason he also bore the Latin name Paul.

Now Ananias instructed him that he must obey this miraculous call from Jesus, and restored his sight to him. Then Saul went back to Jerusalem, where Jesus appeared to him for a second time, as he was praying in the temple. Jesus ordered him to leave Jerusalem and to teach among the Gentile nations. For, having persecuted the Christians in Jerusalem, Saul could not very well remain there, all the more so because his former fellow champions of orthodoxy, the Pharisees, would now set upon him.

And so Paul headed for Asia Minor. When he stayed in a city, he lived by his own handiwork, for he was a tentmaker. Thus he spent more than a year in Antioch. There people began to call Jesus' followers Christians. Paul and his companions were then driven out and went on their way. During the journey Paul also healed the sick. He had to flee from the Jews, who tried to kill him. He passed through Asia Minor and came to Europe, where he taught in the synagogue and exorcised evil spirits. He was thrown into prison and was miraculously set free.

And so he arrived in Athens and proclaimed the gospel of Christ to the Epicureans and Stoics. He preached in Corinth, Ephesus and Troas. In Ephesus, the population rioted in protest against him, because they rightly feared that, if Paul continued to preach, the cult of Diana, goddess of the city, would be wiped out. When, after further journeys, he once more stayed for a time in Jerusalem, he was seized by the Jews and accused of starting an uproar. Saul appeared before the Roman governor Festus and, invoking his Roman citizenship, appealed to Caesar. And so, after being under arrest for almost three years, he was sent to the capital of the empire. On the way there he performed still more great miracles in the name of Jesus. In Rome he was allowed to live in his own lodgings while he awaited the emperor's verdict. He was guarded by only one soldier and had many visits from Jews and Gentiles alike. For two years he lived this way, busily preaching and writing letters to the various Christian communities, until he died a martyr in the reign of Nero.

[Acts 22:3–21 (see also 9:1–23); Philippians 3:5; Acts 22:25–8; 18:3; I Thessalonians 2:9; I Corinthians 9:6; II Corinthians 11:2; Acts 11:26; 21–8; First Letter of Clement 5]

(i) Like Peter, Paul was undoubtedly a historical person. But the meagre biographical details in the authentic Pauline epistles have been amplified into a legend in Luke's Acts of the Apostles. This is perhaps less the case with Paul's travels as a Christian missionary than with his conversion. The accounts in Acts present him as a great prophet called by God. Paul has a vision and hears voices, an experience that leads him to change his life completely. He becomes an eloquent miracle worker. His death (*c.* A.D. 66), like the death of Peter, is not described in the Acts of the Apostles or anywhere else in the New Testament, out of respect for the dogmatic principle that Christ's death on the cross was unique. As with Peter, this event was treated only in apocryphal literature.

(ii) After Peter (see XIII.5 (p. 231)), Paul is the most important Christian hero in the early Church. He must have received a thorough rhetorical training, judging from the authentic Pauline letters (Romans, Corinthians, Galatians, I Thessalonians) and the speeches ascribed to him in the Acts of the Apostles. Together with John, the supposed author of the fourth gospel and three epistles, Paul is the first great theologian of early Christianity. He is also one of the creative mythographers in the history of religion. He couches the great traditional myths in a language accessible to a Hellenistic mind, without falling into a Hellenistic syncretism. His greatest mythopoeic accomplishment lies in his notion of proclaiming the risen Jesus Christ to be the *Kyrios*, God himself (see XIII.1.vii (p. 225)). As a Pharisee, he was familiar with the conceptual world of angels, unseen powers and resurrection from the dead. His vision on the road to Damascus, often falsely called Paul's 'conversion', is a legend used to describe the birth of a new idea. The miracles attributed to Paul resemble the highlights on a portrait: they enhance the figure without being important in themselves. Paul is not inferior to Peter. In any case, the miracle of healing the sick or raising the dead is, for the faithful, only the sensible evidence of divine powers. The apocryphal writings of Paul (*Acta Pauli*), draw a colourful picture of the adventures and miracles of the man whose historical achievement consisted in turning a Jewish sect into the Christian Church.

XIV. The New World

XIV.1. *The New Age*

a. When Uzziah was king in Judah and Jeroboam was king in Israel, two years before the earthquake that shook the land, Amos arose, the shepherd of Tekoa, and said: Woe to those who desire the day of Yahweh. The day of Yahweh is darkness and not light, perilous and not a day of grace.

Yahweh will visit the people of Israel with woe, and cause all sinners to be slain with the sword. But at the same time Yahweh will raise up the fallen hut of David. – And for this reason Amos said: The time is coming – thus says Yahweh – when the ploughman will overtake the reaper, and the treader of grapes him who sows the seed. The mountains will drip sweet wine and the hills bear rich fruit.

[Amos 1:1; 5:18; 9:8–13]

b. The word of the Lord came to Zephaniah in the days of King Josiah in Judah, and Zephaniah proclaimed aloud in the land: Yahweh will come to exterminate all living things in the land, to wipe out the name of Baal and the priests who serve the idols. For the day of Yahweh is near, the day of Yahweh is very near. It is a day of wrath, a day of trouble and distress, of storm and rage, darkness and gloom, clouds and thick darkness.

[Zephaniah 1:1–16]

c. And the word of Yahweh came to the priest Ezekiel, the son of Buzi, at the time when King Jehoiachin of Judah had already been a prisoner in Babylon for five years. Ezekiel prophesied the downfall of Israel, Judah and Jerusalem, the temple, and the sons and daughters of the land, because they had apostatized from Yahweh: Only a remnant of Israel and a remnant of the nations will be left. And the remnant of Israel will become a people of Yahweh, and Yahweh's servant David will be prince for ever in their midst. All nations will see this and praise the name of Yahweh. Even Gog from Magog, the great general – thus says Yahweh – shall perish. Then Yahweh himself will come, and all the fish in the sea will tremble before Yahweh, and the birds in the sky, the beasts in the field, and all living creatures. And the mountains will be thrown down, the precipices and all walls will shatter, so that all nations may acknowledge the name of Yahweh as Lord.

[Ezekiel 1:3; 20–24; 34:15–25; 37–9]

d. And the word of Yahweh came to Zechariah in the second year of the reign of King Darius: See, the world is at peace, all lands are tranquil. Yahweh in his mercy will turn again to Jerusalem, and make it rise again, and he will surround it like a wall of fire, to protect the city and his glory. The city will lie open, and it will teem with men and cattle. – And Zechariah saw all the thieves and perjurers leaving the city. And impiety took flight, after Yahweh had slain all his enemies, and from all sides the men and women who counted themselves among God's people came back to Jerusalem. Then the streets were full of happy old folk and happy children. For once the work of man and beast had been fruitless. There was no peace in the land on account of the armies marching through it, because all men were set against each other. But then Yahweh made peaceful citizens of them, and everyone had his share in the vine and the increase of the earth, and every man spoke truth to his neighbour, and justice ruled in the courts, and fast days became times of joy.

[Zechariah 1:11–16; 2:4–5; 5:1–11; 8:1–19]

e. The word of the Lord also came to Isaiah, the son of Amoz, when Uzziah was king in Judah, and Isaiah prophesied: In the last days the mountain of the Lord's house will be established and overtop all the mountains. And from there Yahweh will judge the nations and govern them. Then they will beat their swords into ploughshares and their spears into pruning hooks. For nation will not make war against nation. And there will be peace even among the animals. The wolf will dwell with the lamb, the leopard will lie down with the kid. A little child will lead calves, young lions and fatlings together out to pasture. The cow and the bear will graze together, and their young ones will play together. The lion will eat straw like the ox. Children will play with adders without being bitten. And the fruitfulness of the land will increase, because the spirit comes over the land from on high.

Isaiah prophesied all this to the remnant who repented and turned to Yahweh. He told them: Yahweh will set the remnant of his people free from a foreign yoke and give them a good and quiet place to dwell, first and foremost to the poor and needy, for whom the sprig from the house of Jesse will come, whose reign endures for ever.

Then Yahweh Sabaoth himself will give a great banquet on Mount Zion for all nations, and take away the veils and coverings from them. He will swallow up death in victory. He will wipe away the tears from all eyes, and his people will be held in honour.

[Isaiah 2:2–4; 11:1–8; 32:15–20; 7:3; 9:2–5; 14:30; 9:6; 14:4; 25:6–9]

(i) The new world is the time of salvation, which Yahweh will bring after his day of judgement. Even where the prophets do not use the term, 'day of Yahweh', they present the concept it stands for (e.g. Isaiah 3:7, 18; 7:17–23; Micah 2:4; Zephaniah 1:7–18; Jeremiah 46:10, etc.). It is a fundamental conviction of all the prophets that judgement and salvation go together. (For the prophets, see Chapter VIII.)

The judgement of Yahweh is the central theme of all the prophets. The myth of Yahweh's violent intervention in history was nourished by the prophets' painful experience. The old social structures and statutes of the Law had broken down, and the newly formed monarchy proved incapable of relieving the people's distress, the crises that broke out with the arrival of theocratic despotism. All nations now fell under the anathema of the great King Yahweh, including Israel, which he judged with special severity.

(ii) For the pre-exilic prophets, judgement, with the time of salvation that follows it, was never understood in a universal or cosmic sense, but as something that occurs in the here and now. The day of judgement had no eschatological significance, even when the images expressing it were borrowed from natural catastrophes (Isaiah 30:30; Zephaniah 1:15–16). The sermons of the prophets were political sermons.

During the Babylonian exile, Ezekiel was the first to give his message eschatological import. Yahweh's judgement begins when the 'time of the nations' (30:3) arrives. Ezekiel does not end with the resettlement of Jerusalem; he has Gog of Magog assault the new Jerusalem in a final charge and come to grief in the course of it (chs. 38–9). The battle is a horrible one, and all of nature is caught up in the carnage. From this the nations will recognize 'that I am Yahweh' (38:23). Here Ezekiel is anticipating the apocalyptic scenes in Daniel (see XI.3 (p. 208)).

(iii) All the prophets, including the cultic prophet Ezekiel, have one mythologem in common: salvation, the great new age of salvation, will not be achieved by means of sacrifice or worship performed according to the traditional religious laws but only through Yahweh's intervention. Prophetic ideals even penetrated the writings of the Priestly Source with Leviticus 26:3–13, where we find that the blessings 'of Yahweh will flow in abundance, if you keep my commandments and walk in my statutes'. In the prophets' fundamental hostility to the priests (which is always hostility to the king as well), we see the survival of the old opposition between the representatives of the central government and those of the rural population (see Introduction, p. 16).

(iv) Another prophetic mythologem is that Yahweh himself brings salvation. The scion of David mentioned in Isaiah is only an administrator or manager. He is never called a king, because Yahweh himself is king. This descendant of David is a prince in Israel, a leader and a human being. Isaiah is outlining here a 'Mirror for Princes' for the occupants of David's throne; he is not drawing up a theory of the eschatological Saviour. Zechariah explicitly names the Persian viceroy Zerubbabel and the first high priest Joshua in a Messianic context. And so the longing for the Messiah has no particular importance in the prophetic doctrine of salvation. Old Testament tradition uses the term Messiah mostly for the high priest and the ordinary human king, as well as for Cyrus, king of the Persians (Isaiah 45:1). The Messiah, that is, the Anointed One, is the person who acts on orders from Yahweh and rebuilds Jerusalem (Daniel 9:25–6), once the time of judgement is past. But even the Messiah must die.

(v) The prophets' kingdom of peace, which was promised at different times and expressed in various terms, is the dialectical nullification of the present. In the myth of the future golden age, which as always in mythology is linked to the dream of paradise lost and the blissful primeval age, the state of perfection is a necessary postulate of an imperfect society. Prophecy sees the possibility of another, better world, not in Promethean revolt or even human activity, but in a gift of grace from Yahweh, who will come to liberate and redeem his people. The idea of redemption by Yahweh makes its appearance with the Exile, with Jeremiah and Second Isaiah. It reaches its climax in the myth of Yahweh's new covenant with Israel (Jeremiah 31; Ezekiel 36).

XIV.2. *The New Man*

a. In the eighteenth year of the reign of King Nebuchadnezzar of Babylon, the word of Yahweh came to the prophet Jeremiah from Anathoth: Days are coming when I will make a new covenant with the house of Judah and the house of Israel. I will put my law deep inside them and write it in their hearts. Then they will be my people, and they will all know me as Yahweh.

[Jeremiah 31:31–4]

b. And not long afterwards Yahweh proclaimed this message through the prophet Ezekiel: House of Israel, I will sprinkle you with pure water to make you clean, and give you a new heart and a new spirit. I will take the stony heart from out of your breast and give you a human one. I will put my spirit in you, and you will live faithfully by my statutes and walk and live in your land, of which it will be said: it is like the garden of Eden.

[Ezekiel 36:24–35]

c. The word of Yahweh came to the prophet Isaiah: See, this is my servant, whom I uphold, whom I have chosen. I have put my spirit upon him, so that he may proclaim the truth among the nations. He will not shout nor cry aloud, his voice will not be heard in the streets. A bruised reed he will not break, a faintly gleaming wick he will not quench or break in pieces. The furthest shores will wait for him. – And the word of Yahweh continued: I have called you and hold you by the hand. I have made you to be a light to the nations, to open blind eyes, to lead prisoners out of captivity and the dead from their prison. Before new things spring forth, I tell you of them.

And Yahweh further commanded Isaiah to say: My servant will be fortunate and ascend to the first ranks of the nations. Many will not wish to believe it, but they will see for themselves. For he sprouted as if from a root in dry ground. He was neither handsome nor appealing that we should pay him heed. Instead, he was despised, rejected, plagued with sickness and pain, so that we turned our faces away from him. But he bore the sickness and pain of others, and he was wounded for the sins of others. He was afflicted, yet he opened not his mouth, like a sheep being led to the slaughter. He was slain and buried with the wicked. But in this way he will bring righteousness to many. He will sit among the great, and he will divide the spoils with the strong.

[Isaiah 42:1–9; 52:13–53:12]

d. A long time after this, after John the Baptist had been put in prison, Jesus came from Nazareth to Galilee, and proclaimed: The hour has come, the kingdom of God, his royal dominion, the kingdom of heaven is nigh. Repent, change your lives, and believe the gospel. And he did not cease to teach this. But he meant that the kingdom of God was within, and so he taught people to pray:

> Our Father, who art in heaven,
> Hallowed be thy name.
> Thy kingdom come,
> Thy will be done,
> On earth as it is in heaven.
> Give us this day our daily bread.
> And forgive us our debts,
> As we forgive our debtors.
> And lead us not into temptation,
> But deliver us from evil.

And he continued: You need have no cares for the future. Seek first the kingdom of God and his righteousness, for then all these other things will come your way.

Jesus taught Nicodemus, who enjoyed high esteem among the Pharisees, that a man could only enter the kingdom of God, if he were born anew of water and the spirit.

[Mark 1:15; Matthew 4:17; Luke 17:20–21; Matthew 6:9–13:33; John 3:1–11]

e. When the apostle Paul wrote a letter to the community in Rome, he taught that the Christian was baptised into the death of Jesus, in order to rise again with him and to live, but now as a new creature, without sin, in truth, love, faith and justice. For if anyone lives with Christ, he is a new creation. The old things have passed away, and all things have been made new.

[Romans 6:1–11; 8:1–13; II Corinthians 5:17]

(i) The prophets Jeremiah and Ezekiel introduced ideas of the new man as a visible sign of God's kingdom into biblical mythology. Yahweh makes man over, he transforms his heart and his spirit. To the Old Testament's way of thinking, that is equivalent to a new creation. With this myth, both prophets laid the foundation for the New Testament typology of the Kingdom of God. Their work is not tied to any eschatological scheme, but is open to empirical-historical interpretation. The mythologem of the 'new man' is, at the same time, the mythologem of the new god. The new man and the new god need no cult, no holy law, no regulations, no priest, and no sacred kingship. God and man know and respect each other. They have made a new covenant.

(ii) Neither prophet provides any information about when this covenant will take place. But one gathers that the prophets still hoped to see this new man in their lifetime. The passage on the new beginning marks a radical, definitive renunciation of the Jerusalem temple and its teaching. At the same time, it rejects the monarchy as a possible mode of leadership. Jeremiah and still more, Ezekiel dissolve the bonds of society. Ezekiel individualizes not only guilt and sin, but also salvation and peace. The individual receives a new spirit and a new heart. His life resembles the life of man in the garden of Eden.

(iii) Jeremiah and Ezekiel present the solution to the problems posed by the Exile in the veiled form of a dream. The vision of the new man is the wish for perfection, born of the imperfect state of the world. The new man is to be like the first man in Paradise, but this does not exhaust the prophetic dialectic. The new man is not placed back in the angelic status of the first man, but remains in the world, goes on working there, lives, begets and dies in it. Prophetic hope is directed solely at the removal of the old social order, all of it; at the future disappearance of lords, priests, kings and slaves, laymen and soldiers; and at the recovery of man's nature, as Yahweh wished it to be.

(iv) The prophet Isaiah, by contrast, proclaims a mythologem of a quite different sort. His 'servant' stands for the entire people of God. Isaiah paints a picture of this new nation, which, quite contrary to expectations, emerges triumphant from oppression and persecution. The nations have scarcely looked at this little nation, scarcely noticed or heard it. Nevertheless the prophet predicts for it a great future, which he sends word of, even before there is a hint of its coming: Yahweh's people are to make the blind see, free prisoners and raise the dead.

And not only that, but Isaiah maintains at the same time that Yahweh has made his people suffer, in order to free the other nations. Through the sufferings of Yahweh's people, the other peoples will be saved from the wrath of God. But this suffering comes to a splendid conclusion: in the end the people of Yahweh sit alongside the great empires, enjoying equal rights with them. Once a nation of the oppressed, it has become a nation of oppressors.

(v) Judaism has always understood these chapters on the Servant in a collective sense as referring to the people of Israel. Christianity, however, has applied the myth of vicarious suffering to Jesus (Matthew 11:2–6; 12:18–21; Romans 10:5–16; 15:21; I Peter 2:24; II Corinthians 3:17) and seen in these prophetic texts a foreshadowing of the Messiah. But originally they were only Isaiah's consoling speeches to his people, for whom he conjured up an image of rich future blessings to counter the cheerless present. All prophetic literature, however, unanimously calls for the end of ritual worship in its vision of the last days.

(vi) As a preacher, Jesus follows in the footsteps of the prophets. But he differs from his predecessors, above all when he declares that the kingdom of God has drawn nigh, has in fact already begun. Like the prophets, Jesus individualizes this kingdom. It is located within man, in his heart and feelings. Hence the main theme of his preaching is: do penance, i.e. be converted, become the new human beings God wishes to make of you. Jesus makes his listeners renounce all speculation about the future. Everything is to change within man here and now, not in some vague eternity. This is also the aim of the so-called Lord's prayer ('Our Father'). It is a call to the future kingdom of God, understood as an inner emotional state.

(vii) Elsewhere in the theological literature of the New Testament, the myth of the new man as a new divine creation is equally far removed from any revolutionary transformation of the world. The personal renewal achieved through baptism is entirely a matter of exclusion: it excludes the individual from the world and encloses him in the Church, the mystical body of Christ. The evidently close contacts between stoicism and Christianity that

Paul reveals in Acts 17:28 are not so much signs that the two systems are interdependent as indications that they both were part of the same socio-economic situation that arose in the Middle East in the wake of Alexander's empire.

XIV.3. *The New Earth*

a. In the days of the kings of Judah the word of Yahweh came to Micah: In the last days the mountain of Yahweh will be established more firmly than all other mountains, and will tower over them all. Many peoples and nations will come to receive justice from Yahweh. Yahweh will make peace among the nations. They will beat their swords into ploughshares and their spears into pruning hooks. Nation will not lift up sword against nation, nor will they learn war any more. But they will sit every man under his vine and under his fig tree and rejoice in Yahweh. For out of the region of Bethlehem–Ephrathah Yahweh will make a ruler in Israel come forth, whose origin is from of old, from time immemorial. He will be a mighty lord over all the earth, and his rule will be salvation. [See also XIV.1.e (p. 237).]

[Micah 4:1–5; 5:2]

b. When Jesus of Nazareth was in Jerusalem he taught his disciples about the end of the world. He told them: In the last days a great battle will take place on the earth, in which every man will fight against his neighbour, and the horrors of desolation in fields and plains will slay every living thing. False teachers and prophets will appear, doing signs and wonders, to prove they are God's elect. Jesus warned against such men. For redemption will only come out of catastrophe, when the sun and moon go dark and the stars fall from heaven. Then the world will see the Son of man coming on the clouds. He will send his angels to the elect and bring them to himself. But the hour of his coming remains the secret of God, the Father of the Son of Man. The day of judgement will come as unexpectedly as the Flood in the time of Noah.

Jesus' disciples believed this message and spread it wherever they went. For Jesus had said that his generation would not pass away until all his prophecies were fulfilled. And they believed that he was the one who would come to redeem them. Thus they waited longingly for his arrival. They also had great difficulty reading the signs of the times. But from the persecution they suffered at the hands of the Jews and others they saw that the end of time had drawn near. And they waited for the new heaven and the new earth, as promised by Jesus and the prophets.

[Mark 13; Matthew 24; II Thessalonians 2: 1–17; I Peter 4:7; II Peter 3:13]

c. At the end of his life, when the aged apostle John was living on the island of Patmos, the heavenly throne room appeared to him in the spirit. On the main throne sat one whose appearance was like the fiery gleam of precious stones. And around the throne twenty-four other thrones were set up, on which sat figures clad in white and wearing crowns. And from the throne lighting came forth, and thunder and mighty voices. The throne stood on a crystal base, around which were four creatures holding it up. They were everywhere full of eyes. The first creature looked like a lion, the second like a bullock, the third like an eagle, and the fourth like a man. Each of them had six wings, and they sang unceasingly: Holy, holy, holy is the Lord God Almighty, the Eternal one. – As they sang, the twenty-four elders cast their crowns before the divine master and adored him as the Lord and Creator of all things.

Then amid this assembly there appeared a lamb that seemed as if it had been slain, and with it were the seven spirits of God. And all fell down before the lamb and worshipped and exalted it to divine honours, intoning a new song of praise to the accompaniment of harps. Then from the great throne a voice rang out like that of a thousand angels: Worthy is the lamb that was slain to receive power, and riches, and wisdom, and strength, and honour, and glory, and blessing.

And only the lamb was powerful enough to open the seven seals of the book that was in the right hand of him who sat on the great throne, and thereby to set in motion the final destiny of the world. When it opened the first six seals, four riders came forth to rule the earth until the resurrection of the dead occurred and the end of the world. The riders were victory, war, famine and death. And the sun turned black and the moon blood red, the stars fell down, the heavens rolled up like a scroll and a powerful earthquake ripped up the mountains and islands from their foundations. Then men fled to the caves and clefts in the mountains.

But before they perished, an angel appeared with the seal of the living God, to separate out the chosen ones and to lead them before the throne of the Almighty. Out of all the tribes of the children of Israel one hundred and forty-four thousand were sealed, twelve thousand from each tribe. The multitude of those who were chosen out of the other nations was beyond counting.

After this the seventh seal was opened, and John saw seven angels standing before the throne of the Almighty. One after another they blew their trumpets, and as they did the destruction of the earth proceeded apace. First, a third of the earth, of the water, of life on land and in the water, of the sun, moon and stars, was annihilated. Then the powers of the abyss arose to torment humanity, and last of all the four angels who had been bound at the Euphrates were set free to kill a third part of the human race.

When the seventh trumpet sounded, then was proclaimed the eternal, all-embracing kingdom of Christ. Michael and his angels defeated Satan, or the devil, as the great dragon, the ancient serpent, was called, and cast him down from heaven to the earth. And at this time a woman appeared in the heavens, standing on a crescent moon, clothed with the sun and crowned with twelve stars. She bore a child, who was to rule the nations. And the child was caught up to heaven. The women fled from the dragon's attack into the wilderness and was miraculously rescued.

And John saw further how God's judgement was poured out on the earth from seven bowls full of God's wrath, with plagues and earthquakes. And the chosen saints stood before his throne and praised and extolled him, like the angels who praised God during these last seven divine chastisements. He saw, too, how the great whore, the magnificent city, that ruled over the kings of the earth, was destroyed like Babylon; and at her downfall a great lament arose on the earth, but in heaven loud jubilation.

Then John saw how Christ, after his great victory over the kings of the earth, established a thousand-year reign of peace. During this time, the ancient dragon was bound and banished to the underworld. After the thousand years were up Satan was released for a short time. He led Gog and Magog into war against the saints, and fire from heaven consumed them. And then, after Satan had been thrown for ever into the sea of fire, all the dead rose up. John saw how they were judged by the one who sat on the white throne, before whom earth and heaven fled away. And there was no more place for them. Death and the kingdom of the dead – that is, all those not chosen to live in the kingdom of the lamb – were cast into the sea of fire. For the first heaven and the first earth had passed away, and the sea was no more.

And the new Jerusalem came down from God's heaven, filled with the glory of God. And the city had no need of either sun or moon, for there was no more night in it, because the glory of God and the lamb were in it. There was no more temple.

John saw how from the throne of God and the lamb a stream issued forth, bringing the water of life. On both banks of the river stood trees that bore fruit the year round, whose leaves were for the healing of the nations. The river flowed through the new city, and its inhabitants will live and reign for ever.

And the angel said to John: Do not seal the words of prophecy of this book, for the time is near.

John shared this promise with the prophet Isaiah, who proclaimed these words as Yahweh's: Behold, I create new heavens and a new earth, so that the former things shall not be remembered. They will rejoice for ever over what I have created. No more will weeping or mourning be heard in the city.

If a child should die, it will be at least a hundred years old. And the wolf and the lamb will feed together. The people will remain before Yahweh, like the new heaven and the new earth, in which Yahweh is well pleased.

[Revelation 4:2–5, 13; 6–9; 11:15–12:17; 14–19:5; 20; 21:1–22:10; Isaiah 65:17–25; 66:22]

(i) Old Testament thinking about the transformation of the world takes a radical turn with Micah and Third (post-exilic) Isaiah. Yahweh does not simply change the world, he creates it anew, creates a new heaven and a new earth. ('New' consistently means that which did not exist before.) This idea came into circulation as a result of earlier post-exilic experiences. The lot of those released from servitude in Babylon was so hard that the yearning for liberation could no longer be quieted with images of an overhaul or alteration of the present world, but called for a vision of a completely new earth. This expectation has remained alive in Judaism till this day.

(ii) Jesus did not share this expectation. His career was shaped by the notion that men must change themselves (see XIII.1.iv (p. 224); XIV.2.d. (p. 240)), to get into the kingdom of God, which was about to break in upon this world. He looked forward to the arrival of this kingdom within the lifetime of his generation. After his death, when this hope was not fulfilled, some of his followers repudiated it and turned to the Old Testament tradition that hoped for a new creation of the world by Yahweh after a second coming by the Messiah as judge and saviour of humanity. By Jesus' time, this expectation had absorbed a good deal of mythological material from apocalyptic Jewish thought, for example, the mythologem of the final battle between the powers of light and darkness or of the last judgement by the divine emissary. Time was no longer understood as a circular succession of periods, but as linear history. The concept of the two ages, or aeons, present and to come, interprets these ages not only temporally but spatially too, and thus leads to the transcendence of the old age. This primitive dialectic dominates all of biblical eschatology.

The so-called 'apocalypses' in Mark 13 and Matthew 24 did not belong to Jesus' original teaching, but were placed in his mouth by his followers in order to make the mystery of the delay of the Parousia (return of Christ) a part of Christ's own teaching.

(iii) The elements of the myth describing the coming of a new heaven and a new earth were already available from the apocalyptic literature of the Old Testament. The four beasts that bring about the destruction of the world, can be found in Daniel 7 (see XI.3 (p. 208)). In Ezekiel (see VIII.6 (p. 165)), the lion, eagle, bull and man also support Yahweh's throne-chariot. The angels as heavenly hosts likewise embellish the mythical images of the prophets.

Despite the official religious tradition that spoke of Yahweh as having neither shape nor form, Daniel's old man on a throne had evidently become such a popular symbol of a certain notion of God that John could make use of it.

(iv) The lamb in John's apocalypse is plainly Jesus. He is made into a divine hero by the acclamation of the heavenly assembly. This scene reflects what actually happened in history: the human Jesus becomes the divine co-ruler. The voice from God's throne confirms the dignity of the lamb and exalts it. Thereupon the whole court assembly adores the lamb as it formerly adored only the Almighty himself. Not until then can Christ enter upon his reign, which is at first a cruel one. It brings about the slow destruction of the entire world, from which only the elect are spared. They find salvation in the heavenly Jerusalem. The mythologems here are once again borrowed from Old Testament prophecy (see, for example, Ezekiel 38), but given a completely different interpretation.

(v) The queen of heaven was originally not Mary, the mother of Jesus, but stood for the city of Jerusalem. Antiquity was familiar with the idea of the city as mother of its citizens, and, indeed, the ancient city goddesses had once been the 'great mothers'. The twelve stars in the woman's crown point to the twelve tribes of Israel. The other woman, the great whore of Babylon, stands for Rome, a description also found elsewhere in the literature of the Apostolic age. The seven times of terror are conceived by analogy to the seven plagues with which Yahweh afflicted Egypt. The author of Revelation takes it for granted that Rome and the Roman empire will not endure for ever. He proclaims their downfall, although Rome was still at the zenith of its power when the book was written in the second half of the first century A.D.

(vi) The thousand-year reign of peace is the period allotted to the nations to ally themselves with Christ under the command of the martyrs. The number 1,000 for an epoch in world history derives from Iranian tradition. But, in Revelation, it is no longer thought of as a link in a chain of such epochs, but as the unique era of the kingdom, when the Church fights alongside Christ till the process of remaking heaven and earth begins. In this context, 1,000 is not a specific number but a symbol for an infinitely long period of time. Chapter 20 of Revelation was the point of departure for chiliastic speculation by all sorts of Christian sectarians.

(vii) The new earth, the new heaven, the new Jerusalem with its new people is the climax of John's visions and a revival of the hopes of Third Isaiah. The author tries to reopen the Paradise that, in the myth of Adam and Eve, seems to be closed to all future generations. The vivid picture of life in the new city, which is located somewhere in the Beyond, is an attempt to transcend the concrete world. Roman persecution and the sufferings of the nations subjugated by Rome make the lost paradise an escape from reality.

In the new Jerusalem there is eternal life and eternal freedom, and eternal freedom means eternal dominion. The author sees no possibility of further improving the world, and only a single chance for survival: the new creation. His hopes for a new world have a cosmic dimension. There will be no more sun or moon or difference between night and day. Man, too, will be different: no longer free, but obedient to God in everything.

(viii) The position of John's Revelation at the end of the Bible is not an accident; it indicates the viewpoint of Christian mythology: through one man's sin (Romans 5:12–21), death and misery came into the world, and through one man comes liberation from death and the abolition of history since Adam's entrance into the world. Revelation is the book envisaging the exit of man and his god from this world and their passage into another. Revelation differs from the more or less contemporaneous Gnostic doctrines of redemption on a single, but critical, point: John attributes all redemptive activity to God and his emissary, whereas the Gnostics believed that redemption could be attained through *gnosis*, the knowledge of divine mysteries.

XV. The Evolution of Biblical Mythology

The end of the world Christians looked for did not arrive. The earth remains the same old earth, with the same heaven overarching it that in the days of the patriarchs had been the tent roof beneath which dwelt the human race.

The image of the sky as a tent – a familiar metaphor to wandering herdsmen for a hospitable, secure and protected place – remained alive. But in the first centuries of the Christian era and the centuries that followed, the inhospitableness of society also remained unchanged. The slave-holding society of the Roman Empire did experience a rapid succession of soldier emperors from the house of the Flavians and Julians, as well as the effects of armed contests for the throne; but it was a long time before it saw the end of merciless and inhuman tyranny. Along with the slaves, Jews and Christians suffered even more than other groups in the empire because they rejected the cultic worship of the emperor as a god. Their situation as outlawed victims of persecution and their expectation that the world would soon end united Christians more closely than the ties binding together the countless other religious organizations in the empire. Herein lie the 'roots of that community of goods reminiscent of primitive communism' (Engels), which we find in the first two centuries of Christianity. During this time, the new faith spread across the entire Roman Empire and even leapt over its frontiers. Christian congregations were small at first and limited in effectiveness both because of imperial edicts and self-imposed isolation. In addition, the various centres of Christianity were essentially different, one from another. Their modes of piety differed, their cultic practices were subject to different influences in the East from those in the West. This pluralistic development came to an end when Christianity was first sanctioned by an edict of Constantine the Great in 313, and later in 325 when the first general council of the Church, convoked and run by the non-Christian emperor, met in Nicaea. Constantine tried to use this council to unify the individual churches in a common doctrine. He needed a centralized Church to match his empire.

On the theological front, Nicaea witnessed the victory of the church father Athanasius over his opponent Arius. Athanasius taught that Jesus as the son of God and the Christ was of the *same* nature as God, his father, while Arius taught that Christ's nature was only *similar* to God's. On 28 February in the year 380, Theodosius ordered all his subjects to accept the Christian religion. This edict marks the birth of the established Church. All other cults were forbidden and abolished, and their property reverted to the state. The conciliar resolutions of Nicaea meant that the Church's separation from Judaism would be permanent. The imperial Church received as its lord a proper god. The orientals fought in vain for Jesus' humanity. Everyone now had to believe that Jesus' nature was divine. For this reason, the so-called Lord's Supper acquired a sacramental character and became a divine gift of grace. The offering of the bread and wine – now the divine body and blood – in the sacrament of the Eucharist made an institutional priesthood necessary. The Church underwent a further process of organization along the lines of the imperial administration, with its articulation into prefectures, dioceses and provinces. It became a powerful economic force after the Synod of Constantinople in 381, where, by means of the doctrine that the Holy Spirit was consubstantial with God the Father and God the Son, the Church awarded itself full authority in matters religious and intellectual. In the unbroken line of clerical succession stretching back to the apostles, the Church felt it had a guarantee that the same Holy Spirit bestowed on Jesus' first disciples had been bequeathed to the bishops and priests. From now on the attainment of eternal salvation, of immortality, required participation in the Church's sacraments, which divinized the individual person. This is why godlike powers were attributed to saints and martyrs after their death and even while they were alive. The saints replaced the innumerable regional cult heroes and gods of earlier times; the sacrifices once offered to these pagan divinities now fell to the Church. In its first three centuries, Christianity and the churches had moved so far from the New Testament's anticipation of a new heaven and a new earth and had become so committed to the idea of individual salvation, derived from late antiquity, that they made ideal partners for the unification of the empire under Constantine the Great.

From the third century on, bishops and priests, as a general rule, no longer earned their bread by working, but were taken care of by their congregations and dioceses. In addition, because of imperial influence on church administration, there was no way to avoid choosing bishops primarily from rich and prosperous families. Upon their death, these men would leave their property to their congregations. For, after the end of the fourth century, if not before, bishops had to live as celibates. Priestly celibacy had already become common in the ancient world before the time of Christ, because of the belief that sexual intercourse rendered one unfit to celebrate divine worship. So long as sacrifice and the liturgy were limited to a few days or feasts in the year, priests could restore their ritual purity by means of certain 'holiness laws'. But the introduction of daily mass after the eleventh century put an insurmountable obstacle in the way of this. Participation in the life of the Christian congregation was originally a voluntary, egalitarian affair, but this increasingly gave way to a strictly hierarchical and legally regulated system. The class structure of the Empire was mirrored in the ecclesiastical rules and dogmas (doctrinal principles that had to be accorded the same respect as Holy Writ), which were often declared on the Emperor's initiative. Jesus Christ, now God's equal, advanced to full partnership in his father's royal dominion. Since he was intrinsically one with his father, he was represented as the Pantocrator, the ruler of the world, surrounded by angels, saints, martyrs and a 'cloud of witnesses', as well as by the Holy Spirit in visible form. Jesus, who had once taught, 'Render to Caesar the things that are Caesar's', was now, as Jesus the Christ, set over the emperor as his Lord. Five years after helping the Church to power with his edict, Theodosius had to put up with a public excommunication until he did penance.

Jesus' mother Mary, the carpenter's wife, was now no longer an ordinary mother, but, according to the decrees of the Council of Chalcedon, the bearer of Christ and mother of a god. She could not be denied divine honours. And because she had given birth to the Saviour and Redeemer, she was indirectly responsible for the redemption of the world. Thus the list of her titles grew – 'co-redemptrix', 'mediatrix of all graces', 'mother of sorrows' – and with it the honours that put her on a level with the 'great mothers', Diana of Ephesus or the goddess Isis. This process reached its culmination in 1950 when Pope Pius XII promulgated the dogma that, like Christ, Mary had 'ascended into heaven', and now sat enthroned at her son's right hand.

This evolution of Christian mythology in the centuries that followed the completion of the New Testament canon can only be briefly outlined here, not dealt with in any detail. Over the course of church history, the apostle Peter, the married fisherman from Lake Kinneret, became Christ's deputy, first bishop of Rome, and for the Roman Church the first pope. Paul had also been martyred in Rome, but he was not granted such a distinction. His widely disseminated writings made him proof against that sort of mythical amplification. Peter, who was less burdened with literary productions, was a better subject for this. All through the Middle Ages, the Church went on weaving this image-filled tapestry. Of course, the Eastern Church, which considered itself the orthodox (i.e. right-thinking) church, broke away from the West in 1054, and thereafter followed its own pattern of development.

The early bourgeois Reformation in Germany after 1517 had only a modest influence on the evolution of biblical mythology, which it used to further its aims. The revolutionary feature of Luther's chorale, 'A Mighty Fortress is Our God', which became the battle-song of the Reformation, was that, as in its model (Psalm 46), a challenge was issued to the supposedly permanent social and political structures of the day. The mighty fortresses and the goodly weapons of the feudal Middle Ages – the psalmist's imagery corresponded perfectly to the symbolism of sixteenth-century society – were now rendered useless, intellectually speaking. The mythic terms, 'God', 'his word', 'the right man, whom God himself has chosen', took the place of the programme – still largely unclear – of the new social forces. The rebellious peasants took the godly warriors of the Old Testament for models. In the radical demands of the prophets, they saw an anticipation and divine authorization of their own demands. Their cause was God's cause.

The Peasants' Rebellion was suppressed by the Protestant and Catholic imperial classes, acting in concert. Their ideals survived only in various little religious splinter groups, but the victors returned very quickly to the old ways. The break with Rome and liturgical reform may have been very advantageous for the development of early bourgeois culture after 1517, but they did not mean the end of Christian mythology. Still, the Church's influence came under restraints. In the parts of Europe affected by the Lutheran–Calvinist Reformation, the *sine qua non* condition for salvation was no longer faithful compliance with the Church's laws and requirements, but belief in the unconditional grace of Jesus Christ, which could not be earned. The Reformed Church's overlords and pastors were now no longer the bishops, cardinals and pope, but the princes and lords of the various regions. The Church had once been a sovereign mistress, like the statue of the *ecclesia triumphans* that still adorned Strasbourg Cathedral, but now it became a maid again, a servant of authority. Protestant piety was also deeply influenced by the bourgeois (and feudal) image of father and son, who, as the possessors of land or guild privileges and workshops, offered a visible guarantee of social continuity. The Reformers wanted God the Father and God the Son to be the centre of religious devotion.

The Reformation proved to be a double-edged sword. On the one hand, it was in accord with the laws of socio-economic development; but, on the other, it showed that ties to the Church, previously considered inviolate, could be severed. In the Protestant churches, the living consciousness of biblical mythology was displaced by the abstract wisdom of the catechism. The Ten Commandments superseded the whole body of Canon Law with its regulations governing fasts – and every other aspect of life. The chief residue from what once had been the plenitude of biblical mythology was a familiarity with dogmas and sayings from the Bible. With the coming of the Enlightenment and rationalism, which in theology was accompanied and eventually replaced by a profound pietism, biblical myths could arouse only a feeble interest.

The first thinker in the German-speaking world to gain access to the beauty of the Bible as literature was Johann Gottfried von Herder. His essay *On the Spirit of Hebrew Poetry* was published in 1782–3. Herder ranked the Bible, like the sacred books of other nations, among the writings, 'in which human imaginative power and poetry offer divine vistas on this world'. Herder does not attempt to justify Hebrew legends and folk tales (as, some have objected and claimed, he faults himself for doing, in his discussion of Samson), but to explain them. He was entranced by the lofty poetry of the Bible and thought it was fair to say that, 'if all stories could be told to children the way the Book of Judges and Samuel tell theirs, children would learn them all as poetry'.

Goethe introduced God the Father as a dramatic character in the 'Prologue in Heaven' (*Faust*, Part I), after Lessing had evaporated God into an idea in *Nathan the Wise*. The social principles of Christianity (of which Marx later said they were cringing and hypocritical in comparison with the revolutionary proletariat), as well as its philosophical pronouncements – the things, in other words, that make Christianity a religion – had receded well into the background, as far as Herder and Goethe were concerned; as, indeed, they have continued to recede ever since. Art superseded the religion of yesterday. The process of dialectical transcendence of religion through aesthetics and art is, of course, almost as old as religion itself. Hesiod was not the first, Hegel not the last, to attempt to do this.

Herder attempted to present the Bible as a cultural treasure. He saw his ideal reader as 'an admirer of the oldest, simplest, and perhaps the most heartfelt poetry on earth, a lover, finally, of the oldest story of the human heart and spirit'. This door to the Bible that Herder opened will remain open for all time. It cannot be closed by any ecclesiastical dogmas, which, for their part – there can be no disputing this – bind men and women to this book so that they see in it the centre of their life and thought.

Yet, like Homer's epics, the biblical myths do not derive their aesthetic importance from their authors' religious convictions, but from the harmony between their subjective creative form and the objective laws of social development. Thanks to this harmony, the myths can find their counterpart in the plastic and pictorial arts whenever they are employed as motifs. In this area, it quickly becomes apparent whether or not a work of art is essentially religious. For every really great, multi-layered art work, and this includes the biblical myths, crosses the threshold of its historical, religiously based limitations as soon as it is given a fresh critical reception. The symbols of the Bible will maintain their rightful place in aesthetic consciousness when pious efforts at integrating biblical myths into the contemporary world have ceased.

Meanwhile, there is no doubt that biblical religion contains knowledge which can enrich art, if understood dialectically. Thus, the great image in biblical mythology for the long awaited, salvific 'time of the end' is the prophet's vision of swords beaten to ploughshares (see XIV.1.e (p. 237)). A Soviet sculptor took this text and built a monument inspired by it for the United Nations headquarters in New York. The image of the dove, bringing peace and reconciliation, has long ago escaped the confines of church altars. And the psalmist's exclamation, 'how good and how pleasant it is for brothers to dwell together in unity', has received valid artistic treatment, and not only in Schiller's 'Ode to Joy', as embodied in the final chorus of Beethoven's Ninth Symphony.

The world did not begin as the biblical myth would have it, nor will it end as the Bible dreamt it would. 'The solution of the riddle of human history' (Marx) is not yet complete. But biblical mythology, like that of the Greeks, anticipates partial findings, in so far as it tries to present the great theme of a human god who wants a human world as the meaning of human history.

Chronological Table

(all dates given are approximate)

A. Up until the Partition of the Kingdom of Israel

Israel	Egypt	Assyria-Babylon
1350 Immigration into Canaan	c. 1400 Egypt rules Palestine	
c. 1300–1050 Period of the Judges	The Hittites threaten Egyptian hegemony in Palestine	c. 1230 Nabu-kudurri-uzur I of Babylon
	c. 1250 Ramses II	
	1225–1215 Merneptah	
	1165–1085 Ramses IV–IX	
c. 1050 Samuel, prophet		
1032–1012 Saul, the first king		
1012–972 David		
972–932 Solomon. Building of the temple		964–933 Tiglath-pileser II (Tukulti-apil-esarra) of Assyria
932 Partition of the kingdom. Emergence of the Elohist, Yahwist and Lay Sources		

B. From the Partition of the Kingdom to 587

Judah	Israel	Egypt, Syria, Assyria, Babylonia
932–916 Rehoboam	932–911 Jeroboam	
	886–875 Omri	
874–850 Josaphat	875–854 Ahab; Elisha Battles with the king of Syria	
	854–853 Ahaziah	

Judah (cont'd)	Israel (cont'd)	Egypt, Syria, Assyria, Babylonia (cont'd)
850–843 Joram		*c.* 845 Hazael of Syria harasses Judah and Israel
843–842 Ahaziah	842 Jehu destroys the house of Ahab and stamps out Baal worship	
842–836 Athaliah		
836–797 Joash	842–815 Jehu	842 Shalmaneser III of Assyria
	799–784 Joash	
779–739 Azariah (Uzziah)	784–744 Jeroboam II. Last golden years of Israel	
	c. 760 Amos	
	c. 750 Book of Hosea	
	744 Kingdom begins to disintegrate	745–727 Tiglath-pileser III of Assyria
	743 Zechariah	
739–734 Jotham		
734–719 Ahaz	733–725 Hosea	733–732 Tiglath-pileser of Assyria destroys the kingdom of Damascus
735–734 Syro-Ephraimite War		
c. 740–690 Isaiah; Micah		727–722 Shalmaneser V of Assyria overthrows Hosea and begins the siege of Samaria
	724–722 Samaria falls. End of the kingdom of Israel	722–705 Sargon II of Assyria

Judah	Syria, Assyria, Babylonia, Egypt
719–691 Hezekiah	705–681 Sennacherib of Assyria
701 Sennacherib advances to Jerusalem	
	681–669 In Egypt, the XXV and XXVI Dynasties of the Nubians and Saites. Esarhaddon of Assyria subjugates Egypt
	669–625 Ashur-bani-pal of Assyria
	c. 660 Egypt under Psammetichus I recovers its independence
	c. 650 Media an autonomous kingdom
638–608 Josiah. Final heyday of Judah	c. 635 Scythian invasions of the Near East
626–580 Jeremiah	625 Babylonia under Nabopolassar becomes independent from Assyria
622 Josiah's reformation. Deuteronomy	614–612 Nabopolassar of Babylon and the king of the Medes put an
c. 620 Nahum	end to the Assyrian empire. Nineveh taken. A part of the population remained until 609 (606?)
	610–594 Necho of Egypt
608 Josiah falls at Megiddo	
608 Jehoahaz	
608–598 Jehoiakim, installed by Necho. Jehoiakim submits to the king of Babylon, later rebels	605 Necho defeated at Carchemish by Nebuchadnezzar II (Nabu-kudurri-uzur)
597 Jehoiachin, Jehoiakim's son, taken off to Babylon. First deportation	605–562 Nebuchadnezzar of Babylon
597–587 Zedekiah	
592–570 Ezekiel. Zedekiah revolts from Babylon	
589–587 Jerusalem besieged and captured. Second deportation. Babylonian captivity	

C. From the Destruction of Jerusalem to Nehemiah

Judah	Babylonia, Persia
	555–539 Nabonidus, last king of Babylon
	558–529 Cyrus II of Persia
	550 conquers Media
	546 destroys the kingdom of Lydia
538 Cyrus allows the Jews to return from Babylon. Joshua and Zerubbabel	538 captures Babylon
	525 Egypt a Persian province until 332. Cambyses conquers Egypt
520–516 Rebuilding of the temple. Haggai and Zechariah	521–486 Darius I of Persia
458 Ezra comes to Jerusalem with full authority from Artaxerxes I	485–465 Xerxes ('Ahasuerus' in the Bible)
	465–424 Artaxerxes I Longimanus (Artakhshatra)
450(?) Malachi	
445 Nehemiah in Jerusalem. Ezra proclaims the Law and commits the nation to its observance	
c. 400 Beginning of final redaction of the Priestly Source	

D. Palestine in the Hellenistic Age

Palestine	Alexander's Empire and Subsequent Governments
	336–331 Darius III Codomannus defeated by Alexander the Great. End of the Persian empire
332 Palestine under Macedonian rule	332 Alexander the Great in Syria, Palestine, Egypt. Founding of the city of Alexandria

Palestine (cont'd)

Alexander's Empire and Subsequent Governments (cont'd)

323–301 Palestine under various rulers

323 Alexander's successors, the Diadochi
323–285 Ptolemy I in Egypt. (Ptolemaic dynasty lasts until 30 B.C.)
312 Seleucus I in Syria (Seleucids rule until 64 B.C.)

301–198 Palestine under Egyptian rule
198 Palestine under Syrian rule

222–187 Antiochus III the Great of Syria
176–164 Antiochus IV Epiphanes of Syria

168 Antiochus IV plunders the temple of Jerusalem and forbids Jewish worship
167 The priest Mattathias of Modin and his five sons begin a war of liberation
166 Judas Maccabaeus conquers the Syrians at Emmaus
165 Judas captures Jerusalem (except for the fortress) and purifies the temple
160 Death of Judas. His brother Jonathan head of the Maccabean party
142 Simon the high priest. Judea's independence recognized
141 The people choose Simon as hereditary high priest, general and leader of the nation. Maccabean or Hasmonean dynasty

164 Antiochus V Eupator of Syria
162 Demetrius I murders Antiochus V and Lysias

63 Pompey takes the temple by storm and brings the kingdom of the Maccabees to an end. Palestine under Roman rule. Hyrcanus II high priest and ethnarch. Antipater the actual ruler of the country
40 Herod, Antipater's son, named king by Rome
37–4 Herod the Great

64 Pompey destroys the kingdom of Syria

30 Herod's position confirmed by Augustus

31 Octavian's victory over Antony at Actium
30 B.C.–A.D. 14 Octavian Augustus

E. Palestine as a Roman Province

Palestine	Roman Empire
4 B.C. Herod dies. His sons:	30 B.C.–A.D. 14 Octavian Augustus
A.D. 6 Archelaus, ethnarch of Judea and Samaria	
A.D. 39 Herod Antipas, tetrarch of Galilee and Peraea	
A.D. 6 Archelaus deposed. Judea under Roman procurators	14–37 Tiberius
26–36 Pontius Pilate, procurator of Judea	
c. 27 First appearance of Jesus	
c. 30 Death of Jesus	
37 Herod Agrippa I, king in Jerusalem (41–4)	37–41 Gaius Caligula
	41–54 Claudius
c. 55 Felix procurator. Paul imprisoned	54–68 Nero
c. 60 Festus procurator	
63 Paul executed in Rome	
64 Peter dies in Rome	
	64 Fire of Rome. Nero's persecution of the Christians
66 Jewish insurrection in Palestine	
67–9 Vespasian in Galilee, Peraea and southern Judea	
	68 Death of Nero. Galba, Otho, Vitellius in Rome
70 Titus besieges and destroys Jerusalem	69 Vespasian proclaimed emperor

Glossary

Adytum (Gk): Holy of Holies, the room in the temple which could not be entered by laymen and non-priestly cult officers.

Altar: In the language of the Bible, a place at which sacrifices are offered to the gods. The first altars, intended for burnt offerings, were built of undressed stones. In the temple of Solomon, the altar of incense was made of gold (I Kings 7:48).

Amarna Letters: From the palace archives of Akhetaton, the capital of Egypt under Amenophis IV Ikhnaton, on the east bank of the Nile between Memphis and Thebes. They provide information about conditions in Palestine and Syria, because the senders were mostly princes from those countries. The letters are, without exception, written in cuneiform. Amarna is the modern name for Akhetaton, which was only inhabited for about twenty years (*c.* 1375–1355 B.C.).

Apocalypses: Texts in the Books of Isaiah, Daniel, Ezekiel and Revelation. Outside the Bible there are apocalypses of Enoch, Baruch, Adam, Ezra, Jacob, Paul and Peter. In each case the authors have only borrowed these names and speak on their own behalf. (See also following entry.)

Apocalyptic Genre (Gk. *apokalyptein* = reveal, unveil): A literary and artistic mode that describes future events. For this reason, apocalyptic images are mythical. The mythologems employed are older than the genre itself. Apocalypses (précis of future hopes) appear some time after the beginning of the third century B.C., once pious believers shift their expectations of a change for the better in their lives to eschatology (q.v.).

Apocrypha (Gk. *apokryptein* = conceal, veil): Sacred scriptures which are non-canonical, i.e., which theologians have not confirmed as divinely revealed. In the Old Testament, this category includes the Books of Judith, Wisdom of Solomon, Tobit, Ecclesiasticus, Baruch, I and II Maccabees, parts of Esther, the story of Susanna and Daniel, of Bel and the Dragon at Babylon, the Prayer of Azariah, the Song of the Three Young Men in the Fiery Furnace, and the Prayer of Manasseh. These works are often retained in editions of Luther's Bible. The Roman Catholic Church calls them deuterocanonical, applying the term apocryphal to what the Jews and members of other Christian confessions label the Pseudepigrapha. This latter group includes the books of Enoch and III and IV Ezra. The list of apocryphal New Testament writings (unanimously recognized as such) is very long.

Apostle (Gk *apostellein* = send forth): Plenipotentiary messenger or envoy. Hence the name apostle is given to Jesus' first twelve disciples, called by Jesus himself (Mark 6:30 and Matthew 10:2), as well as to the first preachers who set out from Jerusalem as missionaries (Acts 14:4).

Aram, Aramaeans: The Bible's collective term for Semitic tribes which pressed into Syria in the twelfth century B.C. and set up a powerful kingdom *c.* 1000 with its capital at Damascus. Their language, Aramaic, was the lingua franca of the Middle East until the first century A.D. Jesus undoubtedly spoke Aramaic.

Ark of the Covenant: The ancient cult idol worshipped in common by the tribes of Israel. It was the tribal palladium (Numbers 10:35–6). Later the ark became a divine throne, when Solomon transferred it to the temple, whence it disappeared in 586 B.C. during the destruction of Jerusalem.

Asherah: Presumably the name of an Amorite goddess, identical to Ishtar and Astarte. She was still venerated in Jeremiah's time as the queen of heaven (Jeremiah 7:18). Numerous clay figurines found in Jerusalem stress her character as a fertility goddess. The word is also applied to the cult tree, which appears along with its masculine counterpart, the *mazzebah*, as part of the furnishings of Canaanite religious worship.

Baal Sidon: The city god of Sidon. Baal (see VIII.2 (p. 155)) is the Canaanite name for a god, and means lord. Most of the Baal literature has come to us from Ugarit. There, Aleyin Baal drives out the ancient god El.

Ban: The divine anathema decreed by Yahweh in order to keep his people uncontaminated by other nations and their gods. It is carried out by the slaughter of every living thing (e.g. I Samuel 15:3). The same rule holds for the New Testament as well (Matthew 18:18). The ban is not lifted until the future kingdom of Revelation (Revelation 22:3).

Burnt offering, also *holocaust:* Probably the most common and frequently offered sacrifice (Leviticus 1:3). Only male animals were sacrificed, but without their skin or fur or feathers. The blood was sprinkled on the altar beforehand.

Canon, biblical: The list of writings recognized by the Church as divinely inspired. It was drawn up at the Council of Florence (1442), which is still considered valid. Luther took over the Catholic canon, but declared the Old Testament apocrypha (q.v.) noncanonical. Calvin excluded these works entirely.

Cherubim: The bearers of the throne, above which God appears. They are described precisely in Ezekiel 10:1–20. They protect the garden of God (Ezekiel 28:13, 14, 16), the garden of Eden (Genesis 3:24) and the inner sanctum of the Jerusalem temple (I Kings 6:23–8).

Chiliasm (Gk *chilioi* = a thousand): Doctrine concerning the coming of a thousand-year kingdom of freedom and blessedness. This teaching arose around the second century B.C. and has close connections with the apocalyptic genre and eschatology (q.v.).

Church: The word comes from the Late Greek (Byzantine) phrase *to [doma] kuriakon,* 'the house of the Lord', and has entered many languages as a loan word. The 'Lord' in this context was always Christ. Originally designating a building, the term was also applied to the congregation of the faithful, otherwise expressed by the Hebrew *qahal* and the Greek *ekklesia*.

Deuteronomy (Gk *deuteronomion* = second law): The adjective deuteronomic characterizes the influence of the ideas in this book on Old Testament texts that were composed at the same time.

Diaspora (Gk): In the first instance, the scattering of the Jews all over the ancient world after the destruction of the Second Temple. The term is also applied to Christianity, meaning life in an environment foreign to one's own religious or denominational standpoint.

Edom: The land of Edom (Genesis 25:30) comprises three parts: (a) Seir, south of the Negeb (Joshua 15:1; Numbers 24:18). (b) The rift valley running south of the Dead Sea to the Gulf of Aqaba (II Kings 3:8). (c) The range of rocky heights east of the valley, Edom proper (Numbers 20:17). Within the borders of Edom lies Petra, with its sanctuaries cut from the rock and Nabataean graves (*see* Nabataeans).

Enneateuch (Gk *ennea* = nine): The first nine books of the Old Testament taken as a unit, namely, the Pentateuch, Joshua, Judges, Samuel and Kings, because the sources of the five Books of Moses reappear in the latter books.

Eschatology (Gk *eschatos* = last): 1. The doctrine of the last things and the end of time. By anticipating the future, eschatology criticizes the present in the most radical way. It is the total negation of the negation that is the world here and now. Eschatology looks for radical change either through God's direct intervention or from a hero sent by God, the Messiah, Christ, Son of Man or Son of David, Servant of God. 2. It also refers to the doctrine of the last things in the sense of the subjective world beyond, of life after death. This meaning never occurs at all in the Old Testament, and only sporadically in the New. Only over the course of Church history did this sense slowly displace the notion of expectation mentioned under (1).

Essenes: Jewish sect active in the century before and after the birth of Christ, with a strongly eschatological orientation. They were in conflict with the temple of Jerusalem. Since the discoveries at Qumran (see XIII.4.iii (p. 230)) much more has been learned about them.

Gnosis (Gk = knowledge): Knowledge of the divine mysteries, reserved to an élite group. In the second century B.C., there was a great number of such groups with various secret doctrines. This movement is called gnosticism. The gnostic believes that he is of divine nature and that through divine gnosis he will be transported out of this world, the kingdom of darkness, into a godlike condition, the kingdom of light.

Gospel (Gk *euangelion* = evangel): Its original meaning, in the New Testament epistles, is the 'good news', Jesus Christ's doctrine of salvation, first understood as his words and sermons, oral tradition. In the second century, the term was transferred to the accounts of Jesus by the 'evangelists'. Thus arose a literary term without parallel in antiquity. Today the term is used in both senses.

Hero (Gk): A godlike, superhuman being. Mythical progenitors, mighty warriors, founders of cities and temples become heroes. Heroes can become gods and vice versa. An eponymous hero is one with the same name as a nation. Generally he is the mythical ancestor of the people.

Hexateuch (Gk): The book of six scrolls, i.e. the Pentateuch plus the Book of Joshua.

Judges (Heb. *shophetim*): Heroes from the early period of Israelite history who guided the destinies of the country between the death of Joshua and the prophet Samuel. Their actual function was that of a leader of the army levied from the tribes. But the stories about them show that they were for the most part not Israelites but kings of smallish regions within the territory controlled by the tribes. Individual tribes probably made defence treaties with such Canaanite kings. The group is divided into six major judges (Othniel, Ehud, Barak, Gideon, Jephthah and Samson) and six minor ones. The number twelve is a mythical quantity and signifies a complete period of time.

Logos (Gk): The Greek word originally meant story, news, word, reckoning, proof, number, value. In the New Testament, it refers to Jesus Christ as God's salvific will for the world, the Word of God itself (John 1; I Corinthians 1:17–18). The New Testament writers thus adapted for their own purpose a notion already current in Judaism, which had since the second century B.C. considered wisdom and 'the word' modes of Yahweh's self-manifestation.

Maccabees: The descendants of Mattathias of Modin from the line of Hasmon. Mattathias led the Jewish opposition to the Seleucid Antiochus IV Epiphanes, who tried to Hellenize Jewish worship. Their story is told primarily in the First Book of Maccabees, which was composed *c.* 100 B.C.

Messiah (the same word in Hebrew as the Gk. *Christos* = the anointed one): God's anointed, the king, high priest, royal saviour and redeemer. Longing for a Messiah is as old as kingship in Israel, and incorporates the most vehement criticism of the monarchy. Beginning with the seventh century B.C., Messianic expectation was combined with hopes for the coming of the Servant of God (q.v.), and became especially intense in the first century B.C.

Nabataeans (Edom): Arabian tribes which in the first century B.C. and the century following built an empire stretching from the country east of the Jordan to Damascus. They were stretching from the country east of the Jordan to Damascus. They were conquered by the Romans in A.D. 106. Their capital was Petra, where every year on 25 December they celebrated the feast of their chief god Dusares, an ancient solar deity.

Nehushtan: The bronze serpent, which was formally worshipped in Jerusalem as late as the reign of King Hezekiah (II Kings 18:4). The name once referred to a female deity, and was also borne by the mother of King Jehoiachin of Judah (II Kings 24:8; see also V.3 (p. 119)).

Nicanor: Important Syrian general and sworn enemy of the temple in Jerusalem. The feast of Nicanor (see XI.2.ii (p. 207)) was celebrated in Jerusalem from 161 B.C. onwards, in memory of his defeat and death at the hands of the Maccabees. This is recounted in detail in the Second Book of Maccabees, which dates from the last third of the first century A.D.

Parousia (Gk = arrival): Jesus' first followers looked for his coming from heaven to sit in judgement and redeem the world in their lifetime. The term acquired the meaning 'second coming' (the first being Jesus' birth).

Patristic (Lat. *pater* = father): Refers to the teaching of the great Christian philosphers and theologians from the first to the seventh century. The earliest are the Apostolic Fathers (immediately following the apostles), the next oldest are the Apologetic Fathers (second century).

Pentateuch (Gk): The five books (scrolls) of Moses, known in Judaism as the Torah (the Law).

Pharisees (Heb. *perushim* = the separated ones): Members of a Jewish movement that grew out of the Hasideans, pious zealots from the time of the Maccabees. Their attacks were levelled against the Hasmonean dynasty (see Maccabees), which they saw as the cause of national apostasy, and against the Sadducees (q.v.), who combined practical observance of the Torah with a pronounced cosmopolitan attitude. In the New Testament, the Pharisees are presented as hypocritical sticklers for the Law.

Prophet: Greek term for the Hebrew *nabi*. The prophet is a conduit for divine revelation, hence Moses is designated a prophet. The early stage of this institution is represented by cultic prophecy, where the prophet is also a priest. Biblical prototypes of this are Samuel, Elijah and Elisha. The wandering literary prophet, e.g. Jeremiah or Ezekiel, usually comes from a priestly family which has come down in the world. In the face of his oppressors (the kings and their priests), he defends the interests of those who have been subjugated as he has. The impassioned commitment of the prophets was forever bringing them into conflict with their environment.

Proto-evangel (Gk *protos* = first): Refers in the first instance to Genesis 3:15, interpreted Christologically. The text, in which the seed of the woman crushes the head of the serpent, was read as a prophecy of Christ. This tradition can be traced back to the fourth-century Church. The apocryphal gospel of James, also called the proto-evangel, is a legendary version of Jesus' childhood, from the third century.

Sadducees: Named after their supposed father, the priest Zadok (installed by Solomon), these Jerusalem priests maintained that all things were permissible for Jews, provided they observed the law of Moses literally. The Sadducees rejected all the additions and supplements to the Law made by the Pharisees. They were on good terms with the Hasmoneans and the Romans. They denied the existence of angels and demons as well as the resurrection of the dead.

Samaritans: The modern descendants of the people who inhabited the land around Samaria, once the capital of the northern kingdom of Israel. They now live in Nablus (Palestine) and have been separated from Jerusalem since the middle of the fourth century B.C. To this day, they are the most conservative group within Judaism in that they have only one sacred book, the Pentateuch. They celebrate the feast of Passover with sacrifices offered on Mount Gerizim in accordance with the pre-Deuteronomic rite, their temple having been destroyed in 128 B.C. They played an important part in the transmission of Jewish ideas among Gnostic sects. One can only be a Samaritan in Nablus: their god Yahweh has remained a local god.

Saraph (Seraphim): Mythical composite creatures with wings. They are the guardians of Yahweh's temple and his servants. They make up the angelic chorus that sings in Yahweh's house. Their name presumably comes from the Hebrew verb *saraph* = to burn.

Septuagint (Lat. = seventy): The Greek translation of the Old Testament. According to the legend contained in the letter of Aristeas, it was composed by seventy Jewish savants in Alexandria in the third century B.C. It is the first complete version of the Old Testament in a non-Semitic language, and has conserved many readings at variance with the Hebrew manuscripts. Some of these variants are older than the Hebrew text now accepted as standard.

Servant of God: This messianic title derives from the Old Testament tradition of God's suffering servant in Isaiah 53. It is not employed directly as a Christological title, but the first Christian authors turned to this tradition for their descriptions of Jesus' activities (Mark 1:10; 8:31; 10:45; Matthew 12:18; Luke 22:37; 23:35; 24:26). This mythopoeic application is genuinely Christian, because Jewish tradition has always understood the Servant of God as Israel itself (cf. XIV.2.c. (p. 240); XIV.2.c.iv (p. 242)).

Son of David: Title of sovereignty applied to Jesus (Mark 10:47 and Matthew 9:27). As we can see from the apocryphal Psalm 17 of Solomon or the Fourth Book of Ezra, Judaism looked for a saviour-king to come in the last age from the house of David (2 Samuel 7:14). The term, 'Son of David', then, has messianic associations.

Son of Man: The term stems from the eschatological longing for a saviour, as in Daniel 7. It also occurs in the apocryphal Ethiopic Book of Enoch, 37–71. The first Christian interpreters applied this term to Jesus and described his work in the context of this tradition, which had Messianic implications even before the time of Christ (Mark 2:10; 8:31, 38; 13:26; 14:62).

Temple prostitute (Gk *hierodoulé*; Heb. *kedeshah*): They were occasionally present in considerable numbers at the temple of Jerusalem. They belonged to the ancient fertility cults and prostituted themselves in the service of such cults. There was also male cultic prostitution.

Testament of Adam – (*Testamentum Adae*): Christian apocryphal work in Syriac, presumably composed in the third century A.D. It was popular in Byzantium, Alexandria and Ethiopia. In the form of an apocalypse, Adam, the first man, reveals all of salvation history and proclaims Christ as the saviour of the world.

Theophoric (Gk. *pherein* = bear): Refers to names and terms that have the name of a god as an integral part. Syntactically speaking, theophoric names are compound names. John, for example, comes from the Hebrew Yohanan, meaning 'Yahweh is gracious'.

Zoroaster: Credited with being the founder of Parseeism. He established a strictly monolatrous religion, centred around Ahura Mazda, the great and good god of light who does battle with the evil Ahriman. With this doctrine, Zoroaster introduced dualism. He was active in Iran, presumably during the eighth century B.C.

Indices

Index of Personal Names

Aaron, 52, 103–12 passim, 115ff., 120, 121, 138, 214, 228
Abd al Malik, 201
Abdihipa, king of Urusalim (Jerusalem), 196, 197
Abel, 56–7, 68, 70
Abiathar, 182, 184
Abigail, 178
Abijam, 188
Abimelech, king of Gerar, 42, 81–2, 85–6
Abimelech, king in Israel, 144, 146–7, 173–4
Abinoam, 142
Abishag of Shunem, 179
Abraham (Abram), 42, 54–5, 57, 79–84, 86, 87–8, 92, 104, 105, 108, 109, 137, 139, 148, 194, 203, 225
Abram, see Abraham
Absalom, 16, 127, 137, 179, 182
Achan, son of Carmi, 50
Achish, king of the Philistines, 178
Acrisius, 86, 92
Adad (Hadad), 61
Adah, 68
Adam, 36, 56, 62–8, 69–70, 73, 192, 197, 218, 247–8
Adonai (for Yahweh), 44
Adonijah, 16, 179, 184
Adoram, 188
Aeneas, 80–81
Aesculapius, 108
Agag, king of Amalek, 175
Ahab, king in Israel, 50, 60, 155
Ahasuerus (Xerxes), king of Persia, 205–207
Ahaziah, king of Judah, 159, 190
Ahijah, 187–9
Ahimelech, 51
Ahinoam, 178
Ahithophel, 179

Ahriman, 266
Ahura Mazda (Ormuzd), 266
Alexander the Great of Macedon, 19, 171, 203, 210, 211, 217, 243
Aleyan Baal, 45, 53, 55, 133
Allah, 196
Alphaeus, 219
Amasa, 179, 181, 182
Amaziah, king of Judah, 194
Amenophis III, Pharaoh, 76
Amenophis IV Ikhnaton, Pharaoh, 39
Amittai, 170, 171
Amnon, 179
Amon, 39
Amos (prophet), 18, 23, 50, 138, 161, 201, 236
Amoz (father of Isaiah), 161, 237
Amphictyon, 92, 93
Amphictyonis, 92
Ananias, 233
Anat, 52, 53, 100
Anathoth, 184
Andrew, 219, 231
Andromeda, 45
Antiochus III the Great, king of Syria, 20
Antiochus IV Epiphanes, king of Syria, 20, 210
Antum, 10
Anu, 10, 11, 55, 73
Anunaki, 133
Aphrodite, 80, 140
Apollo, 29, 108, 119, 156, 215
Apophis, 108
Apsu, 34, 35
Aquila, 21
Aram, 76, 203
Araunah, 181
Arius, 76
Arphaxad, 76

Artaxerxes I Longimanus, king of Persia, 19
Asclepios, 223
Asher, 88, 92, 101, 129
Asherah, 132, 133, 144
Ashur (god), 61
Ashur (son of Shem), 61, 76
Astart, 45, 133
Astarte, 262
Athanasius, 249
Athena, 46, 66, 100
Aton, 39
Attis, 223
Augustine, Aurelius, 214
Augustus, Roman emperor, 20, 218
Azariah, 210
Azariah, king of Judah, *see* Uzziah
Azazel, 214–15

Baal, 94, 100, 132, 133, 145, 155, 174, 190–91, 210, 236
   at Babylon, 210
   Sidon, 155
   Zaphon, 45
   -zebul, 144, 159, 215–16
   see also Aleyan Baal
Baba, 10
Balaam of Pethor, 106, 108, 122–4
Balak, king of Moab, 106, 122–3
Barak, 141–3
Barnabas, 32
Bartholomew, 219
Baruch, 163–4
Bashemath, 87
Bathsheba, 51, 178–9, 181
Beelzebul (Beelzebub), 159, 215–16
Beeri (father-in-law of Esau), 87
Beeri (father of Hosea), 169
Beethoven, Ludwig van, 254
Behemoth, 205
Belial, 212
Belshazzar, 208–9
Belteshazzar, 209
Benaiah, 16
Ben-hadad, king of Syria, 50, 158
Benjamin, 13, 91, 92, 96–7, 99–100, 101, 129
Benoni (Benjamin), 91
Bethuel, 84–5, 87
Bildad, 202

Bilhah, 90, 92, 138
Boaz, 151
Buzi, 165, 236

Caesar, 234, 251
Cain, 56–7, 68–70, 212
Caiphas, 221
Caleb, son of Jephunneh, 110, 120–22, 140
Calvin, John, 252, 262
Canaan, 41, 75, 76, 77
Chemosh, 132, 133, 186
Christ, *see* Jesus Christ
Constantine, Roman emperor, 9, 249, 250
Cronus, 55
Cush, 75, 76
Cybele, 78
Cyrus, king of Persia, 43–4, 194, 209, 239

Dagon, 134
Damkina, 10
Dan, 92, 101, 129, 139, 149
Danae, 86
Daniel, 203, 208–11, 238, 247
Darius I, king of Persia, 19, 194, 209, 237
David, 15–16, 29, 48, 50, 51, 59, 60, 67, 75, 90, 116, 127, 135, 137, 139, 148, 152, 154, 160, 162, 167, 175, 176, 178ff., 182ff., 188ff., 194ff., 201, 211, 213, 214, 218, 220, 223, 224, 226, 227, 236, 239
Deborah, 141–3
Delilah, 150
Demeter, 87
Deucalion, 73, 92
Diabolos, 213
Diana, 234, 251
Dinah, 89, 94, 95
Dione, 140
Dionysus, 74
Dumuzi, 170, *see also* Tammuz
Dusares, 264

Ea, 35, 55, 73
Eanna, 11
Edom, *see* Esau-Edom

Ehud, 263
El (god of Israel), 91
El (god of Ugarit), 52–3, 54, 55
El Elyon, 83
El Shaddai, 28
Elam, 76
Eleazar, 140–41
Eleazar (son of Abinadab), 135
Elhanan, son of Jair, 182
Eli, 134, 153
Elihu, 47, 204
Elijah, 137, 155–9, 190, 220, 229, 230, 231
Elimelech, 151
Eliphaz, 202
Elisha, 137, 156, 157–9, 189, 191
Eliyahu, 157
Elizabeth, 227, 228–9
Elkanah, 153
Elohim, 22, 24, 25, 28, 29, 32ff., 42–3, 47, 53ff., 58, 59, 62ff., 72–3, 81–2, 86, 90–92, 94, 95, 105–6, 114, 117, 130, 135, 142, 145–6, 148, 151, 153, 173–4, 175, 176, 178, 180, 182, 184–5, 187, 194, 196, 201, 208
Elon, 87
Engels, Friedrich, 32, 249
Enki, 10
Enkidu, 170
Enlil, 10, 11, 71, 165, 168–9
Enoch, 68–9, 157
Enosh, 69
Ephraim, 91ff., 97, 98
Ephron, 83
Erasmus of Rotterdam, 31
Esau, 85ff., 91, 93, 100
Esau-Edom, 86
Esh-baal, 178
Esther, 205–7
Eteocles, 57
Europa, 169
Eurybia, 113
Eurydice, 113
Euronyme, 113
Eve (Hava), 56, 64–8, 70, 73, 247
Ezekiel, 27, 46, 61, 165–9, 170, 199, 203, 210, 236, 238, 239, 241
Ezra, 19, 27, 118, 192, 194–5

Festus, 234

Gaal, 173
Gabriel, 211, 227, 229
Gad (prophet), 60, 180
Gad (son of Jacob), 88, 92, 101, 115, 129
Gideon (Jerubbaal), 143–6, 173
Gilead, 147
Goethe, Johann Wolfgang, 253
Gog, 168
Gog and Magog, 236, 238, 245
Goliath, 180, 182
Gomer, 76
Gudea, king of Lagash, 165

Hadad, king of Edom, 185, 187
Hadad (near-eastern god), 44
Hadassah (Esther), 207
Hagar, 79, 81–2, 83
Haggai, 19, 200
Ham, 72, 75, 76
Haman, 206, 207
Hammurabi, king of Babylon, 126
Hannah (mother of Samuel), 153
Hannah (prophetess), 218, 227
Hananiah, 163
Hazael, 155, 158
Hegel, Georg Wilhelm Friedrich, 253
Helios, 168
Hellen, 93
Hera, 108, 119, 152
Heracles, 30, 57, 90, 150, 152, 162, 169, 224
Herder, Johann Gottfried, 32, 253
Hermes, 32
Herod the Great, Jewish king, 20, 195, 199, 218–19, 225, 228–9
Herodias, 229
Hestia, 177
Hezekiah, king of Judah, 18, 120, 160–161, 191–3, 194, 199
Hiba, 197
Hilkiah, 132, 162
Hobab, 103, 115
Homer, 169, 253
Hophni, 153
Horus, 46
Hosea, 52, 140–41, 165, 169–70
Huldah, 132
Humman, 207
Hur, 116

Iapetos, 77
Igigi, 133
Immanuel, 160, 162
Innana, 10, 11
Innana-Ishtar, 10, 170
Iphicles, 57, 90
Iphigeneia, 148
Irad, 68
Isaiah, 23, 44, 159–62, 168, 191, 195, 201, 239, 240, 242, 245ff.
Isaac, 54–5, 80, 81–2, 83, 84–8, 90, 92, 100, 104, 105, 108, 109, 137, 225
Ishmael, 81–2, 83, 87
Isis, 46, 217, 251
Israel, *see* Jacob-Israel
Ishtar, 35, 61, 73, 74, 132, 133, 165, 168, 186, 207, 217
Issachar, 89, 92, 100, 129
Itpn, 52

Jabal, 68
Jabin, king of the Philistines, 141–3
Jacob (also called Israel), 11, 58–9, 80, 82, 85–101 *passim*, 104, 105, 108, 109, 123, 137ff., 143
  Israel, 86, 92ff., 96–7, 113, 123, 143
  House of Jacob, 24, 160
  Jacobel, 87
Jacob, sons of, 88, 90, 92, 105, 107, 108, 138
James (brother of Jesus), 219, 226, 228
James (son of Alphaeus), 219
James (son of Zebedee), 231
Japheth, 72, 75ff.
Javan, 76
Jeconiah, 135
Jedidiah (Solomon), 186
Jehoiachin, king of Judah, 194, 236
Jehoiada, 16
Jehoiakim, king of Judah, 163
Jehu, king of Israel, 155, 158, 190–91
Jephthah, 147–9, 181
Jeremiah, 23, 24, 27, 50, 69, 162–5, 168, 170, 197, 199, 205, 231, 239, 241
Jeroboam, king in Israel, 18, 52, 131, 138, 139, 169, 185f., 187–90, 236
Jeroboam II, king in Israel, 171
Jerome, 31
Jerubbaal, *see* Gideon

Jesse, 152, 160, 179, 180, 188, 237
Jesus, 20–21, 26ff., 30, 32, 55, 59, 162, 168, 183, 195, 197, 212ff., 218–34 *passim*, 240ff., 246–52 *passim*
  Christ, 28, 108, 157, 159, 172, 216ff., 221ff., 226, 231, 234, 235, 241, 242, 245ff., 250ff.
Jethro, 102–8 *passim*
Jezebel, 153, 190
Joab, 179, 181, 184
Joanna, 219
Joash (father of Jerubbaal), 144, 194, 199
Joash, king in Israel, 158, 169
Job, 42, 43, 47, 202–5, 210, 211
Johab, king of Edom, 203
John (the Baptist), 157, 228–31, 240
John (evangelist), 214, 219, 220, 225, 234
John Hyrcanus I, Hasmonean king, 20
John (son of Zebedee), 219, 220, 231
John (visionary), 244–5, 247–8
Jona (John, father of Peter), 231
Jonah, 170–72, 231
Jonathan, 15, 175, 178, 180ff.
Joram, king in Israel, 190
Joseph (father of Jesus), 218–19, 226–7
Joseph (son of Jacob), 12, 89ff., 96–101, 102, 105, 129, 137, 139, 140, 169
Joseph of Arimathea, 221
Joses, 228
Joshua (high priest), 48ff., 58, 104, 120, 129, 130, 134, 137, 157, 239
Joshua (son of Nun), 26, 110, 116, 121–122, 130, 139, 140–41
Josiah, king of Judah, 18, 24, 131–3, 136, 138, 181, 187, 192, 197, 236
Jotham, king of Judah, 174
Jotham (son of Gideon), 146, 147
Jubal, 68
Judah, 88, 92, 96–7, 101, 129, 169, 170
Judas (brother of Jesus), 219, 221, 228
Judas Iscariot, 212, 219, 221
Judith (wife of Esau), 87
Jupiter, 44

Kerényi, Karl, 32
Keturah, 80
Kingu, 35

Kish, 174

Laban, 84–5, 87, 88–9, 90–91
Lamech, 68, 69, 72
Leah, 88–90, 92, 151
Lessing, Gotthold Ephraim, 28
Levi, 88, 92, 94–5, 101, 129
Leviathan, 160, 162, 205
Lot, 79
Lud, Ludim, 76
Luke, 36, 157, 168, 222, 223, 227, 234
Luther, Martin, 36, 251

Madai, 76
Magog, 76, 168, *see also* Gog
Mahalath, 87
Malachi, 157
Manasseh, 91ff., 97, 98, 115
Manoah, 58, 149ff.
Marduk, 35, 46, 55, 61, 74, 168–9, 207, 217
Mardukapalidinna (Merodach-baladan), king of Babylon, 192
Mark, 168, 222, 227
Marx, Karl, 253–4
Mary (mother of Jesus), 151, 168, 218, 226–7, 251
Mary (mother of James), 221, 228
Mary Magdalen, 219, 221
Mattathias of Modin, 263
Matthew, 157, 168, 183, 219, 222, 223, 227, 230
Mehujael, 68
Melchizedek, king of Salem (Jerusalem), 83–4, 197
Meribbaal, 180
Merneptah, Pharaoh, 12
Meshech, 76
Methusael, 68
Micah, 243, 246
Michael, 209, 211, 216–17, 245
Michal, 178
Milcom, 132–3, 186
Miriam (mother of Jesus), *see* Mary
Miriam (sister of Moses), 106, 108, 115–116
Mithra, 223
Mizraim, 75, 76
Molech, 133, 186
Mordecai, 205ff.

Moses, 12, 22, 30, 44, 46, 48, 50, 52–3, 55–6, 101, 102–12, 114–22 *passim*, 125, 127ff., 134, 136, 140–141, 157, 159, 214, 220, 231
M't (Death), 94
Muhammad, 201
Müntzer, Thomas, 145

Naamah, 68
Naaman, 158
Nabal, 178
Nadab, king in Israel, 188
Nahor, 79, 203
Nahum, 24, 46
Naomi, 151–2
Naphtali, 96, 101, 129
Nathan, 179, 180, 182
Nebat, 187
Nebuchadnezzar (Nabu-kudurri-uzur), king of Babylon, 12, 18, 163–4, 167–168, 192, 194, 199, 204, 208, 239
Necho, Pharaoh, 132
Nefertiti, 39
Nehemiah, 19, 118, 192, 195
Nehushtan, 120
Neith, 180
Neleus, 57
Nergal, 10, 168–9
Nero, Roman emperor, 232, 234
Nicanor, 207
Nicodemus, 241
Nimrod, 75–6
Nimshi, 190
Ninlil, 10, 165
Ninurta, 169
Noah, 36, 47, 53, 70–77 *passim*, 203, 210, 243

Obed, 152
Obed-edom, 135
Odysseus, 29
Oholah, 168
Oholibah, 168
Omphale, 162
Omri, 155
Orpah, 151
Osiris, 46, 114, 217
Othniel, 263

Pan, 215

Paul, 32, 68, 93, 232ff., 241, 243, 251
Pelias, 57
Persephone, 108, 119
Perses, 87
Perseus, 45–6
Peter (Simon Peter, also called Cephas), 26, 213, 219, 220, 225, 231–3, 234, 235, 251
Philip, 219
Pinchas, 138, 153
Pius XII, pope, 251
Plato, 100
Plutarch, 100, 154
Polyneices, 57
Pontius Pilate, 21, 221
Poseidon, 29, 113, 148, 168
Potiphar, 98
Potipherah, 98
Proetus, 86
Prometheus, 77
Put, 76
Python, 108, 119

Ra, 107–8, 113–14
Rachel, 88ff., 96–7, 138, 151
Rahab, 49
Ramses II, Pharaoh, 10, 13
Raphael, 59
Rebekah, 84ff., 143
Rehoboam, king of Judah, 17, 139, 187–188, 194, 199
Remus, 57
Reuben, 13, 88, 90, 92–3, 97ff., 115, 129
Reuel, 102, 104
Rezon of Zobah, king of Damascus, 185, 187
Rilke, Rainer Maria, 189
Romulus, 57
Ruach, 35
Ruth, 151–2

Sabazius, 223
Salome (daughter of Herodias), 229
Salome (wife of Zebedee), 221
Samson, 58, 139, 148, 149–51, 253
Samuel, 15, 26, 137, 138, 151, 153–4, 174–5, 179–80, 182, 230, 253
Sarah, 42, 54, 79ff.
Sargon, king of Akkad, 11

Sargon II, king of Assyria, 18
Satan, 42, 43, 202, 204, 205, 212–14, 216–17, 219, 231, 245
Saul, king of Israel, 11, 15, 51, 137, 153, 154, 174–7, 178ff., 189
Saul, 233–4, see also Paul
Schiller, Friedrich, 254
Schweitzer, Albert, 222
Scylla, 29
Selene, 74, 93
Seleucus, king of Syria, 210
Semele, 177
Sennacherib, 161, 191–2, 199
Set (Egyptian god), 177, 227
Seth (son of Adam), 36, 69, 70
Seti I, Pharaoh, 10
Shamash, 11, 40, 94, 133, 150–51
Shaphan, 131
Shaphat, 157
Shear-jashub, 160
Shechem, 94–5, 130, 138, 173
Shedim, 214
Shedu, 215
Shem, 72ff., 203
Shemaiah, 188
Shimei of Bahurim, 184
Shishak (Sheshonk), Pharaoh, 194, 199
Sihon, king of Heshbon, 106
Simeon, 218, 232
Simeon (son of Jacob), 88, 92ff., 99, 101, 129, 227
Simon (brother of Jesus), 228, 231–3, see also Peter
Simon (high priest), 219
Simon bar Kochba, 21
Sin, 11, 151, 165
Sisera, 142–3
Solomon, 16, 17, 27, 40, 48, 52, 66
Susanna (from the Book of Daniel), 210
Susanna (from Jesus' circle), 210, 219

Tamar, 179
Tammuz, 133, 165
Teiresias, 123–4
Terah, 79
Teshub, 44
Themis, 73–4
Theodosius, Roman emperor, 9, 250
Theseus, 154
Thomas, 219

Thutmose, 107
Tiamat, 34–5
Tiglath-pileser I, king of Assyria, 16, 75
Tiras, 76
Titus, Roman emperor, 21, 27
Tubal, 76
Tubal-cain, 68
Tukulti-Ninurta I, king of Assyria, 13

Uraeus, 108, 119
Uriah, 51, 178–9
Uriel, 214
Urijah, 163
Urukagina, king of Lagash, 10
Utnapishtim, 71, 73
Utu, 10
Uz, 203
Uzzah, 135–6
Uzziah (Azariah), king of Judah, 60, 146, 159, 236, 237

Vashti, 207
Venus, 81
Vespasian, Roman emperor, 21
Virgil, 223

Yam, 45
Yahweh, 17, 22–9 *passim*, 32, 37ff., 41–
67 *passim*, 70, 71, 74ff., 79, 80, 82–9
passim, 94, 98, 101ff., 106–23 *passim*,
125–49 *passim*, 151ff., 158–72 *passim*,
174, 175, 178–92 *passim*, 194ff.,
198–205 *passim*, 210, 212ff., 223ff.,
236–43 *passim*, 245ff.

Zacharias, 228–9
Zadok, 179
Zalmunna, 145
Zebah, 145
Zebedee, 219, 231
Zebul (god of Ekron), 159
Zebul (governor of Shechem), 173
Zebulun, 13, 89, 92, 101, 129
Zechariah, 196, 200, 237, 239
Zedekiah, 194
Zephaniah, 236
Zeruiah, 213
Zeus, 29, 32, 44, 45, 55, 73, 74, 87, 113,
140, 150, 169, 215
  of Dodona, 140
  of Olympus, 210
Zillah, 68
Zilpah, 88, 90, 92
Zipporah, 55, 56
Zophar, 202
Zoroaster, 211, 213

Index of Tribal and Place Names

Abel-Beth-Maacah, 179
Abel-Meholah, 157
Abu Simbel, 13
Aelia Capitolina (Jerusalem), 21
Ai, 50
Aijalon, 49
Akkad, 10, 11, 75
Alexandria, 19
Amalek, Amalekites, 50, 116, 121, 140, 175, 178
Amarna (Akhetaton), 39
Ammon, Ammonites, 15, 16, 80, 106, 122, 147, 148, 167, 174, 186
Anakim, 120
Anamim, 75
Anathoth, 162, 239
Anatole, 26
Antioch, 233
Aphek, 134
Aqaba, 262
Aram (Syria), Arameans (Syrians), 10, 84, 87, 155, 158-9, 179
Argos, 86
Ashdod, 134
Asher, 13, 144
Assyria, Assyrians, 10, 11, 12, 13, 18, 52, 61, 150, 161, 168, 171, 189, 191-2, 194, 200, 207
Athens, 234
Atlantis, 74
Attica, 12, 154
Aulis, 148

Babylon, Babylonians, 10, 11, 12, 18-19, 24, 26, 29, 34ff., 39, 44, 48, 50, 55, 59, 61, 64, 69, 72-3, 75, 76, 79, 82, 112, 119, 121, 122, 126, 133, 156, 162ff., 165ff., 171, 192, 194, 196, 197, 199, 200, 205, 207, 208ff., 236, 238, 245, 246

Bahurim, 184
Basle, 31
Beersheba, 54, 81-2, 85-6
Benjamin, 175, 233
Bethel, 18, 52, 59, 79, 90ff., 93, 132, 137, 138, 139, 141, 153, 188-9
Bethlehem, 151, 179, 180, 218-19, 226, 227
Bethlehem-Ephrathah, 243
Bethsaida, 231
Beth-shemesh, 135
Bezer, 136-7
Buto, 108, 119
Byzantium, 265

Caesarea, 20, 231
Calah, 75
Calebites, 13, 68, 108, 121-2, 137
Canaan, Canaanites, 12-13, 14, 15, 16, 21-3, 29, 39, 41, 42, 46, 48, 51, 52-3, 54, 59, 65, 66-8, 70, 77, 79, 81ff., 87, 89ff., 95ff., 99, 109, 110-11, 115, 121, 123, 126, 131, 133, 135, 136-43 passim, 147-8, 159, 173-4, 176, 182
Capernaum, 231
Carmel, 155, 156
Casluhim, 75
Cassites, 11, 41
Chalcedon, 251
Chaldea, Chaldeans, 201, 208
Chebar, 165
Cherith, 16, 155
Cilicia, 233
Constantinople, 250
Corinth, 214, 234
Crete, Cretans, 15, 16, 56, 66, 77
Cyprus, 15, 23

Damascus, 16, 83, 158, 160, 185, 187, 233, 235

Dan (city), 18, 83, 137, 188, 189
Dan (tribe), 13, 52, 58
Dead Sea, 16, 230
Delphi, 14, 108, 119, 201
Dodona, 140

Ebal, 129, 130
Eden, 56, 62–3, 240, 241
Edom, Edomites, 16, 106, 117, 142, 158, 167, 185, 187, 204
Egypt, 10ff., 16ff., 26, 35, 39, 40, 41, 45–6, 52, 53, 55, 79, 84, 89, 91, 92, 96–100 passim, 102–3, 105, 109, 112, 113–14, 116–17, 119, 121, 125, 127–8, 130, 133, 156, 163, 167, 171, 184, 185, 187ff., 191, 193, 199ff., 205, 210, 219, 225, 247
El quds, 195, see also Jerusalem
Elam, Elamites, 11, 207
Endor, 175
Ephesus, 234, 251
Ephraim (mountains), 141, 187
Ephraim (tribe), 13, 140, 147–8, 153
Ephratah, 151
Eridu, 10
Eshkol, 120
Etham, 109
Euphrates, 10, 31, 64, 128, 133, 162, 163, 184, 244
Europe, 234

Florence, 262

Gad, 13
Galilee, 21, 219, 221–2, 231, 240
Gath, 134, 178, 180, 182
Gath-Hepher, 171
Geliloth, see Gilgal
Gennesareth, 231
Gerar, 81, 82, 85
Gethsemane, 197, 221
Gezer, 185
Gibea, 174
Gibeon, 49, 184
Gihon (scene of Solomon's anointing), 179
Gihon (second river of Paradise), 64
Gilboa, 175
Gilead, 147, 148, 155, 190
Gilgal, 15, 134, 137–9, 153, 156, 175

Gob, 182
Golan, 136–7
Golgotha, 197, 221
Gomorrah, 79–80, 83
Goshen, 89, 97, 99
Greece, Greeks, 54, 55, 92, 93, 108, 113, 119, 123, 156, 196, 197, 201, 210, 225, 227, 231

Haran, 79, 82, 88–9, 92, 139
Hebrews, 19, 31, 76, 84, 105, 108, 120, 253
Hebron, 13, 15, 83, 86, 88, 90, 92, 93, 97, 120, 136–7, 150, 155, 178
Hiddekel, 64
Hinnom, 132–3
Hittites, 13, 83, 126, 178, 197
Hor, 111, 118
Horeb, 46, 106, 116–17, 127–8, 156, 157
Hurri-Mittani, 13
Hyksos, 13

Indus, 64
Iran, 247
Ishmaelites, 13, 96
Israel (nation), 10–20 passim, 22ff., 27ff., 35ff., 43, 45, 48–53 passim, 57, 58, 67, 70, 74, 76, 80, 84, 100, 105ff., 109, 113–23 passim, 125–31 passim, 133–43 passim, 145, 147ff., 151–60 passim, 163, 165, 166, 168, 169, 178, 179, 182, 185, 187ff., 194, 195, 199, 214, 215, 236, 238, 243
  (Northern kingdom), 167, 170, 171, 173, 210, 239, see also Joseph, House of Joseph
  (People of God), 164, 165, 168ff., 174, 180, 190, 196, 199, 214, 215, 242, 244, 247
Issachar, 13

Jabbok, 93
Jabesh, 174
Jamnia (Jaffa), 21
Jebusites, 178, 181, 193
Jerahmeelites, 13
Jericho, 48, 49, 58, 111, 115, 117, 118, 134, 137, 138, 156, 158

Jerusalem, 13ff., 18–24 *passim*, 34, 38, 39, 44, 45, 48–53 *passim*, 60, 61, 65, 70, 72ff., 78, 80ff., 84, 87, 88, 90, 92, 93, 100, 101, 107, 112, 116ff., 123, 127–33 *passim*, 135ff., 154, 157, 160ff., 168, 169, 173, 178, 180ff., 186ff., 191, 192, 194–201 *passim*, 208ff., 218, 220–28 *passim*, 230, 232–9 *passim*, 241, 243, 245, 247, 248

Jews, 19, 20, 48, 74, 82, 96, 108, 163, 195ff., 199, 201, 206ff., 218, 219, 221, 223, 228, 230, 231, 233, 234, 243, 246, 249

Jezreel, 178, 190

Jordan, 13

Joseph, Josephites, 108
  House of Joseph (for Ephraim and Machir-Manasseh), 13
  House of Joseph (for the nation of Israel or the northern kingdom), 100, 102f.

Judah (southern kingdom), 10, 13, 15–21 *passim*, 29, 36, 38, 40, 44, 5off., 67, 68, 74, 78, 94, 129, 131ff., 138, 139, 145, 158ff., 162, 163, 166ff., 179, 181, 182, 186–92 *passim*, 194, 196, 199, 200, 204, 210, 223, 236 (tribe), 22, 68, 70, 120, 143, 164, 178

Kadesh, 106ff., 119, 120

Kedesh, 136, 137, 141

Kedumim, 142

Keilah, 180

Kenites, 13, 57, 68, 107, 141

Kibroth-hattavah, 104

Kiriath-jearim, 135

Kish, 68

Kishon, 142, 155

Korahites, 111, 115, 118

Lagash, 10

Laish, 139

Larsa, 10, 11

Lasha, 76

Lebanon, 10, 146, 198

Leningrad, 31

Levites, 13, 107, 11off., 118, 129

Lud, Ludim, 75

Luz (Bethel), 90, 92, 138

Machir-Manasseh, 13, 144

Machpelah, 83, 89, 92, 97

Magog, 76

Mamre, 57, 79, 83, 87, 89, 92, 97, 139, 140

Manasseh, 92, 97, 115, 144

Maon, 178, 180

Marah, 116

Massah, 116

Media, Medes, 162, 206, 207, 209

Megiddo, 142

Memphis, 39

Meribah, 116

Meroz, 142

Mesopotamia, 11, 12, 16, 53, 59, 73, 76, 83, 87

Midianites, 14, 108, 111, 112, 115, 130, 143–4

Mizpah, 148, 153, 175

Moab, Moabites, 16, 54, 80, 107, 111, 118, 122–3, 133, 148, 151–2, 158, 167, 186

Moriah, 55

Mount of Olives, 221

Mycene, 66

Nabateans, 80, 262, 264

Nablus, 20

Naphtali, 13, 141–2, 144

Nazareth, 219ff., 226, 228, 233, 240

Nebo, 104, 111, 118

Negeb, 262

Nicaea, 249–50

Nile, 10, 16, 31, 64, 76, 98, 102, 105, 109, 113, 114, 128, 133, 162

Nineveh, 75–6, 170–71

Nob, 51

Olympia, 169, 197, 210, 224

Ophrah, 144, 146

Othnielites, 13

Palestine, 10, 13, 2off., 41, 69, 100, 104, 133, 146, 171, 210, 222, 223

Paran, 110, 118, 120, 140

Patmos, 244

Pelethites, 16

Persia, Persians, 11, 18, 19, 61, 76, 118, 168, 171, 195, 203, 205ff., 209, 211, 213

Petra, 262, 264
Philistia, Philistines, 14ff., 75, 77, 81, 82, 85, 86, 105, 134, 135, 141, 149, 150, 153, 159, 167, 175, 178, 180, 181, 184, 191
Phoenicia, Phoenicians, 20, 54, 56, 171, 200
Pihahiroth, 114
Pisgah, 107
Pishon, 64
Pniel, 91, 94

el quds, *see* Jerusalem
Qumran, 31, 230–31

Ramah, 91, 141, 154, 180, 182
Ramoth, 136, 137, 190
Ras Shamra, *see* Ugarit
Rephidim, 116
Reuben, Reubenites, 90
Rome (city), 20, 21, 201, 222, 231, 234, 241, 247, 251, 252
Rome (empire), 30, 81, 195, 196, 198, 199, 217, 221, 223, 226, 233, 234, 247, 249

Sabeans, 202
Sais, 100
Salem, *see* Jerusalem
Samaria, 19, 132, 155, 158, 160, 168, 190
Samaritans, 20, 130
Seir, 142
Sheba, 185
Shechem, 79, 89, 90ff., 95ff., 101, 130, 136, 137, 139, 140, 141, 144ff., 154, 173, 174, 187, 188
Shechem-Ramah, 17, 153
Shedim, 214, 215
Shiloh, 134, 135, 141, 153, 187, 188, 189
Shinar, 74
Shunem, 158
Sidon, 17, 22, 155, 167, 200
Simeon, 13

Sin, 117
Sinai, 45, 52, 103, 107ff., 115ff., 119, 125, 127
Sodom, 57, 58, 75, 79, 80, 83
Strasbourg, 252
Sudan, 10
Succoth, 89, 113, 114
Sumer, 10, 11, 165, 170
Susa, 205, 206
Syria, 19, 20, 41, 190, 207, 210, *see also* Aram

Taanach, 142
Tabor (mountain), 142
Tabor (oak tree), 174
Tanis, 16
Tarshish, 170
Tarsus, 233
Tekoah, 236
Tell Abib, 166
Thebes, 16, 19, 35, 39
Thebez, 173
Tigris, 10, 31, 64
Timnah, 149
Timrath-serah, 141
Tishbe, 155
Tob, 148
Troas, 234
Troy, 29, 81, 169
Tyre, 17, 22, 167, 169, 178, 185, 198ff.

Ugarit (Ras Shamra), 22, 23, 52, 55, 94, 159
Ur, 10, 11, 79, 81
Uruk, 10, 75, 76
Uz, 202, 203

Zarephath, 155
Zebulun, 144
Zereda, 187
Ziklag, 178
Zion, 178, 193, 196, 198, 237
Zoar, 16
Zorah, 58, 149
Zuph, 174

MORE ABOUT PENGUINS
AND PELICANS

For further information about books available from Penguins please write to Dept EP, Penguin Books Ltd, Harmondsworth, Middlesex UB7 ODA.

In the U.S.A.: For a complete list of books available from Penguins in the United States write to Dept CS, Penguin Books, 625 Madison Avenue, New York, New York 10022.

In Canada: For a complete list of books available from Penguins in Canada write to Penguin Books Canada Ltd, 2801 John Street, Markham, Ontario, L3R 1B4.

In Australia: For a complete list of books available from Penguins in Australia write to the Marketing Department, Penguin Books Australia Ltd, P.O. Box 257, Ringwood, Victoria 3134.

In New Zealand: For a complete list of books available from Penguins in New Zealand write to the Marketing Department, Penguin Books (N.Z.) Ltd, P.O. Box 4019, Auckland 10.

A Pelican Book

GODS AND MYTHS OF NORTHERN EUROPE

H. R. Ellis Davidson

Tiw, Woden, Thunor, Frig . . . these ancient northern deities gave their names to the very days of our week. Nevertheless most of us know far more of Mars, Mercury, Jupiter, Venus, and the classical deities.

Recent researches in archaeology and mythology have added to what was already a fairly consistent picture (largely derived from a twelfth-century Icelandic account) of the principal Scandinavian gods and goddesses. This study – the first popular treatment of the subject to appear in English for many years – is the work of a scholar who has long specialized in Norse and Germanic mythology. She describes the more familiar gods of war, of fertility, of the sky and the sea and the dead, and also discusses those most puzzling figures of Norse mythology – Heimdall, Balder, and Loki.

All these deities were worshipped in the Viking Age; and the author has endeavoured to relate their cults to daily life and to see why these pagan beliefs gave way in time to the Christian faith.

A Pelican Book

THE GREEK MYTHS
Volumes 1 and 2
Robert Graves

Few modern writers are better qualified than Robert Graves to retell the Greek legends of gods and heroes for a modern audience. In the two volumes of *The Greek Myths*, with a dazzling display of relevant knowledge, he provides a complete 'mythology' to replace Smith's *Dictionary of Classified Mythology* of the nineteenth century. Graves's work covers, in nearly two hundred sections, the creation myths, the legends of the birth and lives of the great Olympians, the Theseus, Oedipus and Heracles cycles, the Argonaut voyage, the tale of Troy, and much else.

All the scattered elements of each myth have been assembled into a harmonious narrative, and many variants are recorded which may help to determine its ritual or historical meaning. Full references to the classical sources, and copious indexes, make the book as valuable to the scholar as to the general reader; and a full commentary on each myth explains and interprets the classical version in the light of today's archaeological and anthropological knowledge.

A Pelican Book

THE NATURE OF GREEK MYTHS
G. S. Kirk

What are myths?

Theories abound. They have been seen as echoes of cosmological and meteorological events; as attempts to explain some of the odder things that go on in the world – a sort of primitive science; as stories invented to validate existing customs or institutions; as evocative tales of a creative past; as justification for primitive rituals. Psychologists and structural anthropologists have all had a say.

Professor Kirk examines such universal theories in this Pelican. They are all, he admits, illuminating, but none is adequate by itself, because these 'traditional tales' are of such variety that no single theory can embrace them all. His general analysis of the nature of myth is followed by a splendid account of the Greek myths – myths about Gods, myths about heroes and, in greater detail, the myths about the unique God-hero Heracles.

In the final chapter of this unusually rigorous study Professor Kirk speculates on the manner in which an age dominated by myth gave way to an age dominated by philosophy.

A Peregrine Book

THE USES OF ENCHANTMENT

Bruno Bettelheim

The enchanted world of fairy tales, with its princesses and stepmothers, its magic forests and wise old kings, has been an integral part of childhood for hundreds of years. Worn smooth by time, these stories are not only extremely beautiful, but of great help to the child in dealing with the emotional turmoils of his early years.

Dr Bettelheim has written this book to help adults become aware of the irreplaceable importance of fairy tales. By revealing the true content of such stories, he shows how children may make use of them to cope with their baffling emotions, whether it be the feelings of smallness and helplessness, or the anxieties the child feels about strangers and the mysteries of the outside world. Taking the best-known stories in turn, he demonstrates how they work, consciously or unconsciously, to support and free the child. Thus, in fairy tales, the young begin to sense for themselves the meaning of justice, fidelity, love or courage: not as lessons imposed, but as discovery and experience. The great fairy tales should, argues Dr Bettelheim, be retained for the benefit of future generations, a priceless source of aesthetic pleasure and moral sustenance.

The Uses of Enchantment was awarded the Critics' Choice Prize for the best work of criticism published in the United States in 1976, and the National Book Award in 1977.

A Peregrine Book

RELIGION AND THE DECLINE OF MAGIC

Keith Thomas

Witchcraft, astrology and every kind of popular magic flourished in sixteenth- and seventeenth-century England. At the same time men began to reach for a scientific explanation of the universe, and the Protestant Reformation attempted to take the magic out of religion.

'In his impressive new study Keith Thomas examines the magical tradition from a new but equally fascinating viewpoint. He considers reactions to magical practices, and their social meaning, at all levels of English society, and particularly among the lower classes. As a result he has produced one of the most original and thought-provoking books on English sixteenth- and seventeenth-century history to appear for decades' – *The Times Literary Supplement*

Keith Thomas won one of the two Wolfson Literary Awards for History in 1972 with *Religion and the Decline of Magic*.

A Penguin Reference Book

THE PENGUIN SHORTER ATLAS OF THE BIBLE

Luc. H. Grollenberg

Translated by Mary F. Hedlund

The Penguin Shorter Atlas of the Bible is a distillation of the knowledge that archaeology and textual scholarship have brought to our understanding of scripture. With the aid of more than one hundred plates and full colour maps, Luc. Grollenberg carries the story forward from the time of the Patriarchs until the beginnings of the Christian church. Each episode is interpreted in the light of our knowledge of conditions in Palestine at the time, an exercise which vastly expands our appreciation of the Bible.

This translation was first published under the title of *Shorter Atlas of the Bible*.